Wine

FOR

DUMMIES®

5TH EDITION

by Ed McCarthy
Certified Wine Educator

and
Mary Ewing-Mulligan
Master of Wine

WILEY

John Wiley & Sons, Inc.

Wine For Dummies® 5th Edition

Published by
John Wiley & Sons, Inc.
111 River St.
Hoboken, NJ 07030-5774
www.wiley.com

WILEY

About the Authors

Ed McCarthy and **Mary Ewing-Mulligan** are two wine lovers who met at an Italian wine tasting in New York City's Chinatown and subsequently merged their wine cellars and wine libraries when they married. They have since coauthored 11 wine books in the *Wine For Dummies* series (including two of their favorites, *French Wine For Dummies* and *Italian Wine For Dummies*) as well as *Wine Style: Using Your Senses to Explore and Enjoy Wine* (Wiley); taught hundreds of wine classes together; visited nearly every wine region in the world; run five marathons; and raised 12 cats. Along the way, they have amassed more than half a century of professional wine experience between them.

Mary is president of International Wine Center, a New York City wine school for wine professionals and serious wine lovers. As U.S. director of the Wine & Spirit Education Trust (WSET), the world's leading wine educational organization, she works to make the courses she offers in New York available in more and more parts of the United States. She is also a wine journalist, having been the wine columnist of the *NY Daily News* for more than a decade. Mary's most impressive credential is that she's the first female Master of Wine (MW) in the United States, and one of only 30 MWs in North America (with 298 worldwide).

Ed, a New Yorker, graduated from City University of New York with a master's degree in psychology. He taught high school English in another life, while working part-time in wine shops to satisfy his passion for wine and subsidize his growing wine cellar. That cellar is especially heavy in his favorite wines — Bordeaux, Barolo, and Champagne. Besides coauthoring 11 wine books with Mary, Ed went solo as author of *Champagne For Dummies,* a topic on which he's especially expert.

Ed also writes for *Beverage Media,* a trade publication. Both Ed and Mary are columnists for the online wine magazine *WineReviewOnline.com,* and both are accredited as Certified Wine Educators (CWE).

When they aren't writing, teaching, or visiting wine regions, Mary and Ed maintain a busy schedule of speaking, judging at professional wine competitions, and tasting as many new wines as possible. They admit to leading thoroughly unbalanced lives in which their only non-wine pursuits are hiking in the Berkshires and the Italian Alps. At home, they wind down to the tunes of U2, k.d. lang, Bob Dylan, and Neil Young in the company of their feline roommates, Ponzi and Pinot.

Dedication

We dedicate this book to all who have the courage to buy a book called *Wine For Dummies*. You are intelligent, not dummies, because you have the wisdom to realize that in the complex world of wine, everyone has something more to learn.

Authors' Acknowledgments

The wine world is dynamic — it's constantly changing. Because six years have passed since the fourth edition of *Wine For Dummies*, we decided to revise and update the book. We especially felt an obligation to write this fifth edition because of all the readers who have personally told us how valuable *Wine For Dummies* has been to them over the years. We are grateful to have the opportunity to contribute to your knowledge of wine.

But this book would not have been possible without the team at Wiley. We sincerely thank Publisher Kathy Nebenhaus, who engaged us to write the fifth edition of *Wine For Dummies*, along with Acquisitions Editor Stacy Kennedy and Assistant Editor David Lutton. Really special thanks go to our project editor, Georgette Beatty, who made excellent suggestions to improve the text, and to our diligent copy editor, Jennette ElNaggar.

We thank our technical reviewer and colleague, Mary Gorman-McAdams, MW, for her expertise and her thoroughness in combing through our manuscript. We know that it's a better, more accurate book because of you.

Special thanks to Steve Ettlinger, our agent and friend, who brought us to the *For Dummies* series in the first place and who is always there for us.

We thank all our friends in the wine business for your information and kind suggestions for our book; the reviewers, whose criticism has been so generous; and our readers, who have encouraged us with your enthusiasm for our previous books in this series.

Mary offers special thanks to Linda Lawry and everyone else at International Wine Center, who enabled her to have the time and the peace of mind to work on this book. Thanks also to Elise McCarthy, E.J. and Kim McCarthy, and Cindy McCarthy Tomarchio and her husband, David, for their encouragement and support.

Publisher's Acknowledgments

We're proud of this book; please send us your comments at http://dummies.custhelp.com. For other comments, please contact our Customer Care Department within the U.S. at 877-762-2974, outside the U.S. at 317-572-3993, or fax 317-572-4002.

Some of the people who helped bring this book to market include the following:

Acquisitions, Editorial, and Vertical Websites

Senior Project Editor: Georgette Beatty
(Previous Edition: Traci Cumbay)

Acquisitions Editor: Stacy Kennedy

Copy Editor: Jennette ElNaggar

Assistant Editor: David Lutton

Editorial Program Coordinator: Joe Niesen

Technical Editor: Mary Gorman-McAdams, MW

Editorial Manager: Michelle Hacker

Editorial Assistant: Alexa Koschier

Art Coordinator: Alicia B. South

Cover Photo: ©Jupiterimages/Photos.com

Cartoons: Rich Tennant
(www.the5thwave.com)

Composition Services

Project Coordinator: Patrick Redmond

Layout and Graphics: Carl Byers, Noah Hart, Joyce Haughey, Corrie Niehaus, Lavonne Roberts

Proofreaders: Lindsay Amones, Bonnie Mikkelson

Indexer: Estalita Slivoskey

Illustrator: Lisa S. Reed

Publishing and Editorial for Consumer Dummies

Kathleen Nebenhaus, Vice President and Executive Publisher

Kristin Ferguson-Wagstaffe, Product Development Director

Ensley Eikenburg, Associate Publisher, Travel

Kelly Regan, Editorial Director, Travel

Publishing for Technology Dummies

Andy Cummings, Vice President and Publisher

Composition Services

Debbie Stailey, Director of Composition Services

Contents at a Glance

Table of Contents

Introduction

We love wine. We love the way it tastes, we love the amazing variety of wines in the world, and we love the way wine brings people together at the table. We want you and everyone else to enjoy wine, too — regardless of your experience or your budget.

But we'll be the first to admit that the trappings of wine — the ceremony, the fancy language, the paraphernalia — don't make it easy for regular people to enjoy wine. You have to know strange names of grape varieties and foreign wine regions. You have to figure out whether to buy a $20 wine or an $8 wine that seem to be pretty much the same thing. You usually even need a special tool to open the bottle when you get it home!

All this complication surrounding wine will never go away, because wine is a very rich and complex field. But you don't have to let the complication stand in your way. With the right attitude and a little understanding of what wine is, you can begin to buy and enjoy wine. And if, like us, you decide that wine is fascinating, you can find out more and turn it into a rewarding hobby.

Because we hate to think that wine, which has brought so much pleasure into our lives, could be the source of anxiety for anyone, we want to help you feel more comfortable around wine. Some knowledge of wine, gleaned from the pages of this book and from our shared experiences, will go a long way toward increasing your comfort level.

Ironically, what will *really* make you feel comfortable about wine is accepting the fact that you'll never know it all — and that you've got plenty of company. You see, after you really get a handle on wine, you discover that *no one* knows everything there is to know about wine. There's just too much information, and it's always changing. And when you know that, you can just relax and enjoy the stuff.

About This Book

If you already have a previous edition of *Wine For Dummies,* you might be wondering whether you need this book. We believe that you do. We wrote the first edition of *Wine For Dummies* in 1995, and the world of wine has changed tremendously since then. It has even changed a lot since our fourth edition in 2006:

- ✔ The wine world has an exciting new face thanks to the communities of wine lovers who share opinions, chat, and blog on Internet sites, and these voices are shaping new trends. New styles of popular wine are emerging, and a whole new approach to food and wine pairing has taken root.

- ✔ The wines of South America have come on strong, and they offer some of the best values around. We've ramped up our coverage of Chile and Argentina to give you the inside track on these explosive wine regions.

- ✔ Dozens of California wineries have opened, a few have gone out of business, many have improved, and a few have slipped. Our recommendations reflect all these changes.

- ✔ Remember those prices we listed for wines worth trying in our earlier editions? Well, big surprise: Just about all those prices have increased. But we point out some bargains, especially in Parts III, IV, and V.

- ✔ Several new vintages have occurred; we give you the lowdown on them throughout the book, and especially in our vintage chart in Appendix C.

We wrote this book to be an easy-to-use reference. You don't have to read it from cover to cover for it to make sense and be useful to you. Simply turn to the section that interests you and dig in.

Conventions Used in This Book

To help you navigate this book, we established the following conventions:

- ✔ **Boldface** indicates key words in bulleted lists and actions to take in numbered steps.

- ✔ *Italic* is used for emphasis and to highlight new words or terms that are defined.

- ✔ `Monofont` is used for web addresses.

- ✔ Sidebars, which are shaded boxes of text, consist of information that's interesting but not necessarily critical to your understanding of the topic.

When this book was printed, some web addresses may have needed to break across two lines of text. If that happened, rest assured that we haven't put in any extra characters (such as hyphens) to indicate the break. So, when using one of these web addresses, just type in exactly what you see in this book, pretending that the line break doesn't exist.

What You're Not to Read

We don't want you to read any part of this book that could make you uncomfortable because the information seems too technical or complicated. If you're not into knowing explanations and backstories, for example, don't read the text that's flagged with the Technical Stuff icon. If you want to just drink wine rather than collect it or visit wineries, don't read Part VI, "When You've Caught the Bug." And if you don't like sweet wines, don't read Chapter 16 about dessert wines.

Seriously though, you can skip over the sidebars (those shaded gray boxes) as you read, because they complement the story line but are not strictly part of it. You can always come back to them later.

We hope that you'll read everything — but only if you want to.

Foolish Assumptions

We assume that you picked up this book for one of several reasons:

- ✔ You know very little about wine but have a strong desire to find out more.
- ✔ You do know something about wine, more than most people, but you want to understand it better, from the ground up.
- ✔ You're already very knowledgeable but realize that you can always discover more.

We also assume that you don't have a lot of ego invested in wine — or maybe you do, and you're buying this book "for your sister-in-law." And we assume (correctly, we hope) that you are someone who doesn't appreciate a lot of mumbo jumbo and jargonistic language about wine — that you're someone who wants straight talk instead.

How This Book Is Organized

This book is a wine textbook of sorts, a user's manual, and a reference book, all in one. We include very basic information about wine for readers who know nothing (or next to nothing) about wine — but we also include tips, suggestions, and more sophisticated information for seasoned wine drinkers who want to take their hobby to a more advanced level. Depending on where you fall on the wine-knowledge gradient, different chapters will be relevant to you. Parts I and II are the most fundamental and practical, Parts III to V are intermediate but also practical because they discuss specific wine regions and types, and Part VI contains the most advanced discussions.

Part I: Getting to Know Wine

The five chapters in Part I get you up and sipping even if you've never tasted wine in your life. We tell you the basic types of wine, how to taste it, which grapes make wine, why winemaking matters, and how wines are named.

Part II: Wine and You: Up Close and Personal

This part deals with practical wine matters — in the wine shop, in the restaurant, and in your home. Find out how to handle snooty wine clerks, decode restaurant wine lists, remove those stubborn corks, and pair wine with food. In addition, we show you how to decipher cryptic wine labels.

Part III: The "Old World" of Wine

Visit this part for a tour of the major wine regions of Europe: France, Italy, Spain, Portugal, Germany, Austria, and Greece.

Part IV: Discovering the "New World" of Wine

Here we adventure to Australia, New Zealand, Chile, Argentina, and South Africa, and then we take a look at the major wine areas in the United States: California, Oregon, Washington, and New York.

Part V: Wine's Exotic Face

Some of the most exciting and fascinating wines are in this part, including Champagne, Sherry, Port, Sauternes, and other exotic dessert wines.

Part VI: When You've Caught the Bug

You find a wealth of practical advice in this part, including recommendations on where and how you can buy wine beyond your local wine shops. We tell you how to describe and rate wines you taste, how to store wine properly, and how to pursue your love and knowledge of wine beyond this book.

Part VII: The Part of Tens

What *For Dummies* book would be complete without this part? It's a synopsis of interesting tips and recommendations about wine to reinforce our suggestions earlier in the book. We're particularly happy to debunk ten prevalent myths about wine so that you can become a savvier consumer and a more satisfied wine drinker.

Part VIII: Appendixes

In Part VIII, we show you how to pronounce foreign wine words, and you can look up unfamiliar wine terms in the glossary. You can also consult the vintage chart to check out the quality and drinkability of your wine.

Icons Used in This Book

The pictures in the margins of this book are called *icons,* and they point out different types of information.

A bargain's not a bargain unless you really like the outfit, as they say. To our tastes, the wines we mark with this icon are bargains because we like them, we believe them to be of good quality, and their price is low compared to other wines of similar type, style, or quality. You can also interpret this logo as a badge of genuineness, as in "This Chablis is the real deal."

Some issues in wine are so fundamental that they bear repeating. Just so you don't think that we repeated ourselves without realizing it, we mark the repetitions with this symbol.

Wine snobs practice all sorts of affectations designed to make other wine drinkers feel inferior. But you won't be intimidated by their snobbery if you see it for what it is. (And you can discover how to impersonate a wine snob!)

This odd little guy is a bit like the 2-year-old who constantly insists on knowing "Why, Mommy, why?" But he knows that you may not have the same level of curiosity that he has. Where you see him, feel free to skip over the technical information that follows. Wine will still taste just as delicious.

Advice and information that will make you a wiser wine drinker or buyer is marked by this bull's-eye so that you won't miss it.

There's very little you can do in the course of moderate wine consumption that can land you in jail — but you could spoil an expensive bottle and sink into a deep depression over your loss. This symbol warns you about common pitfalls.

Unfortunately, some of the finest, most intriguing, most delicious wines are made in very small quantities. Usually, those wines cost more than wines made in large quantities — but that's not the only problem; the real frustration is that those wines have very limited distribution, and you can't always get your hands on a bottle even if you're willing to pay the price. We mark such wines with this icon, and hope that your search proves fruitful.

Where to Go from Here

We recommend that you go to Chapter 1 and start reading there. But if you don't have time because you're about to head out to a fancy restaurant, then begin at Chapter 7. If you already have bottle in hand, wine in glass, and want to know more about what you're about to sip, turn to Chapter 4 to decode the words on the label, and then consult the index to find the regional section that corresponds to your wine to read about the wines of that area. Or — because so many wines today are named after grape varieties — start with Chapter 3, which explains the major grape varieties for wine.

In other words, start wherever you wish, closer to the beginning if you're a novice and closer to the middle if you know something about wine already. On the journey of wine appreciation, *you* get to decide how far to go and how quickly — and you get to choose the route to get there. The final destination is pleasure.

Part I
Getting to Know Wine

The 5th Wave   By Rich Tennant

"Oh, come on, you're just drinking it!
You're not even tasting it..."

In this part . . .

To grasp the material in this part of the book, you need some preliminary knowledge: what a grape is and where your tongue and nose are located.

If you have those bases covered, you're ready to begin understanding and enjoying wine — even if you've never tasted wine before in your life. Through the chapters in this part, you find out about the technique of wine tasting, get familiar with grape varieties, understand how to read wine names and labels, and take a sneak peek at the process of winemaking. We start slowly so that you can enjoy the scenery along the way.

Chapter 1

Wine 101

*W*e know plenty of people who enjoy drinking wine but don't know much about it. (Been there, done that ourselves.) Knowing a lot of information about wine definitely isn't a prerequisite to enjoying it. But familiarity with certain aspects of wine can make choosing wines a lot easier, enhance your enjoyment of wine, and increase your comfort level. You can master as much or as little as you like. The journey begins here.

How Wine Happens

Wine is, essentially, nothing but liquid, fermented fruit. The recipe for turning fruit into wine goes something like this:

1. **Pick a large quantity of ripe grapes from grapevines.**

   You could substitute raspberries or any other fruit, but 99.9 percent of all the wine in the world is made from grapes, because grapes make the best wines.

2. **Put the grapes into a clean container that doesn't leak.**

3. **Crush the grapes somehow to release their juice.**

   Once upon a time, feet performed this step.

4. **Wait.**

In its most basic form, winemaking is that simple. After the grapes are crushed, *yeasts* (tiny one-celled organisms that exist naturally in the vineyard and, therefore, on the grapes) come into contact with the sugar in the grapes' juice and gradually convert that sugar into alcohol. Yeasts also produce carbon dioxide, which evaporates into the air. When the yeasts are done working, your grape juice is wine. The sugar that was in the juice is no longer there — alcohol is present instead. (The riper and sweeter the grapes, the more alcohol the wine will have.) This process is called *fermentation*.

Fermentation is a totally natural process that doesn't require man's participation at all, except to put the grapes into a container and release the juice from the grapes. Fermentation occurs in fresh apple cider left too long in your refrigerator, without any help from you. We read that even milk, which contains a different sort of sugar than grapes do, develops a small amount of alcohol if left on the kitchen table all day long.

Speaking of milk, Louis Pasteur is the man credited with discovering fermentation in the 19th century. That's discovering, not inventing. Some of those apples in the Garden of Eden probably fermented long before Pasteur came along. (Well, we don't think it could have been much of an Eden without wine!)

Now if every winemaker actually made wine in as crude a manner as we just described, we'd be drinking some pretty rough stuff that would hardly inspire us to write a wine book. But today's winemakers have a bag of tricks as big as a sumo wrestler's appetite, which is one reason no two wines ever taste exactly the same.

- ✔ The men and women who make wine can control the type of container they use for the fermentation process (stainless steel and oak are the two main materials) as well as the size of the container and the temperature of the juice during fermentation — and every one of these choices can make a big difference in the taste of the wine.

- ✔ After fermentation, winemakers can choose how long to let the wine *mature* (a stage when the wine sort of gets its act together) and in what kind of container. Fermentation can last three days or three months, and the wine can then mature for a couple of weeks or a couple of years or anything in between. (If you have trouble making decisions, don't ever become a winemaker.)

Obviously, one of the biggest factors in making one wine different from the next is the nature of the raw material, the grape juice. Besides the fact that riper, sweeter grapes make a more alcoholic wine, different *varieties* of grapes (Chardonnay, Cabernet Sauvignon, or Merlot, for example) make different wines. Grapes are the main ingredient in wine, and everything the winemaker does, he does to the particular grape juice he has. Chapter 3 covers specific grapes and the kinds of wine they make.

The skinny on sulfites

Sulfur dioxide, a compound formed from sulfur and oxygen, occurs naturally during fermentation in very small quantities. Winemakers add it, too. Sulfur dioxide is to wine what aspirin and vitamin E are to humans — a wonder drug that cures all sorts of afflictions and prevents others. Sulfur dioxide is antibacterial, preventing the wine from turning to vinegar. It inhibits yeasts, preventing any sugar in a wine from fermenting in the bottle. It's an antioxidant, keeping the wine fresh and untainted by the demon oxygen. Despite these magical properties, winemakers try to use as little sulfur dioxide as possible because many of them share a belief that the less you add to wine, the better (just as many people prefer to ingest as little medication as possible).

Now here's a bit of irony for you: Today, wine-making hygiene is so advanced that winemakers need to rely on sulfur dioxide's help less than ever before, yet most wine labels in the United States state *Contains Sulfites* (meaning sulfur dioxide). That's because Congress passed a law in 1988, requiring that phrase on the label of wines sold in the United States. So now, many wine drinkers understandably focus on the fact that sulfur is in the wine when, in reality, sulfur dioxide use is probably at an all-time low.

A small percent of asthmatics are extremely sensitive to sulfites. To protect them, Congress mandated that any wine containing more than 10 parts per million of sulfites carry the *Contains Sulfites* phrase on its label. Considering that about 10 to 20 parts per million occur naturally in wine, that covers just about every wine. (The exception is organic wines from the United States, which are intentionally made without the addition of sulfites; some of them are low enough in sulfites that they don't have to use the mandated phrase. Organic wines from Europe can contain added sulfur. You can read about organic wines in Chapter 5.)

Actual sulfite levels in wine range from about 30 to 150 parts per million (about the same as in dried apricots); the legal max in the United States is 350. White dessert wines have the most sulfur — followed by medium-sweet white wines and blush wines — because those types of wine need the most protection. Dry white wines generally have less, and dry reds have the least.

Of course, grapes don't grow in a void. Where they grow — the soil and climate of each wine region, as well as the traditions and goals of the people who grow the grapes and make the wine — affects the nature of the ripe grapes and the taste of the wine made from those grapes. That's why so much of the information about wine revolves around the countries and regions where wine is made. In Parts III and IV, we cover all the world's major wine regions and their wines.

What Color Is Your Appetite?

Your inner child will be happy to know that when it comes to wine, it's okay to like some colors more than others. You can't get away with saying "I don't like green food!" much beyond your sixth birthday, but you can express a general preference for white, red, or pink wine for all your adult years.

(Not exactly) white wine

Whoever coined the term *white wine* must have been colorblind. All you have to do is look at it to see that it's not white; it's yellow. But we've all gotten used to the expression by now, so *white wine* it is.

White wine is wine without any red color (or pink color, which is in the red family). This means that White Zinfandel, a popular pink wine, isn't a white wine. But yellow wines, golden wines, and wines that are as pale as water are all white wines.

Wine becomes white wine in one of two ways: First, white wine can be made from white grapes — which, by the way, aren't white. (Did you see that one coming?) *White* grapes are greenish, greenish yellow, golden yellow, or sometimes even pinkish yellow. Basically, white grapes include all the grape types that aren't dark red or dark bluish. If you make a wine from white grapes, it's a white wine.

The second way a wine can become white is a little more complicated. The process involves using red grapes — but only the *juice* of red grapes, not the grape skins. The juice of almost all red grapes has no red pigmentation — only the skins do — therefore, a wine made with only the juice of red grapes can be a white wine. In practice, though, very few white wines come from red grapes. (Champagne is one exception; Chapter 15 addresses the use of red grapes to make Champagne.)

In case you're wondering, the skins are removed from the grapes either by pressing large quantities of grapes so that the juice flows out and the skins stay behind — sort of like squeezing the pulp out of grapes, the way kids do in the cafeteria — or by crushing the grapes in a machine that has rollers to break the skins so that the juice can drain away.

You can drink white wine anytime you like, but typically, people drink white wine in certain situations:

- ✔ Most people drink white wines without food or with lighter foods, such as fish, poultry, or vegetables. Chapter 9 covers the dynamics of pairing wines with food and has suggestions of foods to eat with white wine.

- ✔ White wines are often considered *apéritif* wines, meaning that people consume them before dinner, in place of cocktails, or at parties. (If you ask the officials who busy themselves defining such things, an apéritif wine is a wine that has flavors added to it, as vermouth does. But unless you're in the business of writing wine labels for a living, don't worry about that. In common parlance, an apéritif wine is just what we said.)

- ✔ A lot of people like to drink white wines when the weather is hot because they're more refreshing than red wines, and they're usually drunk chilled (the wines, not the people).

White wine styles: There's no such thing as plain white wine

White wines fall into four general taste categories, not counting sparkling wine or the really sweet white wine that you drink with dessert (see Chapters 15 and 16 for more on each of those). If the words we use to describe these taste categories sound weird, take heart — they're all explained in Chapter 2. We also explain the styles in plentiful detail in our book *Wine Style: Using Your Senses to Explore and Enjoy Wine* (Wiley). Here are our four broad categories:

- **Fresh, unoaked whites:** These wines are crisp and light, with no sweetness and no oaky character. (Turn to Chapter 3 for the lowdown on oak.) Most Italian white wines, like Soave and higher-end Pinot Grigio, and some French whites, like Sancerre and some Chablis, fall into this category.

- **Earthy whites:** These wines are dry, fuller-bodied, unoaked or lightly oaked, with a lot of earthy character. Some French wines, such as Mâcon or whites from the Côtes du Rhône region (covered in Chapter 10), have this taste profile.

- **Aromatic whites:** These wines are characterized by intense aromas and flavors that come from their particular grape variety, whether they're *off-dry* (that is, not bone-dry) or dry. Examples include a lot of German wines and wines from flavorful grape varieties, such as Riesling or Viognier and, in some cases, Sauvignon Blanc.

- **Rich, oaky whites:** These wines are dry or fairly dry and full-bodied with pronounced oaky character. Most Chardonnays and some French wines — like many of those from the Burgundy region of France — fall into this group.

We serve white wines cool, but not ice cold. Sometimes, restaurants serve white wines too cold, and we actually have to wait a while for the wine to warm up before we drink it. If you like your wine cold, fine; but try drinking your favorite white wine a little less cold sometime, and we bet you'll discover it has more flavor that way. In Chapter 8, we recommend specific serving temperatures for various types of wine.

Red, red wine

In this case, the name is correct. Red wines really are red. They can be purple red, ruby red, or garnet, but they're red.

Red wines are made from grapes that are red or bluish in color. So guess what wine people call these grapes? Black grapes! We suppose that's because black is the opposite of white.

Popular white wines

These types of white wine are available almost everywhere in the United States. We describe these wines in Parts III and IV.

- ✔ **Chardonnay:** Can come from California, Australia, France, or almost any other place
- ✔ **Pinot Grigio** or **Pinot Gris:** Can come from Italy, France, Oregon, California, and other places

- ✔ **Riesling:** Can come from Germany, California, New York, Washington, France, Austria, Australia, and other places
- ✔ **Sauvignon Blanc:** Can come from California, France, New Zealand, South Africa, Italy, and other places
- ✔ **Soave:** Comes from Italy

The most obvious difference between red wine and white wine is color. The red color occurs when the colorless juice of red grapes stays in contact with the dark grape skins during fermentation and absorbs the skins' color. Along with color, the grape skins give the wine *tannin,* a substance that's an important part of the way a red wine tastes. (See Chapter 2 for more about tannin.) The presence of tannin in red wines is actually the most important taste difference between red wines and white wines.

Red wines vary quite a lot in style — partly because winemakers have so many ways of adjusting their red winemaking to achieve the kind of wine they want. For example, if winemakers leave the juice in contact with the skins for a long time, the wine becomes more *tannic* (firmer in the mouth, like strong tea; tannic wines can make you pucker). If winemakers drain the juice off the skins sooner, the wine is softer and less tannic.

Red wine tends to taste better when it's consumed as part of a meal or with accompanying food than as a drink on its own.

Thanks to the wide range of red wine styles, you can find red wines to go with just about every type of food and every occasion when you want to drink wine. The one exception is times when you want to drink a wine with bubbles: Although bubby red wines do exist, most bubbly wines are white or pink. In Chapter 9, we give you some tips on matching red wine with food.

One sure way to spoil the fun in drinking most red wines is to drink them too cold. Those tannins can taste really bitter when the wine is cold — just as in a cold glass of very strong tea. On the other hand, many restaurants serve red wines too warm. (Where do they store them? Next to the oven?) If the bottle feels cool to your hand, that's a good temperature. For more about serving wine at the right temperature, see Chapter 8.

Pink wines, from rosé to "blush"

Pink wines are made from red grapes, but they don't end up red because the grape juice stays in contact with the red skins for a very short time — only a few hours, compared to days or weeks for red wines. Because this *skin contact* (the period when the juice and the skins intermingle) is brief, pink wines also absorb very little tannin from the skins. Therefore, you can chill these wines and drink them as you'd drink white wines.

Traditionally, pink wines are called *rosé* wines. But today, not all of them are. (That would be too simple.) Many pink wines today are called *blush* wines — a term invented by wine marketers to avoid the word *rosé,* because back in the '80s, rosé wines weren't very popular. Lest someone figure out that *blush* is a synonym for *rosé,* the labels on "White" Zinfandels and other such blush wines call these wines *white.* But even a child can see that White Zinfandel is really pink.

The blush wines that call themselves *white* are fairly sweet. Wines labeled *rosé* can be sweetish, too, but some wonderful rosés from Europe (and a few from the United States) are *dry* (not sweet). Some hard-core wine lovers used to shun rosé wine, but today, rosé wines, especially the dry ones, can be so good that many wine drinkers are discovering what a pleasure — not to mention what a versatile food partner — a good rosé wine can be.

Red wine styles: There's no such thing as plain red wine, either

Here are four red wine styles:

- *Soft, fruity reds* are relatively light-bodied, with a lot of fruitiness and fairly little tannin (like Beaujolais Nouveau wine from France, some Bardolinos or Valpolicellas from Italy, and many under-$12 U.S. wines).

- *Mild-mannered reds* are medium-bodied with subtle, un-fruity flavors (like less expensive wines from Bordeaux, France, and some inexpensive Italian reds).

- *Spicy reds* are flavorful, fruity wines with spicy accents and some tannin (such as some Malbecs from France or Argentina and Dolcettos from Italy).

- *Powerful reds* are full-bodied and tannic (such as the most expensive California Cabernets; Barolo, from Italy; Priorat from Spain; the most expensive Australian reds; and lots of other expensive reds).

Popular red wines

You find descriptions and explanations of these popular and widely available red wines all through this book.

- ✔ **Beaujolais:** Comes from France
- ✔ **Bordeaux:** Comes from France
- ✔ **Cabernet Sauvignon:** Can come from California, Australia, France, Chile, and other places
- ✔ **Chianti:** Comes from Italy

- ✔ **Côtes du Rhône:** Comes from France
- ✔ **Lambrusco:** Comes from Italy
- ✔ **Merlot:** Can come from California, France, Washington, New York, Chile, and other places
- ✔ **Pinot Noir:** Can come from California, France, Oregon, New Zealand, and other places
- ✔ **Zinfandel:** Usually comes from California

Which color of wine when?

Your choice of a white wine, red wine, or pink wine will vary with the season, the occasion, and the type of food you're eating (not to mention your personal taste!). Choosing a color usually is the starting point for selecting a specific wine in a wine shop or in a restaurant. As we explain in Chapters 6 and 7, most stores and most restaurant wine lists arrange wines by color before making other distinctions, such as grape varieties, wine regions, or taste categories.

Although certain foods can straddle the line between white wine and red wine compatibility — grilled salmon, for example, can be delicious with a rich white wine or a fruity red — your personal preference for red, white, or pink wine will often be your first consideration in pairing food with wine, too.

Pairing food and wine is one of the most fun aspects of wine, because the possible combinations are almost limitless. (We get you started with the pairing principles and a few specific suggestions in Chapter 9.) Best of all, your personal taste rules!

Other Ways of Categorizing Wine

We sometimes play a game with our friends: We ask them, "Which wine would you want to have with you if you were stranded on a desert island?" In other words, which type of wine could you drink for the rest of your life without getting tired of it? Our own answer is always Champagne, with a capital *C* (more on the capitalization later in this section).

In a way, Champagne is an odd choice because, as much as we love Champagne, we don't drink it *every day* under normal circumstances. We welcome guests with it, we celebrate with it after our team wins a Sunday football game, and we toast our cats with it on their birthdays. We don't need much of an excuse to drink Champagne, but it's not the type of wine we drink every night.

What we drink every night is regular wine — red, white, or pink — without bubbles. These wines have various names. In the United States, they're called *table* wines, and in Europe, they're called *light* wines. Sometimes, we refer to them as *still* wines, because they don't have bubbles moving around in them.

In the following sections, we explain the differences between three categories of wines: table wines, dessert wines, and sparkling wines.

Table wine

Table wine, or light wine, is fermented grape juice whose alcohol content falls within a certain range. Furthermore, table wine isn't bubbly. (Some table wines have a very slight carbonation but not enough to disqualify them as table wines.) According to U.S. standards of identity, table wines may have an alcohol content no higher than 14 percent; in Europe, light wine must contain from 8.5 percent to 14 percent alcohol by volume (with a few exceptions). So unless a wine has more than 14 percent alcohol or has bubbles, it's a table wine or a light wine in the eyes of the law.

The regulation-makers didn't get the number 14 by drawing it from a hat. Historically, most wines contained less than 14 percent alcohol — either because the juice didn't have enough sugar to attain a higher alcohol level or because the yeasts died off when the alcohol reached 14 percent, halting the fermentation. That number, therefore, became the legal borderline between wines that have no alcohol added to them (table wines) and wines that may have alcohol added to them (dessert or fortified wines; see the next section).

Ten occasions to drink pink or rosé

Still not convinced about choosing a pink or rosé wine? Here are some of our favorite reasons to drink pink.

1. When she's having fish and he's having meat (or vice versa)

2. When a red wine just seems too heavy

3. With lunch — hamburgers, grilled cheese sandwiches, and so on

4. On picnics on warm, sunny days

5. To wean your son/daughter, mate, friend (yourself?) off cola

6. On warm evenings

7. To celebrate the arrival of spring or summer

8. With ham (hot or cold) or other pork dishes

9. When you feel like putting ice cubes in your wine

10. On Valentine's Day (or any other pink occasion)

Red wine sensitivities

Some people complain that they can't drink red wines without getting a headache or feeling ill. Usually, they blame the sulfites in the wine. We're not doctors or scientists, but we can tell you that red wines contain far less sulfur than white wines. That's because the tannin in red wines acts as a preservative, making sulfur dioxide less necessary. Red wines do contain numerous substances derived from the grape skins that could be the culprits. But whatever the source of the discomfort, it's probably not sulfites.

Today, however, the issue isn't as clear-cut as it was when the laws were written. Many grapes are now grown in warm climates where they become so ripe and have so much natural sugar that their juice attains more than 14 percent alcohol when fermented. The use of gonzo yeast strains that continue working even when the alcohol exceeds 14 percent is another factor. Many red Zinfandels, Cabernets, and Chardonnays from California now have 14.5 or even 15.5 percent alcohol. Wine drinkers still consider them table wines, but legally, they don't qualify (technically, they're dessert wines and are taxed at a higher rate) — which is just to say that laws and reality don't always keep pace.

Here's our own, real-world definition of table wines: They're the normal, non-bubbly wines that most people drink most of the time.

Dessert wine

Many wines have more than 14 percent alcohol because the winemaker added alcohol during or after the fermentation. That's an unusual way of making wine, but some parts of the world, like the Sherry region in Spain and the Port region in Portugal, have made quite a specialty of it. We discuss those wines in Chapter 16.

Dessert wine is the legal U.S. terminology for these wines, probably because they're usually sweet and often enjoyed after dinner. We find that term misleading because dessert wines aren't *always* sweet and aren't *always* consumed after dinner. (Dry Sherry is categorized as a dessert wine, for example, but it's dry, and we drink it before dinner.)

In Europe, this category of wines is called *liqueur wines,* which carries the same connotation of sweetness. We prefer the term *fortified,* which suggests that the wine has been strengthened with additional alcohol. But until we get elected to run things, the term will have to be *dessert wine* or *liqueur wine.*

Sparkling wine (and a highly personal spelling lesson)

Sparkling wines are wines that contain carbon dioxide bubbles. Carbon dioxide gas is a natural byproduct of fermentation, and winemakers sometimes decide to trap it in the wine. Just about every country that makes wine also makes sparkling wine. In Chapter 15, we discuss how sparkling wine is made and describe the major sparkling wines of the world.

In the United States, Canada, and Europe, *sparkling wine* is the official name for the category of wines with bubbles. Isn't it nice when everyone agrees?

Champagne (with a capital *C*) is the most famous sparkling wine — and probably the most famous *wine,* for that matter. Champagne is a specific type of sparkling wine (made from certain grape varieties and produced in a certain way) that comes from a region in France called Champagne. It is the undisputed Grand Champion of Bubblies.

Unfortunately for the people of Champagne, France, their wine is so famous that the name *champagne* has been borrowed again and again by producers elsewhere, until the word has become synonymous with practically the whole category of sparkling wines. For example, until a recent agreement between the United States and the European Union (E.U.), U.S. winemakers could legally call any sparkling wine *champagne* — even with a capital *C,* if they wanted — as long as the carbonation was not added artificially. Even now, those U.S. wineries that were already using that name may continue to do so. (They do have to add a qualifying geographic term such as *American* or *Californian* before the word *Champagne,* however.)

How to (sort of) find out the alcohol content of a wine

Regulations require wineries to state a wine's alcohol percentage on the label (again, with some minor exceptions). It can be expressed in degrees, like 12.5 degrees, or as a percentage, like 12.5 percent. If a wine carries the words *Table Wine* on its label in the United States but not the alcohol percentage, it should have less than 14 percent alcohol by law.

But for wines sold within the United States — whether the wine is American or imported — there's a big catch. The labels are allowed to lie. U.S. regulations give wineries a 1.5 percent leeway in the accuracy of the alcohol level. If the label states *12.5 percent,* the actual alcohol level can be as high as 14 percent or as low as 11 percent. The leeway doesn't entitle the wineries to exceed the 14 percent maximum, however.

If the alcohol percentage is stated as a number that's neither a full number nor a half-number — 12.8 or 13.2, for example, rather than 12.5 or 13 — odds are it's precise.

For the French, limiting the use of the name *champagne* to the wines of the Champagne region is a *cause célèbre.* E.U. regulations not only prevent any other E.U. country from calling its sparkling wines *champagne* but also prohibit the use of terms that even *suggest* the word *champagne,* such as fine print on the label saying that a wine was made by using the "Champagne method." What's more, bottles of sparkling wine from countries outside the European Union that use the word *champagne* on the label are banned from sale in Europe. The French are that serious about Champagne.

To us, this seems perfectly fair. You'll never catch us using the word *champagne* as a generic term for wine with bubbles. We have too much respect for the people and the traditions of Champagne, France, where the best sparkling wines in the world are made. That's why we stress the capital *C* when we say Champagne. *Those* are the wines we want on our desert island, not just any sparkling wine from anywhere that calls itself champagne.

When someone tries to impress you by serving "champagne" that's not French, don't rush to be impressed. Nearly all the respectable sparkling wine companies in the United States won't call their wines champagne out of respect for their French counterparts. (Of course, many of California's top sparkling wine companies are actually owned by the French — so it's no surprise that *they* won't call their wines champagne — but many other companies won't use the term, either.)

Chapter 2

These Taste Buds Are for You

In This Chapter

▶ How to slurp and gurgle

▶ The meaning and effect of acidity, tannin, alcohol, and other components of wine

▶ Six mysterious concepts of wine quality

*W*e know they're out there — the cynics who are saying, right about now, "Hey, I already know how to taste. I do it every day, three to five times a day. All that wine-tasting humbug is just another way of making wine complicated."

And you know, in a way, those cynics are right. Anyone who can taste coffee or a hamburger can taste wine. All you need are a nose, taste buds, and a brain. Unless you're like our friend who lost his sense of smell from the chemicals he used every day as a cosmetology teacher, you, too, have all it takes to taste wine properly.

You also have all it takes to speak Mandarin; however, having the ability to do something is different from knowing how to do it and applying that know-how in everyday life. In this chapter, we show you how (how to taste wine, that is — you're on your own for the Mandarin).

The Special Technique for Tasting Wine

You drink beverages every day, tasting them as they pass through your mouth. But when it comes to wine, drinking and tasting are not synonymous. Wine is much more complex than other beverages: There's more going on in a mouthful of wine. For example, most wines have a lot of different (and subtle) flavors, all at the same time, and they give you multiple simultaneous sensations, such as softness and sharpness together.

If you just drink wine by gulping it down the way you do soda, you miss a lot of what you paid for. But if you *taste* wine, you can discover its nuances. In fact, the more slowly and attentively you taste wine, the more interesting it tastes.

And with that, we have the two fundamental rules of wine tasting:

1. Slow down.

2. Pay attention.

The process of tasting a wine — of systematically experiencing all the wine's attributes — has three steps, which we discuss in the following sections. The first two steps don't actually involve your mouth at all: First, you look at the wine, and then you smell it. Finally, you get to sip it.

Savoring a wine's appearance

We enjoy looking at the wine in our glass, noticing how brilliant it is and the way it reflects the light, trying to decide precisely which shade of red it is and whether it will stain the tablecloth permanently if we tilt the glass too far.

To observe a wine's appearance, tilt a (half-full) glass away from you and look at the color of the wine against a white background, such as the tablecloth or a piece of paper (a colored background distorts the color of the wine). Notice how dark or how pale the wine is, what color it is, and whether the color fades from the center of the wine out toward the edge, where it touches the glass. Also notice whether the wine is cloudy, clear, or brilliant. (Most wines are clear. Some *unfiltered* wines — Chapter 5 explains filtering — can be less than brilliant but shouldn't be cloudy.) Eventually, you'll begin to notice patterns, such as deeper color in younger red wines.

If you have time, at this point you can also swirl the wine around in your glass (see the following section) and observe the way the wine runs back down the inside of the glass. Some wines form *legs* or *tears* that flow slowly down. Once upon a time, these legs were interpreted as the sure sign of a rich, high-quality wine. Today, we know that a wine's legs are a complicated phenomenon having to do with the surface tension of the wine and the evaporation rate of the wine's alcohol. If you're a physicist, feel free to show off your expertise and enlighten your fellow tasters — but otherwise, don't bother drawing conclusions from the legs.

The nose knows

After you observe a wine's appearance, you get to the really fun part of tasting wine: swirling and sniffing. This is the stage when you can let your imagination run wild, and no one will ever dare to contradict you. If you say that a wine smells like wild strawberries to you, how can anyone prove that it doesn't?

Before we explain the smelling ritual, and the tasting technique that goes along with it (described in the next section), we want to assure you that (a) you don't have to apply this procedure to every single wine you drink; (b) you won't look foolish doing it, at least in the eyes of other wine lovers (we can't speak for the remaining 90 percent of the human population); and (c) it's a great trick at parties to avoid talking with someone you don't like.

To get the most out of your sniffing, swirl the wine in the glass first. But don't even *think* about swirling your wine if your glass is more than half full.

Keep your glass on the table and rotate it three or four times so that the wine swirls around inside the glass and mixes with air. Then quickly bring the glass to your nose. Stick your nose into the airspace of the glass and smell the wine. Free-associate. Is the aroma fruity, woodsy, fresh, cooked, intense, light? Your nose tires quickly, but it recovers quickly, too. Wait just a moment and try again. Listen to your friends' comments and try to find the same things they find in the smell.

As you swirl, the aromas in the wine vaporize, enabling you to smell them. Wine has so many *aromatic compounds* that whatever you find in the smell of a wine is probably not merely a figment of your imagination.

The point behind this whole ritual of swirling and sniffing is that what you smell should be pleasurable to you, maybe even fascinating, and that you should have fun in the process. But what if you notice a smell that you don't like? Hang around wine geeks for a while, and you'll start to hear words like *petrol, manure, sweaty saddle, burnt match,* and *asparagus* used to describe the aromas of some wines. "Yuck!" you say? Of course you do! Fortunately, the wines that exhibit such smells are not the wines you'll be drinking for the most part — at least not unless you really catch the wine bug. And when you do catch the wine bug, you may discover that those aromas, in the right wine, can really be a kick. Even if you don't come to enjoy those smells (some of us do, honest!), you'll appreciate them as typical characteristics of certain regions or grapes.

Wine can also have bad smells that nobody will try to defend. It doesn't happen often, but it does happen, because wine is a natural, agricultural product with a will of its own. Often, when a wine is seriously flawed, it shows immediately in the nose of the wine. Wine judges have a term for such wines. They call them *DNPIM — Do Not Put in Mouth.* Not that you'll get ill, but why subject your taste buds to the same abuse that your nose just took? Sometimes a bad cork is to blame, and sometimes the problem lies with some issue in the winemaking or even the storage of the wine. Just rack it up to experience and open a different bottle.

Tips for smelling wine

Try these techniques for getting more out of wine when you sniff:

- Be bold. Stick your nose right into the airspace of the glass where the aromas are captured.

- Don't wear a strong scent; it will compete with the smell of the wine.

- Don't knock yourself out smelling a wine when strong food aromas are present. The meat you smell in the wine could really be a stew cooking on the stove.

- Become a smeller. Smell every ingredient when you cook, everything you eat, the fresh fruits and vegetables you buy at the supermarket, even the smells of your environment — like leather, wet earth, fresh road tar, grass, flowers, your wet dog, shoe polish, and your medicine cabinet. Stuff your mental database with smells so you'll have aroma memories at your disposal when you need to draw on them.

- Try different techniques of sniffing. Some people like to take short, quick sniffs, while others like to inhale a deep whiff of the wine's smell. Keeping your mouth open a bit while you inhale can help you perceive aromas. (Some people even hold one nostril closed and smell with the other, but we think that's a bit kinky.)

While you're choosing the next bottle, make up your own acronyms: SOTYWE (Serve Only to Your Worst Enemies), for example, or ETMYG (Enough to Make You Gag), or our own favorite, SLADDR (Smells Like a Dirty Dish Rag).

When it comes to smelling wine, many people are concerned that they aren't able to detect as many aromas as they think they should. Smelling wine is really just a matter of practice and attention. If you start to pay more attention to smells in your normal activities, you'll get better at smelling wine.

The mouth action

After you've looked at the wine and smelled it, you're finally allowed to taste it. This is the stage when grown men and women sit around and make strange faces, gurgling the wine and sloshing it around in their mouths with looks of intense concentration in their eyes. You can make an enemy for life if you distract a wine taster just at the moment when he's focusing all his energy on the last few drops of a special wine.

Here's the procedure to follow:

1. Take a medium-sized sip of wine.

2. Hold the wine in your mouth, purse your lips, and draw in some air across your tongue, over the wine.

(Be utterly careful not to choke or dribble, or everyone will strongly suspect that you're not a wine expert.)

3. Swish the wine around in your mouth as if you're chewing it.

4. Swallow the wine.

The whole process should take several seconds, depending on how much you are concentrating on the wine. (Wondering what to concentrate on? The next two sections tell you, along with the section "Parlez-Vous Winespeak?" later in this chapter.)

Feeling the tastes

Taste buds on the tongue can register various sensations, which are known as the basic tastes — sweetness, sourness, saltiness, bitterness, and umami, a savory characteristic. Of these tastes, sweetness, sourness, and bitterness are those most commonly found in wine. By moving the wine around in your mouth, you give it a chance to hit all your taste buds so that you don't miss anything in the wine (even if sourness and bitterness sound like things you wouldn't mind missing).

As you swish the wine around in your mouth, you're also buying time. Your brain needs a few seconds to figure out what the tongue is tasting and make some sense of it. Any sweetness in the wine registers in your brain first because many of the taste buds on the front of your tongue — where the wine hits first — capture the sensation of sweetness; *acidity* (which, by the way, is known to normal people as *sourness*) and bitterness register subsequently. While your brain is working out the relative impressions of sweetness, acidity, and bitterness, you can be thinking about how the wine feels in your mouth — whether it's heavy, light, smooth, rough, and so on.

Wines have noses — and palates, too

With poetic license typical of wine tasters, someone once dubbed the smell of a wine its *nose* — and the expression took hold. If someone says that a wine has a huge nose, he means that the wine has a very strong smell. If he says that he detects lemon *in the nose* or *on the nose,* he means that the wine smells a bit like lemons.

In fact, most wine tasters rarely use the word *smell* to describe how a wine smells because the word *smell* (like the word *odor*) seems pejorative. Wine tasters talk about the wine's nose

or aroma. Sometimes they use the word *bouquet,* although that word is falling out of fashion.

Just as a wine taster might use the term *nose* for the smell of a wine, he might use the word *palate* in referring to the taste of a wine. A wine's palate is the overall impression the wine gives in your mouth, or any isolated aspect of the wine's taste — as in, "This wine has a harmonious palate," or "The palate of this wine is a bit acidic." When a wine taster says that he finds raspberries *on the palate,* he means that the wine has the flavor of raspberries.

Ten aromas (or flavors) associated with wine

The following are some of the most common aromas you can find in wine:

Fruits	Herbs
Flowers	Earth
Grass	Tobacco
Butterscotch	Toast
Vanilla	Coffee, mocha, or chocolate

Tasting the smells

Until you cut your nose in on the action, all you can taste in the wine are those three sensations of sweetness, acidity, and bitterness and a general impression of weight and texture. Where have all the wild strawberries gone?

They're still there in the wine, right next to the chocolate and plums. But to be perfectly correct about it, these flavors are actually *aromas* that you taste, not through tongue contact, but by inhaling them up an interior nasal passage in the back of your mouth called the *retronasal passage* (see Figure 2-1). When you draw in air across the wine in your mouth, you're vaporizing the aromas just as you did when you swirled the wine in your glass. There's a method to this madness.

Figure 2-1:
Wine flavors are actually aromas that vaporize in your mouth; you per-ceive them through the rear nasal passage.

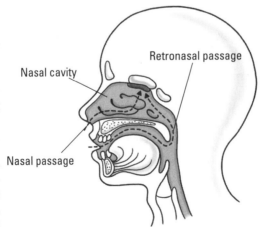

Retronasal passage

Nasal cavity

Nasal passage

Illustration by Lisa S. Reed

After you go through all this rigmarole, it's time to reach a conclusion: Do you like what you tasted? The possible answers are yes, no, an indifferent shrug of the shoulders, or "I'm not sure, let me take another taste," which means that you have serious wine-nerd potential.

Parlez-Vous Winespeak?

Now we have to confess that there is one step between knowing how to taste wine and always drinking wine that you like. And it's a doozy. That step is putting taste into words. You wouldn't have to bother with this detail if only you could always choose your wines the way that customers choose cheese in a gourmet shop. ("Can I try that one? No, I don't like it; let me taste the one next to it. Good. I'll take half a pound.")

"Like/Don't like" is a no-brainer when you have the wine in your mouth. But most of the time, you have to buy the stuff without tasting it first. So unless you want to drink the same wine for the rest of your life, you're going to have to decide what you like or don't like in a wine and communicate that to another person who can steer you toward a wine you'll like.

There are two hurdles here: Finding the words to describe what you like or don't like and then getting the other person to understand what you mean. Naturally, it helps if everyone speaks the same language.

Unfortunately, Winespeak is a dialect with an undisciplined and sometimes poetic vocabulary whose definitions change all the time, depending on who's speaking. In case you really want to get into this wine thing, we treat you to some sophisticated wine language in Chapters 5 and 19. In the following sections, we provide a few basic words and concepts to get you started.

Is it sweetness or fruitiness?

Beginning wine tasters sometimes describe dry wines as sweet because they confuse fruitiness with sweetness. Here's the difference:

✔ A wine is *fruity* when it has distinct aromas and flavors of fruit. You smell the fruitiness with your nose; in your mouth, you "smell" it through your retronasal passage (see the earlier section "Tasting the smells").

✔ Sweetness, on the other hand, is a tactile impression on your tongue. When in doubt, try holding your nose when you taste the wine; if the wine really is sweet, you'll be able to taste the sweetness despite the fact that you can't smell the fruitiness.

Touchy-feely

Softness and firmness are actually *textural impressions* a wine gives you as you taste it. Just as your mouth feels temperature in a liquid, it also feels texture. Some wines literally *feel* soft and smooth as they move through your mouth, while others feel hard, rough, or coarse. In white wines, acid is usually responsible for impressions of hardness or firmness (or crispness); in red wines, tannin is usually responsible. Low levels of either substance can make a wine feel pleasantly soft — or too soft, depending on the wine and your taste preferences. Unfermented sugar also contributes to an impression of softness, and alcohol can, too. But very high alcohol — which is fairly common in wines these days — can give a wine an edge of hardness.

The sequential palate

The tastes of a wine reveal themselves sequentially as the tongue detects them, and they register in your brain. We recommend that you follow the natural sequence we describe in the next sections when you try to put words to what you're tasting.

Sweetness

As soon as you put the wine into your mouth, you can usually notice sweetness or the lack of it. In Winespeak, *dry* is the opposite of sweet. Classify the wine you're tasting as either *dry, off-dry* (in other words, somewhat sweet), or *sweet*.

Acidity

All wine contains acid (mainly *tartaric acid,* which exists in grapes), but some wines are more acidic than others. Acidity is more of a taste factor in white wines than in reds. For white wines, acidity is the backbone of the wine's taste (it gives the wine firmness in your mouth). White wines with a high amount of acidity feel *crisp,* and those without enough acidity feel *flabby.*

You generally perceive acidity in the middle of your mouth — what wine-tasters call the *mid-palate.* You can also sense the consequences of acidity (or the lack of it) in the overall style of the wine — whether it's a tart little number or a soft and generous sort, for example. Classify the wine you're tasting as *crisp, soft,* or *couch potato.*

Tannin

Tannin is a substance that exists naturally in the skins, seeds (or *pips*), and stems of grapes. Because red wines are fermented with their grape skins and pips, and because red grape varieties are generally higher in tannin than white varieties, tannin levels are far higher in red wines than in white wines. Oak barrels can also contribute tannin to wines, both reds and whites.

Have you ever taken a sip of a red wine and rapidly experienced a drying-out feeling in your mouth, as if something had blotted up all your saliva? That's tannin.

To generalize a bit, tannin is to a red wine what acidity is to a white: a backbone. Tannins alone can taste bitter, but some tannins in wine are less bitter than others. Also, other elements of the wine, such as sweetness, can mask the perception of bitterness (see the section "Balance," later in this chapter). You sense tannin — as bitterness or as firmness or richness of texture — mainly in the rear of your mouth and, if the amount of tannin in a wine is high, on the inside of your cheeks and on your gums. Depending on the amount and nature of its tannin, you can describe a red wine as *astringent, firm,* or *soft.*

Body

A wine's body is an impression you get from the whole of the wine — not a basic taste that registers on your tongue. It's the impression of the weight and size of the wine in your mouth, which is usually attributable mainly to a wine's alcohol. We say *impression* because, obviously, one ounce of any wine will occupy exactly the same space in your mouth and weigh the same as one ounce of any other wine. But some wines *seem* fuller, bigger, or heavier in the mouth than others. Think about the wine's fullness and weight as you taste it. Imagine that your tongue is a tiny scale and judge how much the wine is weighing it down. Classify the wine as *light-bodied, medium-bodied,* or *full-bodied.*

The flavor dimension

Wines have flavors (er, we mean *mouth aromas*), but wines don't come in a specific flavor. Although you may enjoy the suggestion of chocolate in a red wine that you're tasting, you wouldn't want to go to a wine store and ask for a chocolaty wine, unless you don't mind the idea of people holding their hands over their mouths and trying not to laugh aloud at you.

TIP

Is it acid or tannin?

Red wines have acid as well as tannin, and distinguishing between the two as you taste a wine can be a real challenge. When you're not sure whether you're perceiving mainly tannin or acid, pay attention to how your mouth feels *after* you swallow the wine. Acid makes you salivate (saliva is alkaline, and it flows to neutralize the acid). Tannin leaves your mouth dry.

Instead, you should refer to *families of flavors* in wine. You have your *fruity wines* (the ones that make you think of all sorts of fruit when you smell them or taste them), your *earthy wines* (these flavors make you think of minerals and rocks, walks in the forest, turning the earth in your garden, dry leaves, and so on), your *spicy wines* (cinnamon, cloves, black pepper, or Indian spices, for example), your *herbal wines* (mint, grass, hay, rosemary, and so on), and so on, and so on. So many flavors exist in wines that we could go on and on (and we often do!), but you get the picture, don't you? (By the way, chocolate-like flavors would fall into the family of nuts or kernels, along with flavors of coffee and of nuts themselves.)

If you like a wine and want to try another wine that's similar but different (and it will always be different, we guarantee you), one method is to decide what families of flavors in the wine you like and mention that to the person selling you your next bottle. In Parts III, IV and V, you find wines that fit these specific flavors.

Another aspect of flavor that's important to consider is a wine's *flavor intensity* — how much flavor the wine has, regardless of what those flavors are. Some wines are as flavorful as a Big Mac, while others have flavors as subtle as fillet of sole. Flavor intensity is a major factor in pairing wine with food, as you can read in Chapter 9, and it's also an issue in determining how much a wine appeals to you.

The Quality Issue

Did you notice, by any chance, that nowhere among the terms we use to describe wines in the previous section are the words *great, very good,* or *good?* Instead of worrying about crisp wines, earthy wines, and medium-bodied wines, wouldn't it just be easier to walk into a wine shop and say, "Give me a very good wine for dinner tonight"? Isn't *quality* the ultimate issue — or at least, quality within your price range, also known as *value?*

In fact, much of the marketing of wine revolves around the notion of quality, except in the case of the least expensive wines. Wine producers constantly brag about the quality ratings that their wines receive from critics, because a high rating — implying high quality — translates into increased sales for a wine.

However, quality wines come in all colors, all degrees of sweetness and dryness, and all flavor profiles. Just because a wine is high quality doesn't mean that you'll actually enjoy it, any more than a three-star rating means that you'll love a particular restaurant. We've purchased highly rated wines and ended up pouring them down the sink because we didn't care to drink them. Personal taste is simply more relevant than quality in choosing a wine.

Taste is personal

Literally! The perception of the basic tastes on the tongue varies from one person to the next. Research has proven that some people have more taste buds than others, and are, therefore, more sensitive to characteristics such as sourness or bitterness in food and beverages. The most sensitive tasters are called, somewhat misleadingly, *supertasters* — not because they're more expert, but because they perceive sensations such as bitterness more acutely. If you find diet sodas very bitter, or if you need to add a lot of sugar to your coffee to make it palatable, you might fall into this category — and you, therefore, might find many red wines unpleasant, even if other people consider them great.

Degrees of quality do exist among wines. But a wine's quality is not absolute: How great a wine is or isn't depends on who's doing the judging.

The instruments that measure the quality of a wine are a human being's nose, mouth, and brain, and because everyone is different, everyone has a different opinion on how good a wine is. The combined opinions of a group of trained, experienced palates (also known as wine experts) is usually considered a definitive judgment of a wine's quality. (Turn to Chapter 19 for more about expert opinion.)

In the following sections, we explore what makes a good wine good and what makes a poor wine taste bad.

What's a good wine?

A good wine is, above all, a wine that you like enough to drink, because the whole purpose of a wine is to give pleasure to those who drink it. After that, how good a wine is depends on how it measures up to a set of (more or less) agreed-upon standards of performance established by experienced, trained experts. These standards involve mysterious concepts like *balance, length, depth, complexity, finish,* and *trueness to type* (*typicity* in Winespeak, *typicité* in Snobwinespeak), which we explain in the following sections. None of these concepts is objectively measurable, by the way.

Balance

The three words *sweetness, acidity,* and *tannin,* which we talk about in the "Parlez-Vous Winespeak?" section earlier in this chapter, represent three of the major *components* (parts) of wine. The fourth is *alcohol.* Besides being one of the reasons we usually want to drink a glass of wine in the first place, alcohol is an important player in wine quality.

Balance in action

For firsthand experience of how the principle of taste balance works, try this: Make a very strong cup of black tea and chill it. When you sip it, the cold tea will taste bitter, because it's very tannic. Now add lemon juice; the tea will taste astringent (constricting the pores in your mouth), because the acid of the lemon and the tannin of the tea are accentuating each other. Now add a lot of sugar to the tea. The sweetness should counterbalance the acid-tannin impact, and the tea will taste softer than it did before.

Balance is the relationship of these four components to one another. A wine is balanced when nothing sticks out, such as harsh tannin or too much sweetness, as you taste the wine. Most wines are balanced to most people. But if you have any pet peeves about food — if you really hate anything tart, for example, or if you never eat sweets — you might perceive some wines to be unbalanced. If you perceive them to be unbalanced, then they are unbalanced for you. (Professional tasters know their own idiosyncrasies and adjust for them when they judge wine.)

Tannin and acidity are *hardening elements* in a wine (they make a wine taste firmer in the mouth), while alcohol and sugar (if any) are *softening elements.* The balance of a wine is the interrelationship of the hard and the soft aspects of a wine, and a key indicator of quality.

Length

When we call wines *long* or *short,* we're not referring to the size of the bottle or how quickly we empty it. *Length* describes a wine that gives an impression of going all the way on the palate — you can taste it across the full length of your tongue — rather than stopping short halfway through your tasting of it. Many wines today are very *upfront* on the palate — they make a big impression as soon as you taste them, but they don't go the distance in your mouth. In other words, they're *short.* Generally, high alcohol or excess tannin is to blame. Long length is a sure sign of high quality.

Depth

Depth is another subjective, unmeasurable attribute of a high-quality wine. We say a wine has *depth* when it seems to have a dimension of verticality — that is, it doesn't taste flat and one-dimensional in your mouth. A "flat" wine can never be great.

Complexity

Nothing is wrong with a simple, straightforward wine, especially if you enjoy it. But a wine that keeps revealing different things about itself, always showing you a new flavor or impression — a wine that has *complexity* — is usually considered better quality. Some experts use the term *complexity* specifically to indicate that a wine has a multiplicity of aromas and flavors, while others use it in a more holistic (but less precise) sense, to refer to the total impression a wine gives you.

Finish

The impression a wine leaves in the back of your mouth and in your throat after you swallow it is its *finish* or *aftertaste.* In a good wine, you can still perceive the wine's flavors, such as fruitiness or spiciness, at that point. Some wines may finish *hot,* because of high alcohol, or *bitter,* because of tannin — both shortcomings. Or a wine may have nothing much at all to say for itself after you swallow.

Typicity

In order to judge whether a wine is true to its type, you have to know how that type is supposed to taste. So you have to know the textbook characteristics of wines made from the major grape varieties and wines of the world's classic wine regions. (For example, the Cabernet Sauvignon grape typically has an aroma and flavor of black currants, and the French white wine called Pouilly-Fumé typically has a slight gunflint aroma.) Turn to Chapter 3 and Parts III, IV, and V for all those details.

What's a bad wine?

Strangely enough, the right to declare a wine *good* because you like it doesn't carry with it the right to call a wine *bad* just because you don't. In this game, you get to make your own rules, but you don't get to force other people to live by them.

The fact is that very few bad wines exist in the world today, compared to even 20 years ago. And many of the wines we could call *bad* are actually just bad *bottles* of wine — bottles that were handled badly so that the good wine inside them got ruined.

Here are some characteristics that everyone agrees indicate a bad wine (or a bad bottle). We hope you never meet one.

✔ **Moldy fruit:** Have you ever eaten a raspberry from the bottom of the container that had a dusty, cardboardy taste to it? That same taste of rot can be in a wine if the wine was made from grapes that weren't completely fresh and healthy when they were harvested. Bad wine.

✔ **Vinegar:** In the natural evolution of things, wine is just a passing stage between grape juice and vinegar. Most wines today remain forever in the wine stage because of technology or careful winemaking. If you find a wine that has crossed the line toward vinegar, it's bad wine.

✔ **Chemical or bacterial smells:** The most common are acetone (nail polish thinner) and sulfur flaws (rotten eggs, burnt rubber, bad garlic). Bad wines.

✔ **Oxidized wine:** This wine smells flat, weak, or maybe cooked, and it tastes the same. It might have been a good wine once, but air — oxygen — got in somehow and killed the wine. Bad bottle.

✔ **Cooked aromas and taste:** When a wine has been stored or shipped in heat, it can actually taste cooked or baked as a result. Often there's telltale leakage from the cork, or the cork has pushed up a bit. Bad bottle. (Unfortunately, every other bottle of that wine that experienced the same shipping or storage will also be bad.)

✔ **Corky wine:** The most common flaw, *corkiness* comes across as a smell of damp cardboard that gets worse with air, as well as a diminished flavor intensity. It's caused by a bad cork, and any wine in a bottle that's sealed with a cork is at risk for it. Bad bottle.

Let's not dwell too long on what can go wrong with a wine. If you find a bad wine or a bad bottle — or even a wine that's considered a good wine, but you don't like it — just move on to something you like better. Drinking a so-called great wine that you don't enjoy is as stupid as watching a television show that bores you. Change the channel. Explore.

Chapter 3

Pinot Envy and Other Secrets about Grape Varieties

We love to visit wine country. Gazing across manicured rows of grape-vines in Napa Valley or pondering craggy terraces of rugged hillside vines in Portugal inspires us — and reinforces for us the fact that wine is an agricultural product, born of the earth, the grapevine, and the hard work of humans. Literally and emotionally, grapes are the link between the land and the wine. As you read in this chapter, grapes also happen to give us one of the easiest ways of classifying wine and making sense of the hundreds of different types of wine that exist.

The Importance of Grape Varieties

Grapes are the starting point of every wine. The grapes that make a particular wine dictate the genetic structure of that wine and how it will respond to everything the winemaker does to it. Think back to the last wine you drank. What color was it? If it was white, the odds are that's because it came from white grapes; if it was pink or red, that's because the wine came from red grapes. Did it smell herbal or earthy or fruity? Whichever, those aromas came mainly from the grapes. Was it firm and tannic or soft and voluptuous? Thank the grapes — with a nod to Mother Nature and the winemaker.

The specific grape variety (or varieties) that makes any given wine is largely responsible for the sensory characteristics the wine offers — from its appearance to its aromas, flavors, and alcohol-tannin-acid profile. How the grapes grow — the amount of sunshine and moisture they get, for example, and how ripe they are when they're harvested — can emphasize certain of these characteristics rather than others. So can winemaking processes, such as oak aging (see Chapter 5). Each type or *variety* of grape reacts in its own way to the farming and winemaking techniques that it faces.

Of genus and species

By *grape variety,* we mean the fruit of a specific type of grapevine: the fruit of the Cabernet Sauvignon vine, for example, or of the Chardonnay vine.

The term *variety* actually has specific meaning in scientific circles. A variety is a subdivision of a species. Most of the world's wines are made from grape varieties that belong to the species *vinifera* — itself a subdivision of the genus *Vitis.* This species originated in Europe and western Asia; other distinct species of *Vitis* are native to North America.

Grapes of other species can also make wine; for example, the Concord grape, which makes Concord wine as well as grape juice and jelly, belongs to the native American species *Vitis labrusca.* But the number of non-vinifera wines is small because the flavor of those grapes is less popular in wine.

A variety of varieties

Snowflakes and fingerprints aren't the only examples of Nature's infinite variety. Within the genus *Vitis* and the species *vinifera,* as many as 10,000 varieties of wine grapes exist. If wine from every one of these varieties were commercially available and you drank the wine of a different variety every single day, it would take you more than 27 years to experience them all!

Not that you would want to. Within those 10,000 varieties are grapes that have the ability to make extraordinary wine, grapes that tend to make very ordinary wine, and grapes that only a parent could love. Most varieties are obscure grapes whose wines rarely enter into international commerce.

An extremely adventuresome grape nut who has plenty of free time to explore the back roads of Spain, Portugal, Italy, and Greece might be able to encounter only 1,500-plus different grape varieties (over four years' worth of drinking) in his lifetime. The grape varieties you might encounter in the course of your normal wine enjoyment probably number fewer than 50.

How grapes vary

All sorts of attributes distinguish each grape variety from the next. These attributes fall into two categories: personality traits and performance factors. *Personality traits* are the characteristics of the fruit itself — its flavors, for example. *Performance factors* refer to how the grapevine grows, how its fruit ripens, and how quickly it can get from 0 to 60 miles per hour.

The phylloxera threat

If endangered species lists had existed at the end of the 19th century, *Vitis vinifera* certainly would have been on them. The entire species was nearly eradicated by a tiny louse called *phylloxera* that immigrated to Europe from America and proceeded to feast on the roots of vinifera grapevines, wiping out vineyards all across the continent.

To this day, no remedy exists to protect vinifera roots from phylloxera. What saved the species was grafting vinifera vines onto rootstocks of native American species that are resistant to the bug. The practice of grafting the fruit-bearing part of *Vitis vinifera* onto the rooting part of other, phylloxera-resistant species continues today everywhere in the world where phylloxera is present and fine wine is made. Miraculously, each grape variety maintains its own character despite the fact that its roots are alien.

Personality traits of grape varieties

Skin color is the most fundamental distinction among grape varieties. Every grape variety is considered either a white variety or a red (or black) one, according to the skin color of the ripe grapes. (A few red-skinned varieties are further distinguished by having red pulp rather than white pulp, but almost all red varieties have white pulp.)

Individual grape varieties also differ from one another in other ways:

- ✔ **Aromatic compounds:** Some grapes (like Muscat) contribute floral aromas and flavors to their wines, for example, while others contribute herbaceous notes (as Sauvignon Blanc can) or fruity character. Some grapes have neutral aromas and flavors and, therefore, make fairly neutral wines.

- ✔ **Acidity levels:** Some grapes are naturally disposed to higher acid levels than others, which makes for crisper, leaner wines.

- ✔ **Thickness of skin and size of the individual grapes (called *berries*):** Black grapes with thick skins naturally have more tannin than those with thin skins; ditto for small-berried varieties compared to large-berried varieties, because their skin-to-juice ratio is higher. More tannin in the grapes translates into a firmer, more tannic red wine.

The composite personality traits of any grape variety are fairly evident in wines made from that grape. A Cabernet Sauvignon wine is usually more tannic and slightly lower in alcohol than a comparable Merlot wine, for example, because that's the nature of those two grapes.

The ripening process

When grapes are not yet ripe, they contain high amounts of acid and very little sugar — which is true for any fruit — and their flavor is tart. As ripening progresses, they become sweeter and less acidic (although they always retain some acid), and their flavors become richer and more complex. Their skins get thinner, and even their seeds and stems "ripen." In red grape varieties, the tannin in the skins, stems, and pips (seeds) becomes richer and less astringent. The stage of ripeness that the grapes attain is a big factor in the style of the wine.

Performance factors of grape varieties

How a particular grape variety performs in the field is vitally important to the grape grower because the vine's growing tendencies determine how easy or challenging it will be to cultivate in a particular site. The issues include

- How much time a variety typically needs to ripen its fruit. (In regions with short growing seasons, early-ripening varieties do best.)

- How dense and compact the grape bunches are. (In warm, damp climates, dense bunches can have mildew problems.)

- How much vegetation a particular variety tends to grow. (In fertile soils, a vine that's disposed to growing a lot of leaves and shoots can have so much vegetation that the grapes don't get enough sun to ripen.)

The reasons some grape varieties perform brilliantly in certain places (and make excellent wine as a result) are extremely complex. The amount of heat and cold, the amount of wind and rain (or lack of it), and the slant of the sun's rays on a hillside of vines are among the factors affecting a vine's performance. In any case, no two vineyards in the world have precisely the same combination of these factors — precisely the same *terroir* (see Chapter 4). The issue simply defies simple generalizations.

Grape royalty

Bees have their queens, gorillas have their silverbacks, and humans have their royal families. The grape kingdom has nobles, too — at least as interpreted by the people who drink the wine made from those grapes. *Noble* grape varieties (as wine people call them) have the potential to make great — not just good — wine. Every noble grape variety can claim at least one wine region where it's the undisputed king. The wines made from noble grapes on their home turf can be so great that they inspire winemakers in far-flung regions to grow the same grape in their own vineyards. The noble grape might prove itself noble there, too, but frequently it doesn't. Adaptability isn't a prerequisite of nobility.

Classic examples of noble grape varieties at their best are

- ✔ The Chardonnay grape and the Pinot Noir grape in Burgundy, France
- ✔ The Cabernet Sauvignon grape in Bordeaux, France
- ✔ The Syrah grape in France's Northern Rhône Valley
- ✔ The Chenin Blanc grape in France's Loire Valley
- ✔ The Nebbiolo grape in Piedmont, Italy
- ✔ The Sangiovese grape in Tuscany, Italy
- ✔ The Riesling grape in the Mosel and Rheingau regions of Germany

A Primer on White Grape Varieties

This section includes descriptions of the 12 most important white *vinifera* varieties today. In describing the grapes, we naturally describe the types of wine that are made from each grape. These wines can be varietal wines or place-name wines that don't mention the grape variety anywhere on the label (a common practice for European wines; see Chapter 4). These grapes can also be blending partners for other grapes, in wines that are made from multiple grape varieties. (Turn to Chapter 2 for a quick review of some of the descriptors we use in this section.) We discuss these wines in the rough order of their importance.

Chardonnay, do you take this limestone soil?

One key factor in how a grape variety performs is the soil of the vineyard. Over the centuries, some classic compatibilities between grape varieties and types of soil have become evident: Chardonnay in limestone or chalk, Cabernet Sauvignon in gravelly soil, Pinot Noir in limestone, and Riesling in slatey soil. At any rate, these are the soils of the regions where these grape varieties perform at their legendary best.

Soil affects a grapevine in several ways: It provides nutrition for the grapevine; it can influence the temperature of the vineyard; and it's a water-management system for the plant.

A safe generalization is that the best soils are those that have good drainage and aren't particularly fertile. (An extreme example is the soil — if we can call it that — of the Châteauneuf-du-Pape district in France's Rhône Valley: It's just stones.) The wisdom of the ages dictates that the grapevine must struggle to produce the best grapes, and well-drained, less fertile soils challenge the vine to struggle, regardless of what variety the grapevine is.

Chardonnay

Chardonnay is a noble grape for its role in producing the greatest dry white wines in the world and the greatest sparkling wines — white Burgundies, in the first case, and Champagnes (when it's usually part of a blend), in the second case. Today, it also ends up in a huge amount of everyday wine. The Chardonnay grape grows in practically every wine-producing country of the world for two reasons: It's quite adaptable to a wide range of climates, and the name *Chardonnay* on a wine label is a surefire sales tool.

Because the flavors of Chardonnay are very compatible with those of oak — and because white Burgundy (the great prototype) is generally an oaked wine, and because many wine drinkers love the flavor of oak — most Chardonnay wines receive some oak treatment either during or after fermentation. (For the best Chardonnays, oak treatment means expensive barrels of French oak, but for value-priced Chardonnays, it can mean soaking oak chips in the wine or even adding liquid essence of oak. See Chapter 5 for more on oak.) In some places, notably northeastern Italy and France's Chablis and Mâconnais districts, Chardonnay wines are often not oaked. Some winemakers in California, Australia, and elsewhere are also now making un-oaked Chardonnay. But oaky Chardonnay wine is the norm.

Oaked Chardonnay is so common that some wine drinkers confuse the flavor of oak with the flavor of Chardonnay. If your glass of Chardonnay smells or tastes toasty, smoky, spicy, vanilla-like, or butterscotch-like, that's the oak you're perceiving, not the Chardonnay!

Chardonnay itself has fruity aromas and flavors that range from apple — in cooler wine regions — to tropical fruits, especially pineapple, in warmer regions. Chardonnay also can display subtle earthy aromas, such as mushroom or minerals. Chardonnay wine has medium to high acidity and is generally full-bodied. Classically, Chardonnay wines are dry, but most inexpensive Chardonnays these days are actually somewhat sweet.

The top Chardonnay-based wines (except for most Champagnes and similar bubblies) are 100 percent Chardonnay. But less expensive wines that are labeled *Chardonnay* — those selling for less than $12 a bottle in the United States, for example — are likely to have some other, far less distinguished grape blended in, to help reduce the cost of making the wine. (Chapter 4 explains the regulations governing grape variety blending.)

Riesling

The great Riesling wines of Germany and of Alsace, France, have put the Riesling grape on the charts as an undisputedly noble variety. Riesling shows its real class only in a few other places. Austria, Australia's Clare Valley region, and New York's Finger Lake region are among the few.

In some ways, Riesling is the antithesis of Chardonnay. While Chardonnay is usually gussied up with oak, Riesling almost never is; while Chardonnay can be full-bodied and rich, Riesling is more often light-bodied, crisp, and refreshing. Riesling's fresh, vivid personality can make many Chardonnays taste clumsy in comparison.

Trademarks of Riesling are high acidity, low to medium alcohol levels, and aromas/flavors that range from ebulliently fruity to flowery to minerally.

The common perception of Riesling wines is that they're sweet, and many of them are — but plenty of them aren't. (Riesling grapes can be vinified either way, according to the style of wine a producer wants to make.) And some Riesling wines that are not technically dry don't actually taste sweet, because their high acidity undercuts the impression of sweetness. Look for the word *trocken* (meaning dry) on German Riesling labels and the word *dry* on U.S. labels if you prefer the dry style of Riesling. We suggest that you not get hung up on the sweetness issue and just focus on how delicious the wine can be.

If you consider yourself an insider who's hip to new trends, check out the Riesling section of your wine shop rather than the Chardonnay aisle. And definitely look for Riesling wines in top restaurants, because they can be delicious with lighter foods.

Sauvignon Blanc

Sauvignon Blanc is a white variety with very distinctive character. It's high in acidity and has pronounced aromas and flavors. Besides herbaceous notes (sometimes referred to as *grassy*), Sauvignon Blanc wines display mineral aromas and flavors, vegetal character, or — in certain climates — fruity character, such as ripe melon, figs, or passion fruit. The wines are light- to medium-bodied and dry or dryish. Most of them are unoaked.

France has two classic wine regions for the Sauvignon Blanc grape: the Loire Valley, where the two best-known Sauvignon wines are called Sancerre and Pouilly-Fumé (described in Chapter 10), and Bordeaux. In Bordeaux, Sauvignon Blanc is sometimes blended with Sémillon (described in Table 3-1 in the later section "Other white grapes"); some of the Bordeaux wines that are blends of the two grapes and fermented in oak are among the great white wines of the world.

Sauvignon Blanc is also important in northeastern Italy, South Africa, Chile, and parts of California (sometimes labeled as *Fumé Blanc*). New Zealand's Sauvignon Blanc wines are particularly renowned for their intensely flavorful style.

Pinot Gris/Pinot Grigio

Pinot Gris (gree) is one of several grape varieties called *Pinot:* Others include Pinot Blanc (white Pinot), Pinot Noir (black Pinot), and Pinot Meunier (we don't know how that one translates). Pinot Gris (gray Pinot), called *Pinot Grigio* in Italian, is considered a white grape, although its skin color is unusually dark for a white variety.

Pinot Gris wines are medium- to full-bodied and usually not oaky. Those labeled Pinot Grigio typically have fairly neutral aromas and flavors and those called Pinot Gris tend to have more flavor, such as notes of peach, peach-stone, or orange rind.

Pinot Gris is an important grape throughout northeastern Italy and also grows in Germany, where it's called Ruländer. The only region in France where Pinot Gris is important is Alsace, where it really struts its stuff. Oregon enjoys success with Pinot Gris, and more and more winemakers in California are now taking a shot at it. Most of the California versions are mass-market wines labeled Pinot Grigio and modeled after the Italian style, but are less dry, more flavorful, and softer in acidity.

Other white grapes

Table 3-1 describes some other grapes whose names you see on wine labels or whose wine you could drink in place-name wines without realizing it.

Table 3-1	Other White Grapes and Their Characteristics
Grape Type	**Characteristics**
Albariño	An aromatic grape from the northwestern Spanish region of Rías Baixas and Portugal's northerly Vinho Verde region, where it's called Alvarinho. It makes medium-bodied, crisp, stony- and appley-tasting, usually unoaked white wines whose high glycerin gives them silky texture.
Chenin Blanc	A noble grape in the Loire Valley of France, for Vouvray and other wines. The best wines have high acidity and a fascinating oily texture (they feel rather viscous in your mouth). A few good dry Chenin Blanc wines come from California. In South Africa, the wine is often called Steen.

Grape Type	Characteristics
Gewürztraminer (geh-*vairtz*-trah-mee-ner)	A wonderfully exotic grape that makes fairly deep-colored, full-bodied, soft white wines with aromas and flavors of roses and lychee fruit. France's Alsace region is a classic domain of this variety; the wines have pronounced floral and fruity character but are fairly dry. Italy's Alto Adige region makes dry, minerally Gewürztraminer, as do a few wineries in California, Oregon, and New York.
Grüner Veltliner	A native Austrian variety that boasts complex aromas and flavors (vegetal, spicy, mineral), rich texture, and usually substantial weight.
Muscat	An aromatic grape that makes Italy's sparkling Asti (which, incidentally, tastes exactly like ripe Muscat grapes). Extremely pretty floral aromas. In Alsace and Austria, makes a dry wine, and in lots of places (southern France, southern Italy, Australia) makes a delicious, sweet dessert wine. Moscato (the Italian name) from California and Australia is becoming a popular mass-market wine in the U.S.
Pinot Blanc	Fairly neutral in aroma and flavors yet can make characterful wines. High acidity and low sugar levels translate into dry, crisp, medium-bodied wines. Alsace, Austria, northern Italy, and Germany are the main production zones.
Sémillon (seh-mee-yohn)	Sauvignon Blanc's classic blending partner and a good grape in its own right. Sémillon wine is low in acid relative to Sauvignon Blanc and has attractive but subtle aromas — lanolin sometimes, although it can be slightly herbaceous when young. A major grape in Australia, and southwestern France, including Bordeaux (where it's the key player in the dessert wine, Sauternes).
Viognier (vee-ohn-yay)	A grape from France's Rhône Valley that's grown in California, the south of France, South America, and elsewhere. Floral aroma, delicately apricot-like flavor, medium- to full-bodied with low acidity.

Aliases and a.k.a.'s

The same grape variety will often go by different names in different countries or even in different districts within the same country. Often, it's just a case of traditional local synonyms. But sometimes, grape growers call one variety by the name of another because they think that's what they're growing (until a specialized botanist called an *ampelographer* examines their vines and tells them otherwise). In Chile, for example, some of the so-called Merlot turned out to be another grape entirely: Carménère.

A Primer on Red Grape Varieties

If you love red wine, lucky you! You have a wide range from which to choose, because so many red grape varieties make good quality and interesting wines. Some of these varieties grow just about everywhere, while others are specialties of certain countries or regions. You'll encounter these grapes in varietal wines, place-name wines, and sometimes in blends. (See Chapter 4 for a chart listing the grape varieties of major place-name wines. Also, check out Chapter 2 for a guide to some of the descriptors we use in this section.)

International superstars

Four red grape varieties are so renowned that winemakers all over the world have tried their hands at growing them and making wine from them. Read on to discover these four superstars.

Cabernet Sauvignon

Cabernet Sauvignon is a noble grape variety that grows well in many climates, except very cool areas. It became famous through the age-worthy red wines of the Médoc district of Bordeaux (which also contain Merlot and Cabernet Franc, in varying proportions; see Chapter 10). But today, California is an equally important region for Cabernet Sauvignon — not to mention Washington, Italy, Australia, South Africa, Chile, Argentina, and so on.

The Cabernet Sauvignon grape makes medium- to full-bodied wines that are high in tannin. The textbook descriptor for Cabernet Sauvignon's aroma and flavor is *black currants* or *cassis*. Many of the finest wines have a marked note of minerality, and many have toasty or smoky aromas and flavors from oak.

Cabernet Sauvignon wines come in all price and quality levels. The least-expensive versions are usually fairly soft and very fruity. The best wines are rich and firm with great depth and classic, concentrated Cabernet flavor. Serious Cabernet Sauvignons can age for 15 years or more.

Because Cabernet Sauvignon is fairly tannic (and because of the blending precedent in Bordeaux), winemakers often blend it with other grapes; usually Merlot — being less tannic — is considered an ideal partner. Australian winemakers have an unusual practice of blending Cabernet Sauvignon with Syrah. (More on that in Chapter 13.)

Cabernet Sauvignon often goes by just its first name, *Cabernet* (although it isn't the only Cabernet) or even by its nickname, *Cab*.

Merlot

Deep color, full body, high alcohol, and soft tannin are the characteristics of wines made from the Merlot grape. The aromas and flavors can be plummy or sometimes chocolatey, or they can suggest tea leaves.

Some wine drinkers find Merlot easier to like than Cabernet Sauvignon because it's less tannic. (But some winemakers feel that Merlot isn't satisfactory in its own right, and thus often blend it with Cabernet Sauvignon, Cabernet Franc, or both.) Merlot makes both inexpensive, simple wines and, when grown in the right conditions, very serious wines.

Merlot is actually the most-planted grape variety in France's Bordeaux region, where it excels in the Right Bank districts of Pomerol and St.-Emilion. Merlot is also important in Washington, California, New York's Long Island district, northeastern Italy, and Chile, among other regions.

Pinot Noir

The late Andre Tchelitscheff, the legendary winemaker of some of California's finest Cabernets, once told us that if he could do it all over again, he'd make Pinot Noir rather than Cab. He's probably not alone. Cabernet is the sensible wine to make — a good, steady, reliable wine that doesn't give the winemaker much trouble and can achieve excellent quality — while Pinot Noir is finicky, enigmatic, and challenging. But a great Pinot Noir can be one of the greatest wines ever.

The prototype for Pinot Noir wine is red Burgundy, from France, where tiny vineyard plots yield rare treasures of wine made entirely from Pinot Noir. Oregon, California, New Zealand, and parts of Australia and Chile also produce good Pinot Noir. But Pinot Noir's production is relatively limited, because this variety is very particular about climate and soil.

Pinot Noir wine is lighter in color than Cabernet or Merlot. It has fairly high alcohol, medium to high acidity, and medium to low tannin (although oak barrels can contribute additional tannin to the wine). Its flavors and aromas can be very fruity — often like a mélange of red berries and black berries — or earthy and woodsy, depending on how it's grown and/or vinified. Pinot Noir is rarely blended with other grapes in making red wine, but most Champagnes combine Pinot Noir with Chardonnay. (Chapter 15 explains how a red grape can make a white sparking wine.)

Syrah/Shiraz

The northern part of France's Rhône Valley is the classic home for great wines from the Syrah grape, but these days, Australia can be considered the grape's second home. Syrah also grows in California, Washington, Italy, Spain, Chile, Argentina, Israel, Greece — you name it.

Syrah produces deeply colored wines with full body, firm tannin, and aromas/flavors that can suggest berries, smoked meat, black pepper, tar, or even burnt rubber (believe it or not). In Australia, Syrah (called Shiraz) comes in several styles; some Shirazes are charming, vibrantly fruity wines that are quite the opposite of the northern Rhône's powerful Syrah wines, such as Hermitage and Côte-Rôtie, while others are even more powerful than those classic French wines. Turn to Chapter 13 for more on Shiraz.

Syrah doesn't require any other grape to complement its flavors, although in Australia, it's often blended with Cabernet, and in the southern Rhône Valley, it's often part of a blended wine with Grenache and other varieties (see the later section "Other red grapes" for more about Grenache).

Local heroes

Some red grape varieties don't translate well outside their home regions, usually because growing conditions elsewhere aren't ideal. But they can make exciting wines on their home turf — wines that offer a terrific change of pace from the more standard "international" red varieties. Here are five of them, in random order.

Zinfandel

Zinfandel is one of the oldest grapes in California. Its aura is enhanced by its mysterious history: For decades, authorities were uncertain of its origins and thought that it might exist only in the United States. DNA research finally proved that Zinfandel is an obscure Croatian grape called Crljenak Kastelanski. (In case you're wondering, that's pronounced soorl-*yen*-ak kash-tel-*ahn*-ski.)

Zin — as lovers of red Zinfandel call it — makes rich, dark wines that are high in alcohol and medium to high in tannin. They can have a blackberry or raspberry aroma and flavor, a spicy or tarry character, or even a jammy flavor. Some Zins are lighter than others and meant to be enjoyed young, and some are serious wines with a tannin structure that's built for aging. (You can tell which is which by the price.) The Zinfandel grape also makes the popular pink wine called White Zinfandel.

Nebbiolo

Outside of scattered sites in northwestern Italy — mainly the Piedmont region — Nebbiolo just doesn't make remarkable wine. But the extraordinary quality of Barolo and Barbaresco, two Piedmont wines, proves what greatness Nebbiolo can achieve under the right conditions.

The Nebbiolo grape is high in both tannin and acid, which can make a wine tough. Fortunately, it also gives enough alcohol to soften the wine. Its wines can be deep in color when young but can develop orangey tinges within a few years. Its complex aroma is fruity (strawberry, cherry), earthy and woodsy (tar, truffles), herbal (mint, eucalyptus, anise), and floral (roses).

Lighter versions of Nebbiolo are meant to be drunk young — wines labeled *Nebbiolo d'Alba* or *Roero,* and some wines labeled *Nebbiolo delle Langhe,* for example — while Barolo and Barbaresco are wines that really deserve a *minimum* of 8 years' age before drinking.

Sangiovese

Sangiovese is an Italian grape that has proven itself in the Tuscany region of Italy, especially in the Brunello di Montalcino and Chianti districts. Sangiovese makes wines that are medium to high in acidity and firm in tannin; the wines can be light-bodied to full-bodied, depending on exactly where the grapes grow and how the wine is made. The aromas and flavors of the wines are fruity — especially cherry, often tart cherry — with floral nuances of violets and sometimes a slightly nutty character.

Tempranillo

Tempranillo is Spain's candidate for greatness. It gives wines deep color, fairly low acidity, and only moderate alcohol. Modern renditions of Tempranillo from the Ribera del Duero region and elsewhere in Spain prove what depth of color and fruit intensity this grape has. In more traditional wines, such as some of those in the Rioja region, much of the grape's color and flavor is lost due to long wood aging and to blending with varieties that lack color, such as Grenache.

Malbec

This grape originated in Bordeaux and is key in the southwestern French region of Cahors. But today, wine drinkers know it far better as Argentina's signature red grape variety. Malbec is a dark variety that makes deeply colored red wines with very firm tannin and spicy, dark-berry aromas and flavors. In the sunny, high elevations of Argentina's Mendoza region, the wines tend to have softer tannin and richer fruit flavors than in France.

Other red grapes

Table 3-2 describes additional red grape varieties and their wines, which you can encounter either as varietal wines or as wines named for their place of production.

Table 3-2	Other Red Grapes and Their Characteristics
Grape Type	*Characteristics*
Aglianico	From southern Italy, where it makes Taurasi and other age-worthy, powerful red wines, high in tannin.
Barbera	Italian variety that, oddly for a red grape, has little tannin but very high acidity. When fully ripe, it can give big, fruity wines with refreshing crispness. Many producers age the wine in new oak.
Cabernet Franc	A parent of Cabernet Sauvignon, and often blended with it to make Bordeaux-style wines. Ripens earlier, and has more expressive, fruitier flavor (especially berries), as well as less tannin. A specialty of the Loire Valley in France, where it makes wines with place-names such as Chinon and Bourgeuil.
Carménère	Originated in Bordeaux, but today is a key player only in Chile. Makes dark, flavorful wines with dark berry and spice notes and fairly soft tannins. Some wines can have herbal flavors if the grapes weren't ripe enough.
Gamay	Excels in the Beaujolais district of France. It makes grapey wines that can be low in tannin — although the grape itself is fairly tannic. Neither the grape called Gamay Beaujolais in California nor the grape called Napa Gamay is true Gamay.
Grenache	A Spanish grape by origin, called Garnacha there. (Most wine drinkers associate Grenache with France's southern Rhône Valley more than with Spain, however.) Sometimes Grenache makes pale, high-alcohol wines that are weak in flavor. In the right circumstances, it can make deeply colored wines with velvety texture and fruity aromas and flavors suggestive of raspberries.

Chapter 4

Wine Names and Label Lingo

● ●

In This Chapter

▶ A quick trick to decoding wine names

▶ The secret cult of *terroir*

▶ The truth behind impressive terms like *reserve* and *estate-bottled*

▶ PDO, PGI, and other strange designations

● ●

*W*e browse the shelves of wine stores all the time, not only to shop for dinner but also to keep an eye on what kinds of wines are hitting the shelves. Never before have we seen such an astounding proliferation of wine labels! New brands of wine seem to appearing out of the blue every week. All this choice is terrific — or it's completely paralyzing, depending on how you approach the situation.

One sure way to become more comfortable when confronted by shelf upon shelf of unfamiliar wine labels is to figure out how to decode the information on those labels. Reading wine labels isn't difficult, because regulations specify what items must, can, and cannot appear on a label. Master that with the help of this chapter, and you'll be basking in the richness of choices that today's wine market offers.

The Wine Name Game

All sorts of names appear on wine labels. These names often include the following:

✔ The name of the *grape* from which the wine was made

✔ A *brand name,* which is traditionally the name of the company or person that made the wine (called the *producer*); for less expensive wines, it's likely to be an invented name

✔ Sometimes a special, fanciful name for that particular wine (called a *proprietary name*)

> ✔ The name of the *place,* or *places,* where the grapes grew (the wine region, and sometimes the name of the specific vineyard property)

Then there's the *vintage* year (the year the grapes for that wine grew), which is part of the wine's identity; and sometimes you see a descriptor like *reserve,* which either has specific legal meaning or means nothing at all, depending on where the wine came from. You discover details about all these items in the following sections.

Grape names and place-names

Most of the wines you find in your wine shop or on restaurant wine lists are named in one of two basic ways: either for their *grape variety* or for the *place where the grapes grew.* That information, plus the name of the producer, becomes the shorthand name we use in talking about the wine.

Robert Mondavi Cabernet Sauvignon, for example, is a wine made by the Robert Mondavi Winery and named after the Cabernet Sauvignon grape. Fontodi Chianti Classico is a wine made by the Fontodi winery and named after the place called Chianti Classico.

You may recognize some names as grape names (see Chapter 3) and other names as place-names right off the bat; but if you don't, don't panic. That information is the kind of thing you can look up. (Parts III, IV, and V will help.)

Hello, my name is Chardonnay: Varietal wines

A *varietal* wine is named after either the *principal* or the *sole* grape variety that makes up the wine. Each country (and in the United States, some individual states) has laws that stipulate the minimum percentage of the named grape that a wine must contain if that wine wants to call itself by a grape name. The issue is truth in advertising.

U.S. federal regulations fix the legal minimum percentage of the named grape at 75 percent (which means that your favorite California Chardonnay can have as much as 25 percent of some *other* grape in it). In Australia and in the countries that form the European Union (E.U.), the minimum is 85 percent.

Some varietal wines are made *entirely* from the grape variety for which the wine is named. There's no law against that anywhere.

Most of the time, the labels of varietal wines don't tell you whether other grapes are present in the wine — let alone what those grapes are or the percentage of the wine that they account for. All you know is that the wine contains at least the minimum legal percentage of the named variety.

Interestingly, if a wine sold in the United States is named for two or more grape varieties — a Semillon-Chardonnay, for example — the label must state the percentages of each, and these percentages must total 100 percent. Now that's an honest varietal wine!

Why name a wine after a grape variety? Grapes are the raw material of a wine. Except for whatever a wine absorbs from oak barrels (certain aromas and flavors, as well as tannin) and from certain winemaking processes described in Chapter 5, the juice of the grapes is what any wine *is.* So to name a wine after its grape variety is logical.

Naming a wine for its grape variety is also satisfying to exacting consumers. Knowing what grape a wine is made from is akin to knowing what type of oil is in the salad dressing, whether your cupcake has any trans fats, and how much egg is in your egg roll.

Most California (and other U.S.) wines carry varietal names. Likewise, most Australian, South American, and South African wines are named by using the *principal* principle. Even some countries that don't normally name their wines after grapes, such as France, are jumping on the varietal-name bandwagon for certain wines that they especially want to sell to Americans.

A common perception among some wine drinkers is that a varietal wine is somehow *better* than a non-varietal wine. Actually, the fact that a wine is named after its principal grape variety is absolutely *no indication of quality.*

Hello, my name is Bordeaux: Place-name wines

Unlike American wines, most European wines are named for the *region* where their grapes grow rather than for the grape variety itself. Many of these European wines come from precisely the same grape varieties as American wines (like Chardonnay, Cabernet Sauvignon, Sauvignon Blanc, and so on), but they don't say so on the label. Instead, the labels say Burgundy, Bordeaux, Sancerre, and so on: the *place* where those grapes grow.

Is this some nefarious plot to make wine incomprehensible to English-only wine lovers who have never visited Europe and flunked geography in school?

Au contraire! The European system of naming wines is actually intended to provide more information about each wine, and more understanding of what's in the bottle, than varietal naming does. The only catch is that to harvest this information, you have to learn something about the different regions from which the wines come. (Turn to Parts III, IV, and V for some of that information.)

In the following sections, we list reasons for naming wines after places, describe the concept of *terroir,* and talk about place-names on American wines.

Why name a wine after a place?

Grapes, the raw material of wine, have to grow somewhere. Depending on the type of soil, the amount of sunshine, the amount of rain, and the many other characteristics that each *somewhere* has, the grapes will turn out differently. If the grapes are different, the wine is different. Each wine, therefore, reflects the place where its grapes grow.

In Europe, grape growers/winemakers have had centuries to figure out which grapes grow best where. They've identified most of these grape-location matchups and codified them into regulations. Therefore, the name of a *place* where grapes are grown in Europe automatically connotes the grape (or grapes) used to make the wine of that place. The label on the bottle usually doesn't tell you the grape (or grapes), though. Which brings us back to our original question: Is this some kind of nefarious plot to make wine incomprehensible to non-Europeans?

The most common place-names on wine labels

Here's a list of the place-names you're most likely to find on wine labels:

Beaujolais	Chianti	Rioja
Bordeaux	Côtes du Rhône	Sancerre
Burgundy (Bourgogne)	Mosel	Sauternes
Chablis	Port (Porto)	Sherry
Champagne	Pouilly-Fuissé	Soave
Châteauneuf-du-Pape	Rhine (Rheingau, Rheinhessen)	Valpolicella

Decoding common European place-names

The following table lists common place-names on wine labels, the European countries in which the places are located, and the grape varieties used to make the wines.

Wine Name	Country	Grape Varieties
Beaujolais	France	Gamay
Bordeaux (red)	France	Cabernet Sauvignon, Merlot, Cabernet Franc, and others*
Bordeaux (white)	France	Sauvignon Blanc, Sémillon, Muscadelle*
Burgundy (red)	France	Pinot Noir
Burgundy (white)	France	Chardonnay
Chablis	France	Chardonnay
Champagne	France	Chardonnay, Pinot Noir, Pinot Meunier*
Châteauneuf-du-Pape	France	Grenache, Mourvèdre, Syrah, and others*
Chianti	Italy	Sangiovese, Canaiolo, and others*
Côtes du Rhône	France	Grenache, Mourvèdre, Carignan, and others*
Port (Porto)	Portugal	Touriga Nacional, Tinta Barroca, Touriga Franca, Tinta Roriz, Tinto Cão, and others*
Pouilly-Fuissé, Mâcon, St.-Véran	France	Chardonnay
Rioja (red)	Spain	Tempranillo, Grenache, and others*
Sancerre/Pouilly-Fumé	France	Sauvignon Blanc
Sauternes	France	Sémillon, Sauvignon Blanc*
Sherry	Spain	Palomino
Soave	Italy	Garganega and others*
Valpolicella	Italy	Corvina, Molinara, Rondinella*

*Indicates that a blend of grapes is used to make these wines.

The terroir game

Terroir (pronounced ter-wahr) is a French word that has no direct translation in English, so wine people just use the French word, for expediency (not for snobbery). *Terroir* has no fixed definition; it's a concept, and, like most concepts, people tend to define it more broadly or more narrowly to suit their own needs. The word itself is based on the French word *terre,* which means soil; so some people define *terroir* as, simply, dirt (as in, "Our American dirt is every bit as good as their French dirt").

Places large and small

When we travel to other countries, we realize that people in different places have different ways of perceiving space and distance. If someone tells us that we'll find a certain restaurant "just up ahead," for example, we figure it's the equivalent of about three blocks away — but they might mean three miles.

Discussing place-names for European wines can be just as problematic. Some of the *places* are as small as several acres, some are 100 square miles big, and others are the size of New Jersey. Certain words used to describe wine zones imply the relative size of the place (in descending order of size and ascending order of specificity): country, region, district, subdistrict, commune, and vineyard.

But *terroir* is really much more complex (and complicated) than just dirt. *Terroir* is the combination of immutable natural factors — such as topsoil, subsoil, climate (sun, rain, wind, and so on), the slope of the hill, and altitude — that a particular vineyard site has. Chances are that no two vineyards in the entire world have precisely the same combination of these factors. So we consider *terroir* to be the *unique* combination of natural factors that a particular vineyard site has.

Terroir is the guiding principle behind the European concept that wines should be named after the place they come from (thought we'd gotten off the track, didn't you?). The thinking goes like this: The name of the place connotes which grapes were used to make the wine of that place (because the grapes are set by regulations), and the place influences the character of those grapes in its own unique way. Therefore, the most accurate name that a wine can have is the name of the place where its grapes grew. It's not some nefarious plot; it's just a whole different way of looking at things.

Place-names on American wine labels

France doesn't have a monopoly on the concept that wines should be named after their place of origin, nor does greater Europe. Wine labels from non-European countries also tell you where a wine comes from — usually by featuring the name of a place somewhere on the label. But a few differences exist between the European and non-European systems.

First of all, on an American wine label (or an Australian, Chilean, or South African label, for that matter), you have to go to some effort to find the place-name on the label. The place of origin isn't the fundamental name of the wine (as it is for most European wines); the grape usually is.

Second, place-names in the United States mean far less than they do in Europe. Okay, if the label says *Napa Valley,* and you've visited that area, Napa Valley will mean something to you. But *legally,* the name Napa Valley means only that at least 85 percent of the grapes came from an area defined by law as the Napa Valley wine zone. The name Napa Valley doesn't define the type of wine, nor does it imply specific grape varieties, the way a European place-name does. (Good thing the grape name is there, as big as day, on the label.)

Place-names on labels of non-European wines, for the most part, merely pay lip service to the concept of *terroir.* In fact, some non-European wine origins are ridiculously broad. We have to laugh when we think how European wine-makers must react to all those wine labels that announce a wine's place of origin simply as "California." *Great. This label says that this wine comes from a specific area that is 30 percent larger than the entire country of Italy! Some specific area!* (Italy has more than 300 specific wine zones.)

When the place on the label is merely *California,* in fact, that information tells you next to nothing about where the grapes grew. California's a big place, and those grapes could come from just about anywhere. Same thing for all those Australian wines labeled *South Eastern Australia* — an area only slightly smaller than France and Spain *combined.*

Branded, proprietary, generic: Wines named in other ways

Now and then, you may come across a wine that's named for neither its grape variety nor its region of origin. Such wines usually fall into three categories: *branded wines, wines with proprietary names,* or *generic wines.*

> ✔ **Branded wines:** Most wines have brand names, including those wines that are named after their grape variety — like Cakebread (brand name) Sauvignon Blanc (grape) — and those that are named after their region of origin — like Masi (brand name) Valpolicella (place). These brand names are usually the name of the company that made the wine, called a *winery.* Because most wineries make several different wines, the brand name itself isn't specific enough to be the actual name of the wine. But sometimes a wine has *only* a brand name. For example, the label says *Salamandre* and *red French wine* but provides little other identification.
>
> Wines that have *only* a brand name on them, with no indication of grape or of place — other than the country of production — are generally the most inexpensive, ordinary wines you can get.

✔ **Wines with proprietary names:** Fanciful wine names such as Tapestry, Conundrum, Insignia, Isosceles, and Trilogy are *proprietary names* (often trademarked) that producers create for special wines. In the case of American wines, the bottles with proprietary names usually contain wines made from a *blend* of grapes; therefore, no one grape name can be used as the name of the wine. In the case of European wines, the grapes used to make the wine were probably not the approved grapes for that region; therefore, the regional name couldn't be used on the label.

Wines with proprietary names usually are made in small quantities, are quite expensive ($40 to $75 or more a bottle), and are high in quality.

✔ **Generic wines:** A generic name is a wine name that's been used inappropriately for so long that it has lost its original meaning in the eyes of the government. Burgundy, Chianti, Chablis, Champagne, Rhine wine, Sherry, Port, and Sauterne are all wine names that rightfully should apply only to wines made in those specific European places, but they've been adopted by large American wineries. Although the U.S. government has finally agreed that these names can no longer be used for American wines, any wine that bore such a name prior to March 2006 may continue to carry that name for domestic commerce. In time, these generic names will become less common on wine labels.

Wine Labels, Forward and Backward

Most wine bottles have two labels. The front label names the wine and grabs your eye as you walk down the aisle, and the back label gives you a little more information, ranging from really helpful suggestions like "this wine tastes delicious with food" to oh-so-useful data such as "this wine has a total acidity of 6.02 and a pH of 3.34."

Grape names on European wines

Although most European wines are named after their place of origin, grape names do sometimes appear on labels of European wines. In Italy, for example, the official name of a wine could be a combination of place and grape — like the name Barbera d'Alba, which translates as Barbera (grape) of Alba (place).

In France, some producers have deliberately added the grape name to their labels, even though the grape is already implicit in the wine name. For example, a white Bourgogne (place-name) may also have the word *Chardonnay* (grape) on the label, for those wine drinkers who don't know that white Bourgogne is 100 percent Chardonnay. And German wines usually carry grape names along with their official place-names.

But even if a European wine does carry a grape name, the most important part of the wine's name, in the eyes of the people who make the wine, is the place.

The government authorities in the United States (and other governments) require certain information to appear on the front label of all wine bottles — basic stuff, such as the alcohol content, the type of wine (usually *red table wine* or *white table wine*), and the country of origin. But sometimes producers put all that information on the smaller of two labels and call that one the front label. Then they place a larger, colorful, dramatically eye-catching label — with little more than the name of the wine on it — on the other side of the bottle. Guess which way the so-called front label ends up facing when the bottle is placed on the shelf?

We don't feel at all outraged about this situation. We'd rather look at colorful labels on the shelf than boring information-laden ones any day. And we're not so lazy that we can't just pick up the bottle and turn it around to find out what we need to know. If you notice that a wine label contains very little information, just look for the information on the bottle's other label. The following sections explain what kind of data you can expect to find — on one label or the other.

The mandatory sentence

The federal government mandates that certain items of information appear on labels of wines sold in the United States. Such items are generally referred to as *the mandatory.* These items include the following:

- A brand name
- Indication of class or type (table wine, dessert wine, or sparkling wine)
- The percentage of alcohol by volume (unless it's implicit — for example, the statement *table wine* implies an alcohol content of less than 14 percent; see Chapter 1 for details)
- Name and location of the bottler
- Net contents (expressed in milliliters; the standard wine bottle is 750 milliliters, which is 25.6 ounces)
- The phrase *Contains Sulfites* (with very, very few exceptions)
- The government warning (that we won't dignify by repeating here; just pick up any bottle of wine, and you'll see it on the back label)

Figure 4-1 shows you how all the details come together on a label of an American varietal wine.

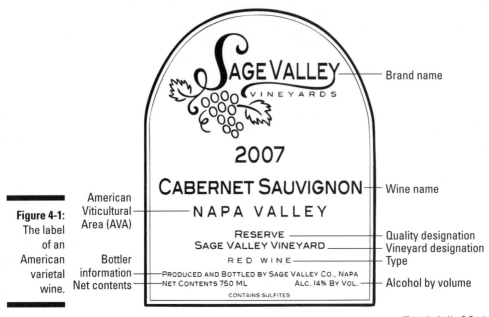

Figure 4-1: The label of an American varietal wine.

Brand name

2007

CABERNET SAUVIGNON — Wine name

NAPA VALLEY

RESERVE — Quality designation
SAGE VALLEY VINEYARD — Vineyard designation
RED WINE — Type

American Viticultural Area (AVA)

Bottler information
Net contents

PRODUCED AND BOTTLED BY SAGE VALLEY CO., NAPA
NET CONTENTS 750 ML   ALC. 14% BY VOL. — Alcohol by volume
CONTAINS SULFITES

Illustration by Lisa S. Reed

Wines made outside the United States but sold within it must also carry the phrase *imported by* on their labels, along with the name and business location of the importer.

Canadian regulations are similar, and many of these required items must be indicated in both English and French.

The mandatory information required on U.S. and Canadian wine labels is also required by the E.U. authorities for most wines produced in European Union countries. (The requirements are looser for the most generic and least expensive wines.) Furthermore, the labels of those finer wines must contain one additional item of information not required on labels of wines from elsewhere. This additional item is a phrase that indicates that the wine comes from an officially recognized wine zone (see the next section for the scoop).

Indications of origin

The European Union has set up a system to recognize and protect agricultural products (such as wine, cheese, olives, hams, and so forth) that come from specific places so that companies in other places can't make products with the same name, and thus confuse consumers. Wines from all the classic wine regions of E.U. member countries (France, Italy, Spain, Germany, and so forth) are protected under this system. When you see the label of a European wine that's from a recognized, protected place, you'll find a phrase to that effect.

Will the real wine producer please stand up?

Although U.S. labeling laws require wine labels to carry the name and address of the bottler, this information doesn't necessarily tell you who made the wine.

Of the various phrases that may be used to identify the bottler on labels of wine sold in the United States, only the words *produced by* or *made by* indicate the name of the company that actually fermented 75 percent or more of the wine (that is, who really *made* the wine); words such as *cellared by* or *vinted by* mean only that the company subjected the wine to cellar treatment (holding it for a while, for example).

Actually, two different phrases exist because European wines from protected places fall into two categories:

✔ Wines named for places where production is highly regulated so that the very place-name of the wine not only defines the territory of production but also connotes the wine's grape varieties, grape-growing methods, and winemaking techniques

✔ Wines that carry the protected names of larger places where winemakers have more freedom in terms of the grape varieties and production methods they use

The E.U.'s mandated phrases for these two types of place-name wines are:

✔ *Protected Designation of Origin (PDO),* for the most regulated wines. The classic wines mentioned in the sidebar "Decoding common European place-names," for example, are all in this category.

✔ *Protected Geographic Indication (PGI),* for the less regulated wines from registered regions.

In theory, every bottle of European wine — except for the most generic, least expensive wines — carry one of these two phrases on its label.

But in practice, the situation is much more complicated, especially at the moment. How?

✔ For one thing, each country can, and does, translate the words *Protected Designation of Origin* and *Protected Geographic Indication* into its own language on its labels.

✔ Second, because these E.U. designations went into full effect only in 2012, many wine labels still carry the phrases that were previously used by each country to designate a wine's category of origin.

✔ And finally, each country can permit its wineries to continue using the former phrases rather than the new phrases.

If you're getting into French, Italian, or other European wines and see a phrase on the label that's adjacent to the place-name or region of the wine, know that it indicates an officially protected geographic zone. If you really want to know which of the two protected categories the wine falls into, refer to the lists in the next two sections.

Incidentally, the phrase for a registered place-name in the United States is *American Viticultural Area (AVA)*. But the phrase *doesn't* appear on wine labels (refer to Figure 4-1). Nor does any such phrase appear on labels of Australian or South American wines. Nor do two different degrees of regulation exist, as they do in the European Union. (Refer to the section "Place-names on American wine labels," earlier in this chapter.)

Label terms that mean PDO (Protected Designation of Origin)

Here are the phrases — first in the new terminology and then in the original terminology — that you might find on labels of PDO wines from the major European countries. In all cases, the phrases translate more or less as "Protected Designation of Origin":

✔ **France:** *Appellation d'Origine Protégée (AOP)* or *Appellation Contrôlée* or *Appellation d'Origine Contrôlée (AC or AOC,* in short)

✔ **Italy:** *Denominazione di Origine Protetta (DOP)* or *Denominazione di Origine Controllata (DOC);* and for certain wines of an even higher status, *Denominazione di Origine Controllata e Garantita (DOCG)*

✔ **Spain:** *Denominación de Origen Protegida (DOP)* or *Denominación de Origen (DO),* as well as *Denominación de Origen Calificada (DOCa)* for regions with the highest status (of which only two exist: Rioja and Priorat; see Chapter 12 for even more words on Spanish labels)

✔ **Portugal:** *Denominação de Origem Protegida (DOP)* or *Denominação de Origem Controlada (DOC)*

✔ **Germany:** *geschützte Ursprungsbezeichnung (gU)* or *Qualitätswein;* and for wines of higher ripeness, *Qualitätswein mit Prädikat (QmP)* (see Chapter 12 for more on Germany's complex appellation system)

Figure 4-2 shows a European wine label as it would appear in the United States, using the original place-name terminology.

Brand name

Wine name

PDO category

Type

Vintage

Producer information

Net contents

Bottler information

Importer information

Illustration by Lisa S. Reed

Figure 4-2:
The label of
a European
wine to
be sold in
the United
States.

Alcohol by volume

Label terms that mean PGI (Protected Geographic Indication)

Here are the phrases — first in the new terminology and then in the original terminology — that you might find on labels of PGI wines from the major European countries. In all cases, the phrases translate more or less as "Protected Geographic Indication":

- **France:** *Indication Géographique Protégée (IGP)* or *Vin de Pays* followed by the name of an approved area
- **Italy:** *Indicazione Geografica Protetta (IGP)* or *Indicazione Geografica Tipica (IGT)* and the name of an approved area
- **Spain:** *Indicación Geográfica Protegida (IGP)* or *Vino de la Tierra* followed by the name of an approved area

- ✔ **Portugal:** *Indicaçõa Geográfica (IG)* to refer to a region, but on a label, the original phrase, *Vinho Regional* (regional wine) and the name of an approved area

- ✔ **Germany:** *geschützte geografische Angabe (ggA)* or *Landwein* and the name of an approved area

Some optional label lingo

Besides the mandatory information required by government authorities, all sorts of other words can appear on wine labels. These words can be meaningless phrases intended to make you think that you're getting a special quality wine, or words that provide useful information about what's in the bottle. Sometimes the same word can fall into either category, depending on the label. This ambiguity occurs because some words that are strictly regulated in some producing countries aren't at all regulated in others.

Vintage

The word *vintage* followed by a year, or the year listed alone without the word *vintage,* is the most common optional item on a wine label (refer to Figure 4-2). Sometimes the vintage appears on the front label, and sometimes it has its own small label above the front label.

The *vintage year* is nothing more than the year in which the grapes for a particular wine grew; the wine must have 75 to 100 percent of the grapes of this year, depending on the country of origin. (*Non-vintage* wines are blends of wines whose grapes were harvested in different years.) But an aura surrounds vintage-dated wine causing many people to believe that any wine with a vintage date is by definition better than a wine without a vintage date. *In fact, no correlation exists between the presence of a vintage date and the wine's quality.*

Generally speaking, *what* vintage a wine is — that is, whether the grapes grew in a year with perfect weather or whether the grapes were meteorologically challenged — is an issue you need to consider (a) only when you buy top-quality wines, and (b) mainly when those wines come from parts of the world that experience significant variations in weather from year to year — such as many European wine regions.

Reserve

Reserve is our favorite meaningless word on U.S. wine labels. The term is used to convince you that the wine inside the bottle is special. This trick usually works because the word *does* have specific meaning and *does* carry a certain amount of prestige on labels of wines from many other countries:

✔ In Italy and Spain, the word *reserve* (or its foreign language equivalent, which looks something like *reserve*) indicates a wine that has received extra aging at the winery before release. Implicit in the extra aging is the idea that the wine was better than normal and, therefore, worthy of the extra aging. Spain even has *degrees* of reserve, such as Gran Reserva.

✔ In France, the use of *reserve* isn't regulated. However, its use is generally consistent with the notion that the wine is better in quality than a given producer's norm.

In the United States, the word *reserve* has historically been used in the same sense — as in, Beaulieu Vineyards Georges de Latour Private Reserve, the best Cabernet that Beaulieu Vineyards makes. But these days, the word is bandied about so much that it no longer has meaning. For example, some California wines labeled *Proprietor's Reserve* sell for $6 a bottle. Those wines are not only the *least* expensive wines in a particular producer's lineup but also some of the least expensive wines, period. Other wines are labeled *Special Reserve, Vintage Reserve, Vintner's Reserve,* or *Reserve Selection* — all utterly meaningless phrases.

Estate-bottled

Estate is a genteel word for a wine farm, a combined grape-growing and wine-making operation. The words *estate-bottled* on a wine label indicate that the company that grew the grapes and made the wine also bottled the wine. In other words, *estate-bottled* suggests accountability from the vineyard to the winemaking through to the bottling. In many countries, the winery doesn't necessarily have to own the vineyards, but it has to control the vineyards and perform the vineyard operations.

Estate-bottling is an important concept to those who believe that you can't make good wine unless the grapes are as good as they can possibly be. If *we* made wine, we'd sure want to control our own vineyards.

We wouldn't go so far as to say that great wines *must* be estate-bottled, though. Ravenswood Winery — to name just one example — makes some terrific wines from the grapes of small vineyards owned and operated by private landowners. And some large California landowners are quite serious about their vineyards but don't make wine themselves; they sell their grapes to various wineries. None of those wines would be considered estate-bottled.

Sometimes French wine labels carry the words *domaine-bottled* or *château-bottled* (or the phrase *mis en bouteille au château/au domaine*). The concept is the same as estate-bottled, with *domaine* and *château* being equivalent to the U.S. term *estate*.

Vineyard name

Some wines in the medium-to-expensive price category — costing about $25 or more — might carry on the label the name of the specific vineyard where the grapes for that wine grew. Sometimes one winery will make two or three different wines that are distinguishable only by the vineyard name on the label. Each wine is unique because the *terroir* of each vineyard is unique (we discuss *terroir* earlier in this chapter). These single vineyards might or might not be identified by the word *vineyard* next to the name of the vineyard.

Italian wines, which are really into the single-vineyard game, will have *vigneto* or *vigna* on their labels next to the name of the single vineyard. Or they won't. It's optional.

Even more optional words on the label

You'll be pleased to know that we have just about exhausted our list of terms that you could find on a wine label.

One additional expression on some French labels is *Vieilles Vignes* (vee-yay veen), which translates as "old vines," and appears as such on some Californian and Australian labels. Because old vines produce a very small quantity of fruit compared to younger vines, the quality of their grapes and of the resulting wine is considered to be very good. The problem is the phrase is unregulated. Anyone can claim that his vines are old.

The word *superior* can appear in French *(Supérieure)* or Italian *(Superiore)* as part of a PDO place-name (refer to the section "Indications of origin," earlier in this chapter, for a refresher on this acronym). It traditionally meant that the wine attained a higher alcohol level than a nonsuperior version of the same wine would have — a distinction not worth losing sleep over. Now, the term is also used in Italy to designate a specific type of wine, such as Soave Superiore, a wine that's distinct from the wine Soave by virtue of its vineyard location, winemaking, and so forth.

The word *Classico* appears on the labels of some Italian PDO wines when the grapes come from the heartland of the named place.

Chapter 5

Behind the Scenes of Winemaking

In This Chapter

▶ Separating the meaningful wine terms from the mumbo jumbo

▶ Wondering no more about the meaning of words related to winemaking and grape growing

▶ Showing off with technical terms to wow your friends

The most frustrating thing about wine has got to be the technical lingo. All you want is a crisp, fruity white wine to serve with tonight's mac 'n' cheese. But to find it, you have to fight your way through a jungle of jargon, which you encounter on the back labels of wine bottles, in the words the sales clerk uses to explain his recommendations, and on the signs all around the wine shop. Why on earth is everyone making wine so complicated?

Here's the story: Wine is two products. Some wine is just a beverage, and it should taste good — period. Other wine is an art form that fascinates and intrigues people. Many people who make and sell wine want you to think that their wines are in the second category, because such wines are more prestigious. Complicated technical language is supposed to make you think that a wine is special — something more than just a beverage.

How much of this information (if any) is pivotal in helping you get the kind of wine you want, and how much is pretentious technobabble? Read on.

Grape Growing, Winemaking, and the Jargon That Surrounds Them

Winemakers use numerous techniques to make wine. These techniques vary according to the grapes the winemakers have and the type of wine they're making. (If a winemaker is producing a huge quantity of a wine that will sell for $5.99 a bottle, for example, he probably won't put the wine into new oak barrels because the cost of the barrels can add as much as $5 to the price of every bottle.)

No winemaking procedure is inherently good or inherently bad. Any technique can be right or wrong depending on the grapes and the type of wine being made — that is, the wine's price level, the taste profile the winemaker is seeking, and the type of wine drinker the winery is targeting.

Different wines appeal to different wine drinkers at different times:

- ✔ Some wines are intended to taste good right away, while others are intended to taste best down the road, after the wine has aged (see Chapter 17).
- ✔ Some wines are intended to taste good to casual wine drinkers, while others are intended for more experienced wine lovers.

How the wine tastes is the ultimate validation of any method used to produce a wine: The procedures themselves are meaningless if they don't create a wine that's appealing to the wine drinkers for whom that wine is intended.

The *taste* of the wine involves not only its flavors but also its aroma, body, texture, length, and so on (see Chapter 2). And the taste of a wine is a subjective experience.

Because every winemaking technique does affect the taste of the wine in one way or another, most of the technical words that are bandied about in wine circles represent procedures that *are* relevant to the taste of a wine. But — here's the key point — these technical words each represent isolated elements in the making of the wine, which are only *parts* of the total picture that begins with the grapes and ends when you put the wine in your mouth.

The rest of this chapter explains the meaning behind those isolated elements of winemaking that you're most likely to hear or read about when you're buying wine.

The World of Viti-Vini

Producing wine actually involves two separate steps: the growing of the grapes, called *viticulture,* and the making of the wine, called *vinification.* (In some wine courses, students nickname the dual process *viti-vini.*) Sometimes, one company performs both steps, as is the case with *estate-bottled* wines (see Chapter 4). And sometimes, the two steps are completely separate. For example, some large wineries buy grapes from private grape growers. These growers don't make wine; they just grow grapes and sell them to whatever wine company offers them the highest price per ton.

In the case of the very least expensive wines, the winery named on the label may not have even purchased grapes but rather wine (from bulk wine producers) and then blended the wines and bottled the final product as its own.

(As we mention in Chapter 4, only the terms *produced by* or *made by* on the label assure you that the company named on the label actually vinified most of that wine.) In the following sections, we discuss terms that are associated with viticulture and vinification.

Vine-growing variations

Growing grapes for wine is a fairly intricate process that viticulturalists are constantly refining to suit their particular soil, climate, and grape varieties. Many of the technical terms spill over into discussions about wine or crop up on wine labels. Here are expressions you're likely to encounter as you dig farther into wine:

- **Microclimate (known increasingly as *mesoclimate*):** Every wine region has climatic conditions (the amount and timing of sun, rain, wind, humidity, and so on) that are considered the norm for that area. But individual locations within a region — the south-facing side of a particular hill, for example — can have a climatic reality that's different from that of the area as a whole. The unique climatic reality of a specific location is called its *microclimate,* or, in technical circles, its *mesoclimate. Microclimate* is the more common term on back labels and in colloquial usage.

- **Canopy:** Left untended, grapevines would grow along the ground, up trees, wherever — they're *vines,* after all! Commercial viticulture involves attaching the shoots of vines to wires or trellises in a systematic pattern. The purpose of *training* the vine — as this activity is called — is to position the grape bunches so that they get enough sun to ripen well and so that the fruit is easy for the harvesters to reach.

  An *open canopy* is a trellising method that maximizes the sunlight exposure of the grapes. *Canopy management,* which is the practice of maneuvering the leaves and fruit into the best position for a given vineyard, is a popular buzzword meant to signify that great care went into the growing and ripening of the grapes.

- **Ripeness:** Harvesting grapes when they're perfectly ripe is one of the crucial points in wine production. (See Chapter 3.) But ripeness is a subjective issue.

  In cooler climates, a high degree of ripeness doesn't happen every year; wines from "riper" vintages should, therefore, be richer and fuller-bodied than the norm for that type of wine. In warmer climates, ripeness is almost automatic; the trick becomes not letting the grapes get too ripe too fast, which causes them to be high in sugar but still physiologically immature and undeveloped in their flavors (like a physically precocious but immature teenager). There's no fixed definition of perfect ripeness.

✔ **Low yields:** Generally, the more grapes a grapevine grows (the higher its *yield* of grapes), the less concentrated the flavors of those grapes will be, and the lower in quality (and less expensive) their wine will be. Just about any wine producer anywhere can claim that his yields are low, because it's too complicated to prove otherwise. The proof is usually in the wine's concentration of flavor: If the wine tastes thin or watery, we'd be suspicious of the "low yield" claim.

✔ **Organic:** Grape growers increasingly farm their vineyards *organically,* that is, without using chemical pesticides, herbicides, and so forth. Their reasons have to do with the health of the land, as well as their belief that organically grown grapes are superior to conventionally farmed grapes and that they make better wine. For a wine label in the Unites States to state that the grapes for that wine were grown organically, the vineyard must be certified as organic by a government-approved organization.

A related term is *biodynamic;* this means that the vineyards are organic and also are farmed in keeping with the principles established in the early 20th century by Austrian philosopher Rudolph Steiner, which involve, among other issues, cosmic aspects such as respecting the movement of the moon and the planets in the timing of the work on the land. Biodynamic wines enjoy almost a cult following.

Winemaking wonder words

The vinification end of wine production falls into two parts:

✔ **Fermentation:** The period when the grape juice turns into wine

✔ **Maturation (or *finishing*):** The period following fermentation when the wine settles down, loses its rough edges, goes to prep school, and gets ready to meet the world

Depending on the type of wine being made, the whole process can take three months or five years — or even longer if the bank isn't breathing down the winery's neck.

Winemakers don't have as many options in making wine as chefs do in preparing food — but almost! Of all the jargon you're likely to hear about fermentation and maturation, information about oak is probably the most common. The following sections give you the details.

When wood becomes magic

Winemakers use oak barrels, 60 gallons in size, as containers for wine during fermentation and/or maturation. The barrels lend oaky flavor and aroma to the wine, which many people find very appealing; they can also affect the texture of the wine and its color. The barrels are expensive — about $800 per barrel if they're made from French oak. (Most people consider French oak to be the finest.) We suppose the expense is one good reason to boast about using the barrels.

But not all oak is the same. Oak barrels vary in the origin of their oak, the amount of *toast* (a charring of the inside of the barrels) each barrel has, how often the barrels have been used (their oaky character diminishes with use), and even the size of the barrels. Even if all oak *were* the same, a wine can turn out differently depending on whether unfermented juice or actual wine went into the barrels, and how long it stayed there.

In fact, the whole issue of oak is so complex that anyone who suggests that a wine is better simply because it's been oaked is guilty of gross oversimplification.

Barrel-fermented versus barrel-aged

You don't have to venture very far into wine before you find someone explaining to you that a particular wine was barrel-fermented or barrel-aged. What in the world does he mean, and should you care?

- ✔ The term *barrel-fermented* means that grape juice went into barrels (almost always oak) and changed into wine there.
- ✔ The term *barrel-aged* usually means that wine (already fermented) went into barrels and stayed there for a maturation period — from a few months to a couple of years.

Cloning the perfect grapevine

Hang around wine people long enough and you're sure to hear talk about *clones* or *clonal selection* of grape varieties. Has the brave New World of grape growing arrived? Not really. In botanical terms, a *clone* is a subdivision of a variety. Within a single variety, such as Chardonnay, differences can exist from one plant to the next. For example, some plants might ripen their fruit slightly more quickly or produce grapes with slightly different aromas and flavors than the next.

When nurseries propagate grapevines by taking cuttings from a *mother plant* and allowing those cuttings to root (until the plant is mature enough to be grafted onto a phylloxera-resistant rootstock, as we discuss in Chapter 3), the new plants are genetically identical to the mother plant. Naturally, grape growers purchase the most ideal plants for their situation, in terms of ripening time, fruit flavor, disease resistance, heartiness — or whatever they're looking for. Voilá! They've made a clonal selection. Increasingly, growers plant several different clones of a variety to foster complexity in the wine made from that vineyard's grapes.

Because most wines that ferment in barrels remain there for several months after fermentation ends, *barrel-fermented* and *barrel-aged* are often used together. The term *barrel-aged* alone suggests that the fermentation happened somewhere other than the barrel — usually in stainless steel tanks.

Classic barrel-fermentation — juice into the barrel, wine out — applies mainly to white wines, and the reason is very practical. As we mention in Chapter 2, the juice of red grapes ferments together with the grape skins in order to become red, and those solids are mighty messy to clean out of a small barrel! Red wines usually ferment in larger containers — stainless steel tanks or large wooden vats — and then *age* in small oak barrels after the wine has been drained from the grape skins. (Some light, fruity styles of red wine may not be oaked at all.) Some winemakers do partially ferment their reds in barrels; they start the fermentation in tanks then drain the juice from the skins and let that juice finish its fermentation in barrels, without the skins. When a red wine is described as being barrel-fermented, that's usually the process.

Here's why you might care whether a white wine is barrel-fermented or just barrel-aged. Wines that ferment in barrels actually end up tasting *less* oaky than wines that simply age in barrels, even though they might have spent more time in oak. (A barrel-fermented and barrel-aged Chardonnay might have spent 11 months in oak, for example, and a barrel-aged Chardonnay might have spent only 5 months in oak.) That's because juice interacts with the oak differently than wine does.

A lot of people who are supposed to know more about wine than you confuse the effects of the two processes and tell you that the barrel-fermented wine tastes oakier. If you have a strong opinion about the flavor of oak in your wine, be sure you know the real story.

Even More Winemaking Terms

Become a wine expert overnight and dazzle your friends with this amazing array of wine jargon. (Just don't fool yourself into believing that any one of the procedures described here necessarily creates a high-quality wine. The merit of each procedure depends on the complete set of winemaking techniques for that wine and on the particular type of wine being made.)

- **Temperature control:** The modern age of winemaking began when winemakers were able to control scientifically the temperature of their fermentations by using stainless steel tanks rigged with cooling jackets or by using various computer-operated cooling devices. Because the temperature of the fermentation (about 54 to 77 degrees Fahrenheit or 12 to 25 degrees Celsius for white wines and 77 to 93 degrees Fahrenheit or 25 to 34 degrees Celsius for reds) affects the final style of the wine, temperature control is critical. But, hey, this process was revolutionary and exciting almost half a century ago. Today, it's just ho-hum par for the course.

✔ **Stainless steel:** Large tanks made of shiny, hygienic stainless steel are the vessels of choice for most fermentations, whether for red wine or white. When you hear a winemaker or wine expert say that a particular wine was fermented in stainless steel, understand him to mean that one of three things is true:

- The wine was not oaked at all (which is common for many aromatic-style white wines — such as Rieslings, for example — to preserve the grapes' own flavors).

- The wine was barrel-aged rather than barrel-fermented (see the preceding section).

- The winery sunk a lot of money into its equipment and wants you to know it.

✔ **Lees:** *Lees* is the name for various solids, such as dead yeast cells, that precipitate to the bottom of a wine after fermentation. These solids can interact with the wine and create more complex flavors in the wine. (Sometimes, the winemaker stirs the lees around in the wine periodically to prevent off flavors.) A white wine with extended lees contact is usually richer in texture and tastes less overtly fruity than it would otherwise.

✔ **ML or malolactic:** *Malolactic,* nicknamed *ML* or *malo,* is a secondary fermentation that weakens the acids in a wine, making the wine softer and less acidic. ML usually happens naturally, but a winemaker can also incite it or prevent it.

Red wines almost always undergo malolactic fermentation, but for white wines, ML is a stylistic judgment call on the winemaker's part. Sometimes, ML can contribute a buttery flavor to a white wine, but it diminishes the wine's fresh fruitiness.

✔ **pH:** The chemical term *pH* means exactly the same thing for wine as it does in other scientific fields. ("Our facial cream is pH-balanced for sensitive skin.") If you want a technical explanation, look up your former chemistry teacher. If you'll settle for the general concept, *pH* is a measurement of acidity; wines with low pH (approximately 3.4 or less) have stronger acidity, and wines with higher pH have weaker acidity. But all wines have acidity.

✔ **Soft tannins:** Tannin in red wines varies not only in its quantity but also in its nature. Some tannins give wines rich texture and an impression of substance without tasting bitter; other tannins are astringent and mouth-drying. *Soft tannins*, or *ripe tannins,* are buzzphrases for the good kind. Winemakers achieve soft tannins by harvesting red grapes fully ripe, by controlling fermentation time and temperature, and by using other techniques.

✔ **Micro-oxygenation:** You hear this term, sometimes abbreviated as *micro-ox,* thrown around in technical circles. This high-tech winemaking technique involves feeding miniscule, controlled amounts of oxygen into a wine during or after fermentation. One effect is that it can mimic the gentle, steady exposure to oxygen that barrel-aged red wines receive as they mature in wood and can, thus, help red wines develop softer tannins and more stable color without any actual use of oak. For some winemakers, it's a useful tool, but some critics consider it manipulative.

✔ **Fining and filtering:** Winemakers *fine* and *filter* most wines near the end of their maturation period. The purpose of these procedures is to *clarify* the wine — that is, to remove any cloudiness or solid matter in the wine — and to *stabilize* it — to remove any yeast, bacteria, or other microscopic critters that may change the wine for the worse after it's bottled.

A popular belief among anti-tech wine lovers is that fining and filtration strip a wine of its character — and that unfined, unfiltered wines are inherently better, even if they're not brilliant in appearance. But it's a complex issue. (For one thing, there are *degrees* of fining and filtration, like *light* fining and *gentle* filtration.) These processes, when carried out carefully, are generally not detrimental to wine.

✔ **Natural wine:** It's fashionable for winemakers to claim that their wine is *natural* (as if other wines are unnatural?). They mean to suggest that their winemaking techniques — and their grape growing, for that matter — are non-manipulative and low tech. But even the advocates and practitioners of so-called natural wine don't agree about what the term *natural* actually means. For example, some use sulfur to keep their wine sound (read about sulfites in Chapter 1), while others don't, and sometimes to the detriment of the wine. Take the term with a grain of (natural) salt.

✔ **Blending:** This term usually applies to the process of making a wine from more than one grape variety. Winemakers typically ferment the different grapes separately and then blend their wines together.

The reasons for blending wines of different grapes are either to reduce costs — by diluting an expensive wine, like Chardonnay, with something else far less expensive, for example — or to improve the quality of the wine by using complementary grapes whose characteristics enhance each other. Many of Europe's traditional wines, such as red Rioja, red Bordeaux, Châteauneuf-du-Pape, and Champagne, are blended wines that owe their personalities to several grapes.

Wine terms that mean nothing

Sometimes winemakers or salespeople use words to describe their wines that, frankly, have no real meaning. When you hear these terms, understand them to mean that the person using them really wants you to believe his wine is special. Then decide for yourself, by tasting, whether it is.

✔ Handcrafted

✔ Artisanal

✔ Limited edition, limited selection, limited release

✔ Vintner's select, vineyard select, "anything" select

Part II
Wine and You: Up Close and Personal

The 5th Wave   By Rich Tennant

"The wine is supposed to breathe, Martin, not hyperventilate."

In this part . . .

With some of the basics under your belt — such as grape varieties, wine types, and wine names — you're ready to apply your knowledge at the practical level. Corkscrews, wine glasses, restaurant wine lists, wine shops, and Internet wine retail sites won't be any challenge at all, after you get the hang of them by browsing through the pages of this part. And choosing a wine for your favorite dish? Easy as pie. We promise.

Chapter 6

Buying Wine to Drink at Home

. . . .

. . . .

*U*nless you enjoy a permanent, dependent relationship with an indulgent wine expert, the day will come when you have to purchase a bottle of wine yourself. If you're lucky, the shop owner will just happen to be some enlightened guy or gal whose life's purpose is to make wine easy and accessible to others. The odds are, however, that most of the time you'll feel as if you're dancing in the dark.

When we wrote the fourth edition of *Wine For Dummies,* we bought almost all our wine in wine shops that we visited in person. Although we still buy much of our wine in wine shops, these days we use the Internet to find shops that sell the wines we want at the best prices, and then we often purchase wine online.

In this chapter, we tell you about various types of wine retailers and how to choose the best ones for you. We also explain how to overcome any intimidation you might feel about buying wine, and we provide a number of strategies that you can use, no matter where you shop for wine.

Buying Wine Can Intimidate Anyone

Common sense suggests that buying a few bottles of wine should be less stressful than, say, applying for a bank loan or interviewing for a new job. What's the big deal? It's only grape juice.

But memories tell us otherwise. One time, a particular wine shop wouldn't take back one of the two bottles of inexpensive wine that we bought the week before, even when we explained how awful the first bottle had been. (Needless to say, that was the last time we shopped in that store.) And then another time when we pretended we knew what we were doing, we bought a full case — 12 bottles — of a French wine based on the brand's general reputation, not realizing that the particular vintage we purchased was a miserable aberration from the brand's usual quality. (Why didn't we just ask someone in the store? We *might* have received good advice.) And we still recall the many times we spent staring at shelves lined with bottles whose labels might as well have been written in Greek, for all that we could understand from them. Fortunately, our enthusiasm for wine caused us to persevere. We eventually discovered that wine shopping can be fun.

Our experience has taught us that the single, most effective way to ensure that you have more good wine-buying experiences than bad ones is to come to terms with your knowledge — or lack thereof — of the subject.

Too much information about wine — new vintages each year, hundreds of new wineries, new brands, and so on — is constantly changing for *anyone* to presume that he knows it all, or for anyone to feel insecure about what he doesn't know.

If we'd all quit pretending that we know more than we do and give up our defensiveness about what we don't know, buying wine would become the simple exchange that it should be.

Wine Retailers, Large and Small

Buying wine in a store to drink at home is great for a number of reasons, not the least of which is that stores usually have a much bigger selection of wines than restaurants do, and they charge you less for them. You can examine the bottles carefully and compare the labels. And you can drink the wine at home from the glass — and at the temperature — of your choosing.

On the other hand, you have to provide your own wine glasses, and you have to open the bottle yourself (see Chapter 8 for the lowdown on all of that). And that big selection of wines in the store can be downright daunting.

Depending on where you live, you can buy wine at all sorts of stores: supermarkets, wine superstores, discount warehouses, liquor stores, or small specialty wine shops. Each type of store has its own advantages and disadvantages in terms of selection, price, or service.

Wine is a regulated beverage in many countries, and governments often get involved in deciding where and how wine may be sold. Some states within the United States and some provinces in Canada have raised government control of alcoholic beverage sales to a fine art, deciding not only *where* you can buy wine but also *which wines* are available for you to buy. If you love wine and live in one of those areas (you know who you are), take comfort in the fact that (a) you have a vote; (b) freedom of choice lies just across the border; and (c) if the Iron Curtain can topple, there's hope for freedom of wine buying.

We'll assume a healthy, open-minded, free-market economy for wine in our discussion of retail wine sales in the following sections. We hope that scenario applies where you live, because your enjoyment of wine will blossom all the more easily if it does.

On the other hand, now that wine is available on the Internet, even if you live in a state or province that controls your choice of wines, you can simply avoid buying wines in your home state or province — provided that your state allows you to legally obtain wine from elsewhere!

Supermarkets, superstores, and so on

In truly *open* wine markets, you can buy wine in supermarkets, like any other food product. Supermarkets and their large-scale brethren, discount warehouses and superstores, make wine accessible to everyone.

When wine is sold in supermarkets, superstores, or discount stores, the mystique surrounding the product evaporates: Who can waste time feeling insecure about a wine purchase when much more critical issues are at hand, such as how much time is left before the kids turn into monsters and which is the shortest line at the checkout? And the prices, especially in large stores, are usually quite reasonable.

The downside of buying wine in these stores is that your selection is often limited to wines produced by large wineries that generate enough volume to supply supermarket chains. And you'll seldom get any advice on which wines to buy. Basically, you're on your own.

Discount stores are good places to find *private label* wines — wines that are created especially for the chain and that carry a brand name that's owned by the store. These wines are usually decent (but not great), and if you like the wines, they can be excellent values. Some of the "club" chains may also offer — in smaller quantities — higher-end wines that are not the usual supermarket fare.

Supermarket survival tips

If you're shopping in a supermarket with no one to turn to for advice, do one or more of the following:

✔ Consult a list of recommended wines from a wine article that impressed you.

✔ Call a wine-knowledgeable friend on your cellphone (assuming that his or her palate and yours get along).

✔ If you have a smartphone, scan the QR code on the bottle (if there is one) for more information about the wine you're thinking of buying.

The bottom line is that supermarkets and discount warehouses can be great places to buy everyday wine for casual enjoyment. But if what you really want is to become knowledgeable about wine as you buy it, or if you want an unusually interesting variety of wines to satisfy your rapacious curiosity, you'll probably find yourself shopping elsewhere.

Wine specialty shops

Wine specialty shops are small- to medium-sized stores that sell wine and liquor and, sometimes, wine books, corkscrews, wine glasses, and maybe a few specialty foods. The foods sold in wine shops tend to be gourmet items rather than just run-of-the-mill snack foods.

If you decide to pursue wine as a serious hobby, you'll probably end up buying your wine at wine specialty shops because they offer many advantages. For instance, wine specialty shops almost always have wine-knowledgeable staffers on the premises. Also, you can usually find an interesting, varied selection of wines at all price levels.

Many times, wine shops organize their wines by country of origin and — in the case of classic wine countries, such as France — by region (Bordeaux, Burgundy, Rhône, and so on). Red wines and white wines are often in separate sections within these country areas. You can usually find a special section for Champagnes and other sparkling wines and another section for dessert wines. Some stores are now organizing their wine sections by style, such as *Aromatic Whites, Powerful Reds,* and so forth. A few organize the wines according to grape varieties.

Some wine shops have a special area (or even a super-special, temperature-controlled room) for the finer or more expensive wines. In some stores, this area is a locked vaultlike room. In others, it's the whole back area of the store.

Over in a corner somewhere, often right by the door to accommodate quick purchases, you might see a *cold box,* a commercial refrigerator where bottles of best-selling white and sparkling wines sit. Unless you really *must* have an ice-cold bottle of wine immediately (the two of you have just decided to elope, the marriage minister is a mile down the road, and the wedding toast is only ten minutes away), avoid the cold box. The wines in there are usually too cold and, therefore, might not be in good condition. You never know how long the bottle you select has been sitting there under frigid conditions, numbed lifeless.

Near the front of the store, you might also see boxes or bins of special *sale* wines. Sometimes, sale wines are those the merchant is trying to unload because he's had them for too long, or they're wines that he got a special deal on (because the distributor is trying to unload them). When in doubt, try one bottle first before committing to a larger quantity. (We provide more wine shopping strategies later in this chapter.)

Online merchants

The online wine-buying experience today mainly involves purchasing wines from the websites of established brick-and-mortar wine shops or choosing wines from flash sites that offer an ever-changing, limited selection. Because of state-by-state regulations governing the sale of alcoholic beverages, you won't find a slew of sites that are the wine equivalent of Zappos.com. The few exceptions, such as Wine.com, ShopWineDirect.com and Vinfolio (`www.vinfolio.com`), prove the rule.

In actuality, most websites of established wine shops are all-purpose online shopping sites. Most sites can ship wine to almost any location, although some destinations might be off-limits because of regulations within those states.

Some wine-selling sites specialize in certain types of wine, such as elite European wine or collector-level wine. (You can read about both of these types of wines in Chapter 17.) Some sites convey an air of refinement and prestige, while others seem intent on making the shopping experience fun. What kind of site you choose to buy wine is really all about your preference.

Flash sites offer a limited selection of wines at any given moment, usually at very affordable prices. Flash sites are the wine equivalent of shopping for sale items at the mall: If you find something you want, buy it before someone else does. Most flash sites enable you to sign up for e-mail alerts so that you can stay abreast of their offerings.

We shop on wine websites as a convenient way not only to buy wine but also to find out info about the particular wines we're planning to buy. We're especially interested in knowing the alcohol content of wines, which you can find on wine labels when you're in a shop but not always in the glowing product descriptions you read online. By Googling the name of the wine, we can usually find technical info such as the alcohol content of the wine. (Personally, we generally try to avoid buying wine with high alcohol, or anything over 14 percent. However, sometimes we do make exceptions.)

Criteria for Choosing Wine Merchants

Buying wine on the Internet is terrific if you know something about wine. If you're a complete novice, you're much better off relying on a knowledgeable wine merchant to help you select your wines. Whichever route you prefer, certain guidelines can help you choose a good retailer.

Sizing up a wine merchant is as simple as sizing up any other specialty retailer, whether online or face to face. As you find out in the following sections, the main criteria are fair prices, a wide selection, staff expertise, and service.

In the wine shop

When you're a novice wine buyer, your best strategy is to shop around with an eye to service and reliable advice more than to price. After you've found a merchant who has suggested several wines you've liked, stick with him, even if he doesn't have the best prices in town. Paying a dollar or so more for wines recommended by a reliable merchant (wines that you'll probably like) makes more sense than buying wines in a cut-rate or discount store and saving a buck, especially if that store has no special wine adviser or if the advice you receive is suspect.

When you have more knowledge of wine, you'll have enough confidence to shop at stores with the best prices. But even then, price must take a backseat to the storage conditions of the wine (see the section "Judging wine storage conditions," later in this chapter).

Evaluating selection and expertise

You won't necessarily know on your first visit whether a particular store's selection is adequate for you. If you notice a lot of wines from many different countries at various prices, give the store's selection the benefit of the doubt. If you outgrow the selection as you discover more about wine, you can seek out a new merchant at that point.

Don't be too ready to give a merchant the benefit of the doubt when it comes to expertise, however. Although some retailers are extremely knowledgeable about the specific wines they sell and about wine in general, others know less than their customers. Just as you expect a butcher to know his cuts of meat, you should expect a wine merchant to know wine. Be free with your questions (such as, "Can you give me some specific information about this wine?" or "How are these two wines different?"), and judge how willing and able the merchant is to answer them.

Expect wine merchants to have *personal* knowledge and experience of the wines they sell. These days, a lot of retailers use the ratings of a few critics as a crutch in selling wines. They plaster their shelves with the critics' scores (usually a number like 90 on a scale of 100) and advertise their wines by these numbers (see Chapter 19 for details). Selling by the numbers is a quick way of communicating what one critic thought about the wine — but that doesn't mean *you'll* like the wine! Personally, we often disagree with the point ratings of individual wines. Retailers' knowledge and experience of the wines simply must go beyond the critics' scores, or they're not doing their jobs properly.

Expecting service with a smile

Most knowledgeable wine merchants pride themselves in their ability to guide you through the maze of wines and help you find a wine you will like. Trust a merchant's advice at least once or twice and see whether his choices are good ones for you. If he's not flexible enough — or knowledgeable enough — to suggest wine that suits your needs, obviously you need another merchant. And all the experiment will have cost you is the price of a bottle or two of wine. (Much less costly than choosing the wrong doctor or lawyer!)

Any reputable wine merchant will accept a bottle back from you if he's made a poor recommendation or if the wine seems damaged. After all, he wants to keep you as a customer. But with the privilege comes responsibility: Be reasonable. Ask ahead of time about the store's defective and unopened wine policy. You should return an *open* bottle only if you think the wine is defective — in which case the bottle should be mostly full! Hold on to the store's receipt. And don't wait several months before returning an unopened bottle of wine. By that time, the store may have a hard time re-selling the wine. After a week or two, consider the wine yours, whether you like it or not.

Judging wine storage conditions

Here's a fact about wine that's worth understanding early on: Wine is a perishable product. It doesn't go moldy like cheese, and it can't host E. coli bacteria as meat can. It normally poses no health hazard beyond those associated with alcohol and certain individuals' sensitivities, even when it's past its prime. But if wine isn't stored properly, its taste can suffer. (For advice on storing wine in your own home, see Chapter 17.)

In sizing up a wine shop, especially if you plan to buy a lot of wine or expensive wine, check out the store's wine storage conditions. What you don't want to see is wines stored in a warm area, such as near the boiler where they cook all winter or on the top floor of the building where the sun can smile on them all summer.

The very best shops will have climate-controlled storerooms for wine, although, frankly, these shops are in the minority. If a shop does have a good storage facility, the proprietor will be happy to show it off to you because he'll be rightfully proud of all the expense and effort he put into it.

In better wine shops, you'll see most of the bottles (except for the inexpensive, large, jug-like bottles) lying in a horizontal position so that their corks remain moist, ensuring a firm closure. A dry cork can crack or shrink and let air into the bottle, which will spoil the wine. A short time upright doesn't affect wine much, so stores with a high turnover can get away with storing their fast-selling wines that way, but slower-selling, expensive bottles, especially those intended for long maturation in your cellar or storage space, will fare better in the long run by lying down.

Unfortunately, the problem of wine spoilage doesn't begin at the retail outlet. Quite frequently, the *wholesaler* or *distributor* — the company from which the retailer purchases wine — doesn't have proper storage conditions. And in some instances, wine has been damaged by extreme weather even before it got to the distributor, while sitting on the docks in the dead of winter (or the dead of summer). A good retailer will check out the quality of the wine before he buys it, or he'll send it back if he discovers the problem after he's already bought the wine.

On the Internet

When you purchase wine online rather than at a store, the service and storage components are tough to evaluate. Selection, availability, and price are the criteria you use to determine which online store deserves your loyalty.

When we're shopping for a specific wine online, our first stop is Wine-Searcher.com. This search engine site enables you to look for specific wines, and even specific vintages, and discover which of the site's member retailers (including most major wine shops across the United States and online retailers) are selling that wine and at what price. You can then contact that retailer online or by phone to purchase the wine. We don't always select the shop with the lowest price, however. We live in the New York area, so sometimes shipping charges from a West Coast store negate the low price, especially if that wine is available for only a dollar or two more in nearby New Jersey. (***Note:*** You won't find offerings of flash sites on Wine-Searcher.com because the wines offered by such sites change too quickly.)

The pros and cons of wine clubs

When you're on the wine circuit, you'll get many offers to join various wine clubs. These clubs are wine-buying programs, sometimes sponsored by respected publications, that send you a few preselected wines every month or so. They sound like a good deal: The club selects wines for you, offers them at attractive prices, and delivers them to your door. You'll probably like some of the wines. The catch is that the wines are unknown entities, and they're not necessarily bargains. The wines are usually private-label wines that are exclusive to the club (no comparative shopping is possible) and were purchased at really low prices. You have no say in the wine selection. Yes, wine clubs are convenient. But when you know about wine, you'll want to make your own selections, preferably with the aid of a knowledgeable wine merchant whom you trust.

Wine.com was one of the first and still is one of the most reliable sources for buying wine on the Internet. Another dependable site for buying wine on the Internet is ShopWineDirect.com. Both of these sites offer a wide range of wines at competitive prices. Another relatively new site for buying wine is Vinfolio (www.vinfolio.com); besides offering a large selection of current releases, this site offers many older wines that are normally not available, and it provides storage for wines that you aren't ready to ship home.

Some flash sites that you should check out include Lot 18 (www.lot18.com), WinesTilSoldOut (www.winestilsoldout.com), invino (www.invino.com), The Wine Spies (www.thewinespies.com), and Vitis (www.vitis.com; a new operation, offering some very good wines). All these sites generally list wines at very affordable prices (some highly discounted) and even sometimes with free shipping.

Strategies for Wine Shopping

When you get beyond all the ego-compromising innuendo associated with buying wine, you can really have fun in wine shops, especially when you use the strategies in the following sections. We remember when we first caught the wine bug. We spent countless hours on Saturdays, visiting different wine stores near our home. (To a passionate wine lover, 50 miles can be near.) Trips to other cities offered new opportunities to explore. So many wines, so little time. . . .

How to avoid encounters with poorly stored wine

If you don't know how a wine has been stored — and let's face it, most of the time you don't — you can do two things to minimize the risk of getting a bad bottle:

✔ First, patronize retailers who seem to care about their wine and who provide their customers with good service.

✔ Second, be attentive to seasonal weather patterns when buying wine or when having it shipped to you. We're very cautious about buying wine at the end of, or during, a very hot summer, unless the store has a good climate-control system. And we never have wine shipped to us (other than quick deliveries from our local shop) at the height of summer or winter.

Another way of knowing that the wine you're buying is sound is just to buy the best-selling, most popular wines (assuming you don't mind being a slave to taste trends). Wines that move through the distribution chain very quickly have less opportunity to be damaged along the way.

When we first started buying wine, our repertoire was about as broad as a 2-year-old child's vocabulary. We'd buy the same brands again and again because we knew what to expect from them, and we liked them well enough (both good reasons to buy a particular wine). But in retrospect, we let ourselves get stuck in a rut because we were afraid to take a chance on anything new. If wine was really going to be fun, we realized we had to be a little more adventuresome.

If you want to experience the wonderful array of wines in the world, experimenting is a must. New wines can be interesting and exciting. Now and then you might get a lemon, but at least you'll know not to buy that wine again! Keep in mind that if you're trying a wine for the first time, never buy more than a bottle or two. The wine isn't a great buy unless you like it. Personally, we seldom buy more than three bottles of a particular wine, even if we know the wine. We like variety, rather than drinking the same wine over and over.

Explain what you want

Communication is key in the wine-buying experience. The most knowledgeable wine expert in the world can't recommend a wine you'll like unless you can give him some clues about what you like.

The following is a familiar scene that occurs in nearly every wine shop every day (and ten times every Saturday):

Customer: I remember that the wine had a yellow label. I had it in this little restaurant last week.

Wine Merchant: Do you know what country it's from?

Customer: I think it's Italian, but I'm not sure.

Wine Merchant: Do you recall the grape variety?

Customer: No, but I think it has a deer or a moose on the label. Maybe if I walk around, I can spot it.

Needless to say, most of the time that customer never finds the wine he or she is looking for.

When you come across a wine you like in a restaurant or at a friend's house, write down from the label as much information about the wine as you can or snap a picture of the label with your cellphone. Don't trust your memory. If your wine merchant can see the name, she can give you that wine or something very similar to it.

It's clearly to your advantage to be able to tell your wine retailer anything you can about the types of wine that you've liked previously or that you want to try. Describe what you like in clear, simple terms. For example, for white wine, you might use such words as *crisp, dry,* or *fruity, ripe, oaky, buttery, full-bodied.* For red wines, you might say *big, rich, tannic,* or *medium-bodied, soft.* Turn to Chapter 2 for other helpful descriptors. For detailed guidance in describing the taste of wines, read our book *Wine Style: Using Your Senses to Explore and Enjoy Wine* (Wiley).

Tell your wine merchant what kind of food you plan to have with the wine. Doing so will narrow down your choices even more. The wine you drink with your flounder isn't the one you want with spicy chili! A good wine merchant is invaluable in helping you match your wine with food. (Chapter 9 tells you more about pairing wine with food.)

In-store samplings

In general, we're all for tasting wines before buying them, whenever possible. But the wine tastings that some retailers arrange in their stores do have their limitations. In addition to the fact that you usually get a miniscule serving in a little plastic cup more suited to dispensing pills in a hospital, you get to taste only the wines that the wine merchant (or one of his suppliers) happens to be pushing that day. Sometimes it's a wine that the store made an especially good buy on (translation: the store is making a good profit), or a wine that a local distributor is particularly interested in selling.

Whether you like the wine or not, you may feel pressured to buy it after trying it. Our advice to you is not to succumb to any conscious or unconscious sales pressure. Buy the wine only if you really like it — and even then, buy only one bottle to start. The wine may taste completely different to you when you're having dinner that night. If it tastes even better than you thought, you can always buy more bottles later.

Five questions you should ask in a wine shop

Here are five questions that we believe will give you vital information about the wine you are planning to buy.

✔ **If a wine costs more than $20: What kind of storage has this wine experienced?** Hemming and hawing on the part of the wine merchant should be taken to mean *poor*.

✔ **How long has this wine been in your store?** This question is especially important if the store doesn't have a climate-control system.

✔ **What are some particularly good buys this month?** (Provided you trust the wine merchant, and you don't think he's dumping some overstocked, closeout wine on you.)

✔ **If applicable: Why is this wine selling at such a low price?** The merchant may know that the wine is too old, or is otherwise defective; unless he comes up with a believable explanation, assume that's the case.

✔ **Will this wine go well with the food I'm planning to serve?** The more information about the recipe or main flavors you can provide, the better your chance of getting a good match.

Name your price

Because the price of a bottle of wine can range from about $4 to literally hundreds of dollars, it's a good idea to decide approximately how much you want to spend and to tell your wine merchant. Fix two price ranges in your mind: one for everyday purposes and one for special occasions. These prices will probably change over time; the $8 to $12 range you start with for everyday wines often rises to $12 to $20 as you discover finer wines. A good retailer with an adequate selection should be able to make several wine suggestions in your preferred price category.

A good wine merchant is more interested in the repeat business he'll get by making you happy than he is in trading you up to a bottle of wine that's beyond your limits. If what you want to spend is $10 a bottle, just say so, and stand firm, without embarrassment. Plenty of decent, enjoyable wines can be found at that price.

Chapter 7

Confronting a Restaurant Wine List

. . . .

In This Chapter

▶ Showing the wine list who's boss

▶ Choosing the right wine

▶ Surviving the wine presentation ritual

▶ A few tips for drinking wine in a restaurant

▶ Checking out wine bars

. . . .

*W*hen you buy a bottle of wine in a restaurant, you get to taste it right then and there — instant gratification. If you've chosen well, you have a delicious wine that pairs beautifully with the food you've selected. You also can bask in the compliments of your family and friends during the entire meal and go home feeling good about yourself. If you haven't chosen well . . . well, we all know *that* feeling! Fortunately, practice *does* make perfect, at least most of the time.

How Wine Is Sold in Restaurants

In most restaurants, you have to choose your wine from a menu that tells you only the names of the wines and the price per bottle — and manages to make even that little bit of information somewhat incomprehensible. Welcome to the *restaurant wine list*.

Restaurant wine lists can be infuriating. Typically, they don't tell you enough about the wines. Sometimes, nothing on the list is worth drinking, at least in your price range; other times, you have so many choices that you're immobilized. All too frequently, the lists simply aren't accurate; you spend ten good minutes of your life deciding which wine to order, only to discover that it's "not available tonight" (and probably hasn't been for months).

Believe it or not, restaurateurs really do want you to buy their wine. They usually make a sizable profit on every sale; their servers earn bigger tips and become happier employees; and you enjoy your meal more, going home a more satisfied customer. But traditionally (and, we trust, unwittingly), many restaurants have done more to hinder wine sales than to encourage them. Fortunately, the old ways are changing.

Wines available for sale in a restaurant these days generally fall into four categories, as you discover in the following sections:

- ✔ **House wines:** House wines usually include one white and one red and sometimes a sparkling wine. These wines can be purchased *by the glass* or in a *carafe* (a wide-mouthed, handle-less pitcher). You get a restaurant's house wine when you simply ask for a glass of white or a glass of red.

- ✔ **Premium wines by the glass:** These wines offer a wider selection than the house wines and are generally better quality. They're usually also available by the bottle.

- ✔ **Standard, or regular, wines:** These wines are available by the bottle from the restaurant's *standard,* or regular, *wine list.*

- ✔ **Reserve wines:** Reserve wines include older or rarer wines and are available by the bottle. You often have to request these wines from a special wine list, sometimes called a *reserve wine list* (not every restaurant has this list).

Wines by the glass: House and premium wines

We've noticed that restaurants are selling more wines by the glass than ever before. This is a win-win situation for both the restaurant and the customer. The restaurant makes more of a profit selling wines by the glass, and the customer has more diversity in his wine selection. Wines available by the glass are either house wines or premium wines. We discuss both of these categories in the following sections.

The choice of the house

Imagine this scenario: The wine list looks so imposing that you hand it back to the server and say (either a bit sheepishly, because you're acknowledging that you can't handle the wine list, or with defiant bravado, signifying that you're not going to waste your time on this nonsense), "I'll just have a glass of white wine (or 'Chardonnay')." Smart move or big mistake?

You'll probably know the answer to this question as soon as the house wine hits your lips. It might be just what you wanted — and you avoided the effort of plowing through that list — but in theory, we'd say, "Mistake."

Often, a restaurant's *house wines* are very ordinary stuff that the restaurant owner makes an enormous profit on. (Cost-per-ounce is usually a restaurant owner's main criterion in choosing a house wine.) House wines can range in price from $6 up to $10 a glass (with an average of about $8). Often, the entire bottle costs the proprietor the price of one glass or less! No wonder the "obliging" server fills your glass to the brim.

If you do choose a house wine, you usually save money if you buy it by the carafe, if it's offered that way. On the other hand, you may not want an entire carafe of the house wine!

One of the main problems we encounter with wines by the glass is that they often taste tired (in other words, old or lifeless). Always ask the server, "How long has this bottle been open?" If he or she doesn't know, that's a bad sign. Ideally, the wine was opened that day.

We've found that only a small percentage of restaurants offer a house wine worth drinking. And it's practically never a good value. Under most circumstances, avoid the house wine. For the same reasons, avoid asking for "a glass of Chardonnay" or "a glass of Merlot."

If circumstances are such that a glass of wine makes the most sense (if you're the only one in your group who's having wine with dinner, for example), chances are you'll need to order the house wine, unless you're at a restaurant that offers premium selections by the glass as well (see the next section). If the house wine is your only option, ask the server what it is. Don't be satisfied with a simple response, such as "It's Chardonnay"; ask for specifics: Chardonnay from where? What brand? Ask to see the bottle.

Premium pours

A restaurant's premium wines are red and white wines that are a lot better in quality than its basic house wines. As such, a restaurant sells premium wines at a higher price, usually in the range of $9 to $18 per glass. Usually, a restaurant's house wines aren't listed on its wine list, and so under the category *Wines by the Glass,* you'll find its premium wines (we use the term *premium* to distinguish these wines from the restaurant's house wines).

A restaurant might offer only one premium white and one red, or it might offer several choices. These premium wines aren't anonymous beverages, like the house red and white, but are identified for you somehow — on the wine list, on a separate card, verbally, or sometimes even by a display of bottles. In some informal restaurants, premium wines by the glass are listed on a chalkboard.

The wine-by-the-glass challenge

We're delighted to see that most restaurants these days offer interesting selections of wine by the glass. Selling wine by the glass is a growing trend, despite the challenges it presents to restaurateurs. Their main problem is preserving the wine in all those open bottles. The more wines a restaurant offers by the glass, the greater the odds that wine will be left over in each bottle at the end of the evening, and those wines won't be fresh enough to serve the next day. Unless a restaurant sets up some sort of wine preservation system, it will waste an enormous amount of wine by selling it by the glass. Its wine profits will go right down the drain (or into the stew)!

Ordering premium wines by the glass is a fine idea, especially if you want to have only a glass or two or if you and your guests want to experiment by trying several wines. Sometimes, we order a glass of a premium white wine or a glass of Champagne or sparkling wine as a starter and then go on to a bottle of red wine.

We love a good wines-by-glass listing in restaurants. We don't always agree on which bottle to choose, and so ordering wines by the glass solves that problem. And sometimes, we don't want to drink an entire bottle; for example, at lunch, when one of us has to return to work, just a glass of wine is perfect.

You end up paying more for the wine if you order a bottle's worth of individual glasses than you would if you ordered a whole bottle to begin with. If two or three of you are ordering the same wine by the glass — and especially if you might want refills — ask how many ounces are poured into each glass (usually 5 to 8 ounces) and compare the price with that of a 25.4-ounce (750-ml) bottle of the same wine. (You usually do have the option of buying an entire bottle.) Sometimes, for the cost of only three glasses, you can have the whole bottle.

Special, or reserve, wine lists

Some restaurants offer a *special,* or *reserve,* wine list of rare wines to supplement their standard wine list. These special lists appeal to two types of customers: very serious wine connoisseurs and "high rollers." If you're not in either category, don't even bother asking whether the restaurant has such a list. Then again, if you're not paying for the meal or if you seriously want to impress a client or a date, you may want to look at it! Try to get help with the list from some knowledgeable person on the restaurant staff, though: Any mistake you make can be a costly one.

The (anything but) standard wine list

Most of the time, you'll probably end up turning to the restaurant's standard wine list to choose your wine. We use the term *standard wine list* to distinguish a restaurant's basic wine list from its special, or reserve, wine list. Unfortunately, nothing is standard about wine lists at all. They come in all sizes, shapes, and degrees of detail, accuracy, and user friendliness. Some standard wine lists offer some wines by the glass as well as by the bottle and indicate these wines on the list, with prices for *by the glass* and *by the bottle* given. (Later in this chapter, we explain some strategies for dealing with wine lists.)

How to Read a Wine List

Your first step in the encounter between you and the wine list is to size up the opposition. You can do so by noting how the wine list is organized.

Check out the style of the list: Is it pretentious or straightforward? Figure out how the wines are categorized and how they're arranged within each category. Notice the number of wines on it — whether it's 12 or 200. (An indirect benefit of this procedure is that the purposeful look in your eyes will convince your guests that you know what you're doing.)

When the restaurant doesn't have an alcohol license, BYOB

In most places, establishments that sell alcoholic beverages — both retail stores and restaurants — must be licensed by the government, to assure that appropriate taxes are paid and to aid in the enforcement of local laws. Some restaurants don't have liquor licenses due to circumstance or choice, and, therefore, can't sell wine. In those restaurants, you can BYOB (bring your own bottle) to enjoy with your meal. (If you're not sure of the restaurant's policy on BYOB, call ahead.)

Many Chinese restaurants fall into this category. (Asian cuisine can be difficult to match with wine, but Champagne and sparkling wine generally go well, as do Alsace Gewurztraminer or off-dry German Riesling.) Other examples include restaurants that have recently opened and haven't yet received their liquor licenses or restaurants that for some reason don't qualify for a license. (They may be located too close to a school or a church, for example.)

We love BYOB restaurants! Not only do we save money, but we can also bring the bottle of our choice. You might have to pay a small fee when you bring your own wine — after all, the service staff handles your bottle for you (see the later section "Restaurant Wine Tips" for more about corkage fees) — but in most cases, you still get a good deal.

Wine list power struggles

In many restaurants, the servers don't give you enough time to study the wine list. (Really good restaurants recognize that choosing a bottle of wine can take some time.) If your waiter asks, somewhat impatiently, "Have you selected your wine yet?" simply tell him (firmly) that you need more time. Don't be bullied into making a hasty choice.

Usually, your table will receive only one wine list. An outmoded convention dictates that only the host (the masculine is intentional) needs to see the list. (This convention is part of the same outmoded thinking that dictates that females should receive menus with no prices on them.) At our table of two, we have *two* thinking, curious, decision-making customers. We always ask for a second list.

Invariably, the wine list is handed to the oldest or most important-looking male at the table. If you're a female who is entertaining business clients, this situation can be insulting and infuriating. Speak up and ask for a copy of the wine list for yourself. If it's important enough to you, slip away from the table and inform the server that you are the host of the table.

As soon as your server comes to the table, ask to see the wine list. Besides communicating to the server that you feel comfortable with wine (whether it's true or not), asking for the list quickly gives you more time to study it. Also, if you wait until the food is served to order a wine, you might get the wine when you're almost finished eating!

What the wine list should tell you

You can't predict exactly what you'll find on the wine list, other than prices. Generally speaking, though, you might discover the wines arranged in the following categories:

- ✔ Champagne and sparkling wines
- ✔ (Dry) white wines
- ✔ (Dry) red wines
- ✔ Dessert wines

Some restaurants further subdivide the wines on their list according to country, especially in the white and red wine categories: French red wines, Italian red wines, California reds, and so on. These country sections may then be subdivided by wine region. France, for example, may have listings of Bordeaux, Burgundy, and possibly Rhône all under *French Red Wines. U.S. Reds* may be divided into California wines, Oregon wines, and Washington wines.

The more serious a restaurant is about its wine selection, the more information it gives you about each wine. Here's some information you're likely to find on the wine list:

- ✔ **Item number for each wine:** These numbers are sometimes called *bin numbers,* referring to the specific location of each wine in the restaurant's cellar or wine storage room.

- ✔ **The name of each wine:** The names of wines may be grape names or place-names (see Chapter 4 for details on how wines are named), but they had better also include the name of each producer (Château this or that, or such-and-such Winery), or you'll have no way of knowing exactly which wine any listing is meant to represent.

- ✔ **A vintage indication — the year the grapes were harvested — for each wine:** If the wine is a blend of wines from different years, it may say *NV,* for *non-vintage.* (Chapter 4 tells you why non-vintage wines exist.)

We're always annoyed when we see lists that don't name the wine's vintage. Often, we order a vintage-dated wine and the server shows up with a newer vintage. The restaurant just didn't bother to update its wine list. This can be a problem if the newer vintage isn't as good as the one we ordered, or if it's just too young to drink. We don't hesitate to order a different bottle from the list if this happens.

- ✔ **Description of each wine:** Sometimes, you might find a brief description of the wines; however, this is unlikely if dozens of wines are on the list.

- ✔ **Food pairings for each wine:** Sometimes, a wine list might include suggestions from the restaurateur for certain wines to pair with certain dinner entrées. In our experience, this information is helpful at times, but you might not always like — or agree with — the wine suggestion.

- ✔ **Prices for each wine:** Wine lists *always* include prices.

Tips for using the wine list

The wine list that you find in your hands might be comprehensive, featuring a large selection of wines and all the information we list in the previous section. Or it might be sparse. Depending on the nature of that list, here are some tips that we hope will be helpful:

- ✔ **Be aware of low to high pricing.** Often, you'll find that within each category, the wines appear in ascending order of price with the least expensive wine first. Many a restaurateur is betting that you won't order that first wine out of fear of looking cheap. They figure you'll go for the second, third, or fourth wine down the price column or even deeper if you're feeling insecure and need the reassurance that your choice is a good one. (Meanwhile, that least expensive wine may be perfectly fine. Don't hesitate to order it.)

✔ **Check out the regional skews.** If a restaurant features a particular country's cuisine, the wines of that country, say Italian, may be listed first (and given certain prominence), followed by a cursory listing of wines from other areas. You'll usually find the best values in those regional wines.

✔ **Notice the appearance.** Once upon a time, the best wine lists consisted of hand-lettered pages inside heavy leather covers embossed with the words *Carte des Vins* in gold. Today, the best wine lists are more likely to be laser-printed pages or cards that more than make up in functionality what they sacrifice in romance.

The more permanent and immutable a wine list seems, the less accurate its listings are likely to be — and the less specific.

✔ **Don't worry if no separate list exists.** Sometimes, the list of wines is actually part of the restaurant's menu, especially if the menu is a computer-printed page or two that changes from week to week or from month to month. Restaurants featuring immediate, up-to-date wine listings like this can be a good bet for wine.

✔ **Pay attention to the numbers.** Item numbers for each wine make it easier for the server to locate and pull the wine quickly for you. They're also a crutch to help the server bring you the right wine in case he doesn't have a clue about wine, not to mention a crutch for *you* in ordering the wine in case you don't have a clue how to pronounce what you've decided to drink. (You can always pretend that you're using the number for the waiter's benefit.)

Digital browsing

Increasingly, some restaurants are daring to go where no wine list has gone before: into the digital realm. Their wine lists — at least a few copies of them — are on tablet computers that enable you not only to see the list of available wines and their prices but also to access background information on each wine; you can even search for wines that are suitable for the food you're ordering. Of course, these lists have their downside: They're so much fun that you risk offending your friends by playing with the list for too long!

Many restaurants that are serious about wine publish their wine lists on the Internet. Before a special meal, you can go to the restaurant's website and make a short list of possible wines for your meal — a guaranteed way to boost your comfort level.

The lowdown on high wine prices

Most restaurateurs count on wine and liquor sales to provide a disproportionate percentage of their business profit. The typical restaurant charges two to two-and-a-half (sometimes three!) times the retail store price for a bottle of wine. That means that the restaurant is earning *three to four times* the price it paid for the bottle.

Admittedly, restaurateurs incur costs for wine storage, glasses, breakage, service, and so on.

But those costs don't justify such extraordinary markups, in the eyes of most wine drinkers.

Some savvy restaurateurs have discovered that by marking up their wines less, they actually sell *more* wine and make *more money* in the end. We try to patronize *those* restaurants.

Ordering Your Wine

If, after sizing up the wine list, you decide that you aren't familiar with most of the wines on it, *ask for help with your selection.*

If the restaurant is a fancy one, ask whether a *sommelier* (pronounced som-mel-yay) is on staff — technically, a specially trained, high-level wine specialist who's responsible for putting the wine list together and for making sure that the wines offered on the list complement the cuisine of the restaurant. (Unfortunately, usually only the more wine-conscious restaurants employ one.) If the restaurant isn't particularly fancy, ask to speak with the wine specialist. Often someone on the staff, frequently the proprietor, knows the wine list well.

If someone on the restaurant staff knows the wine list well, this person is your best bet to help you select a wine. He will usually know what wines go best with the food you're ordering. He'll also be extremely appreciative of your interest in the list. For these reasons, even though we're familiar with wine, we often consult the sommelier, proprietor, or wine specialist for suggestions from the wine list. The sommelier (or wine specialist) often can save you money by recommending a good-value wine on the list that you didn't know about.

Following are a few ways you can request help when choosing a wine:

- ✔ If you aren't sure how to pronounce the wine's name, point to it on the list, or use the wine's item or bin number (if one exists).

- ✔ Point out two or three wines on the list to the sommelier or server and say, "I'm considering these wines. Which one do you recommend?" Doing so is also a subtle way of communicating your price range.

✔ Ask to *see* one or two bottles; your familiarity with the labels, seeing the name of an importer whose other wines you've enjoyed, or some other aspect of the label might help you make up your mind.

✔ Mention the food you plan to order and ask for suggestions of wines that would complement the meal.

We realize that you can't remember *all* the wines we recommend in this book when you're dining out, so in Table 7-1, we list a few types of wine that are on most restaurant wine lists and that we believe are consistently reliable choices with food. For more information on all these wines, refer to Parts III and IV.

Table 7-1 Reliable Wine Choices when Ordering in a Restaurant

When You Want...	Order...
A crisp, dry white wine that isn't very flavorful to accompany delicately flavored fish or seafood	Soave, Pinot Grigio, or Sancerre
Dry, flavorful white wine that's perfect with mussels and other shellfish	Sauvignon Blanc from South Africa or New Zealand or an Albariño from Spain
Medium-bodied, characterful, dry white wine for simple poultry, risotto, and dishes that are medium in weight	Mâcon-Villages, St.-Véran, Sancerre, or Pouilly-Fuissé
Full-bodied, rich white wine for lobster or rich chicken entrées	California or Australian Chardonnay
Medium-dry white wine for Asian-inspired dishes	Chenin Blanc, Vouvray, or German Riesling
Easy-drinking, inexpensive red, perfect with roast chicken	Beaujolais
Versatile, flavorful, relatively inexpensive red that can stand up to spicy food	California red Zinfandel
A lighter red that's delicious, young, and works with all sorts of light- and medium-intensity foods	Oregon Pinot Noir, Malbec
The basic French version of Pinot Noir; try it with simple cuts of steak	Bourgogne Rouge
Dry, spicy, grapey, and relatively inexpensive red wine that's perfect with pizza	Barbera or Dolcetto
A very dry, medium-bodied red that's great with pasta and simple cuts of meat	Chianti Classico

Twice the price

A few profit-minded restaurateurs train their servers to maximize wine sales in every way possible — even at the customers' expense. For example, some servers are trained to refill wine glasses liberally so that the bottle is emptied before the main course arrives. (This can happen all the more easily when the glasses are large.) Upon emptying the bottle, the server asks, "Shall I bring another bottle of the same wine?" Depending on how much wine is in everyone's glass and how much wine your guests tend to drink, you may not *need* another bottle, but your tendency will be to say "yes" to avoid looking stingy.

An even trickier practice is to refill the glasses starting with the host so that the bottle runs dry before each of the guests has had a refill. How can you refuse a second bottle at the expense of your guests' enjoyment?! You'll have to order that second bottle — and you should let the manager know how you feel about it when you leave. (But remember, these nefarious restaurant practices are the exception rather than the rule.)

Handling the Wine Presentation Ritual

The wine presentation used to occur with such ceremony that you'd think you were involved in high church or temple services. The hushed tones of the waiter, the ritualized performance, the seriousness of it all can make you want to laugh (but that seems wrong — almost like laughing in church). Fortunately, most wine servers aren't taking the ritual so seriously these days. But the process and the logic behind it remain the same. Step by step, the ritual (and the logic) goes like this:

1. **The waiter or sommelier presents the bottle to you (assuming that you are the person who ordered the wine) for inspection.**

   The point is to make sure that the bottle *is* the bottle you ordered. Check the label carefully. In our experience, 10 to 15 percent of the time, we receive the wrong bottle or vintage. Feel the bottle with your hand, if you like, to determine whether its temperature seems to be correct; see Chapter 8 for details on proper serving temperature. (This is also a good time for you to pretend to recognize something about the label, as if the wine is an old friend, even if you've never seen it before.) If you're satisfied with the bottle, nod your approval to the server.

2. **The server removes the cork and places it in front of you.**

   The purpose of this step is for you to determine, by smelling and visually inspecting the cork, whether the cork is in good condition, and whether the cork seems to be the legitimate cork for that bottle of wine.

In rare instances, a wine might be so corky (see Chapter 2 for detailed wine taste descriptions) that the cork itself has an unpleasant odor. On even rarer occasions, the cork might be totally wet and shriveled or very dry and crumbly; either situation suggests that air has gotten into the wine and spoiled it.

Once in a while, you might discover an incorrect vintage year or winery name on your cork. But most of the time, the presentation of the cork is inconsequential.

If the cork does raise your suspicions, you should still wait to smell or taste the wine itself before deciding whether to reject the bottle.

Once, when one of our wiseguy friends was presented the cork by the server, he proceeded to put it into his mouth and chew it, and then he pronounced to the waiter that it was just fine!

3. **If your wine needs decanting, the server decants it.**

   For more information on decanting, see Chapter 8.

4. **The server pours a small amount of wine into your glass and waits.**

   At this point, you're *not* supposed to say, "Is that all you're giving me?!" You're expected to take a sniff of the wine, perhaps a little sip, and then either nod your approval to the waiter or murmur, "It's fine." Actually, this step is an important part of the ritual because if something *is* wrong with the wine, *now* is the time to return it — not after you've finished half the bottle! For a review of wine-tasting techniques, turn to Chapter 2 before you head out to the restaurant.

   If you're not really sure whether the condition of the wine is acceptable, ask for someone else's opinion at your table and then make a group decision; otherwise, you risk feeling foolish by either returning the bottle later when it's been declared defective by one of your guests or drinking the stuff when it becomes clear to you later that something is wrong with it. Take as long as you need to on this step.

   If you do decide that the bottle is out of condition, describe to the server what you find wrong with the wine, using the best language you can. (*Musty* or *dank* are descriptors that are easily understood.) Be sympathetic to the fact that you're causing more work for him, but don't be overly apologetic. (Why should you be? You didn't make the wine!) Let him smell or taste the wine himself if he wants, but don't let him make you feel guilty.

   Depending on whether the sommelier or captain agrees that it's a bad bottle or whether he believes that you just don't understand the wine, he might bring you another bottle of the same, or he might bring you the wine list so you can select a different wine. Either way, the ritual begins again from the top.

5. **If you do accept the wine, the waiter pours the wine into your guests' glasses and then finally into yours.**

   Now you're allowed to relax.

Ladies first?

Almost all restaurant waiters pour, and repour, wine for the women at the table first. What's wrong with that? Well, one of us, who otherwise is not a male chauvinist, doesn't like that idea because most of the time the females at the table aren't drinking as much wine as he is. Quite frequently, the last part of the bottle goes into the glasses of the women, who often don't drink it, while the males have empty glasses in front of them, forcing them to order another bottle or do without. Because we're all for equality between the sexes, how about pouring the wine into the emptiest glasses, regardless of gender?

Restaurant Wine Tips

Drinking wine in a restaurant requires so many decisions that you really do need a guidebook. Should you leave the wine in an ice bucket? What should you do if the wine is bad? And can you bring your own wine? Let the following list guide you:

- ✔ **Can I kick the ice-bucket habit?** Most servers assume that an ice bucket is necessary to chill white wines and sparkling wines. But sometimes the bottle is already so cold when it comes to you that the wine would be better off warming up a bit on the table. If your white wine goes into an ice bucket and you think it's getting *too* cold, remove it from the bucket, or have the waiter remove it. Just because that ice bucket is sitting there on your table (or next to your table) doesn't mean that your bottle has to be in it!

  Sometimes, a red wine that's a bit too warm can benefit from five or ten minutes in an ice bucket. (But be careful! It can get too cold very quickly.) If the server acts as if you're nuts to chill a red wine, ignore him.

- ✔ **What's with these tiny glasses?** When various glasses are available, you can exercise your right to choose a different glass from the one you were given. If the restaurant's red wine glass is quite small, a stemmed water glass might be more appropriate for the red wine.

- ✔ **Should the wine "breathe"?** If a red wine you ordered needs aeration to soften its harsh tannins (see Chapter 8), merely pulling the cork will be practically useless in accomplishing that (because the air space at the neck of the bottle is too small). Decanting the bottle or pouring the wine into glasses is the best tactic. Don't be afraid to ask for your wine to be decanted.

- ✔ **Where's my bottle?** We prefer to have our bottle of wine on or near our table, not out of our reach. We can look at the label that way, and we don't have to wait for the server to remember to refill our glasses, either. (Okay, call us controlling.)

- **What if the bottle is bad?** Refuse any bottle that tastes or smells unpleasant (unless you brought it yourself!). A good restaurateur will always replace the wine, even if he thinks nothing is wrong with it. (See the preceding section for details on returning a bad bottle during the wine presentation ritual.)

- **May I bring my own wine?** Many restaurants allow you to bring your own wine — especially if you express the desire to bring a special wine or an older wine. Restaurants will usually charge a *corkage* fee (a fee for wine service, use of the glasses, and so on) that can vary from $10 to $25 a bottle, or higher, depending on the attitude of the restaurant. You should never bring a wine that's already on the restaurant's wine list; it's cheap and insulting. (Call and ask the restaurant when you're not sure whether the wine is on its list.) Anyway, you certainly should call ahead to determine whether bringing wine is possible (in some places, the restaurant's license prohibits it) and to ask what the corkage fee is.

- **What if I'm traveling abroad?** If you journey to countries, such as France, Italy, Germany, Switzerland, Austria, Greece, Spain, or Portugal, where wine is made, by all means try the local wines. They'll be fresher than the imports, in good condition, and the best values on the wine list. It doesn't make sense to order French wines, such as Bordeaux or Burgundy, in Italy, for example, or California Cabernets in Paris.

Exploring Wine Bars

Wine bars are popping up everywhere, not just in London, Italy, and Paris. Just about every major city in the United States has several wine bars; New York City has more than we can count! Wine bars are establishments that offer an extensive choice of wines by the glass — from 12 to 100 — as well as simple food to accompany the wines. The wine bottles are usually either hooked up to an inert-gas injection system after being opened, which keeps the wine fresh, or are topped up with inert gas from a free-standing dispenser at the end of each evening.

In wine bars, you're sometimes offered a choice of two different *sizes* of wines by the glass. You can have a *taste* of a wine (about 2½ ounces) for one price, or a *glass* of a wine (often 5 ounces) for another price. And you can often order a *flight* of wines — several similar wines served side by side so you can compare them.

Wine bars are the ideal way to try lots of different wines by the glass — an educational as well as satisfying experience. We love them! The fact that their numbers are increasing year by year proves that other wine drinkers love them, too.

Chapter 8

Serving Wine

. . . .

In This Chapter

▶ Corkophobia and other barriers to getting the wine out

▶ Breathing lessons for your bottle

▶ Tulips, flutes, trumpets, and other types of wine glasses

▶ Appropriate temps and serving suggestions for wine

▶ Survival tactics for leftover wine

. . . .

*H*ave you ever broken a cork while trying to extract it from the bottle or taken an unusually long time to remove a stubborn cork while your guests smiled at you uneasily? This has certainly happened to us from time to time and probably to just about everyone else who has ever pulled a cork out of a bottle of wine. It's enough to give anyone a case of corkophobia!

Removing the cork from a wine bottle is the first challenge you face in your quest to enjoy wine, and it's a big one. (Fortunately, when you get the hang of it, it's easy — most of the time.) Then you have the niggling details of wine service, such as which type of glass to use and what to do if you don't finish the whole bottle. But help is at hand in this chapter.

Getting the Cork Out

Before you can even think about removing the cork from a wine bottle, you need to deal with whatever covers the cork. Most wine bottles have a colorful covering over the top of the bottle that's called a *capsule*. Wineries place capsules on top of the corks for two reasons: to keep the corks clean and to create a fetching look for their bottles.

These days, most wineries use colored foil or plastic capsules rather than the traditional lead capsules. Whether the capsule is plastic, foil, or even cellophane, we usually remove the entire capsule so that no wine can possibly come into contact with the covering when we pour. (We use the small knife that's part of most *corkscrews* — the devices that exist solely for opening wine bottles.) Sometimes, we encounter a plastic plug atop the cork rather than a capsule, and we just flick it off with the tip of the knife.

After removing the capsule or plug, we wipe clean the top of the bottle with a damp cloth. Sometimes the visible end of the cork is dark with mold that developed under the capsule, and in that case, we wipe all the more diligently. (That mold is actually a good sign: It means that the wine has been stored in humid conditions. See Chapter 17 for info on humidity and other aspects of wine storage.)

Sometimes wine lovers just can't bring themselves to remove the whole capsule out of respect for the bottle of wine that they're about to drink. (In fact, traditional wine etiquette dictates that you don't remove the entire capsule.) Many people use a gizmo called a foil cutter that sells for about $6 to $9 in wine shops, kitchen stores, or online.

After all the preceding prep, it's time to actually remove the cork. In the following sections, we warn you about the corkscrew you shouldn't use and recommend corkscrews that are worth your time and money.

The corkscrew not to use

The one corkscrew we absolutely avoid happens to be the most common type of corkscrew around. We don't like it for one very simple reason: It mangles the cork, almost guaranteeing that brown flakes will be floating in your glass of wine. (We also don't like it because it offends our sense of righteousness that an inferior product should be so popular.)

That corkscrew is the infamous Wing Type Corkscrew, a bright silver-colored, metal device that looks like a cross between a pair of pliers and a drill; when you insert this corkscrew into a cork, two "wings" rise up from the side of the corkscrew. The major shortcoming of this device is its very short worm, or *auger* (the curly prong that bores into the cork), which is too short for many corks and overly aggressive on all of them.

Instead of finding out the hard way that this corkscrew just doesn't cut it (or, literally, cuts it too much!), as we did, invest a few dollars in a decent corkscrew right off the bat. The time and hassle you'll save will be more than worth the investment. Of the many types of wine-bottle openers available, we recommend the three described in the following sections.

The corkscrew to buy

One very reliable corkscrew is the Screwpull. About six inches long, it consists of an arched piece of plastic (which looks like a clothespin on steroids) straddling an inordinately long, 5-inch worm that's coated with Teflon (see Figure 8-1). It also comes in chrome or nickel — more expensive but worth it because it will last forever. The plastic one usually breaks after a few years.

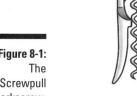

Figure 8-1:
The
Screwpull
corkscrew.

Illustration by Lisa S. Reed

To use this corkscrew, you simply place the plastic frame over the bottle top (having removed the capsule), until a lip on the plastic is resting atop the bottle. Screw the worm downward until it touches the cork. Then hold on to the plastic firmly while turning the lever atop the worm clockwise into the cork. Then you simply keep turning the lever in the same clockwise direction, and the cork magically emerges from the bottle. To remove the cork from the Screwpull, simply turn the lever counterclockwise while holding on to the cork.

The Screwpull comes in many colors and costs about $15 in wine shops, kitchen stores, and online. The chrome or nickel version costs about $50. It's very simple to use and doesn't require a lot of muscle.

Other corkscrews worth owning

We have two other corkscrews for the corks that the Screwpull can't remove. (Flange-top bottles, for example, really challenge the Screwpull because of their unusual width at the top.) Our two alternative corkscrews (described in the following sections) are smaller devices that — besides working better now and then — can conveniently fit into a pocket. Their size is one reason that servers in restaurants favor them.

You can buy some really fancy corkscrews — some which attach to a counter or a bar — that will cost you $100-plus. Yes, most of them work very well after you get the hang of them, but frankly, we don't see the need to spend that much on a corkscrew. We'd rather spend it on the wine!

The two-pronged Ah-So

One corkscrew we recommend is called, unofficially, the Ah-So because — according to wine legend, anyway — when people finally figure out how it works, they say, "Ah, so that's how it works!" (It's also known as the "Butler's Friend" — but where have all the butlers gone?) The Ah-So sells for around $10 to $15.

It's a simple device made up of two thin, flat metal prongs, one slightly longer than the other (see Figure 8-2). To use it, you slide the prongs down into the tight space between the cork and the bottle (inserting the longer prong first), using a back-and-forth seesaw motion until the top of the Ah-So is resting atop the cork. Then you twist the cork while gently pulling it up.

Figure 8-2:
The Ah-So
corkscrew.

Illustration by Lisa S. Reed

One advantage of the Ah-So is that it delivers an intact cork — without a hole in it — that can be reused to close bottles of homemade vinegar or to make cutesy bulletin boards.

Although more difficult to operate than the Screwpull, the Ah-So really comes into its own with very tight-fitting corks that no other corkscrews, including the Screwpull, seem to be able to budge. Also, the Ah-So can be effective with old, crumbly corks that don't give other corkscrews much to grip.

The Ah-So is useless with loose corks that move around in the bottle's neck when you try to remove them. It just pushes those corks down into the wine. At that point, you'll need another tool called a *cork retriever* (which we describe in the section "Waiter, there's cork in my wine!" later in this chapter).

The most professional corkscrew of them all

Our final recommended corkscrew, probably the most commonly used corkscrew in restaurants all over the world, is simply called the Waiter's Corkscrew. A straight or gently curved base holds three devices that fold into it, like a Swiss Army knife: a lever, a worm, and a small knife (see Figure 8-3). The latter is especially handy for removing the capsule from the bottle.

Figure 8-3:
The
Waiter's
Corkscrew.

Illustration by Lisa S. Reed

Using the Waiter's Corkscrew requires some practice. First, grasp the bottle's neck. The trick then is to guide the worm down through the center of the cork by turning the corkscrew; turn slowly at first, until you're sure that the worm is not off center and is actually descending down the middle of the cork. After the worm is fully descended into the cork, place the lever on the lip of the bottle and push against the lever while pulling the cork up. Give a firm tug at the very end or wiggle the bottom of the cork out with your hand.

If your cork ever breaks and part of it gets stuck in the neck of the bottle, the Waiter's Corkscrew is indispensable for removing the remaining piece. Use the method we just described, but insert the worm at a 45-degree angle. In most cases, you will successfully remove the broken cork.

The Waiter's Corkscrew sells for about $10 to $12, but designer versions can cost a lot more. Those of us in the wine business get many of them as promotional items. We have a ton of them. We use them frequently because they're the fastest to use, after you get the hang of them.

Why is my cork blue?

Have you ever opened a bottle of wine and discovered that the "cork" isn't cork at all but is instead plastic — and iridescent, to boot?

Although we appreciate the touch of whimsy that an orange or blue cork contributes, we're not fans of plastic corks. Winemakers are understandably disillusioned with cork itself because it can sometimes give off-aromas to a wine. But if you're going to invent an alternative to cork, why plug the bottle neck with yet another closure that's a rude barrier between wine drinkers and their wine, demanding the same, complicated tool as a cork does — and can be even more difficult to remove?! Fortunately, new versions of synthetic corks are becoming more user friendly than earlier types. But screw caps are even more user friendly. We're a big fan of screw caps, especially for wines that aren't meant for long aging; however, we have increasingly noticed a number of producers, particularly in Australia and New Zealand, using screw caps even on wines destined for long cellaring. (See the later section "The Comeback of the Screw Cap" for details.)

Waiter, there's cork in my wine!

Every now and then, even if you've used the right corkscrew and used it properly, you can still have pieces of cork floating in your wine. They can be tiny dry flakes that crumbled into the bottle, actual chunks of cork, or even the entire cork.

Before you start berating yourself for being a klutz, you should know that "floating cork" has happened to all of us at one time or another, no matter how experienced we are. Cork won't harm the wine. And besides, you can get a wonderful instrument called a *cork retriever* (no, it's not a small dog from the south of Ireland!) that sells for about $15 online.

One type of cork retriever consists of three 10-inch pieces of stiff metal wire with hooks on the ends. This device is remarkably effective for removing floating pieces of cork from the bottle. We have even removed a whole, fallen cork through the neck with a cork retriever.

Alternatively, you can just pick out the offending piece(s) of cork with a spoon after you pour the wine into your glass. (That's one occasion when serving your guest first is rude, because the first glass has more cork pieces in it.) Or you can pour the wine through a paper coffee filter (preferably the natural brown-paper type), into a decanter or pitcher to catch the remaining pieces of cork.

A special case: Opening Champagne and sparkling wine

Opening a bottle of sparkling wine is usually an exciting occasion. Who doesn't enjoy the ceremony of a cold glass of bubbly? But you need to use a completely different technique than you'd use to open a regular wine bottle. The cork even looks different. Sparkling wine corks have a mushroom-shaped head that protrudes from the bottle and a wire cage that holds the cork in place against the pressure that's trapped inside the bottle.

Be careful when you remove the wire cage, and keep one hand on top of the cork as a precaution, from the moment you loosen the cage. (We had a hole in our kitchen ceiling from one adventure with a flying cork.) Be sure to point the bottle away from people and other fragile objects.

If you like to hear the cork pop, just yank it out. When you do that, however, you'll lose some of the precious wine, which will froth out of the bottle. Also, the noise can interfere with your guests' conversation. Besides, it ain't too classy!

Removing the cork from sparkling wine with just a gentle sigh rather than a loud pop is fairly easy. Simply hold the bottle at a 45-degree angle with a towel wrapped around it if it's wet. (Try resting the base of the bottle on your hipbone.) Twist the bottle while holding on to the cork so that you can control the cork as it emerges. When you feel the cork starting to come out of the bottle, *push down against the cork* with some pressure, as if you don't want to let it out of the bottle. In this way, the cork will emerge slowly with a hiss or sigh sound rather than a pop.

Never, ever use a corkscrew on a bottle of sparkling wine. The pressure of the trapped carbonation, when suddenly released, can send the cork *and* corkscrew flying right into your eye, with serious consequences.

Here are some other tips for opening bottles of bubbly:

✔ Never shake a bottle of sparkling wine before opening. If your bottle of bubbly has just traveled, let it rest for a day. Controlling the cork is difficult when the carbonation has been stirred up.

If you're in the midst of a sparkling wine emergency and need to open a bottle that has traveled, calm down the carbonation by submerging the bottle in an ice bucket for about 30 minutes. (Fill the bucket with one-half ice cubes and one-half ice-cold water.)

✔ Every once in a while, you'll come across a really tight sparkling wine cork that doesn't want to budge. Try running the cork under warm water for a few moments or wrapping a towel around the cork to create friction. Either action will usually enable you to remove the cork.

> ✔ Another option for a tight cork is to use a fancy gadget that you place around the part of the cork that's outside the bottle. (Actually, three types of gadgets can do the trick: Champagne Pliers, a Champagne Star, and a Champagne Key.) Or you can probably try using regular pliers, although lugging in the toolbox will surely change the mood of the occasion.

The Comeback of the Screw Cap

Formerly, only cheap, lower-quality wines had screw cap closures. But in the past ten years, more and more wine producers have switched from corks to screw caps for their fine wines. Many wineries throughout the world are now using screw caps, especially for their white wines. Some Swiss producers have been using screw caps for their quality wines for decades now, especially for half-bottles.

Rather than imitation cork (see the earlier sidebar "Why is my cork blue?" for details), we prefer to see real screw caps on wine bottles. Screw caps are perfectly sound closures, technically speaking, and they're easier to remove than corks. They also prevent *cork taint,* a chemical flaw affecting a small percentage of corks and, consequently, the wine in those bottles. A *corky* wine — that is, one affected with cork taint — is damaged either slightly or flagrantly. In the worst-case scenarios, corky wines give off an offensive odor similar to moldy or damp cardboard.

Don't expect to see bottles of particularly fine, age-worthy red wines sporting screw caps anytime soon, because many winemakers are still reluctant to use them for such wines. But don't shy away from screw-capped bottles of other fine wines when you find them.

Does Wine Really Breathe?

Most wine is alive in the sense that it changes chemically as it slowly grows older. Wine absorbs oxygen, and, like our own cells, it oxidizes. When the grapes turn into wine in the first place, they give off carbon dioxide, just like us. So we suppose you could say that wine breathes. But that's not what the server means when he asks, "Shall I pull the cork and let the wine breathe?"

The term *breathing* refers to the process of aerating the wine, exposing it to air. Sometimes the aroma and flavor of a very young wine improves with aeration. But just pulling the cork out of the bottle and letting the bottle sit there is a truly ineffective way to aerate the wine. The little space at the neck of the bottle is way too small to allow your wine to breathe very much.

In the following sections, we explain how to aerate your wine and list the wines that benefit from aerating.

How to aerate your wine

If you really want to aerate your wine, do one or both of the following:

- Pour the wine into a *decanter* (a fancy word for a glass container that is big enough to hold the contents of an entire bottle of wine).

  Practically speaking, it doesn't matter what your decanter looks like or how much it costs. In fact, very inexpensive, wide-mouthed carafes are fine.

- Pour some of the wine into large glasses at least ten minutes before you plan to drink it.

Which wines need aerating?

Many red wines but only a few white wines — and some dessert wines — can benefit from aeration. You can drink most white wines upon pouring, unless they're too cold, but that's a discussion for later (see the section "Not Too Warm, Not Too Cold").

Young, tannic red wines

Young, tannic red wines (see Chapter 2 for more on tannin) — such as Cabernet Sauvignons, Bordeaux, many wines from the northern Rhône Valley, and many Italian wines — actually taste better with aeration because their tannins soften and the wine becomes less harsh.

The younger and more tannic the wine is, the longer it needs to breathe. As a general rule, most tannic, young red wines soften up with one hour of aeration. A glaring exception to the one-hour rule would be many young Barolos or Barbarescos (red wines from Piedmont, Italy, which you can read about in Chapter 11); these wines are frequently so tannic that they can really make your mouth pucker. They often can benefit from three or four hours of aeration.

Older red wines with sediment

Many red wines develop *sediment* (tannin and other matter in the wine that solidifies over time) usually after about 8 years of age. You want to remove the sediment because it can taste a bit bitter. Also, the dark particles floating in your wine, usually at the bottom of your glass, don't look very appetizing.

To remove sediment, keep the bottle of wine upright for a day or two before you plan to open it so that the sediment settles at the bottom of the bottle. Then decant the wine carefully: Pour the wine out of the bottle slowly into a decanter while watching the wine inside the bottle as it approaches the neck. You watch the wine so that you can stop pouring when you see cloudy wine from the bottom of the bottle making its way to the neck. If you stop pouring at the right moment, all the cloudy wine remains behind in the bottle.

To actually see the wine inside the bottle as you pour, you need to have a bright light shining through the bottle's neck. Candles are commonly used for this purpose, and they're romantic, but a flashlight standing on end works even better. (It's brighter, and it doesn't flicker.) Or simply hold the bottle up to a bright light, and pour slowly. Stop pouring the wine into the decanter when you reach the sediment, toward the bottom of the bottle.

The older the wine, the more delicate it can be. Don't give old, fragile-looking wines excessive aeration. (Look at the color of the wine through the bottle before you decant; if it looks pale, the wine could be pretty far along its maturity curve.) The flavors of really old wines will start fading rapidly after 10 or 15 minutes of being exposed to air.

If the wine needs aeration after decanting (that is, it still tastes a bit harsh), let it breathe in the open decanter until the wine softens to your taste.

A few white wines

Some very good, dry white wines — such as full-bodied white Burgundies and white Bordeaux wines, as well as the best Alsace whites — also get better with aeration. For example, if you open a young Corton-Charlemagne (a great white Burgundy), and it doesn't seem to be showing much aroma or flavor, chances are that it needs aeration. Decant it and taste it again in half an hour. In most cases, the wine dramatically improves.

Vintage Ports

One of the most famous fortified wines is Vintage Port (properly called "Porto"). We discuss this wine and others like it in Chapter 16.

For now, we'll just say that, yes, Vintage Port needs breathing lessons, and needs them very much, indeed! Young Vintage Ports are so brutally tannic that they demand many hours of aeration (eight would not be too many). Even older Ports improve with four hours or more of aeration. Older Vintage Ports require decanting for another reason: They're chock-full of sediment. (Often, large flakes of sediment fill the bottom — about 10 percent of the bottle.) Keep Vintage Ports standing for several days before you open them to allow the sediment to settle.

Does the Glass Really Matter?

If you're just drinking wine as refreshment with your meal, and you aren't thinking about the wine much as it goes down, the glass you use probably doesn't matter too much. We've used plastic glasses dozens of times on picnics, not to mention in airplanes (where the wine's quality usually doesn't demand great glasses, anyway).

But if you have a good wine, a special occasion, friends who want to talk about the wine with you, or the boss at your home for dinner, *stemware* (glasses with stems) is called for. And it's not just a question of etiquette and status: Good wine tastes better out of good glasses. Really.

Think of wine glasses as being like stereo speakers. Any old speaker brings the music to your ears, just like any old glass brings the wine to your lips. But can't you appreciate the music so much more, aesthetically and emotionally, from good speakers? The same principle holds true with wine and wine glasses. You can appreciate a wine's aroma and flavor complexities so much more out of a fine wine glass. The medium is the message.

The right color: None

Good wine glasses are always clear. Those pretty pink or green glasses may look nice in your china cabinet, but they interfere with your ability to distinguish the true colors of the wine.

Thin but not tiny

Believe it or not (we didn't always), the taste of a wine changes when you drink the wine out of different types of glasses. A riot almost broke out at one wine event we organized because the same wine tasted so different in different glasses that the tasters thought we served them different wines — and that we had just pretended it was all the same wine, to fool them. We learned that three aspects of a glass are important: its size, its shape, and the thickness of the glass.

Size

For dry red and white wine, small glasses are all wrong — besides that, they're a pain in the neck. You just can't swirl the wine around in little glasses without spilling it, which makes appreciating the aroma of the wine almost impossible. And furthermore, who wants to bother continually refilling them? Small glasses can work adequately only for sherry or dessert wines, which have strong aromas to begin with and are generally consumed in smaller quantities than table wines.

Matching glass size to wine works like this:

- ✔ Glasses for red wines should hold a minimum of 12 ounces; many of the best glasses have capacities ranging from 16 to 24 ounces, or more.
- ✔ For white wines, 10 to 12 ounces should be the minimum capacity.
- ✔ For sparkling wines, an 8- to 12-ounce capacity is fine.

Thickness

Stemware made of very thin, fine crystal costs a lot more than normal glassware. That's one reason many people don't use it, and why some people do. The better reason for using fine crystal is that the wine tastes better out of it. We're not sure whether the elegant crystal simply heightens the aesthetic experience of wine drinking or whether some more scientific reason exists.

Shape

The shape of the bowl also matters. Some wine glasses have very round bowls, while others have more elongated, somewhat narrower bowls. Often, when we're having dinner at home, we try our wine in glasses of different shapes, just to see which glass works best for that wine. We discuss the functions of various glass shapes in the next section.

Tulips, flutes, trumpets, and other picturesque wine-glass names

You thought that a tulip was a flower and a flute and a trumpet were musical instruments? Well, they also happen to be types of glasses designed for use with sparkling wine (see Figure 8-4).

- ✔ The tulip is the ideally shaped glass for Champagne and other sparkling wines. It is tall, elongated, and narrower at the rim than in the middle of the bowl. This shape helps hold the bubbles in the wine longer, not allowing them to escape freely (the way the wide-mouthed, sherbet-cuplike, so-called Champagne glasses do).

Figure 8-4: Glasses for sparkling wine (from left): Tulip, flute, and trumpet.

Illustration by Lisa S. Reed

The flute is another type of sparkling wine glass, but it's less ideal than the tulip because it doesn't narrow at the mouth.

✔ The trumpet actually widens at the mouth, making it less suitable for sparkling wine but very elegant looking. Another drawback of the trumpet glass is that, depending on the design, the wine can actually fill the whole stem, which means the wine warms up from the heat of your hand as you hold the stem. We avoid the trumpet glass. And we use a flute only when tulip glasses are unavailable.

An oval-shaped bowl that's narrow at its mouth (see Figure 8-5) is ideal for many red wines, such as Bordeaux, Cabernet Sauvignons, Merlots, Chiantis, and Zinfandels, and most white wines. On the other hand, some red wines, such as Burgundies, Pinot Noirs, and Barolos — and the better Chardonnays and white Burgundies — are best appreciated in wider-bowled, apple-shaped glasses (see Figure 8-5). Which shape and size works best for which wine has to do with issues such as how the glass's shape controls the flow of wine onto your tongue.

How many glasses do I need, anyway?

So what's a wine lover to do: Buy a different type of glass for each kind of wine? Fortunately, some all-purpose red and white wine glasses combine the best features, in terms of size, thickness, and shape, of most glasses.

Figure 8-5:
The Bordeaux glass (left) and the Burgundy glass (right).

Illustration by Lisa S. Reed

Half empty or half full?

"Fill 'er up" may be the rule for your gas tank, but not for your wine glass. We are annoyed when servers fill our glasses to the top. We guess they don't want to bother repouring the wine too often. Or maybe they want to give us our money's worth. But how can we stick our noses into full glasses without looking like idiots?

To leave some margin of safety for swirling and smelling the wine, fill the glass only partially. One-third capacity is the best fill level for serious red wines. (This goes back to that idea of aerating the wine.) White wine glasses can be filled halfway, while sparkling wine glasses can be two-thirds full.

If you want something finer, try Riedel or Spiegelau Crystal. Riedel is an Austrian glass manufacturer that specializes in making the right wine glass for each kind of wine. Spiegelau, a German company now owned by Riedel, operates similarly, but its glasses are less expensive than Riedel's. Another company, Ravenscroft Crystal, based in New York City, offers quality crystal wine glasses at moderate prices. You can buy these glasses in many department stores, specialty shops, or glass companies.

Washing your wine glasses

Detergents often leave a filmy residue in glasses, which can affect the aroma and flavor of your wine. We strongly advise that you clean your good crystal glasses by hand, using washing soda or baking soda. (Washing soda is the better of the two; it doesn't cake up like baking soda.) Neither product leaves any soapy, filmy residue in your glass. You can find washing soda in the soap/detergent section of supermarkets.

Not Too Warm, Not Too Cold

Just as the right glass enhances your wine experience, serving wine at the ideal temperature is a vital factor in your enjoyment of wine. Frequently, we have tasted the same wine at different temperatures and have loved the wine on one occasion but disliked it the other time!

Most red wines are best at cool room temperature, 62 to 65 degrees Fahrenheit (16 to 18 degrees Celsius). Once upon a time, in drafty old English and Scottish castles, that was simply room temperature. (Actually, it was probably warm, high-noon room temperature!) Today when you hear *room temperature,* you think of a room that's about 70 degrees Fahrenheit (21 degrees Celsius), don't you? Red wine served at this temperature can taste flat, flabby, lifeless, and often too hot — you get a burning sensation from the alcohol.

Ten or 15 minutes in the fridge does wonders to revive red wines that have been suffering from heat prostration. But don't let the wine get too cold. Red wines served too cold taste overly tannic and acidic and decidedly unpleasant. Light, fruity red wines, such as the most simple Beaujolais wines, are most delightful when served slightly chilled at about 58 to 60 degrees Fahrenheit (14 to 15.5 degrees Celsius).

Are you wondering how to know when your bottle is 58 to 60 degrees Fahrenheit? You can buy a nifty digital thermometer that wraps around the outside of the bottle and gives you a color-coded reading. Or you can buy something that looks like a real thermometer that you place into the opened bottle (in the bottle's mouth, you might say). We have both of those, and we never use them. Just feel the bottle with your hand and take a guess. Practice makes perfect.

Just as many red wines are served too warm, most white wines are definitely served too cold, judging by the service that we have received in many restaurants. The higher the quality of a white wine, the less cold it should be so that you can properly appreciate its flavor. Table 8-1 indicates our recommended serving temperatures for various types of wines.

Table 8-1	Serving Temperatures for Wine	
Type of wine	*Temperature °F*	*Temperature °C*
Most Champagnes and sparkling wines	45°F	7°C
Older or expensive, complex Champagnes	52°F	11°C
Inexpensive sweet wines	50°–55°F	10°–12.8°C
Rosés and blush wines	50°–55°F	10°–12.8°C
Simpler, inexpensive, quaffing-type white wines	50°–55°F	10°–12.8°C
Dry Sherry, such as fino or manzanilla	55°–56°F	12°–13°C
Fine, dry white wines	58°–62°F	14°–16.5°C
Finer dessert wines, such as a good Sauternes	58°–62°F	14°–16.5°C
Light, fruity red wines	58°–60°F	14°–14.5°C
Most red wines	62°–65°F	16°–18°C
Sherry other than dry fino or manzanilla	62°–65°F	16°–18°C
Port	62°–65°F	16°18°C

To avoid the problem of warm bubbly, keep an ice bucket handy. Or put the bottle back in the refrigerator between pourings.

Entertaining with Wine

When you're hosting a dinner party, you probably serve more wines than you would in the course of a normal dinner. Instead of just one wine all through the meal, you may want to serve a different wine with every course. Many people serve two wines at the table: a white with the first course and a red with the entrée. (And if they love wine, they use a cheese course as an excuse to serve a second, knockout red.)

Because you want every wine to taste even better than the one before it — besides blending perfectly with the food you're serving — you should give some thought to the sequence in which the wines will be served. The classic guidelines are the following:

- ✔ Champagne or sparkling wine first
- ✔ White wine before red wine
- ✔ Light wine before heavy wine
- ✔ Dry wine before sweet wine
- ✔ Simple wine before complex, richly flavored wine

Each of these principles operates independently. A very light red wine served before a rich, full-bodied white can work just fine. If the food you're serving calls for white wine, there's really no reason that both wines couldn't be white: a simpler, lighter white first and a richer, fuller-bodied white second. Likewise, both wines could be red, or you could serve a dry rosé followed by a red.

We provide more details on how to serve wine when entertaining in the following sections.

First things first

Even if you don't plan to serve hors d'oeuvres, you probably want to offer your guests a drink when they arrive to set a relaxing tone for the evening.

We like to serve Champagne (notice the capital *C*) as the apéritif because opening the bottle of Champagne is a ceremony that brings everyone together. Champagne honors your guests. And a glass of Champagne is compelling enough that to spend a thoughtful moment tasting it doesn't seem rude; even people who think it's absurd to talk about wine understand that Champagne is too special to be ignored. Also, Champagne is complex enough that it stands alone just fine, without food. But we often accompany the bubbly with nuts or a dip with chips.

How much is enough?

A simple rule is to figure, in total, a full bottle of wine per guest (total consumption). That quantity may sound high, but if your dinner is spread over several hours and you're serving a lot of food, it really isn't immoderate. If you're concerned that your guests may overindulge, be sure to keep their water glasses full so that they have an alternative to automatically reaching for the wine.

If your dinner party is special enough to have several food courses and several wines, we recommend giving each guest a separate glass for each wine. The glasses can be different for each wine, or they can be alike. All those glasses really look festive on the table. And with a separate glass for each wine, no guest feels compelled to empty each glass before going on to the next wine. (You also can tell at a glance who is drinking the wine and who isn't really interested in it, and you can adjust your pouring accordingly.)

Keeping Leftover Wine

A sparkling-wine stopper, a device that fits over an opened bottle of bubbly wine, is really effective in keeping any remaining Champagne or sparkling wine fresh (often for two or three days) in the refrigerator. But what do you do when you have red or white wine left in a bottle?

You can put the cork back in the bottle if it still fits, and put the bottle into the refrigerator. (Even red wines will stay fresher there; just take the bottle out to warm up about two hours before serving it.) But two other methods are also reliable in keeping your remaining wine from oxidizing; these techniques are all the more effective if you put the bottles in the fridge after using them:

- ✔ If you have about half a bottle of wine left, simply pour the wine into a clean, empty half-sized wine bottle and recork the smaller bottle. We sometimes buy wines in half-bottles, just to make sure that we have the leftover, empty half-bottles around.

- ✔ Buy small cans of inert gas, available in some wine stores and online. Just squirt a few shots of the gas into the bottle and put the cork back in the bottle. The gas displaces the oxygen in the bottle, thus protecting the wine from oxidizing. Simple and effective.

An aside about atmospheric pressure

File this under FYI ("For Your Information") — or maybe under "Believe It or Not."

Several years ago, we were enjoying one of our favorite red wines, an Italian Barbera, in the Alps. It was a perfect summer day in the mountains — crisp, clear, and cool. The wine was also perfect — absolutely delicious with our salami, bread, and cheese. A couple of days later, we had the very same wine at the seashore, on a cloudy, humid, heavy-pressure day. The wine was heavy, flat, and lifeless.

What had happened to our wonderful mountain wine? We made inquiries among some of our wine-drinking friends and discovered that they have had similar experiences. For red wines, at least, atmospheric pressure apparently influences the taste of the wine: thin, light pressure, for the better; heavy pressure, heavy humidity, for the worse. So the next time one of your favorite red wines doesn't seem quite right, check the barometer!

To avoid all this bother, just drink the wine! Or, if you're not too fussy, just place the leftover wine in the refrigerator and drink it in the next day or two — before it goes into a coma.

Chapter 9

Marrying Wine with Food

*E*very now and then, we encounter a wine that stops us dead in our tracks. It's so sensational that we lose all interest in anything but that wine. We drink it with intent appreciation, trying to memorize the taste. We wouldn't dream of diluting its perfection with a mouthful of food. But 999 times out of 1,000, we drink our wine with food. Wine is meant to go with food. And good food is meant to go with wine.

Good. We've settled that. Wine goes with food, and food goes with wine. Any questions?

Of course, we're being facetious. The world has thousands of wines, and every one is different. And the world has thousands of basic foods, each one different — not to mention the infinite combinations of foods in prepared dishes (what we really eat). In reality, food-with-wine is about as simple an issue as guy-meets-gal. Find out more about pairing wine with food in this chapter.

With Wine and Food, Rules Do Not Apply

Back in the era of the TV show *Mad Men,* a few simple — and simplistic — rules guided people in selecting wines for their meals. Wine was simpler then, and food was simpler, too. Today, the enormous range of wines available and the eclectic gamut of food choices render yesterday's easy rules obsolete. Not only that, but today, science has documented that people have inborn sensitivities or inborn tolerances to some of the fundamental tastes present in foods and wines. The bitterness of strong, black coffee or tannic red wine can be almost painful to people with the most sensitive taste buds, for example, while the most tolerant tasters enjoy that bitterness. The guidelines for pairing food and wine today must be extremely flexible to accommodate individual likes and dislikes.

We can tell you what we like and what works for us in pairing food and wine. And we can tell you how certain components of food interact with certain styles of wine. But you have to be your own judge of what works for you, through your firsthand experience of eating and drinking. (As they say, it's a tough job, but somebody's gotta do it.)

The Dynamics of Food and Wine

Every dish is dynamic — it's made up of several ingredients and flavors that interact to create a (more or less) delicious whole. Every wine is dynamic in exactly the same way. When food and wine combine in your mouth, the dynamics of each change; the result is completely individual to each dish-and-wine combination. When wine meets food, several things can happen:

- ✔ The food can exaggerate a characteristic of the wine. For example, if you eat walnuts (which are tannic) with a tannic red wine, such as a Bordeaux, the wine tastes so dry and astringent that most people would consider it undrinkable.

- ✔ The food can diminish a characteristic of the wine. Protein diminishes the impression of tannin, for example, and an overly tannic red wine — unpleasant on its own — could be delightful with rare steak or roast beef.

- ✔ The flavor intensity of the food can obliterate the wine's flavor or vice versa. If you've ever drunk a big, rich flavorful wine with a delicate filet of sole, you've had this experience firsthand.

- ✔ The wine can contribute new flavors to the dish. For example, a red Zinfandel that's gushing with berry fruit can bring its berry flavors to the dish, as if another ingredient had been added.

- ✔ The combination of wine and food can create an unwelcome third-party flavor that wasn't in the wine or the food originally; for example, we get a metallic flavor when we eat plain white-meat turkey with red Bordeaux.

Fortunately, certain elements of food react in predictable ways with certain elements of wine, giving us a fighting chance at making successful matches. The major components of wine (alcohol, sweetness, acid, and tannin) relate to the basic tastes of food (sweetness, sourness, bitterness, and saltiness) the same way that the principle of balance in wine operates: Some of the elements exaggerate each other, and some of them compensate for each other. (See the discussion of balance in Chapter 2.)

The fifth wheel: Umami

The common belief has been that humans can perceive four basic tastes: sweet, sour, salty, and bitter. But people who study food have concluded that a fifth taste exists, and maybe many more than that. The fifth taste is called *umami* (pronounced oo-*mah*-me), and it's associated with a savory character in foods. Shellfish, oily fish, meats, mushrooms, and cheeses are some foods high in umami taste.

Umami-rich foods can increase the sensation of bitterness in wines served with them. To counteract this effect, try adding something salty (such as salt itself) or sour (such as vinegar or lemon) to your dish. Although this suggestion defies the adage that vinegar and wine don't get along, the results are the proof of the pudding.

The following sections note some ways that food and wine interact, based on the components of the wine. Keep in mind that each wine and each dish has more than one component, and the simple relationships we describe can be complicated by other elements in the wine or the food. Whether a wine is considered tannic, sweet, acidic, or high in alcohol depends on its dominant component. (See Chapter 2 for details.)

Tannic wines

Tannic wines include most wines based on the Cabernet Sauvignon grape (including red Bordeaux), northern Rhône reds, Barolo and Barbaresco, and any wine — white or red — that has become tannic from aging in new oak barrels. These wines can

- ✔ Taste softer and less tannic when served with protein-rich, fatty foods, such as steak or cheese
- ✔ Taste less bitter when paired with salty foods
- ✔ Taste astringent, or mouth-drying, when drunk with spicy-hot foods

Sweet wines

Many so-called dry wines today actually have some sweetness, particularly inexpensive (about $12 or less) wines from California. Wines with unmistakable sweetness include most Moscato wines, White Zinfandel, many Rieslings (unless they're labeled *dry* or *trocken*), and medium-dry Vouvray. Sweet wines also include dessert wines such as Port, sweetened Sherries, and late-harvest wines. Depending on their level of sweetness, these wines can

- ✔ Taste less sweet but fruitier when matched with salty foods

✔ Make salty foods more appealing

✔ Go well with foods as sweet as they are, but not sweeter

Acidic wines

Acidic wines include most Italian white wines; Sancerre, Pouilly-Fumé, and Chablis; traditionally made red wines from Rioja; most dry Rieslings; and wines based on Sauvignon Blanc that are fully dry. These wines can

✔ Counterbalance oily or fatty heaviness in food

✔ Taste less acidic when served with salty foods

✔ Stand up to foods that have some acidity

✔ Make foods taste slightly saltier

High-alcohol wines

High-alcohol wines include many California wines, both white and red; southern Rhône whites and reds; Barolo and Barbaresco; fortified wines such as Port and Sherry; and most wines produced from grapes grown in warm climates. These wines can

✔ Overwhelm lightly flavored or delicate dishes

✔ Go well with slightly sweet foods

Birds of a Feather, or Opposites Attract?

Besides considering the predictable reactions between components of foods and those of wine (see the preceding section), many people choose a wine for a dish (or vice versa) in a more general way, by trying to match or to contrast particular characteristics of a wine with those in the food.

"A châque son gout" — personal taste rules

We once happened to discuss food pairings for red Bordeaux wine with the owner of one of the five First Growths of Bordeaux (see Chapter 10 for an explanation of First Growths). "I don't like Bordeaux with lamb," the distinguished gentleman proclaimed. We were confused; "But Bordeaux and lamb is a classic combination!" we said. "No, I don't agree," he answered, holding his ground. After a moment, he added, "Of course, I don't like lamb."

Wine from Venus, food from Mars

Sooner or later you're bound to experience food-and-wine disaster — when the two taste miserable together. We've had many opportunities to test our solution to food-and-wine disaster, and it works: As long as the wine is good and the food is good, eat one first and drink the other afterward — or vice versa.

The characteristics of a wine that can either resemble or contrast with the characteristics of a dish include the following:

- ✓ **The wine's flavors:** Earthy, herbal, fruity, vegetal, and so on
- ✓ **The intensity of flavor in the wine:** Subtle flavor intensity, moderately flavorful, or very flavorful
- ✓ **The wine's texture:** Crisp and firm, or soft and supple
- ✓ **The weight of the wine:** Light-bodied, medium-bodied, or full-bodied

To match or contrast the characteristics of the wine with those of the food, of course, you have to have a good idea of what the food is going to taste like and what various wines taste like. That second part can be a real stumbling block for people who don't devote every ounce of their free energy to learning about wine. The solution is to ask your wine merchant. He might not have the world's greatest knack in wine and food pairings (then again, he might), but at least he should know what his wines taste like.

Complementary designs

You probably use the like-with-like principle often without realizing it: You choose a light-bodied wine to go with a light dish, a medium-bodied wine to go with a fuller dish, and a full-bodied wine to go with a heavy dish. Here are some other ways to match one of the wine's characteristics to the dish:

- ✓ **Dishes with flavors that resemble those in the wine:** Think about the flavors in a dish the same way you think about the flavors in wine — as families of flavors. If a dish has mushrooms, it has an earthy flavor; if it has citrus or other elements of fruit, it has a fruity flavor (and so on). Then consider which wines would offer their own earthy flavor, fruity flavor, herbal flavor, spicy flavor, or whatever. The earthy flavors of white Burgundy complement risotto with mushrooms, for example, and an herbal Sancerre complements chicken breast with fresh herbs.

- **Foods with texture that's similar to that of the wine:** A California Chardonnay with a creamy, rich texture could match the rich, soft texture of lobster, for example.

- **Foods and wines with similar flavor intensity:** A very flavorful Asian stir-fry or Tex-Mex dish would be at home with a very flavorful (rather than subtle) wine, such as a German Riesling or a rich Zinfandel.

Going for contrast

The contrast principle seeks to find flavors or textures in a wine that aren't in a dish but that would enhance it. A dish of fish or chicken in a rich cream and butter sauce, for example, could be matched with a dry Vouvray, a white wine whose crispness (thanks to its uplifting, high acidity) would counterbalance the heaviness of the dish. A dish with earthy flavors, such as portobello mushrooms and fresh fava beans (or potatoes and black truffles), could contrast nicely with the pure fruit flavor of an Alsace Riesling.

You also apply the contrast principle every time you decide to serve simple food, like unadorned lamb chops or hard cheese and bread, with a gloriously complex aged wine.

The Wisdom of the Ages: Classic Pairings of Wine and Food

No matter how much you value imagination and creativity, there's no sense reinventing the wheel. In wine-and-food terms, it pays to know the classic pairings because they work (assuming that you like the food and the wine). Here are some famous and reliable combinations:

- Oysters and traditional, unoaked Chablis
- Lamb and red Bordeaux (we like Chianti with lamb, too)
- Port with walnuts and Stilton cheese
- Salmon with Pinot Noir
- Amarone with Gorgonzola cheese
- Grilled fish with Vinho Verde
- Foie gras with Sauternes or with late-harvest Gewürztraminer
- Braised beef with Barolo

✔ Dry amontillado Sherry with rich soup

✔ Grilled chicken with Beaujolais

✔ Toasted almonds or green olives with fino or manzanilla Sherry

✔ Goat cheese with Sancerre or Pouilly-Fumé

✔ Dark chocolate with California Cabernet Sauvignon

Look for various additional suggestions on wine and food pairings scattered throughout Parts III, IV, and V.

Part III
The "Old World" of Wine

The 5th Wave   By Rich Tennant

In this part . . .

We're flattered if you've gotten to this point by reading every word we've written so far. But we realize that you might have landed here by skipping a lot of earlier stuff. That's okay with us — the meat and potatoes of this book start right here.

The three chapters in this part are chock-full of information about the world's original wine regions — those of France, Italy, Spain, and other European countries. We explain what the classic grape varieties are for each region and describe the wines, as well as name some top brands. Get your wish list ready!

Chapter 10

Doing France

· ·

In This Chapter

▶ *Crus,* classified growths, *châteaux,* and domaines

▶ Why Bordeaux wines are legendary

▶ The scarcity issue in fine Burgundy

▶ Robust red Rhônes

▶ White gems of the Loire and Alsace

▶ The Languedoc and Provence

· ·

*F*rance. What comes to mind when you hear that word? Strolling along Paris's grand boulevard, the Champs Elysées? Romance? Sky-blue water and golden sun on the French Riviera?

When we think of France, we think of wine. Bordeaux, Burgundy, Beaujolais, Chablis, Champagne, and Sauternes are not only famous wines but also places in France where people live, work, eat, and drink wine. France still has one of the highest per capita wine consumption rates of any major country in the world (although not as high as it used to be). The French have set the standard for the rest of us.

The French Model

Why did France become the most famous place in the world for wine?

✔ For one thing, the French have been doing it for a long time — making wine, that is. Even before the Romans conquered Gaul and planted vineyards, the Greeks arrived in France with their vines.

✔ Equally important is French *terroir,* the magical combination of climate and soil that, when it clicks, can yield grapes that make breathtaking wines. And what grapes! France is the birthplace of almost all the renowned varieties in the world — Cabernet Sauvignon, Chardonnay, Merlot, Pinot Noir, Syrah, and Sauvignon Blanc, just to name a few. (See Chapter 3 for more information on these grape varieties.)

France is the model, the standard setter, for the world's wines: Most wine-producing countries now make their own versions of wines from Cabernet Sauvignon, Chardonnay, Merlot, Pinot Noir, and so on, thanks to the success of these grapes in France. The following sections describe the French model for wine in more detail.

Understanding French wine law

France's system of defining wine regions — the *Appellation d'Origine Contrôlée,* or AOC (translated as "regulated place-name" or "regulated origin name") system, established in 1935 — has been the legislative model for most other European countries. The European Union's (E.U.'s) framework of wine laws, within which the AOC system now operates, is also modeled on the French system.

To understand French wines and wine laws, you need to know five things:

✔ Most French wines are named after places. (These aren't arbitrary places; they're places registered and defined in French wine regulations.)

✔ Most of the time, the wine and the region have the same name (as in Burgundy wine, from Burgundy).

✔ The French wine system is hierarchical. Some wines (that is, the wines of some places) officially have higher rank than other wines.

✔ Generally, the smaller and more specific the place for which a wine is named, the higher its rank.

✔ Just because a wine carries a high rank doesn't necessarily mean that it's better than the next wine; it just means that it *should* be better. The laws rank the potential of the place where the wine comes from and are not infallible indications of a wine's actual quality.

French wines that come from approved and regulated wine regions have two possible ranks. You can determine which rank a French wine has by seeing which of the following French phrases appears on the label. (Wines of higher rank generally cost more.) From highest to lowest, the rankings are

✔ **Appellation Contrôlée,** or AC (or AOC) — known in the new system (described in Chapter 4) as **Appellation d'Origine Protégée,** or AOP. This is the higher grade. On the label, the place-name of the wine usually appears in the middle of the French phrase.

✔ **Vin de Pays,** meaning "country wine" — known in the new system as **Indication Géographique Protégée,** or IGP. On the label, the phrase is followed by a place-name, such as *Vin de Pays* (or *IGP*) *de l'Hérault,* which indicates the area where the grapes grew; the places or regions are generally much larger than the places or regions referred to in the higher ranking.

One very small category, which ranked second in quality after AOC, was eliminated at the end of 2011. This was *Vin Délimité de Qualité Supérieure,* or VDQS, wine (translated as "demarcated wine of superior quality").

If a French wine does not have one of the preceding official terms on its label — in either the original or new version — then it is simply *Vin Français* (a wine from anywhere in France) rather than from a more specific region.

Fine distinctions in the ranks

France's system of place-naming its wines is actually a bit more complex than the two neat categories described in the preceding section might imply. Although all AOC or AOP wines/places hold exactly the same legal status — say, they're all generals in the French wine army — the market accords some AOCs higher regard (and higher prices) than others, based on the specificity of their *terroirs.*

Some large AOC territories have smaller AOC zones nestled within them. When territories overlap, wines produced from grapes grown within the larger area might carry that AOC place-name (assuming that the proper grape varieties are used and the wine conforms to the regulations in all other respects), while wines whose grapes come from the smaller territory within the larger one might carry a more specific AOC name. For example, within the large AOC territory of Bordeaux, some wines can carry the name of a smaller district, such as Haut-Médoc. That district can itself encompass even smaller AOC zones; wines made from grapes grown in these more limited zones may use yet another AOC name, such as Pauillac, a village. (They're all generals, but some of them have silver stars.)

The more specific the place described in the wine name, the finer the wine is generally considered to be in the eyes of the market, and the higher the price the winemaker can ask. Naturally, a winemaker will use the most specific name to which his wine is entitled.

In increasing order of specificity, an AOC or AOP name can be the name of

- ✔ A region (Bordeaux or Burgundy, for example)
- ✔ A district (Haut-Médoc or Côte de Beaune)
- ✔ A subdistrict (Côte de Beaune-Villages)
- ✔ A village or commune (Pauillac or Meursault)
- ✔ A specific vineyard (Le Montrachet)

Unfortunately, unless you're an expert at French geography and place-names, you won't know which type of place an AOC/AOP name refers to just by looking at the label.

France's Wine Regions

France has five wine regions that are extremely important for the quality and renown of the wines they produce. Each region specializes in certain grape varieties for its wines, based on climate, soil, and local tradition.

- ✔ The three major regions for red wine are Bordeaux, Burgundy, and the Rhône Valley.
- ✔ For white wines, Burgundy is again a major region, along with the Loire Valley and Alsace.

Apart from these prestigious regions, France has several more regions that make interesting wines worth knowing about. Again, each region cultivates certain grape varieties for its wines according to its climate, soil, and local tradition.

- ✔ Two significant French wine regions are Provence and Languedoc-Roussillon, both in the South of France.
- ✔ Wine districts in southwest France, such as Cahors, produce good-value wines and, in some cases, seriously good wines.

We cover all these regions in this chapter, in more or less detail according to the importance of the region. For more specific information on French wines, see our book *French Wine For Dummies* (Wiley).

Bordeaux: The Incomparable

To really know wine, you must know French wine — French wines are *that* important in the wine world. Likewise, you must know Bordeaux to know French wine. Bordeaux is a wine region in western France named after the fourth-largest French city (see Figure 10-1). Bordeaux produces more than 700 million bottles a year from more than 10,000 producers. This one region accounts for about 25 percent of all AOC wine. Most Bordeaux wines (about 89 percent of them) are dry reds; the remaining 11 percent of the region's production are dry whites, with a small proportion of sweet white wines, such as Sauternes, and a tiny amount of rosés and sparkling wines.

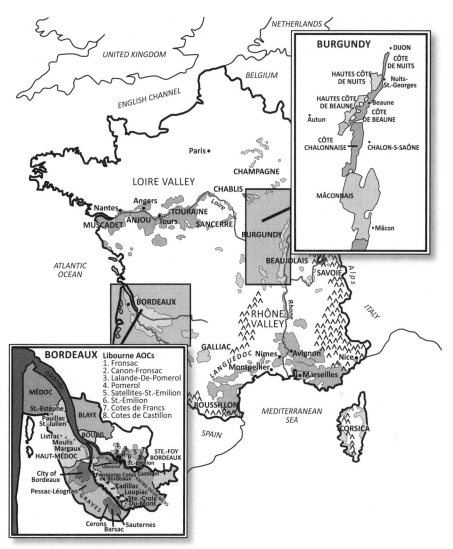

Figure 10-1:
The wine regions of France.

Illustration by Lisa S. Reed

Because the Bordeaux region is situated on the Atlantic coast, it has a maritime climate, with warm summers and fairly mild winters. The maritime weather brings rain, often during harvest time. As the weather varies from year to year, the character and quality of the vintages also vary; when all goes well, such as in 2000, 2005, 2009, and 2010, the wines can be truly great.

The taste of really great Bordeaux

When young, the finest red Bordeaux wines have a deep ruby hue and aromas of black currants (cassis), plums, spice, and cedar. For the first ten years or so, these wines can be very dry in texture, almost austere, with tannin masking the fruity flavors. Eventually, the wines turn garnet, develop an extraordinarily complex bouquet and flavor, and soften in texture. The very finest red Bordeaux wines will frequently take 20 to 25 years or more before reaching their maturity; some have lasted well over 100 years (see Chapter 17 for a discussion of collector-level wines).

Bordeaux's reputation as one of the greatest wine regions in the world revolves around the legendary elite red wines of Bordeaux — *grands vins* (great wines) made by historic *châteaux* (wine estates) and capable of improving for many decades (see Chapter 17). Prices for these wines run up to almost $4,000 a bottle for Château Pétrus — the most expensive red Bordeaux wine. (Old vintages of Pétrus can cost even more!)

These legendary wines represent the pinnacle of a red Bordeaux pyramid; quantitatively, they're only a very small part of the region's red wine production, which also includes medium-priced and inexpensive wines. Middle-level Bordeaux wines start at about $30 a bottle when they're first available and are ready to drink within 10 to 15 years of the harvest. The least expensive Bordeaux reds, which can cost as little as $9 a bottle, are enjoyable young, within two to five years of the vintage date.

The subregions of red Bordeaux

Two distinct red wine production zones exist within the Bordeaux region; these two areas have come to be called the Left Bank and the Right Bank — just as in Paris. While the least expensive Bordeaux reds come from grapes grown anywhere in the Bordeaux region — and thus carry the regionwide AOC designation, Bordeaux — the better wines come from specific AOC *districts* or AOC *communes* that are located in either the Right Bank or the Left Bank.

The Left Bank vineyards lie west of the Garonne River (the more southerly of the two rivers depicted in the Bordeaux inset of Figure 10-1) and the Gironde Estuary, which empties into the Atlantic Ocean. The Right Bank vineyards lie east and north of the Dordogne River (the more northerly of the two rivers depicted in the inset), and east of the Gironde Estuary. (The middle ground in between the two rivers makes white wine as well as red.)

Of the various wine districts on the Left Bank and the Right Bank, four (two on each bank) are the most important:

Cabernet ↑

- ✔ Left Bank (the western area): Haut-Médoc, Pessac-Léognan *, Graves*
- ✔ Right Bank (the eastern area): St.-Emilion, Pomerol *, Fronsac*

The Left Bank and the Right Bank differ mainly in soil composition: Gravel predominates on the Left Bank, and clay prevails on the Right Bank. As a result, Cabernet Sauvignon, which has an affinity for gravel, is the principal grape variety in the Haut-Médoc (oh-may-doc) and Pessac-Léognan (pay-sac-lay-oh-nyahn). Merlot, which does well in clay, dominates the St.-Emilion (sant-ay-meal-yon) and Pomerol (pohm-eh-roll) wines. (Both areas grow Cabernet Sauvignon *and* Merlot, as well as Cabernet Franc and three less significant grapes, Petit Verdot, Malbec, and Carménère, the last two of which are rarely used in Bordeaux today. See Chapter 3 for more information on grape varieties.)

Left Bank and Right Bank Bordeaux wines are, therefore, markedly different from one another. But wines from the Haut-Médoc and Pessac-Léognan are quite similar; likewise, it can be difficult to tell the difference among wines from Pomerol and St.-Emilion (on the Right Bank).

Each bank — in fact, each of the four districts — has its avid fans. The more established Left Bank generally produces firm, tannic wines with more pronounced black currant and mineral flavor. Left Bank wines usually need many years to develop and will age for a long time, often for decades — typical of a Cabernet Sauvignon–based wine.

Bordeaux wines from the larger Right Bank are better introductory wines for the novice Bordeaux drinker. Because they're mainly Merlot, they're more approachable; you can enjoy them long before their Left Bank cousins, often as soon as five to eight years after the vintage. They're less tannic, richer in texture, and plummier in flavor, and they generally contain a bit more alcohol than Left Bank reds.

Because of its dominance in Right Bank red Bordeaux wines, Merlot is in fact the most widely used variety in all of Bordeaux. Cabernet Sauvignon is the second, followed by Cabernet Franc. Even on the Left Bank, a trend for many Bordeaux red wines is a higher amount of Merlot in the blend, thus making them more accessible at an earlier age.

Historically, the Haut-Médoc district, on the Left Bank, is Bordeaux's most important area, and it deserves special attention. The Haut-Médoc is the southern part of the Médoc peninsula. The name *Médoc* has two meanings. It refers to the entire area west of the wide Gironde Estuary (refer to Figure 10-1), and it's also the name for the northernmost district of the Left Bank. In other words (in the same word, actually), Médoc is frequently used as an umbrella term for the combined districts of Médoc and Haut-Médoc (the two districts that occupy the Médoc peninsula).

Of the two districts, the Haut-Médoc is by far the more important for wine. This district encompasses four famous wine communes: St.-Estèphe (sant-eh-steff), Pauillac (poy-yac), St.-Julien (san-jhoo-lee-ehn), and Margaux (mahr-go). Table 10-1 gives a general description of each commune's wines.

Table 10-1	The Four Principal Communes in the Haut-Médoc
Commune	**Wine Characteristics**
St.-Estèphe	Firm, tannic, earthy, chunky, and slow to mature; typical wine — Château Montrose
Pauillac	Rich, powerful, firm, and tannic, with black currant and cedar aromas and flavors; very long-lived; home of three of Bordeaux's most famous wines — Lafite-Rothschild, Mouton-Rothschild, and Latour
St.-Julien	Rich, flavorful, elegant and finesseful, with cedary bouquet; typical wine — Château Ducru-Beaucaillou
Margaux	Fragrant, supple, harmonious, with complex aromas and flavors; typical wine — Château Palmer

Two other communes in the Haut-Médoc — Listrac (lee-strahk) and Moulis (moo-lees) — make less-well-known wines. Vineyards that aren't located in the vicinity of these six communes carry the districtwide appellation, *Haut-Médoc,* rather than that of a specific commune.

The names of these districts and communes are part of the official name of wines made there and appear on the label.

Classified information

Have you ever wondered what a wine expert was talking about when he smugly pronounced a particular Bordeaux a *Second Growth?* Wonder no more. He's talking about a *château* (as wine estates are called in Bordeaux) that made the grade nearly 160 years ago.

Back in 1855, when an exposition (akin to a World's Fair) took place in Paris, the organizers asked the Bordeaux Chamber of Commerce to develop a classification of Bordeaux wines. The Chamber of Commerce delegated the task to the Bordeaux wine brokers, the companies who buy and resell the wines of Bordeaux. These merchants named 61 top red wines — 60 from the Médoc and one from what was then called Graves (and today is known as Pessac-Léognan). According to the prices of the wines at the time and the existing reputations of the wines, they divided these 61 wines into five categories, known as *crus* or *growths*. (In Bordeaux, a *cru* refers to a classified wine estate.) Their listing is known as the Classification of 1855; to this day, these *classified growths* enjoy special prestige among wine lovers. (The Bordeaux wine brokers also classified Sauternes, the great Bordelais sweet wine; see Chapter 16 for info on Sauternes). The following list names the five First Growths (five châteaux):

- ✔ Château Lafite-Rothschild

- ✔ Château Latour

- ✔ Château Margaux

- ✔ Château Haut-Brion

- ✔ Château Mouton-Rothschild (elevated from a Second Growth in 1973)

Additionally, the classification included 14 Second Growths, 14 Third Growths, 10 Fourth Growths, and 18 Fifth Growths.

The 61 ranked wine estates are sometimes referred to as *Great Growths* or *Grands Crus Classés*. To appreciate the honor attached to being one of the 61 Great Growths, bear in mind that about 8,000 châteaux (and more than 10,000 wine producers) exist in Bordeaux!

The 1855 Classification has held up remarkably well over time. Sure, a few of the 61 properties are not performing up to their historic level today, while some unclassified châteaux now probably deserve to be included. But because of the politics involved, no changes in classification ranking have been made, with one dramatic exception (see the sidebar "The Mouton exception").

Just to confuse things even more: Although the 1855 Classification completely ignored the wines of St.-Emilion, the AOC commission classified those wines a century later, in 1955. St.-Emilion wines, unlike the wines covered by the 1855 Classification, are reclassified approximately every ten years. (A reclassification will take place in 2012.) The wines fall into three quality categories, which are indicated on the labels:

- Currently, 15 châteaux have the highest ranking, *Premier Grand Cru Classé*. Two of the 15, Château Ausone and Château Cheval Blanc, are on a pedestal as "Category A"; the other 13 are "Category B" *Premier Grand Cru Classé* wines.

- A middle category, *Grand Cru Classé,* consists of 46 châteaux.

- The third category, simply *Grand Cru,* encompasses some 200 properties.

The wines of Pessac-Léognan were classified in 1953 and again in 1959. The wines of Pomerol have never been officially classified.

Bordeaux to try when you're feeling flush

If you're curious to try a prestigious red Bordeaux, let the following lists guide you. In addition to all five First Growths listed in the previous section, we recommend the following classified growths from the Médoc, as well as some wines from the three other principal districts: Pessac-Léognan, Pomerol, and St.-Emilion. Consult the later section "Practical advice on drinking red Bordeaux" before you drink the wine.

The Mouton exception

The one dramatic change to the 1855 Classification occurred in 1973. That year, the late Baron Philippe de Rothschild, finally (and rightfully) triumphed in his 50-year battle with the French government to have his beloved Château Mouton-Rothschild upgraded from a Second Growth to a First Growth. The Minister of Agriculture (at that time, Jacques Chirac) decreed that Château Mouton-Rothschild was indeed a First Growth — which Bordeaux wine lovers considered it to be all along, in quality if not in official status.

The Baron's motto, written in French on his family crest, had to change. Before 1973, it read:

> First, I cannot be; second, I do not deign to be; Mouton, I am.

The Baron changed the motto on his 1973 Château Mouton-Rothschild to read:

> First, I am; second, I was; Mouton does not change.

A postscript to this heartwarming story: We adopted an adorable little kitten, a Blue Point Siamese, in 1973. Because Mouton-Rothschild is one of our favorite wines, and because our little kitten demonstrated the same firm, tenacious qualities as the wine, we named him Mouton. He was with us for 20 years, proving that he had the same longevity as the wine for which he was named. He is buried in the backyard in an old wooden crate that once held 1973 Mouton-Rothschild.

Médoc wines

Château Léoville-Las-Cases	Château Clerc-Milon	Château Lynch-Bages
Château Léoville-Barton	Château Pichon-Lalande	Château Ducru-Beaucaillou
Château Palmer	Château Lagrange	Château Grand-Puy-Lacoste
Château Léoville-Poyferré	Château Pichon-Baron	Château Branaire-Ducru

Pessac-Léognan wines

Château La Mission-Haut-Brion	Château Haut-Bailly	Château de Fieuzal
Château Pape-Clément	Domaine de Chevalier	Château La Louvière
Château La Tour-Haut-Brion	Château Smith-Haut-Lafitte	

Pomerol wines

Château Pétrus*	Château Trotanoy	Château L'Evangile
Château Lafleur*	Château Clinet	Château La Fleur de Gay
Château Latour à Pomerol	Vieux-Château-Certan	Château La Conseillante
Château Certan de May	Château Lafleur-Pétrus	

* Very expensive

St.-Emilion wines

Château Cheval Blanc	Château La Dominique	Château Canon-La-Gaffelière
Château Ausone	Château Grand Mayne	Château Pavie-Macquin
Château Figeac	Château Troplong Mondot	Château Magdelaine

The value end of the Bordeaux spectrum

As you probably suspected, the best buys in Bordeaux wines are not the illustrious classified growths. As of this writing, the least expensive classified-growth Bordeaux wines retail for $50 a bottle and go up to $1,600 to $2,000 a bottle for First Growths, such as Château Lafite-Rothschild and Château Latour. For really good values (and wines that you can drink within a few years of the vintage), look for Bordeaux wines that were not included in the 1855 Classification.

Cru Bourgeois: The middle class of the Médoc

In 1932, a group of producers in the Médoc whose wines weren't recognized by the 1855 Bordeaux Classification obtained their own legally recognized classification, *Cru Bourgeois.* For decades, the wines in this category were reliable alternatives to the classified growths — less noble but considerably less expensive and some of them even as good as the lesser-quality classified growths. Their prices were mainly in the $10 to $40 range.

The term *Cru Bourgeois* no longer exists as a legal classification. In 2003, the Bordeaux Chamber of Commerce tried to reclassify the *Cru Bourgeois* wines, and the selection was so severe that almost half of the 490 châteaux applying for classification did not make the grade. This attempted reclassfication created such a stir — 78 producers actually bitterly contested the reclassifiation in court — that the Bordeaux Chamber of Commerce annulled the reclassification. A group of producers now submit to an annual quality assessment (not an official classification) and use the term *Label Cru Bourgeois* on their wines.

Over the years, we have been very impressed with the price-to-quality ratio that *Cru Bourgeois* wines offer. The nine wines that follow continue to be particularly impressive. These wines retail for about $28 to $40. We firmly believe that many of these wines would qualify for *Grands Cru* status if the 1855 Classification were revised.

Château Chasse-Spleen	Château Phélan-Ségur	Château Poujeaux
Château Les Ormes-de-Pez	Château Haut-Marbuzet	Château de Pez
Château Labegorce-Zédé	Château Potensac	Château Siran

A few notable producers never applied for *Cru Bourgeois* membership. Château Gloria, from St.-Julien, a wine often compared to *Grands Crus Classés* wines in quality, is one; it retails for about $40. An excellent producer from the Haut-Médoc, Château Sociando-Mallet, is another; it costs about $45.

Other moderately priced ($20 to $35) Haut-Médoc wines that we recommend include the following:

Château Monbrison	Château Meyney
Château Coufran	Château Lanessan
Château Haut-Beauséjour	Château Fourcas-Hosten
Château d'Angludet	

Fronsac and Canon-Fronsac

When you leave the Médoc peninsula and the city of Bordeaux and cross over the Dordogne River into the Right Bank region, the first wine districts you encounter are Fronsac and Canon-Fronsac (refer to Figure 10-1). Of the lesser Bordeaux appellations, Canon-Fronsac and Fronsac have the highest reputations for quality, and they're priced accordingly, in the $22 to $35 range. Like St.-Emilion and Pomerol, Fronsac and Canon-Fronsac produce only red wines, and Merlot is the dominant grape variety.

Petits châteaux

Petits châteaux is the general, catchall term for the huge category of reasonably priced wines throughout the entire Bordeaux region that have never been classified. The term is somewhat of a misnomer because it suggests that the wines come from a specific château or vineyard estate; in fact, many *petits châteaux* do come from specific estates, but not all do.

Some of these wines use grapes that have been sourced from all over the region, and others come from specific appellations. Ten *petits châteaux* red appellations, all on the Right Bank, are noteworthy:

Côtes de Bourg	Puisseguin-St.-Emilion
Côtes de Bordeaux: Blaye	Lussac-St.-Emilion
Côtes de Bordeaux: Castillon	Montagne-St.-Emilion
Côtes de Bordeaux: Francs	St.-Georges-St.-Emilion
Lalande de Pomerol	Côtes de Bordeaux: Cadillac

Lalande de Pomerol is a satellite district of Pomerol, and the four districts with *St.-Emilion* appended to their names surround St.-Emilion. The Côtes de Bourg and Côtes de Blaye take their names from the port towns of Bourg and Blaye, on the Right Bank of the Gironde, opposite the Haut-Médoc.

We especially recommend wines from the Côtes de Bourg, Côtes de Blaye, and Lalande de Pomerol as really good values. Most of the wines from all ten appellations retail in the $9 to $15 range, with a few between $15 and $25.

All these wines are primarily Merlot. They are generally fruitier, have softer tannins, and are enjoyable sooner than the Cabernet Sauvignon–dominated wines of the Left Bank. In our book *Wine Style: Using Your Senses to Explore and Enjoy Wine* (Wiley), we describe these wines as "mild-mannered reds." *Petits châteaux* are the Bordeaux wines of choice when you're looking for a young, inexpensive, approachable Bordeaux with dinner.

Reverse chic: Drinking inexpensive Bordeaux

Some wine snobs wouldn't think of ordering anything but classified-growth Bordeaux in restaurants. But if you're just getting acquainted with these wines, splurging on an expensive, top-rated Bordeaux doesn't make sense. Begin with inexpensive, easier-drinking Bordeaux wines first so you can develop a context for evaluating and appreciating the finer wines. The contrast of simpler Bordeaux really helps you understand the majesty of the great Bordeaux wines. Besides, every dinner doesn't call for great Bordeaux. A modest Bordeaux is perfectly suitable for simpler fare, such as stew or a burger.

Generic Bordeaux

Red Bordeaux wines with no specific appellation carry the general *Bordeaux* or *Bordeaux Supérieur* appellations. Their grapes are predominantly Merlot and can grow anywhere throughout the Bordeaux region. These are fairly light-bodied wines that sell for $8 to $14. Sometimes, the labels identify the wines as specifically Merlot or Cabernet Sauvignon. Two leading brands are Mouton-Cadet and Michel Lynch. Generic Bordeaux from good vintages, such as 2005 and 2009, can be really excellent buys.

Practical advice on drinking red Bordeaux

Because the finest red Bordeaux wines take many years to develop, they're not good choices in restaurants where the vintages available tend to be fairly recent. And when mature Bordeaux wines are available in restaurants, they're usually extremely expensive. Order a lesser Bordeaux when you're dining out, and save the best wines for drinking at home.

Red Bordeaux wines go well with lamb, venison, simple roasts, and hard cheeses, such as Comté, Gruyère, or Cheddar. If you plan to serve a fine red Bordeaux from a good but recent vintage (see Appendix C for information), you should decant it at least an hour before dinner and let it aerate (see Chapter 8); serve it at about 62 to 65 degrees Fahrenheit (17 to 19 degrees Celsius). Better yet, if you have good storage conditions (see Chapter 17), save your young Bordeaux for a few years — it will only get better.

Fine recent Bordeaux vintages are 2009, 2005 (both of which show promise of being truly great — especially 2005), 2000, 1996, 1995, 1990, 1989, 1986, and 1982. Another great Bordeaux vintage, which hasn't yet been released as of this writing, is 2010. Some Bordeaux producers think this may be the finest vintage of a very good decade for red Bordeaux wines.

Bordeaux also comes in white

White Bordeaux wine comes in two styles, dry and sweet. The dry wines themselves fall into two categories: inexpensive wines for enjoying young and wines so distinguished and age-worthy that they rank among the great dry white wines of the world.

Two areas of the Bordeaux region are important for white wine production:

- ✔ The large district south of the city of Bordeaux is known as the Graves (pronounced grahv; see the Bordeaux inset in Figure 10-1). The Graves district and the Pessac-Léognan district (directly north of Graves) are home to the finest white wines of Bordeaux, both dry and sweet. (We cover the great dessert wine from the southern Graves, Sauternes, in Chapter 16.)

- ✔ In the middle ground between the Garonne and Dordogne Rivers, east of Graves and Pessac-Léognan, a district called Entre-Deux-Mers (ahn-truh-duh-mair) is also known for its dry, semi-dry, and sweet white Bordeaux wines as well as for inexpensive red Bordeaux wines.

A few white wines also come from the predominantly red wine Haut-Médoc district, such as the superb Pavillon Blanc du Château Margaux. Although special and expensive, they qualify only for simple Bordeaux Blanc appellation because commune-level appellations of the Haut-Médoc apply only to reds.

Sauvignon Blanc and Sémillon, in various combinations, are the two main grape varieties for elite dry white Bordeaux. It's a fortunate blend: The Sauvignon Blanc component offers immediate charm in the wine, while the slower-developing Sémillon gives the wine richness and depth, enabling it to age well. In general, a high percentage of Sémillon in the wine is a good indicator of the wine's age-worthiness. Many inexpensive white Bordeaux — and a few of the best wines — are entirely Sauvignon Blanc.

The top dry white Bordeaux wines are crisp and lively when they're young, but they develop richness, complexity, and a honeyed bouquet with age. In good vintages (see Appendix C for information), the best whites need at least ten years to develop and can live many years more. (See Chapter 17 for more information on older Bordeaux.)

Table 10-2 lists the top 12 white wines of Pessac-Léognan and Graves, in our rough order of preference, and shows their grape blends. We separated the wines into an A and B group because the four wines in the first group literally are in a class by themselves, quality-wise; they possess not only more depth and complexity but also more longevity than other white Bordeaux. Their prices reflect that fact — the A group wines range from $75 to $500 per bottle, whereas the B group wines cost between $30 and $60.

Table 10-2	Top 12 Dry White Bordeaux
Wine	**Grape Varieties**
Group A	
Château Haut-Brion Blanc	Sémillon, 50–55%; Sauvignon Blanc, 45–50%
Château Laville-Haut-Brion	Sémillon, 60%; Sauvignon Blanc, 40%
Domaine de Chevalier	Sauvignon Blanc, 70%; Sémillon, 30%
Château Pape-Clément	Sémillon, 45%; Sauvignon Blanc, 45%; Muscadelle, 10%
Group B	
Château de Fieuzal	Sauvignon Blanc, 50–60%; Sémillon, 40–50%
Château Smith-Haut-Lafitte	Sauvignon Blanc, 100%
Clos Floridene	Sémillon, 70%; Sauvignon Blanc, 30%
Château La Louvière	Sauvignon Blanc, 70%; Sémillon, 30%
Château La Tour-Martillac	Sémillon, 60%; Sauvignon Blanc, 30%; other, 10%
Château Couhins-Lurton	Sauvignon Blanc, 100%
Château Malartic-Lagravière	Sauvignon Blanc, 100%
Château Carbonnieux	Sauvignon Blanc, 65%; Sémillon, 35%

Burgundy: The Other Great French Wine

Burgundy, a wine region in eastern France, southeast of Paris (refer to Figure 10-1), stands shoulder to shoulder with Bordeaux as one of France's two greatest regions for dry, non-sparkling wines.

Unlike Bordeaux, Burgundy's fame is split nearly equally between its white and red wines. Also unlike Bordeaux, good Burgundy is often scarce. The reason is simple: Not counting the Beaujolais area (which is technically Burgundy, but really makes a separate type of wine), Burgundy produces only 25 percent as much wine as Bordeaux.

Burgundy's vineyards are more fragmented than Bordeaux's. The soils of the Burgundy region vary from hillside to hillside and even from the middle of each hill to the bottom. You can find two different vineyards growing the same grape but making distinctly different wines only two meters apart from each other across a dirt road!

Burgundy (or, as the French call it, *Bourgogne,* pronounced boor-guh-nyuh) is also a region of much smaller vineyard holdings than Bordeaux.

The few large vineyards that do exist have multiple owners, with some families owning only two or three rows of vines in a particular vineyard. (One famous Burgundy vineyard, Clos de Vougeot, has about 82 owners!) The typical Burgundy winemaker's production varies from 50 cases to 1,000 cases of wine a year, per type — far from enough to satisfy wine lovers all over the world. Compare that to Bordeaux, where the average château owner makes 15,000 to 20,000 cases of his principal wine annually.

In Burgundy, the winemaker calls his property a *domaine,* certainly a more modest name than *château,* and a proper reflection of the size of his winery.

The grapes: Chardonnay, Pinot Noir, and Gamay

Burgundy has a *continental* climate (warm summers and cold winters) and is subject to localized summer hailstorms that can damage the grapes and cause rot. The soil is mainly limestone and clay. Burgundy's *terroir* is particularly suited to the two main grape varieties of the region, Pinot Noir (for red Burgundy) and Chardonnay (for white Burgundy). In fact, nowhere else in the entire world does the very fickle, difficult Pinot Noir grape perform better than in Burgundy.

In the southerly Beaujolais district of Burgundy, the soil becomes primarily granitic but also rich in clay and sand, very suitable for the Gamay grape of this area.

Districts, districts everywhere

Burgundy has five districts, all of which make quite distinct wines. The districts, from north to south, are the following (refer to Figure 10-1):

- Chablis (shah-blee)
- The Côte d'Or (coat dor)
- The Côte Chalonnaise (coat shal-oh-naze)
- The Mâconnais (mack-coh-nay)
- Beaujolais (boh-jhoe-lay)

The taste of fine red Burgundy

Red Burgundy is paler than Bordeaux, with a less dense ruby or garnet color, because Pinot Noir grapes don't have nearly as much pigmentation as Cabernet Sauvignon or Merlot grapes. It's rather full-bodied in terms of its alcohol and is relatively low in tannin. The characteristic aroma is of red or black berries and woodsy, damp-earth, or mushroomy scents. When a red Burgundy ages, it often develops a silky texture, richness, and a natural sweetness of fruit flavors; sometimes a bouquet of leather, coffee, and game emerges.

With some exceptions (for example, a powerful wine from a great vintage, such as 2009, 2005, 2002, or 1999), red Burgundy should be consumed within ten years of the vintage — and even sooner in a weaker vintage (see Appendix C for vintage ratings).

The heart of Burgundy, the *Côte d'Or* (which literally means "golden slope"), itself has two parts: Côte de Nuits (coat deh nwee) in the north and the Côte de Beaune (coat deh bone) in the south.

The Chablis district makes only white wines, and the Mâconnais makes mainly white wines. The Côte Chalonnaise makes both white and red wines. Beaujolais makes almost exclusively red wines from the Gamay grape.

The term *red Burgundy* refers primarily to the red wines of the Côte d'Or and also to the less-known — and less-expensive — red wines of the Côte Chalonnaise. Likewise, when wine lovers talk about *white Burgundy,* they are usually referring to just the white wines of the Côte d'Or and the Côte Chalonnaise. They'll use the more precise names, Chablis and Mâcon, to refer to the white wines of those parts of Burgundy. On the other hand, when wine lovers talk about the region, Burgundy, they could very well be referring to the whole shebang, including Beaujolais, or all of Burgundy *except* Beaujolais. It's an imprecise language.

Don't ever mistake the inexpensive red California wine that calls itself *burgundy* — or the inexpensive California wine that calls itself *chablis* — for the real McCoys from France. These imposter wines are from various ordinary grapes grown in industrial-scale vineyards 6,000 miles away from the Côte d'Or. We'd be surprised if either one had even a drop of the true grapes of Burgundy — Pinot Noir or Chardonnay — in them.

From the regional to the sublime

Because soils vary so much in Burgundy, a wine's specific vineyard site is extremely relevant to the taste, quality, and price of that wine. A wine made from a tiny vineyard with its own particular character is more precious and rare than a wine blended from several vineyards or a wine from a less-favored site.

The AOC/AOP structure for Burgundy wines recognizes the importance of site. While there are regionwide AOCs, districtwide AOCs, and commune AOCs — just as in Bordeaux — there are also AOC names that refer to individual vineyards. In fact, some of these vineyards are recognized as better than others: Some of them are *Premier Cru* (prem-yay crew), meaning "first growth," while the very best are *Grand Cru,* meaning "great growth."

Bordeaux producers use the terms *premier cru* and *grand cru,* too. In Bordeaux, however, except for St.-Emilion, the terms represent status bestowed on a winery by a classification outside the AOC law (as when a First Growth calls itself a Premier Grand Cru Classé on its label, based on the 1855 Classification; see the earlier section "Classified information" for details). In Burgundy, *Premier Cru* and *Grand Cru* are always official distinctions within the AOC law. Their meaning is extremely precise.

Table 10-3 gives examples of AOC names in Burgundy, listed in order of increasing specificity.

Table 10-3	The Structure of Burgundy AOC Names
Specificity of Site	**Examples**
Regionwide	Bourgogne Rouge
Districtwide	Beaujolais; Mâcon
Village or commune	Chambolle-Musigny; Gevrey-Chambertin; Puligny-Montrachet
Premier Cru*	Chambolle-Musigny Les Amoureuses; Gevrey-Chambertin Clos St.-Jacques; Puligny-Montrachet Les Pucelles
Grand Cru*	Le Musigny; Le Chambertin; Le Montrachet

* Refers to specific vineyard sites.

The availability and price of each category's wines vary in the following ways (the following prices are based on Côte d'Or Burgundies):

- ✔ The two broadest categories — regional and district place-names — account for 53 percent of all Burgundy wines. These wines retail for $15 to $35 a bottle. (You *can* buy affordable Burgundies at this level.)

  Commune-specific (also referred to as *village*) wines, such as Pommard or Gevrey-Chambertin, make up 30 percent of Burgundy and are in the $25 to $70 per bottle price range. Fifty-three communes in Burgundy have AOC status.

- ✔ Premier Crus, such as Meursault Les Perrières or Nuits-St.-Georges Les Vaucrains, account for 15 percent of Burgundy wines; 561 vineyards have Premier Cru status. Most of these wines retail for $40 to $120 per bottle — but the best can go up to $200 per bottle.

- ✔ The 31 Grand Crus, such as Chambertin, represent only about *2 percent* of Burgundy's wines. Prices for Grand Cru Burgundies — both red and white — start at less than $100 and can go to more than $8,000 a bottle for Romanée-Conti, Burgundy's — and the world's — most expensive wine.

Thankfully, you can usually tell the difference between a Premier Cru and a Grand Cru Burgundy by looking at the label. Grand Cru Burgundies carry only the name of the vineyard on the label, and not the commune in which the vineyard is situated. Premier Cru wines generally carry both the name of their commune plus the vineyard name — most often in the same-sized lettering — on the label and, often, the words *Premier Cru* (or *1er Cru*). If a vineyard name is in smaller lettering than the commune name, the wine is generally not a Premier Cru but a wine from a single-vineyard site in that commune; not all single vineyards have Premier Cru status.

If a wine contains grapes from two or more Premier Crus in the same commune, it can be called a *Premier Cru,* but it won't carry the name of a specific Premier Cru vineyard. The label will simply carry a commune name and the words *Premier Cru.*

The Côte d'Or: The heart of Burgundy

The Côte d'Or, a narrow 40-mile stretch of land with some of the most expensive real estate in the world, is the region where all the famous red and white Burgundies originate. The northern part of the Côte d'Or is named the Côte de Nuits, after its most important (commercial) city, Nuits-St.-Georges. This area makes red Burgundies almost exclusively, although one superb white Burgundy, Musigny Blanc, and a couple other white Burgundies do exist on the Côte de Nuits. The following wine communes, from north to south, are in the Côte de Nuits; the names of these communes are also the names of their wines:

- **Marsannay (mahr-sah-nay):** Known for lighter-bodied reds and rosés

- **Fixin (fee-san):** Sturdy, earthy, firm red wines

- **Gevrey-Chambertin (jehv-ray-sham-ber-tan):** Full-bodied, rich red wines; nine Grand Crus, such as Chambertin, Chambertin Clos de Bèze

- **Morey-St.-Denis (maw-ree-san d'nee):** Full, sturdy red wines; Grand Crus are Bonnes Mares (part), Clos de la Roche, Clos St.-Denis, Clos de Tart, Clos des Lambrays

- **Chambolle-Musigny (shom-bowl-moo-sih-nyee):** Supple, elegant red wines; Grand Crus include Musigny and Bonnes Mares (part)

- **Vougeot (voo-joe):** Medium-bodied red wines; Grand Cru is Clos de Vougeot

- **Vosne-Romanée (vone-roh-mah-nay):** Elegant, rich, velvety red wines; the six Grand Crus are Romanée-Conti, La Tâche, Richebourg, Romanée-St.-Vivant, La Romanée, and La Grand Rue

- **Flagey-Échézeaux (flah-jhay-eh-sheh-zoe):** Hamlet of Vosne-Romanée; Grand Crus are Grands Échézeaux and Échézeaux

- **Nuits-St.-Georges (nwee-san-johrj):** Sturdy, earthy, red wines; no Grand Crus; fine Premier Crus

The southern part of the Côte d'Or, the Côte de Beaune, is named after its most important city, Beaune (the commercial and tourist center of the Côte d'Or). The Côte de Beaune makes both white and red Burgundies, but the whites are more renowned. The following communes, from north to south, make up the Côte de Beaune:

- **Ladoix (lah-dwah):** Seldom-seen, inexpensive red and white wines; part of the Grand Cru vineyards, Corton (red) and Corton-Charlemagne (white) are in this commune

- **Pernand-Vergelesses (per-nahn-ver-jeh-less):** Little-known red and white wines; excellent values

- **Aloxe-Corton (ah-luss-cor-tohn):** Full, sturdy wines; several red Grand Crus that all include the name Corton and one magnificent white Grand Cru (Corton-Charlemagne) are here

- **Chorey-lès-Beaune (shor-ay-lay-bone):** Mainly good-value red wine and a little white wine

- **Savigny-lès-Beaune (sah-vee-nyee-lay-bone):** Mostly red wines; fine values here, too

- **Beaune (bone):** Supple, medium-bodied reds; some whites; fine Premier Crus here

- **Pommard (pohm-mahr):** Sturdy, full red wines; some good Premier Crus (Rugiens and Epénots)

- **Volnay (vohl-nay):** Graceful, elegant red wines; good Premier Crus (Caillerets and Clos des Ducs)

- **Auxey-Duresses (awk-see-duh-ress), Monthélie (mohn-teh-lee), St.-Romain (san-roh-man), St.-Aubin (sant-oh-ban):** Four little-known villages producing mainly red wines; fine values

- **Meursault (muhr-so):** The northernmost important white Burgundy commune; full-bodied, nutty wines; some excellent Premier Crus (Les Perrières and Les Genevrières)

- **Puligny-Montrachet (poo-lee-nyee-mon-rah-shay):** Home of elegant white Burgundies; Grand Crus include Montrachet (part), Chevalier-Montrachet, Bâtard-Montrachet (part), and Bienvenues-Bâtard-Montrachet, plus very fine Premier Crus

- **Chassagne-Montrachet (shah-sah-nyuh-mon-rah-shay):** A bit sturdier than Puligny; the rest of the Montrachet and Bâtard-Montrachet Grand Crus are situated here, along with Criots-Bâtard Montrachet Grand Cru; also, some earthy, rustic reds

- **Santenay (sant-nay):** Light-bodied, inexpensive red wines here

- **Maranges (ma-rahnj):** Little-known, mainly red, inexpensive wines

All these red wines are entirely Pinot Noir, and the whites are entirely Chardonnay. The different characteristics from one wine to the next are due to the wines' individual *terroirs*.

Tables 10-4 and 10-5 list the best Burgundy producers and their greatest wines, in rough order of quality.

Table 10-4 Best White Burgundy Producers and Their Greatest Wines

Producer	Recommended Wines
Domaine Ramonet*	Montrachet; Bâtard-Montrachet; Bienvenues-Bâtard-Montrachet; any of his Chassagne-Montrachet Premier Crus
Coche-Dury*	Corton-Charlemagne; Meursault Premier Crus (any)
Domaine des Comtes Lafon	Meursault Premier Crus (any); Le Montrachet
Domaine Leflaive	Chevalier-Montrachet; Bâtard-Montrachet; Puligny-Montrachet Premier Crus (any)
Domaine Étienne Sauzet	Bâtard-Montrachet; Bienvenues-Bâtard-Montrachet; Puligny-Montrachet Les Combettes
Louis Carillon	Bienvenues-Bâtard-Montrachet; Puligny-Montrachet Premier Crus (any)
Michel Niellon	Bâtard-Montrachet; Chevalier-Montrachet; Chassagne-Montrachet Les Vergers
Verget	Bâtard-Montrachet; Chevalier-Montrachet; Meursault Premier Crus (any)

Producer	Recommended Wines
Louis Latour	Corton-Charlemagne; Puligny-Montrachet Premier Crus (any)
Louis Jadot	Corton-Charlemagne; Chassagne-Montrachet Les Caillerets; Beaune Grèves
Joseph Drouhin	All Grand Crus and Premier Crus

* These wines are very expensive and rare.

Table 10-5   Best Red Burgundy Producers and Their Greatest Wines

Producer	Recommended Wines
Domaine Leroy*	Musigny; Richebourg; Chambertin (all Leroy's Grand Crus and Premier Crus)
Domaine de la Romanée-Conti*	Romanée-Conti; La Tâche; Richebourg; Grands Échézeaux
Domaine Comte de Vogüé	Musigny (Vieilles Vignes); Bonnes Mares
Anne Gros	Richebourg; Clos de Vougeot
Georges et Christophe Roumier	Musigny; Bonnes Mares; Chambolle-Musigny Les Amoureuses
Ponsot	Clos de la Roche (Vieilles Vignes); Chambertin; Clos St.-Denis (Vieilles Vignes); Griotte-Chambertin
Armand Rousseau	Chambertin (all his Grand Crus); Gevrey-Chambertin Clos St.-Jacques
Méo-Camuzet	Vosne-Romanée Premier Crus (any of his three); Clos de Vougeot; Richebourg; Corton
Hubert Lignier	Clos de la Roche; Charmes-Chambertin
Domaine Dujac	Clos de la Roche; Bonnes Mares
Joseph Roty	Any of his Grand Cru Chambertins
Joseph Drouhin	All Grand Crus and Premier Crus
Louis Jadot	Especially Romanée-St.-Vivant; Chambertin Clos de Bèze; Musigny
Domaine Marquis d'Angerville	Volnay Clos des Ducs
Domaine Hubert & Etienne de Montille	Volnay and Pommard Premier Crus
Michel Lafarge	Volnay Premier Crus; Beaune Les Grèves
Domaine Robert Chevillon	Nuits-St.-Georges Les St.-Georges; Nuits-Georges Les Vaucrains

(continued)

Table 10-5 *(continued)*

Producer	Recommended Wines
Domaine/Maison J. Faiveley	Nuits-St.-Georges and Mercurey Premier Crus
Bouchard Pere & Fils	All Grand Crus and Premier Crus

* These wines are very expensive.

Côte Chalonnaise: Bargain Burgundies

The sad fact about Burgundy is that many of its best wines are costly. But one of Burgundy's best-kept secrets is the Côte Chalonnaise (the district that lies directly south of the Côte d'Or). Five villages here are home to some very decent Burgundies. True, Côte Chalonnaise Burgundies are not as fine as Côte d'Or Burgundies (they're a bit earthier and less refined in flavor and texture), but they can still be satisfying wines — and we're talking $21 to $36 retail per bottle here. Four villages or communes whose names appear as appellations on wine labels are the following:

- **Mercurey (mer-cure-ay):** Mainly red wine, with about 20 percent white; the best wines of the Chalonnaise come from here, and also the most expensive ($25 to $36); three of the best producers of Mercurey are Aubert de Villaine, J.Faiveley, and Antonin Rodet.

- **Rully (rouh-yee):** Slightly more white wine than red; although a bit earthy, whites are significantly better than the reds; look for the wines of the producer Antonin Rodet.

- **Givry (gee-vree):** Mostly red wine, with less than 10 percent white; reds are better than the whites (but quite earthy); Domaine Joblot's Givry is especially worth seeking out.

- **Montagny (mon-tah-nyee):** All white wine; look for Antonin Rodet's and Louis Latour's Montagny.

The taste of fine white Burgundy

White Burgundy combines a richness of flavor — peaches, hazelnuts, and honey in Meursault; floweriness and butterscotch in a Puligny or Chassagne-Montrachet — with lively acidity and a touch of oak. With age, even more flavor complexity develops. The wine leaves a lingering reminder of all its flavors. Chardonnay wines from other regions and countries can be good, but there's nothing else quite like a great white Burgundy.

Practical advice on buying Burgundy

It's nice of the Burgundians to make everything so stratified and clear, isn't it? Premier Cru Burgundies are always better than commune wines, and Grand Crus are the best of all, right? Well, it ain't necessarily so! In order of importance, these are the criteria to follow when you're buying Burgundy:

✔ **The producer's reputation:** Based on wines he has made in recent years

✔ **The vintage year:** Quality fluctuates greatly from year to year

✔ **The appellation:** The name of the commune or vineyard and its specificity

The producer and the vintage are *considerably* more important than the appellation in Burgundy. Good vintages for red Burgundy are 2009, 2005, 2002, and 1999. For white Burgundy, 2009, 2008 (especially in Chablis), 2004, and 2002 are quite good.

Another village specializes in the Aligoté grape (a second white grape permitted in Burgundy) that makes a particularly crisp and lively wine called Bouzeroon (boo-zer-ohn). Aubert de Villaine is the quality producer here; try his Bourgogne Rouge, Bourgogne Blanc (made from Pinot Noir and Chardonnay, respectively), and especially his Aligoté de Bouzeron.

Chablis: Exceptional white wines

The village of Chablis, northwest of the Côte d'Or, is the closest Burgundian commune to Paris (about a two-hour drive). Although Chablis's wines are 100 percent Chardonnay, just like the white Burgundies of the Côte d'Or, they're quite different in style. For one thing, almost all Côte d'Or white Burgundies ferment and age in oak barrels, but many Chablis producers use stainless steel tanks instead, at least for some of their wines; as a result, those wines do not have oaky character. Also, Chablis's climate is cooler, producing wines that are intrinsically lighter-bodied, relatively austere in flavor, and crisper.

Chablis wine is classically very dry and sometimes has flinty flavors, without quite the richness and ripeness of Côte d'Or white Burgundies. (Recent Chablis vintages — such as 1997, 2000, 2003, and 2007 — have been so warm, however, that the wines sport riper fruit flavor than usual.) For a classic, cool-climate Chablis, try a bottle from the 2008, 2004, or 2002 vintage. Personally, we buy a lot more Chablis (Premier Cru and Grand Cru) than Côte d'Or white Burgundies. They're so much more affordable — great values for the price. Look especially for the cool-climate 2008 Chablis. (The 2009 and 2010 vintages are good vintages, but the weather was not so cool as in 2008.)

Tips on drinking Burgundy

Red Burgundy is a particularly good wine to choose in restaurants. Unlike Bordeaux and Cabernet Sauvignon–based wines, red Burgundy is usually approachable young because of its softness and enticing aromas and flavors of red fruits. Moreover, red Burgundy, like all Pinot Noirs, is a versatile companion to food. It's the one red wine that can complement fish or seafood; it's ideal with salmon, for example. Chicken, turkey, and ham are also good matches for Burgundy. With richer red Burgundies, beef and game (such as duck, pheasant, rabbit, or venison) all go well.

Red Burgundy is at its best when served at cool temperatures — about 60 to 62 degrees Fahrenheit (17 degrees Celsius). It should *not* be decanted. Even older Burgundies seldom develop much sediment, and extra aeration would cause you to lose the wonderful Burgundy aroma, which is one of the greatest features of this wine.

On the other hand, white Burgundy often benefits from decanting, especially Grand Cru and Premier Cru white Burgundies from younger vintages (5 years old or younger). Great young white Burgundies, such as Corton-Charlemagne, just don't evolve completely in their first few years; the aeration will help bring out their aromas and flavors. And remember, don't serve them too cold! The ideal temperature range for serving the better white Burgundies is 58 to 62 degrees Fahrenheit (15 to 17 degrees Celsius).

Chablis is an ideal companion to seafood, especially oysters. Like all other white Burgundies, Chablis should be served cool (58 to 60 degrees Fahrenheit, or 15 degrees Celsius), not cold.

The Chablis worth trying

Chablis is at its best at the Premier Cru and Grand Cru level. Simple village Chablis is less expensive — about $20 to $30 — but you can often find comparable white wines from Mâcon, the Chalonnaise, or the Côte d'Or (Bourgogne Blanc) at that price.

The seven Grand Cru Chablis vineyards are Les Clos, Valmur, Les Preuses, Vaudésir, Grenouilles, Bougros, and Blanchot. Another vineyard that's actually — but not technically — Grand Cru is La Moutonne; this vineyard is a part of the Vaudésir and Les Preuses Grand Cru acreage but isn't recognized as a Grand Cru appellation. Grand Cru Chablis wines range in price from $65 to more than $100, depending on the producer. Grand Cru Chablis from good vintages (see Appendix C) can age and improve for 15 years.

The Chablis district has 22 Premier Cru Chablis appellations, but the six most well known are Fourchaume, Montée de Tonnerre, Vaillons, Mont de Milieu, Montmains, and Les Forêts (also known as Forest). Premier Cru Chablis wines range in price from $35 to $65, depending on the producer, and can age up to ten years in good vintages.

Nine outstanding producers of Chablis

Nine producers really stand out in Chablis. For a true understanding of this underrated wine, try to buy their Grand or Premier Cru Chablis. *Try* is the operative word here; these are small producers whose wines are available only in better stores:

- ✔ **François Raveneau** and **René et Vincent Dauvissat:** Both use oak for fermenting and aging; thus the wines are fairly rich and substantial.
- ✔ **Louis Michel:** Uses stainless steel only, making vibrant, crisp wines.
- ✔ **Jean Dauvissat:** Uses mainly stainless steel.
- ✔ **Jean Collet**, **Jean-Paul Droin**, **Christian Moreau**, **William Fèvre,** and **Verget:** Other consistently fine producers of Chablis.

Mâcon: Affordable whites

If you're thinking that $20 or more is too much to spend for a bottle of white Burgundy or Chablis for everyday drinking, we have an alternative wine for you: white Mâcon. Many of the best white wine buys — not only in France, but in the world — come from the Mâconnais district.

The Mâconnais lies directly south of the Chalonnaise and north of Beaujolais. It has a milder, sunnier climate than the Côte d'Or to the north. Wine production centers around the city of Mâcon, a gateway city to Provence and the Riviera. The hills in the Mâconnais contain the same chalky limestone beloved by Chardonnay that can be found in many Burgundy districts to the north. In Mâcon, you can even find a village called Chardonnay.

Mâcon's white wines, in fact, are 100 percent Chardonnay. Most of them are simply called Mâcon or Mâcon-Villages (a slightly better wine than Mâcon, because it comes from specific villages), and they retail for $12 to $19 a bottle, with a few up to $22. Often better are Mâcons that come from just one village; in those wines, the name of the village is appended to the district name, Mâcon (as in Mâcon-Lugny or Mâcon-Viré).

Mâcon whites are medium-bodied, crisp, fresh, yet substantial wines, often with minerally flavor. They're usually unoaked. You should enjoy them while they're young, generally within three years of the vintage. A few red wines are made in the Mâcon district (mainly from the Gamay grape) and, like the whites, are good values.

The best Mâcon whites come from the southernmost part of the district and carry their own appellations — Pouilly-Fuissé (pwee-fwee-say) and St.-Véran (san-veh-rahn).

- Pouilly-Fuissé is a richer, fuller-bodied wine than a simple Mâcon, is often oaked, and is a bit more expensive (around $24 to $28; up to $45 for the best ones). To try an outstanding example of Pouilly-Fuissé, buy Château Fuissé, which, in good vintages, compares favorably with more expensive Cote d'Or white Burgundies (although different in style).

- St.-Véran, at $16 to $24, is very possibly the best-value wine in all of Mâcon. Especially fine is the St.-Véran of Verget — one of the best producers of Mâconnais wines.

Beaujolais: As delightful as it is affordable

The Beaujolais district is situated south of the Mâconnais, in the heart of one of the greatest gastronomic centers of the world; good restaurants abound in the area, as well as in the nearby city of Lyon. As a wine, Beaujolais is so famous that it stands apart from the other wines of Burgundy. It even has its own red grape, Gamay. The fact that Beaujolais is part of Burgundy is merely a technicality.

The easy-drinking Beaujolais

If you're a white wine, White Zinfandel, or rosé wine drinker (or even a non-wine drinker!), Beaujolais could be the *ideal* first red wine to drink — a bridge, so to speak, to more serious red wines. Beaujolais wines are the fruitiest red wines in France, although they're dry. Beaujolais is truly a fun wine that's delicious and doesn't require contemplation.

Beaujolais and Beaujolais Supérieur (1 percent higher in alcohol) are the easiest Beaujolais wines. Their AOC territories extend across the whole Beaujolais district, but in practice, these wines come from the southern part of Beaujolais where the soil is mainly clay and sand. They're fresh, fruity, uncomplicated, fairly light-bodied wines that sell for $9 to $14 and are best a year or two after the vintage. They're fine wines for warm weather, when a heavier red wine would be inappropriate.

Celebration time: Beaujolais Nouveau

Each year on the third Thursday in November, the new vintage of Beaujolais — called Beaujolais Nouveau — is released all over the world with great fanfare. This youngster — only about six weeks old! — is a very grapey, easy-to-drink, delicious wine with practically no tannin but lots of fruitiness. In the United States, Beaujolais Nouveau graces many a Thanksgiving table because of the timing of its annual debut. It sells for $8 to $11 and is at its best within the first year of the vintage.

The serious versions

Beaujolais has its serious side, too. The best Beaujolais are made in the northern part of the Beaujolais district where the soil is granite based. Beaujolais-Villages is a wine blended from grapes grown in (some of) 39 specific villages that produce fuller, more substantial wine than simple Beaujolais. It costs a dollar or two more but can be well worth the difference.

Beaujolais that's even higher quality comes from ten specific areas in the north. The wines of these areas are known as *Cru* Beaujolais, and only the name of the Cru appears in large letters on the label. (The wines aren't actually named Beaujolais.) Cru Beaujolais have more depth and, in fact, need a little time to develop; some of the Crus can age and improve for four or five years or more. They range in price from about $12 to $28. Table 10-6 lists the ten Cru Beaujolais as they are geographically situated, from south to north, along with a brief description of each wine.

Table 10-6	The Ten Cru Beaujolais
Cru	*Description*
Brouilly (broo-yee)	The largest Cru in terms of production and the most variable in quality; light and fruity; drink within three years
Côte de Brouilly	Distinctly better than Brouilly, fuller and more concentrated; vineyards are higher in altitude; drink within three years
Régnié (ray-nyay)	The newest village to be recognized as a Cru; very similar to Brouilly; not quite so good as Côte de Brouilly
Morgon (mor-gohn)	At its best, full and earthy; can age for five to seven years
Chiroubles (sheh-roob-leh)	One of our favorites; the quintessential, delicate, delicious, perfumed Beaujolais; tastes of young red fruits; very pretty; drink it within two years of the vintage
Fleurie (flehr-ee)	Medium-bodied, rich, with velvety fruitiness; the most popular Cru (and, along with Moulin-à-Vent, the most expensive, at $16 to $25); quite reliable; can age for four years
Moulin-à-Vent (moo-lahn-ah-vahn)	Clearly the most powerful, concentrated Cru, and the one that can age the longest (ten years or more); this is one Beaujolais that really needs three or four years to develop
Chénas (shay-nahs)	Bordering Moulin-à-Vent (in fact, much of it can be legally sold as the more famous Moulin-à-Vent); what is sold as Chénas is usually well priced; drink within four years
Juliénas (jhool-yay-nahs)	The insider's Beaujolais; often the most consistent and the best of the Crus; full-bodied and rich; can last five years or more; seldom disappoints
Saint-Amour (sant-ah-more)	The northernmost Cru; perfectly named for lovers on Valentine's Day (or any other day); supple, light- to medium-bodied, delicious berry fruit; drink within two or three years

---

Beaujolais in action

To really get a feeling for being in France, visit a bistro in Paris or Lyon and order a carafe of young Beaujolais with your charcuterie, pâte, or chicken. No wine slides down the throat as easily! Young, uncomplicated Beaujolais wines should *definitely* be served chilled, at about 55 degrees Fahrenheit (13 degrees Celsius), to capture their fruity exuberance. The fuller Cru Beaujolais, on the other hand, are best at about the same temperature as red Burgundy (58 to 60 degrees Fahrenheit; 14 degrees Celsius).

Most Beaujolais is sold by large *négociants* — firms that buy grapes and wine from growers and then blend, bottle, and sell the wine under their own labels. Two of the largest Beaujolais *négociants* are Georges Duboeuf and Louis Jadot; Jadot also owns a few very fine domaines, in Moulin-à-Vent and in Morgon. Seek out some of the small Beaujolais producers, such as Jean-Paul Brun, to see how good Beaujolis can be.

The Hearty Rhônes of the Valley

The Rhône (rone) Valley is in southeastern France (refer to Figure 10-1), south of Beaujolais, between the city of Lyon in the north and Avignon directly south (just north of Provence). The growing season in the Rhône Valley is sunny and hot. The wines reflect the weather: The red wines are full, robust, and fairly high in alcohol. Even some of the white wines tend to be full and powerful. But the wines from the southern part of the Rhône are distinctly different from those in the northern Rhône Valley, as you find out in the following sections.

For a good, reliable dry red wine that costs about $9 to $17, look no further than the Rhône Valley's everyday red wine, Côtes du Rhône, which comes mainly from the southern part of the region. The Rhône Valley makes more serious wines — mostly red — but Côtes du Rhône is one of the best inexpensive red wines in the world.

Generous wines of the South

Most (in fact, about 95 percent of) Rhône wines come from the southern Rhône, where the wines are generally inexpensive and uncomplicated. They're mainly blends of several grape varieties. The dominant grape variety in the southern Rhône is Grenache, which makes easygoing wines that are high in alcohol and low in tannin — but some blends contain significant amounts of Syrah or other varieties, which makes for somewhat gutsier wines. Almost all Côtes du Rhône wines are red (94 percent red, 3 percent white, 3 percent rosé).

Besides Côtes du Rhône itself, other southern Rhône wines to look for are

- **Côtes du Ventoux** (vahn-too), which is similar to but a bit lighter than Côtes du Rhône
- **Côtes du Rhône-Villages,** from 95 villages, making fuller and a bit more expensive wines than Côtes du Rhône; 19 of these villages are entitled to use their names on the label, such as *Cairanne — Côtes du Rhône-Villages*
- The single-village wines **Gigondas** (jhee-gohn-dahs) and **Vacqueyras** (vah-keh-rahs)

The last two wines are former Côtes du Rhône-Villages wines that graduated into individual appellations.

- Gigondas ($25 to $35) is quite rich and robust and can live for ten years or more in good vintages.
- Vacqueyras is less powerful and robust than Gigondas but also less expensive (mainly $19 to $25); Vacqueyras is a particularly good buy.

Two interesting dry rosé wines of the southern Rhône are Tavel (tah-vel) and Lirac (lee-rahk); Lirac is less well known and, therefore, less expensive. (Tavel retails mainly from $18 to $28; Lirac, from $13 to $22). Lirac can also be white or red, but all Tavel wines are rosés. Both are made from the Grenache and Cinsault grapes. They can be delightful on hot, summer days or at picnics. As with most rosé wines, they are best when they're very young.

But Châteauneuf-du-Pape (shah-toe-nuf-doo-pahp) is the king in the southern Rhône. Its name recalls the 14th century, when nearby Avignon (not Rome) was the home of the Popes. Almost all Châteauneuf-du-Pape is red wine and a blend of grapes: As many as 13 varieties can be used, but Grenache, Mourvèdre, and Syrah predominate. At its best, Châteauneuf-du-Pape is full-bodied, rich, round, and ripe. In good vintages, it will age well for 15 to 20 years. Most red Châteauneuf-du-Pape wines (a small amount of very earthy-style white Châteauneuf-du-Pape is also made) retail in the $37 to $60 price range, but the best ones can cost up to $75 or more. Two of the finest Châteauneuf-du-Papes are Château Rayas (nearly 100 percent Grenache from very old vines) and Château de Beaucastel (which can age 20 years or more).

Noble wines of the north

The two best red wines of the entire Rhône — Côte-Rôtie (coat-roe-tee) and Hermitage (er-mee-tahj) — hail from the northern Rhône Valley. Both are made from the noble Syrah grape (but a small percentage of white Viognier grapes is permitted and sometimes used in Côte-Rôtie).

✔ Although both are rich, full-bodied wines, Côte-Rôtie is the more finesseful of the two. It has a wonderfully fragrant aroma — which always reminds us of bacon, green olives, and raspberries — and soft, fruity flavors. In good vintages (see Appendix C), Côte-Rôtie can age for 20 years or more. Many Côte-Rôties are in the $40 to $65 price range, but a few of the best ones retail for more than $100.

The most famous producer of Côte-Rôtie is Guigal; his single-vineyard Côte-Rôties — La Mouline, La Landonne, and La Turque — are legendary but rare and particularly expensive (over $100 and up to $200).

✔ Red Hermitage is clearly the most full-bodied, longest-lived Rhône wine. It is a complex, rich, tannic wine that needs several years before it begins to develop, and it ages easily for 30 years or more in good vintages (2010, 2009, 2006, 2003, 1999, 1991, 1990, 1989, and 1988 were all excellent vintages in the northern Rhône). The best red Hermitages sell today for $55 to $90, and a few of the top ones are over $100. Hermitages that sell for less than $50 are invariably not as good.

The three best producers of Hermitage are Jean-Louis Chave, Chapoutier, and Paul Jaboulet Aîné (for its top Hermitage, La Chapelle).

Cornas, also made entirely from Syrah, is another fine northern Rhône red wine. Cornas resembles Hermitage in that it is a huge, tannic wine that needs 10 to 20 years of aging. It ranges in price from $45 to $84 for the best examples. Two Cornas producers to look for are Domaine Auguste Clape and Jean-Luc Colombo.

Two relatively less-expensive red wines from the northern Rhône are Crozes-Hermitage, from an area surrounding the Hermitage zone, and St.-Joseph — both made entirely from Syrah. Both sell for $14 to $24 (and higher, for the best examples).

A small amount of white Hermitage is produced from the Marsanne and Roussanne grape varieties. White Hermitage is traditionally a full, heavy, earthy wine that needs 8 to 10 years to fully develop, and can age for 15 years or more. Chapoutier's fine Hermitage Blanc, Chante Alouette, however, is all Marsanne (about $81 to $84) and made in a more approachable style. The one truly great white Hermitage is Chave's; at about $165 to $180, it's complex, rich, and almost as long-lived as the red Hermitage.

Condrieu (cohn-dree-uh), made entirely from Viognier, is the other white northern Rhône wine to try. It's one of the most fragrant, floral dry wines in existence. Its flavors are delicate but rich, with delicious fresh apricot and peach notes; it makes a wonderful accompaniment to fresh fish. Condrieu (which sells for $42 to $70) is best young, however. And, because Condrieu is a small wine zone, the best Condrieu wines are hard to find. Look for them in finer wine shops and better French restaurants.

One wine, Château Grillet, made from Viognier, has its own very small appellation. It's difficult to find, and expensive. The 2008 Château Grillet is selling for $135. You can find some 2006 Château Grillets in the $100 to $110 range. Like Condrieu, the other Viognier wine, Château Grillet is at its best in its youth. But Château Grillet at its best is an exquisite white wine.

The Loire Valley: White Wine Heaven

Have you been Chardonnay-ed out yet? If you're looking for white wine alternatives to Chardonnay, discover the Loire (l'wahr) Valley wine region. A lot of white wines come from there, but virtually none of them are Chardonnay! For the record, you can find red wines and some dry rosés, too, in the Loire, but the region is really known for its white wines.

The Loire Valley stretches across northwest France (refer to Figure 10-1), following the path of the Loire River from central France in the east to the Atlantic Ocean in the west. The rather cool climate, especially in the west, produces relatively light-bodied white wines. The Loire Valley has three sections, each of which features different grape varieties.

The Upper Loire

In the eastern end of the Valley (called the Upper Loire), just south of Paris, are the towns of Sancerre and Pouilly-sur-Loire, located on opposite banks of the Loire River. Here, the Sauvignon Blanc grape makes lively, dry wines that have spicy, green-grass and minerally flavors. The two principal wines in this area are Sancerre (sahn-sair) and Pouilly-Fumé (pwee-foo-may).

- ✔ Sancerre is the lighter and more vibrant of the two. It's perfect for summer drinking, especially with shellfish or light, freshwater fish, such as trout. Look for the Sancerres of Domaines Henri Bourgeois or Lucien Crochet.

- ✔ Pouilly-Fumé is slightly fuller than Sancerre and can have attractive flinty, mineral flavors. Pouilly-Fumé can be quite a fine wine when made by a good producer, such as Didier Dagueneau or Ladoucette. Because of its fuller weight, Pouilly-Fumé goes well with rich fish, such as salmon, or with chicken or veal.

Most Sancerre and Pouilly-Fumé wines sell in the $20 to $35 range, but a few of the better Pouilly-Fumés can cost $50 or more. These wines are at their best when they're young; drink them within four years of the vintage.

The central Loire Valley

The central Loire Valley is known for both its white and red wines. The Chenin Blanc grape makes better wine here than it does anywhere else in the world. The Anjou district produces arguably the world's greatest *dry* Chenin Blanc wine, Savennières (which starts at about $20). A great dessert white wine made from Chenin Blanc, Coulée de Serrant, also comes from Anjou. Bonnezeaux and Quartz-de-Chaume are two other well-known dessert white wines from Anjou that are made from Chenin Blanc.

Near the city of Tours (where you can see beautiful châteaux of former French royalty), lies the town of Vouvray (voo-vray). Vouvray wines, also made from Chenin Blanc, come in three styles: dry (*sec*), medium-dry (*demi-sec*), or sweet (called *moelleux,* pronounced m'wah-leuh). Vouvray sec is a less austere and less full-bodied wine than Savennières, however. Vouvray also can be a sparkling wine.

The best wines of Vouvray, the sweet (moelleux), can be made only in vintages of unusual ripeness, which occur infrequently. These wines need several years to develop and can last almost forever, thanks to their remarkable acidity; their prices begin at about $45 to $50. Three renowned Vouvray producers are Philippe Foreau of Clos Naudain, Gaston Huet-Pinguet, and Didier Champalou.

Less expensive Vouvrays, priced at about $14 to $15, are pleasant to drink young. Even the drier versions are not truly bone-dry and are a good choice if you don't enjoy very dry wines. They go well with chicken or veal in cream sauce, spicy cuisines, or fruit and soft cheese after dinner.

The central Loire Valley also boasts the region's best red wines. Made mainly from Cabernet Franc, they carry the place-names of the villages the grapes come from: Chinon (she-nohn), Bourgueil (boor-guh'y), St.-Nicolas-de-Bourgueil (san-nee-co-lah-deh-boor-guh'y), and Saumur-Champigny (soh-muhr-shahm-pee-n'yee). They're all spicy, great-value ($15 to $35), medium-bodied reds that are famously food friendly.

Pays Nantais

Close to the Atlantic Ocean is the third wine district of the Loire Valley — Pays Nantais (pay-ee nahn-tay), named after the city of Nantes, right where the Loire River empties into the Atlantic Ocean. This area is the home of the Muscadet grape (also known as Melon de Bourgogne). The wine, which is commonly known as Muscadet (moos-cah-day), is light and very dry, with apple and mineral flavors — perfect with clams, oysters, mussels, and river fish (and, naturally, ideal for summer drinking).

Here a Pouilly, there a Pouilly

You may get the two *Pouilly* wines — Pouilly-Fuissé and Pouilly-Fumé — confused, but they're very different wines.

✔ The Chardonnay-based Pouilly-Fuissé, from the Mâcon in Burgundy, is a full-bodied wine and is usually oaky.

✔ Pouilly-Fumé, from the Loire and made from Sauvignon Blanc, is medium-bodied and crisper.

Most Muscadet comes from the Sèvre-et-Maine AOC zone, and those words appear on the label. Frequently, you also see the term *sur lie,* which means that the wine aged on its *lees* (dead fermentation yeasts) and was bottled straight from the tank. This procedure gives the wine liveliness, freshness, and sometimes a slight prickle of carbon dioxide on the tongue.

Muscadet is a terrific warm weather white and a great value. You can buy a really good Muscadet for $9 to $14.

Alsace: Unique Region, Unique Wines

Alsace, in northeastern France, is a picturesque wine region just across the Rhine River from Germany. Alsace wines are unique among French wines in that almost all of them carry a grape variety name as well as a place-name (that is, Alsace). All Alsace wines come in a long-necked bottle called a *flûte*. The wines of Alsace also happen to represent very good value.

Considering Alsace's northerly latitude, you'd expect the region's climate to be cool. But thanks to the protection of the Vosges Mountains to the west, Alsace's climate is quite sunny and temperate, and one of the driest in France — in short, perfect weather for grape growing.

Although some Pinot Noir exists, 91 percent of Alsace's wines are white. Four are particularly important: Riesling, Pinot Blanc, Pinot Gris, and Gewurztraminer. Each reflects the characteristics of its grape, but they all share a certain aroma and flavor, sometimes called a spiciness, that can only be described as the flavor of Alsace.

✔ **Riesling** is the king of Alsace wines. Alsace Riesling has a fruity aroma but a firm, dry, almost steely taste. Although, like most Alsace wines, it can be consumed young, a Riesling from a good vintage can easily age and improve for ten years or more. Rieslings are in the $18 to $40 price range.

- Alsace **Pinot Blanc** is the lightest of the four wines. Some producers make their Pinot Blanc medium-dry to appeal to wine drinkers who are new to the region's wines, while others make classic, bone-dry Pinot Blanc. Either way, it's best young. Pinot Blanc is quite inexpensive, selling for $15 to $22.

- **Pinot Gris** is made from the same variety that you find in Italy as Pinot Grigio. Here in Alsace, it's a rich, spicy, full-bodied, characterful wine. Alsace's Pinot Gris retails for $18 to $35; it goes well with spicy meat dishes and can work with slightly sweet or sour flavors.

- The **Gewurztraminer** grape has such intense, exotic, spicy aromas and flavors that it's a love-it-or-leave-it wine. (One of us loves it — the other leaves it!) But it certainly has its followers. And this grape is clearly at its best in Alsace. If you haven't tried an Alsace Gewurztraminer yet, you haven't tasted one of the most distinctive wines in the world. It's quite low in acidity and high in alcohol, a combination that gives an impression of fullness and softness. It goes best with *foie gras* and strong cheeses, and some people like it with spicy Asian cuisine. Gewurztraminer sells for about the same price as Riesling but doesn't age quite as well.

The South and Southwest

The most dynamic wine regions in France are all located in the southern part of the country. Ironically, this is the oldest wine-producing area in France: The Greeks made wine in Provence in the sixth century BC. The South is also the part of France that makes the most wine. Languedoc-Roussillon, a dual wine region, produces more than 40 percent of France's wine!

Southwest France, the huge area between Bordeaux and the Spanish border, also makes wine (well, it's French, isn't it?), and many wine regions here have also experienced a renaissance. Like the South, it's mainly red wine country, but you can find some interesting whites, rosés, sparkling wines, and dessert wines, as well. You might say that the South and southwestern France are the country's "new" frontiers.

France's bargain basement: Languedoc-Roussillon

The sunny, dry Languedoc-Roussillon (lahn-gweh-doc-roo-see-yohn) region, also known as the Midi (mee-dee), has long been the country's largest wine-producing area. The region (refer to Figure 10-1) makes mainly red wines;

in fact, more than half of France's red wines come from here. Traditionally, these robust red wines came from typical grape varieties of the South, such as Carignan, Cinsault, and Grenache. But in the last two decades, more serious varieties, such as Syrah, Cabernet Sauvignon, and Merlot, have become popular with growers. Winemakers use these grapes both for varietal wines and in blends.

In this region, look especially for the red wines from the AOC zones of Corbières, Minervois, St.-Chinian, Fitou, and Costières de Nîmes. In addition, many varietal wines carrying the designation *Vin de Pays* (or *IGP*) *d'Oc* are often good values. They're made from grapes that come from anywhere in the Languedoc-Roussillon region, rather than from a specific AOC zone. One amazing white varietal wine, Picpoul de Pinet, has its own appellation. It is a racy, lively, minerally wine that sells in the $9 to $12 range. Look for it!

Whichever the appellation, most of these wines are in the $10 to $16 price range, although a few of the better ones cost $20 or more.

Timeless Provence

Provence (pro-vahns) — southeast of the Rhône Valley, east of Languedoc-Roussillon, and west of northern Italy — may be France's most beautiful region. Home of the Riviera, Nice, and Cannes, it's certainly the country's most fashionable and touristy region. But it's also an ancient land, with a thriving old capital, Aix-en-Provence. The excellent light and climate have always attracted great artists — such as Vincent van Gogh — who painted many of their best works here.

Wine has always been part of Provence's culture and economy. Provence is best known for its rosés, which so many tourists enjoy on the Riviera, but Provence's red wines win the most critical acclaim. Rosé wines still dominate in the region's largest AOC wine zone, Côtes de Provence, but in three other important AOC zones — Coteaux d'Aix-en-Provence, Les Baux-de-Provence, and Bandol — red wines rule. Bandol, and its foremost producer, Domaine Tempier, enjoy Provence's greatest reputation for reds. Another amazing red, Château Simone, from the tiny Palette appellation, is a standout. Cassis (no relation to the black currant liqueur of the same name), a small AOC zone on the Mediterranean coast near Marseilles, makes distinctive, aromatic white wines.

Provence's reds and rosés derive from the same grape varieties used in Languedoc-Roussillon — Grenache, Cinsault, Mourvèdre, Carignan, Syrah, and Cabernet Sauvignon. The main varieties in white Cassis are Clairette and Marsanne.

Southwest France

The large area that borders the Atlantic Ocean south of the Bordeaux region is known as southwest France — but it's actually composed of many individual wine districts. Two of the most significant are situated near Bordeaux.

- **Bergerac** (ber-jhe-rak) makes Bordeaux-like red and white wines, without the Bordeaux prices. Merlot dominates Bergerac's red wines, while Sémillon and Sauvignon Blanc are the main varieties for its whites, some of which cost as little as $10 a bottle.

- **Cahors** (cah-or) is southwest France's most prestigious red wine district. The main grape variety is Malbec, and that name increasingly appears on labels. Nowhere else in the world, except Argentina, does this variety play such an important role. The best wines of the traditional Cahors producers, such as Château Lagrezette, are dark, tannic reds that need about ten years of aging before they mature. Prices for Château Lagrezette Cahors wines begin at about $35.

Three other districts in southwest France, Gaillac (gah-yack), Juraçon (joo-rahn-sohn), and Monbazillac (mon-bah-zee-yak), specialize in white dessert wines. Gaillac also makes fruity, lightly sparkling wines. The AOC red wine district of Madiran produces full-bodied, tannic reds, perfect for the local, hearty Gascony cuisine. Tannat is the main variety used in Madiran, along with Cabernet Sauvignon and Cabernet Franc. The last French AOC district before you cross the Pyrénées Mountains into Spain is Irouléguy (ee-roo-leh-gee); spicy, tannic red wines are made here by natives who don't speak French but rather Basque.

Other French Wine Regions

Two of France's three most obscure wine regions have something in common: They're located in the foothills and slopes of the Alps in eastern France, next to Switzerland. In fact, skiers are probably the most familiar with their wines. They are the Jura (joo-rah) and Savoie (sah-v'wah) — sometimes anglicized as *Savoy*.

Jura makes two interesting wines that are the region's specialties:

- **Yellow Wine (*Vin Jaune*),** from the Savagnin grape variety, is comparable to a light Spanish fino Sherry, but it's not fortified (see Chapter 16). **Château Chalon** is the most famous example of Vins Jaunes (van-joh'n).

✔ **Vin de Paille** (van deh pah'ee) is known as *Straw Wine* because of the traditional way in which it's made: The grapes (Savagnin, Chardonnay and others) are harvested late, arranged on straw mats or in baskets, and then placed in attics to dry — similar to Tuscany's specialty, Vin Santo (see Chapter 16). The resulting wine is rich, concentrated, nutty, and raisiny.

Savoie's wines, mainly white, are typically dry and light-bodied. Seyssel (say-sell), Savoie's best-known appellation, is known for its slightly sparkling wines as well as its still whites.

Corsica, renowned historically as the birthplace of Napoleon, is a large, mountainous island 100 miles southeast of Provence (refer to Figure 10-1). It's best known for its medium-bodied, well-priced red and rosé wines. Corsican wines are experiencing their own renaissance. They are great-value wines. They start at $10 to $12, and go up to over $20 for the better wines.

Chapter 11

Italy, the Heartland of Vino

- -

In This Chapter

▶ Italy's big "B" wines

▶ Chianti: Still famous after all these years

▶ A trio from Verona

▶ The *vino bianco* quality revival

- -

More than 2,000 years after Julius Caesar conquered Gaul, the Italians continue to take the world by storm. With passion, artistic flair, impeccable taste, and flawless workmanship as their tools, the Italians have infiltrated the arenas of fashion, film, food, and of course, wine.

Thanks to the popularity of Italian restaurants, most of us have frequent opportunities to enjoy best-selling Italian wines, such as Pinot Grigio, Soave, Valpolicella, and Chianti. But Italy makes other wines, too — many of them among the greatest wines on earth. And just about every one of Italy's thousand-something wines is terrific with food, because Italian wines are made specifically to be enjoyed during a meal. That's how the Italians drink them.

In this chapter, we begin with Italy's three most renowned wine areas — Piedmont, Tuscany, and northeastern Italy. We also discuss some of the other Italian regions and their wines, which you are likely to find in your wine shop or *ristorante*. If you want detailed information on Italian wines, be sure to get our book *Italian Wine For Dummies* (Wiley).

The Vineyard of Europe

Tiny, overachieving Italy — 60 percent the size of France, three-quarters the size of California — makes more than 20 percent of the world's wine! Wine is the lifeblood of the Italian people. Vines grow all over, and no self-respecting dinner can possibly occur without a bottle of wine on the table.

The downside to wine's penetration into Italian culture is that Italians often take wine for granted. Italy took 28 years longer than France to develop a wine classification system, for example; and today, nearly 50 years after creating that system, Italy has yet to incorporate official recognition of her best vineyard sites *(crus)* into her wine laws, as the French have done in Burgundy.

Another handicap of Italian wines, for wine drinkers in other countries who want to learn about them, is that most Italian wines are made from native grape varieties that don't exist elsewhere (and when transplanted, don't perform nearly as well as in Italy). Grapes such as Nebbiolo, Sangiovese, Aglianico, and Barbera, to name just a few, can make outstanding wine in Italy, but their names are unfamiliar, despite the fact that recognition of Italian wines has grown considerably over the past two decades. Table 11-1 lists the grape varieties behind some wines of Italy's most important wine regions.

Table 11-1   Grape Varieties of Some Major Italian Wine Regions

Region/Red Wine	*White Wine*	*Grape Varieties*
Piedmont		
Barolo		Nebbiolo
Barbaresco		Nebbiolo
Gattinara		Nebbiolo, Bonarda*
	Gavi	Cortese
Tuscany		
Chianti, Chianti Classico		Sangiovese, Canaiolo, and others*
Brunello di Montalcino		Sangiovese Grosso
Vino Nobile di Montepulciano		Sangiovese, Canaiolo, and others*
Carmignano		Sangiovese, Cabernet Sauvignon*
Super-Tuscans**		Cabernet Sauvignon, Sangiovese, and others*
Veneto		
	Soave	Garganega, Trebbiano di Soave, and others*
Valpolicella		Corvina, Rondinella, Molinara*
Amarone		(Same grapes as Valpolicella; semi-dried)
Bardolino		Corvina, Rondinella, Molinara*

Region/Red Wine	White Wine	Grape Varieties
	Bianco di Custoza	Trebbiano, Garganega, Friulano*
	Lugana***	Trebbiano di Lugana

* Blended wines, made from two or more grapes.
** Untraditional wines produced mainly in the Chianti district; see the discussion under Tuscany.
*** Much of the Lugana wine zone is actually in Lombardy.

On the upside, Italy is blessed with such a variety of soils and climates — from Alpine foothills in the north to Mediterranean coastlines — that the range of her wines is almost endless. (A curious wine lover could keep busy for a lifetime, exploring the hundreds of wines in Italy!) Italy's hilly landscape provides plenty of high-altitude relief for grapevines, even in the warm south.

In the following sections, we discuss the gamut of Italian wine quality, explain the label terms that appear on labels of Italian wines, and provide an overview of Italy's wine regions.

The ordinary and the elite

Italy's wines, as we outside of Italy know them, fall into two distinct groups:

- ✔ Inexpensive red and white wines for everyday drinking with meals in the casual Italian fashion
- ✔ The better wines, which range from good to great in quality, for special occasions and for quality-conscious wine drinkers

One of the best-known Italian wines in the first category is Pinot Grigio, the ubiquitous dry white wine that has become the largest-selling type of imported wine in the United States. In the second category is Barolo, one of the world's finest red wines, along with many other fine Italian wines.

Categories of Italian wine, legally speaking

Because Italy is a member of the European Union, her official system of categorizing wines (her *appellation* system) must conform to the E.U. system. (See Chapter 4 for more information.) In the upper tier — wines with a Protected Designation of Origin (PDO) — Italy has two categories of wine:

✔ DOCG *(Denominazione di Origine Controllata e Garantita),* translated as "regulated and guaranteed place-name," wines are a group of elite wines. The long Italian phrase corresponding to the initials DOCG appears on the labels of these wines. In the new E.U. system, these wines are simply part of the DOP category (see next bullet), and therefore most producers will likely continue to use the words corresponding to DOCG on their labels rather than the new E.U. term.

✔ DOC *(Denominazione di Origine Controllata* or, in the new E.U. lingo, *Denominazione di Origine Protetta, DOP*), translated as "regulated (or protected) place-name," wines are Italy's basic PDO wines. The phrase *Denominazione di Origine Controllata* (or *Protetta*) appears on the labels of these wines.

The terms DOC and DOCG refer both to wine zones and to the wines of those zones. The DOC Soave, for example, is both a place (a specific production zone defined and regulated by Italian law, named after a town called Soave) and the wine of that place.

In the lower E.U. tier — wines with a Protected Geographic Indication (PGI) — Italy has another category of wine: IGT *(Indicazione Geografica Tipica* or, in the new E.U. lingo, *Indicazione Geografica Protetta, IGP*) wines. These wines have a geographic name on the label, but that name represents a broader territory than that of DOC/DOCG or DOP wines. For example, although the DOCG wine Brunello di Montalcino must derive from grapes grown in a very specific section of the region of Tuscany, an IGT/IGP Tuscan wine may come from anywhere in the whole region of Tuscany. Many IGT/IGP wines carry a grape variety name in addition to the name of the protected geographic area.

Italy's wine regions

Italy is said to have 20 wine regions, which correspond exactly to her political regions (see Figure 11-1). In other words, wine is produced everywhere in Italy. What we would call a wine region in France, such as Burgundy or Alsace, we refer to as a wine *zone* in Italy to avoid confusion with the political region.

Many of the finest wines come from the north: the Piedmont region in the northwest, Tuscany in north-central Italy, and the three regions (informally called the Tre Venezie) of northeastern Italy. But southern Italy also makes some fine wines that are beginning to become better known outside of Italy, as we discuss in the later section "The Sunny South of Italy."

Figure 11-1:
The wine regions of Italy.

Illustration by Lisa S. Reed

Reds Reign in Piedmont

Piedmont's claim to wine fame is the Nebbiolo (neb-bee-*oh*-lo) grape, a noble red variety that produces great wine only in northwestern Italy. The proof of Nebbiolo's nobility is its wines: Barolo (bah-*ro*-lo) and Barbaresco (bar-bah-*res*-co) are two of the world's great red wines. Both are DOCG wines made entirely from the Nebbiolo grape in the Langhe hills around Alba, and each is named after a village within its production zone.

Both Barolo and Barbaresco are robust reds — very dry, full-bodied, and high in tannin, acidity, and alcohol. Their aromas suggest tar, violets, roses, ripe strawberries, and (sometimes) truffles — the kind that grow in the ground, not the chocolate! Barolo is more full-bodied than Barbaresco and usually requires a bit more aging; otherwise, the two wines are very similar. Like most Italian wines, they show at their best with food. Good Barolo and Barbaresco wines usually start at about $40 and run to well over $100.

Most Barolos and Barbarescos are not meant to drink young. Production rules stipulate that Barolo isn't Barolo until it has aged for three years at the winery, or for five years if it's called *Riserva*. (Barbaresco's minimum aging is two years, or four for Riserva.) But both wines benefit from additional aging. When traditionally made, Barolo and Barbaresco often require 10 to 15 years' total aging, from the year of the vintage — and they usually benefit from a few hours of aeration before drinking to soften their somewhat tough tannins. (See Chapter 8 for instructions on aerating wine.)

Both Barbaresco and especially Barolo have something in common with Burgundy in France: *You must find a good producer to experience the wine at its best.* To guide you in that endeavor, we list the producers whom we consider the best of Barolo and Barbaresco, in our rough order of preference.

Barolo

Giacomo Conterno
Giuseppe Mascarello
Giuseppe Rinaldi
Bartolo Mascarello
Bruno Giacosa
Vietti
Ceretto (a.k.a. Bricco Rocche)
Gaja
Marcarini
Aldo Conterno
Roberto Voerzio
Luciano Sandrone
Paolo Scavino
Podere Colla
Elvio Cogno
Renato Ratti
Brovia
E. Pira & Figli
Clerico

Pio Cesare
Prunotto
Elio Altare
Cordero di Montezemolo
Luigi Pira
Manzone
Marchesi di Barolo
Michele Chiarlo
Conterno-Fantino
Giacomo Borgogno
Fontanafredda

Barbaresco

Bruno Giacosa
Gaja
Marchesi di Gresy
Ceretto (a.k.a. Bricco Asili)
Produttori del Barbaresco
DeForville

Some producers — including Giacomo Conterno, both Mascarellos, Giuseppe Rinaldi, and Bruno Giacosa — clearly make traditionally styled wines; others — such as Gaja, Altare, and Clerico — make modern-style wines; and some, such as Ceretto and Vietti, combine aspects of both winemaking styles. (We prefer the traditionally made wines, but all three styles have some excellent producers.) See the nearby sidebar "Traditional, new-style, and middle-ground" for more details about these styles.

Two other good Nebbiolo-based wines, the DOCGs Gattinara (gah-tee-*nah*-rah) and Ghemme (*gae*-mae), come from northern Piedmont, where the Nebbiolo grape is called *Spanna.* Although Gattinara and Ghemme seldom get the praise that the two big B's (Barolo and Barbaresco) enjoy, they offer the same enticing Nebbiolo aromas and flavors — especially Gattinara — in a less full-bodied style. Priced at $28 to $45 a bottle, Gattinara from a good producer may be one of the world's most underrated wines. Look for the Gattinaras by Antoniolo and Travaglini (Antoniolo is more expensive); Antichi Vigneti di Cantalupo (about $35 to $40) is the leading Ghemme producer.

Piedmont offers wines other than Barolo and Barbaresco; in the following sections, we discuss several red and white wines to try.

Weekday reds

The Piedmontese reserve serious wines like Barolo and Barbaresco for Sunday dinner or special occasions. What they drink on an everyday basis are the red wines Dolcetto (dohl-*chet*-to), Barbera (bar-*bear*-ah), and Nebbiolo wines made from grapes grown outside of the prestigious DOCG zones of Barolo and Barbaresco. Of the three, Dolcetto is the lightest-bodied and is usually the first red wine served in a Piedmontese meal.

Traditional, new-style, and middle-ground

One Barolo can differ from another (and one Barbaresco from another) quite a lot according to the wineries' production methods. Traditionally made wines are more tannic and need more time to develop but typically have greater longevity than the new-style wines. The new-style wines are fruitier in flavor but can be oaky and are ready to drink sooner — as soon as three to five years after they're released. Some producers are in one winemaking camp or the other, while many producers make their wines in a middle-ground style. In our experience, new-style wines are declining in popularity, whereas the traditional style is more popular than ever, and the ranks of producers whose wines are in the middle-ground style are growing.

Dolcetto

If you know enough Italian to translate the phrase *la dolce vita,* you may think that the name Dolcetto indicates a sweet wine. Actually, the Dolcetto grape tastes sweet, but the *wine* is distinctly dry and has some noticeable tannin, although the tannin isn't strong when you drink the wine with food. The aromas and flavors of Dolcetto include black pepper spice and red berry fruit. Dolcetto is often compared to Beaujolais (France's easy-drinking red wine; see Chapter 10), but it's drier and more tannic than most Beaujolais wines.

Most Dolcetto wines sell for $13 to $25. The best Dolcetto wines are from the zones of Dogliani, Diano d'Alba, and Alba; the labels of these wines carry the grape name, Dolcetto, along with the name of the area. Just about all our recommended Barolo producers make a Dolcetto, usually Dolcetto *d'Alba* (from Alba).

Two favorite producers of ours who happen to make only Dolcetto di Dogliani are Quinto Chionetti and Luigi Einaudi.

Barbera

While Dolcetto is unique to Piedmont, the Barbera grape is the third-most widely planted red grape variety in all of Italy. (Sangiovese is *the* most planted red variety, followed by Montepulciano.) But it's in Piedmont — specifically the Asti, Alba, and Monferrato wine zones — that Barbera excels. It's a red wine with high acidity and generous black-cherry fruit character. The wine's richness and weight vary according to the area where the grapes grow and, of course, the producer's style; some Barbera wines are impressively rich while others are delightfully easygoing. Barbera happens to be one of our favorite everyday wines, especially with pasta or pizza — or anything tomato-y.

Barbera d'Alba is generally a bit fuller, riper, and richer than the leaner Barbera d'Asti and Barbera di Monferrato. But Barbera d'Asti from certain old vineyards rivals Barbera d'Alba in richness and in power. (Link the *d'* with the word following it when pronouncing these names: *dal*-ba, *dahs*-tee.)

Barbera is more popular in the United States than it has ever been, and we couldn't be more delighted, because it's now easier to find. Two different styles of Barbera are available:

- ✔ Wine aged without wood or in *casks* (large oak containers that impart little, if any, oak flavor to the wine), which sells for about $15 to $28

- ✔ Oak-influenced Barbera wine aged in *barriques* (small, new barrels of French oak), which sells in the $30 to $50 range (somebody has to pay for those expensive barriques!)

Although both types of Barbera are very good, with a few exceptions, we prefer the simpler, less expensive, traditional style — although we do admit that some barrique-aged Barberas are quite good. Barbera is an unusual red grape variety in that it has practically no tannin, and so the tannins from the small oak barrels can complement Barbera wines.

Two particularly good producers of Barbera d'Alba are Vietti and Giacomo Conterno. Vietti makes a terrific single-vineyard Barbera d'Alba called Scarrone and a superb single-vineyard Barbera d'Asti called La Crena. Marchesi di Gresy also makes an excellent Barbera d'Asti.

Nebbiolo

A third weekday red from Piedmont is Nebbiolo (labeled as *Nebbiolo d'Alba* or *Langhe Nebbiolo,* depending on the vineyard location). The wine is lighter in body and easier to drink than either Barolo or Barbaresco, and it sells for about $25 to $30 a bottle. Another variation is Roero, the red version of which comes almost entirely from Nebbiolo. An advantage these Nebbiolo wines have over Barolo or Barbaresco is that you can drink them while they're young, as soon as they've been released for sale.

Whites in a supporting role

Almost all Piedmont's wines are red, but the region does boast two interesting dry whites:

- ✔ **Gavi,** named for a town in southern Piedmont, is a very dry wine with pronounced acidity, made from the Cortese grape. Most Gavis sell for $12 to $24, while a premium Gavi, La Scolca's Black Label, costs around $35.

- ✔ **Arneis** (ahr-*nase*) is a white wine produced in the Roero zone near Alba from a long-forgotten grape also called Arneis, which was rescued by Alfredo Currado, the recently deceased owner of the Vietti winery, more than 40 years ago. Arneis is a dry to medium-dry wine with rich texture. It's best when consumed within two years of the vintage; a bottle sells for $19 to $28. Besides Vietti's, look for Bruno Giacosa's and Ceretto's Arneis.

Another white Piedmontese variety getting attention lately is the previously obscure Timorasso, from the Alessandria area. Walter Massa, a local producer, is championing the cause of Timorasso as a varietal wine. Like most Piedmontese wines, Timorasso is a dry, fruity wine with lively acidity.

Tuscany the Beautiful

Florence, Siena, Michelangelo's David, the leaning tower of Pisa . . . the beautiful region of Tuscany has more than her share of attractions. Only one Italian wine can possibly compare in fame — and that, too, comes from Tuscany: Chianti. In the following sections, we talk about Chianti and a number of other great wines from Tuscany.

Chianti Classico and Chianti: Italy's great, underrated reds

The hills of central Tuscany are some of the most striking vineyard scenery on the face of the earth. And the red wines from this area, based on the Sangiovese grape variety, are among the best known and best loved of all Italian wines. But discussing the wine from this area today is complicated because what was once a single, collective wine zone with several subzones is now officially two distinct wine zones. Although the name *Chianti* once served to cover the entire area, it now refers specifically to one of those two wine zones. (*Chianti Classico* is the other.) Like friends of a family who has experienced a divorce, many wine people find it convenient to use the old family name to cover both parties of the split, although doing so is technically no longer correct.

Chianti Classico

Chianti Classico is a DOCG wine zone where grapes have grown for more than ten centuries. The 100-square-mile zone is hilly and varied: Some parts of the zone, such as the southern part close to the city of Siena, are relatively warm, while other parts are higher in altitude and cooler; the soil varies throughout. Therefore, Chianti Classico wines vary in style — in their degree of power or delicacy — according to where in the zone the grapes grow.

The Sangiovese grape variety must constitute at least 80 percent of any Chianti Classico wine. In practice, some producers use only Sangiovese; of those who use additional grape varieties, some use only native Tuscan varieties, such as Canaiolo or Mammolo, while others use international varieties, such as Cabernet Sauvignon or Merlot. The inclusion of white grape varieties, which had been required in the blend until 2002 and optional until 2006, is no longer permitted.

Besides varying according to their vineyard location and grape blend, Chianti Classico wines also vary in style according to their aging. *Riserva* wines must age for two years or more at the winery, and some of this aging is often in French oak; the best Chianti Classico Riservas have potential for long life.

Chianti Classico wines have aromas and flavors of tart cherries, violets, dry earth, and sometimes a slightly nutty character. They are dry and dry-textured, with firm tannin from the Sangiovese grape. The best Chianti Classico wines have very concentrated fruit character, even if the flavor is not pronounced. The wines usually taste best from five to eight years after the vintage — although in good vintages, they have no problem aging for ten or more years.

Although Chianti Classico is not a powerful wine, today's wines are richer and more concentrated than ever before — in some cases, too rich for us. Recent warm vintages in Europe, such as 1997, 2000, and 2003, have fed a trend toward ripeness, fleshiness of texture, and higher alcohol. The presence of international varieties and the use of French oak barriques for aging — especially for riservas —unduly influence many Chianti Classico wines. More than ever, you must choose your Chianti Classico producers with care.

The two exceptional recent vintages to look for in Chianti Classico are 2004 and 2006. Two very good older vintages are the 1999 and 2001.

We've compiled a list of our favorite Chianti Classico producers, Group A (for us, the best) and Group B (our other favorites), in alphabetical order within each group.

Group A	Group B
Badia a Coltibuono	Antinori
Castellare	Castello di Fonterutoli
Castell'in Villa	Castello di Volpaia
Castello dei Rampolla	Cecchi-Villa Cerna
Castello di Brolio	Fattoria La Massa
Felsina	Monsanto-Il Poggio
Fontodi	Nozzole
Il Palazzino	Querciabella
Isole e Olena	Ruffino
Riecine	San Felice
Riseccoli	Villa Cafaggio
San Giusto a Rentennano	

Another producer we admire greatly is Montevertine, who chose to drop the Chianti name from its labels almost 30 years ago but who produces excellent 100 percent Sangiovese wine in the Chianti Classico region.

Chianti Classico wines are generally between $20 and $30 a bottle, while Chianti Classico Riservas are a bit more costly, ranging from $35 to $50 per bottle. For us, basic Chianti Classico remains the best buy for the money.

Chianti

Chianti is a large wine zone extending through much of central Tuscany and surrounding the Chianti Classico area. The zone — all of it DOCG status, deservedly or not — has seven subzones. Chianti wines may use the name of the subzone where their grapes grow or the simpler appellation, Chianti, if their production does not qualify for a district name (if grapes from two subzones are blended, for example). The subzone that stands out in quality is the tiny Chianti Rufina (*roo*-fee-nah) area (not to be confused with the famous Chianti/Chianti Classico producer Ruffino). Of the remaining subzones, the Colli Senesi and Colli Fiorentini areas (Siena hills and Florence hills, respectively) enjoy the best reputation for their wines.

Chianti wine must contain at least 70 percent Sangiovese grapes and can be entirely Sangiovese. Both native and international varieties can be part of the wine, but depending on the subzone, Cabernet Sauvignon is limited to 10 or 15 percent. Unlike for Chianti Classico, white grape varieties can constitute up to 10 percent of the blend. Riserva wines must age for two years or more at the winery.

Chianti DOCG wines are a mixed lot, stylistically and qualitatively. Some are easy-drinking, fairly light, and inexpensive reds selling for as little as $12, while others are age-worthy and substantial and can cost up to $35. Like Chianti Classico, Chianti DOCG wines often have aromas of cherries and sometimes violets and have a flavor reminiscent of tart cherries. Like most Italian wines, they're delightful with food.

The two outstanding producers making Chianti DOCG wines are Frescobaldi and Selvapiana, both in the Rufina subzone.

Monumental Brunello di Montalcino

Chianti has been famous for centuries, but another great Tuscan wine, Brunello di Montalcino, exploded on the international scene only some 40 years ago, when the Biondi-Santi family, a leading producer, presented some of its oldest wines to writers. The 1888 and 1891 vintages were still drinking well; in fact, they were in excellent shape! The rest is history, as they say.

Today, Brunello di Montalcino (brew-*nel*-lo dee mon-tahl-*chee*-no), a DOCG wine, is one of the greatest, long-lived red wines in existence. It has a price tag to match: from $50 to more than $200 a bottle (for wines by the producer Soldera).

The wine is named for the town of Montalcino, a walled fortress town south of the Chianti Classico zone. Brunello di Montalcino comes from a particular *clone*, or strain, of Sangiovese, Tuscany's great red variety. It's an intensely concentrated, tannic wine that demands aging (up to 20 years) when traditionally made and benefits from several hours of aeration before serving. Lately, some producers in Montalcino have been making a more approachable style of Brunello.

Rosso di Montalcino is a less expensive ($25 to $35), readier-to-drink wine made from the same grape and grown in the same production area as Brunello di Montalcino. Rosso di Montalcino from a good Brunello producer is a great value, offering you a glimpse of Brunello's majesty without breaking the bank.

To really appreciate Brunello di Montalcino, try a wine from one of the producers recommended in the following list (in our rough order of preference). Traditional winemakers, such as Biondi-Santi, Soldera, Costanti, Canalicchio di Sopra, and Pertimali, make wines that need 15 to 20 years of aging in good vintages. (Great vintages include 2006, 2004, 2001, 1999, 1997, 1995, 1990, 1988, 1985, and 1975; all the vintages from 1997 and older are ready to drink). Brunellos from avowed modern-style producers, such as Caparzo, Altesino, and Col d'Orcia, can be enjoyed about ten years from the vintage. Younger than ten years — drink Rosso di Montalcino instead!

Great Brunello di Montalcino Producers

Soldera, Case Basse (very expensive)	Pertimali di Livio Sassetti
Biondi-Santi (expensive)	Castello Banfi
Costanti	Il Greppone Mazzi
Ciacci Piccolomini	Poggio Antico
Canalicchio di Sopra	Caparzo (La Casa Vineyard)
Il Poggione	La Torre
Altesino (Montesoli Vineyard)	Castel Giocondo

Vino Nobile, Carmignano, and Vernaccia

Three more Tuscan wines of note include two reds — Vino Nobile di Montepulciano (*no*-be-lay dee mon-tay-pul-chee-*ah*-no) and Carmignano (car-mee-*nyah*-no) — and Tuscany's most renowned white wine, Vernaccia di San Gimignano (ver-*nah*-cha dee san gee-mee-*nyah*-noh). All three are DOCG wines.

The Montepulciano wine zone, named after the town of Montepulciano, is southeast of the Chianti Classico zone and within the confines of the Chianti zone. Vino Nobile's principal grape is the Prugnolo Gentile, a local name for Sangiovese. Of central Tuscany's big three red DOCG wines — Chianti Classico, Brunello di Montalcino, and Vino Nobile di Montepulciano — Vino Nobile is generally the most delicate in style. From a good producer, its quality can rival that of the better Chianti Classicos.

Brunello with American roots

The largest producer of Brunello di Montalcino is actually an American family — the Mariani family of Long Island, New York. In 1978, they established Castello Banfi in the southern part of the Montalcino zone, and today they are leaders in research into the grapes and *terroirs* of Montalcino.

Sangiovese at the table

Lighter Chianti wines go well with pasta, prosciutto, and roast chicken or squab. With Chianti Classicos and riservas, lamb, roast turkey, veal, steak, and roast beef are fine accompaniments. For the robust Brunello di Montalcino and super-Tuscan wines, try pheasant, steak, game, or chunks of fresh Parmesan cheese. Serve these wines at cool room temperature, 62 to 66 degrees Fahrenheit (16 to 19 degrees Celsius).

Nine Vino Nobile producers we recommend are Boscarelli, Fattoria del Cerro, Avignonesi, Lodola Nuova, La Braccesca, Dei, Tenuta Trerose, Fassati, and Poliziano. Most Vino Nobile producers also make a lighter, readier-to-drink wine, Rosso di Montepulciano.

The Carmignano wine region is directly west of Florence. Although Sangiovese is the main grape of Carmignano — just as it is for Chianti — Cabernet Sauvignon is also one of this wine zone's traditional grapes. As a result, Carmignano's taste is rather akin to that of a Chianti with the finesseful touch of a Bordeaux. Two outstanding producers of Carmignano are Villa di Capezzana and Ambra.

Vernaccia di San Gimignano is named for the medieval walled town of San Gimignano, west of the Chianti Classico zone. Vernaccia is generally a fresh white wine with a slightly oily texture and almond-like flavor; drink it young. For an unusual interpretation, try the oak-aged riserva Terre di Tufo, from Teruzzi & Puthod, a very good Vernaccia (about $15). Most Vernaccias are in the $12 to $16 range. Besides Teruzzi & Puthod, producers to seek are Montenidoli, Mormoraia, Cecchi, and Casale-Falchini.

Two more reds and a white

So many good Tuscan wines exist that we sometimes don't know when to stop talking about them (that's why we wrote *Italian Wine For Dummies!*). Three more deserve a mention here:

- ✔ **Pomino** (po-*mee*-no) is the name of a red and a white wine from a tiny area of the same name, which lies within the Rufina subzone of Chianti. Pomino has long been a stronghold of French varieties, right in the heart of Sangiovese-land. The Frescobaldi family, the major producer of Chianti Rufina, is also the main landowner in Pomino, and makes both a Pomino Rosso and a Pomino Bianco — the red more noteworthy of the two.

  - Pomino Rosso is a blend of Cabernet Sauvignon, Cabernet Franc, Merlot, Sangiovese, Canaiolo — and in Frescobaldi's case, also

Pinot Nero (the Italian name for Pinot Noir). It sounds like a crazy blend, but it works!

- Pomino Bianco blends Chardonnay, Pinot Bianco, Trebbiano, and often Pinot Grigio.

Besides Frescobaldi, another fine producer of Pomino is Fattoria Petrognano. Pomino costs about $21 to $26.

Super-Tuscans

When Chianti sales lost momentum in the 1970s, progressive producers caught the attention of the world by creating new red wines that are still collectively known as *super-Tuscans,* although this term is being used less and less. The pioneering examples include Sassicaia (sas-ee-*kye*-ah), from Marchese Incisa della Rocchetta, plus Tignanello (tee-nyah-*nel*-loh) and Solaia (so-*lye*-ah) from Marchesi Antinori.

The so-called super-Tuscan category includes dozens of wines. Their grape blends vary; some producers use only native Tuscan grapes, mainly Sangiovese, while others use international varieties, such as Cabernet Sauvignon, Merlot, or Syrah, or a blend of Italian and international grapes. The wines can range in taste from very good Chianti-like wines to Bordeaux-type or California Cabernet–type wines, depending on their varying amounts of Sangiovese, Cabernet Sauvignon, Merlot, and so on — and their specific vineyard areas.

What these wines have in common is that most are expensive, ranging from $50 to more than $100. A few of the most famous super-Tuscan wines — Sassicaia, Ornellaia, Masseto, and Solaia — that are prized by wine collectors can cost more than $200 in good vintages (see Appendix C).

Here are ten of our favorite super-Tuscan wines (listed alphabetically, including their grape blend and the producer's name in parentheses). These wines are some of the best made in Tuscany today. Many other so-called super-Tuscans aren't so special and aren't a good value.

- Cepparello — all Sangiovese (Isole e Elena; owner Paolo DiMarchi insists it isn't a super-Tuscan. Whatever it is, it's a great wine.)
- Masseto — all Merlot (Tenuta dell'Ornellaia)
- Ornellaia — mainly Cabernet Sauvignon; some Merlot and/or Cabernet Franc (Tenuta dell'Ornellaia)
- Percarlo — 100 percent Sangiovese (San Giusto a Rentennano)
- Le Pergole Torte — entirely Sangiovese (Montevertine)
- Sammarco — 80 percent Cabernet Sauvignon, 20 percent Sangiovese (Castello dei Rampolla)
- Sassicaia — 75 percent Cabernet Sauvignon, 25 percent Cabernet Franc (Tenuta San Guido)
- I Sodi di San Niccolò — mostly Sangiovese (Castellare di Castellina)
- Solaia — 80 percent Cabernet Sauvignon, 20 percent Sangiovese (Antinori)
- Tignanello — 80 percent Sangiovese, 20 percent Cabernet Sauvignon (Antinori)

✔ **Morellino** (moh-rehl-*lee*-no) is the name for Sangiovese in the hilly area around the town of Scansano (scahn-*sah*-no) in the Maremma region of southwest Tuscany. Most **Morellino di Scansano** wines offer an easy-drinking, inexpensive ($14 to $22) alternative to Chianti — although a few high-end wines exist, such as Fattoria Le Pupille and Moris Farms.

✔ **Vermentino,** an aromatic white grape variety grown in Sardinia and Liguria, has become a hot variety in Tuscany, especially along the coast. The wine is a crisp, medium-bodied, flavorful white from Maremma that's usually unoaked, and sells for $18 to $24. Many leading Tuscan producers, such as Antinori and Cecchi, are making attractive Vermentino wines.

The Tre Venezie

The three regions in the northeastern corner of Italy (refer to Figure 11-1) are often referred to as the *Tre Venezie* — the Three Venices — because they were once part of the Venetian Empire. Colorful historical associations aside, each of these regions, which we discuss in the following sections, produces red and white wines that are among the most popular Italian wines outside of Italy — as well as at home.

Three gentle wines from Verona

Chances are that if your first dry Italian wine wasn't Chianti or Pinot Grigio, it was one of Verona's big three: the white Soave (so-*ah*-vay) or the reds, Valpolicella (val-po-lee-*chel*-lah) or Bardolino (bar-do-*lee*-noh). These once enormously popular wines hail from northeast Italy, around the picturesque city of Verona — Romeo and Juliet's hometown — and the beautiful Lake Garda.

Of Verona's two reds, Valpolicella has more body; Valpolicella wines whose labels state that they're made in the *ripasso* method (a second fermentation of sorts) are the fullest and richest, although still medium-bodied wines. The lighter Bardolino is a particularly pleasant warm-weather wine when served slightly cool. Some producers are now making Bardolino in a heavier style, but we suspect that trend won't gain traction with wine drinkers. In fact, one of our favorite styles of Bardolino, Chiaretto (key-ah-*ret*-toh) — a rosé wine — goes in the completely opposite direction, capturing the vivacity and charm of the Bardolino area.

Soave can be a fairly neutral-tasting unoaked white or a characterful wine with fruity and nutty flavor, depending on the producer. Look for wines labeled as *Soave Classico,* from the hilly heartland of the Soave area, to experience a Soave with the concentration and depth that is bringing new respect to this long-popular area.

Most Valpolicella, Bardolino, and Soave wines are priced from $12 to $18, as are two other white wines of the region, Bianco di Custoza and Lugana. Some of the better Veronese wines, from the following recommended producers, have slightly higher prices:

- ✔ **Valpolicella:** Quintarelli, Allegrini, Le Ragose, Bertani, Alighieri, Tommasi, Masi
- ✔ **Bardolino:** Le Fraghe, Guerrieri-Rizzardi, Corte Gardoni, Cavalchina
- ✔ **Soave:** Pieropan, Gini, Inama, Pra, Suavia, Santa Sofia, Coffele

Amarone della Valpolicella (also simply known as *Amarone*) is a variant of Valpolicella and one of Italy's most full-bodied red wines. It's made from the same grape varieties (refer to Table 11-1), but the ripe grapes dry indoors on mats for several months before fermentation, thus concentrating their sugar and flavors. The resulting wine is a rich, potent (14 to 16 percent alcohol), long-lasting wine, perfect for a cold winter night and a plate of mature cheeses. Some of the best producers of Amarone are Quintarelli, Bertani, Masi, Tommasi, Le Ragose, and Allegrini.

The Austrian-Italian alliance

If you have traveled much in Italy, you probably realize that, in spirit, Italy isn't one unified country but 20 or more politically conjoined entities. Consider Trentino-Alto-Adige. Not only is this mountainous region (the northernmost in Italy; refer to Figure 11-1) dramatically different from the rest of Italy, but also the mainly German-speaking Alto-Adige (or South Tyrol) in the north is completely different from the Italian-speaking Trentino in the south. (Before World War I, the South Tyrol was part of the Austro-Hungarian Empire.) The wines of the two areas are different, too — yet the area is considered a single region!

Alto-Adige produces red wine, but most of it goes to Germany, Austria, and Switzerland. The rest of the world sees Alto-Adige's white wines — Pinot Grigio, Chardonnay, Pinot Bianco, Sauvignon, Kerner, Müller Thurgau, and Gewürztraminer — which are all varietal wines and are priced mainly in the $14 to $22 range.

One local red wine to seek out is Alto-Adige's Lagrein, from a native grape variety of the same name. It's a hearty wine, somewhat spicy and rustic in style, but it offers a completely unique taste experience. Hofstätter and Alois Lageder are two producers who make a particularly good Lagrein.

Alto-Adige produces arguably Italy's best white wines, along with nearby Friuli (see the next section). Four producers to look for are Alois Lageder, Hofstätter, Tiefenbrunner, and Abbazia di Novacella. Here are some highlights of each:

- ✔ Lageder's Pinot Bianco from the Haberlehof vineyard and his Sauvignon from the Lehenhof vineyard are exceptional examples of their grape varieties and are among the best wines from these two varieties that we've tasted.

- ✔ Hofstätter's Gewürztraminer, from the Kolbenhof vineyard, is as fine a wine as you can find from this tricky grape variety. Hofstätter also makes one of Italy's best Pinot Nero wines, Villa Barthenau.

- ✔ Tiefenbrunner's Müller Thurgau (*mool*-lair *toor*-gow) from his Feldmarschall Vineyard (the region's highest in altitude) could well be the wine world's best wine from this otherwise lackluster variety.

- ✔ Abbazia di Novacella, a working Augustinian monastery and Italy's northernmost winery, produces a range of fine white wines, including a world-class Kerner (a viscous, flavorful wine from a Germanic variety), from $19 to $22. Its premium Kerner, Praepositus, is even better ($29 to $32).

Trentino, the southern part of the Trentino-Alto-Adige region, is not without its own notable wines. Some excellent Chardonnay wines come from Trentino; Pojer & Sandri and Roberto Zeni make two of the best. Elisabetta Foradori is a Trentino producer who specializes in red wines made from the local variety, Teroldego (teh-*roll*-day-go) Rotaliano. Her best red wines, Granato and Sgarzon, are based on Teroldego and get rave reviews from wine critics. Also, one of Italy's leading sparkling wine producers, Ferrari, is in Trentino. (See Chapter 15 for more information on sparkling wine producers.)

The far side: Friuli-Venezia Giulia

Italy has justifiably been known in the wine world for its red wines. But the region of Friuli-Venezia Giulia (refer to Figure 11-1), led by the pioneering winemaker, the late Mario Schiopetto, has made the world conscious of the indisputable quality of Italy's white wines as well.

Near the region's border with Slovenia, to its east, the districts of Collio and Colli Orientali del Friuli produce the best white wines of Friuli — as the region is generally called. Red wines do exist in Friuli, but the white wines are renowned. In addition to Pinot Grigio, Pinot Bianco, Chardonnay, and Sauvignon, two local favorites are Friulano (formerly called Tocai Friulano) and Ribolla Gialla (both rich, full, and viscous).

A truly great white wine made here is Silvio Jermann's Vintage Tunina, a blend of five varieties, including Pinot Bianco, Sauvignon, and Chardonnay. Vintage Tunina is a rich, full-bodied, long-lived white of world-class status. It sells in the $55 to $65 range and, frankly, it's worth the money. Give the wine about ten years to age and then try it with rich poultry dishes or pasta.

We list our recommended producers in Friuli alphabetically:

Great Producers in Friuli

Abbazia di Rosazzo/Walter Filiputti

Borgo Conventi

Girolamo Dorigo

Livio Felluga

Gravner

Jermann

Miani

Lis Neris-Pecorari

Plozner

Doro Princic

Ronco del Gelso

Ronco del Gnemiz

Ronco dei Rosetti, of Zamò

Ronco dei Tassi

Russiz Superiore, of Marco Felluga

Mario Schiopetto

Venica & Venica

Vie di Romans

Villa Russiz

Volpe Pasini

The Sunny South of Italy

Rome is generally regarded as the dividing line between northern and southern Italy. Northern Italy is more industrial and affluent, with several major cities, such as Milan and Turin, and it is the home of Italy's most renowned wines — Barolo, Chianti Classico, Brunello di Montalcino, Soave, Valpolicella, Amarone, and so forth (as we discuss earlier in this chapter). Southern Italy, which is mainly agricultural, has only one important city, Naples, plus the beautiful, heart-stopping Amalfi Coast. Until recently, very few "important" wines came from southern Italy.

Italy's South produces more wine than the North. Two southern regions, Puglia and Sicily, are by far the most productive in all of Italy. Historically, many of the wines from southern Italy were pedestrian in quality, and much of the huge production was sold in bulk to northern Italy and other nearby countries.

Pinot Grigio, a marketing miracle

Pinot Grigio — the biggest-selling imported wine in the United States — is produced in all three of the Tre Venezie regions. Santa Margherita was the first brand to establish itself solidly on the American market, and it still sells extremely well in restaurants. Cavit, Folonari, and MezzaCorona, are other leading producers. The wine is so successful that you could say Pinot Grigio is the new Chardonnay.

Some people theorize that the musical name is part of the wine's success — that U.S. wine drinkers like to say "Pinot Grigio" just as they once liked to say "Pouilly-Fuissé." But obviously, people also like the taste of Pinot Grigio. It's fairly light-bodied, with crisp acidity and fairly neutral aromas and flavors — an easy-drinking wine that goes well with most foods. Pinot Grigio is so successful, in fact, that many California wineries are growing the Pinot Gris grape and using the Italian name, Pinot Grigio, on their wine labels. The Californian versions tend to be fruitier, fuller-bodied and sometimes slightly sweet compared to the Italian wines.

But within the last two decades, a wine renaissance has taken place. Sicily and Campania in particular are now making some of Italy's best wines. The richness of the South includes both white wines and reds.

Here we give you a portrait of southern Italy's four most important wine regions:

- ✔ **Sicily:** One of Sicily's most exciting wine zones is Etna, on the slopes of the active volcano, Mount Etna, in the northeastern part of the island. This zone produces superb cool-climate red and white wines. The reds, called Etna Rosso, are based on Nerello Mascalese, a variety indigenous to the area. The same grape is also the mainstay of other red wines, including the great Faro wine produced by Palari near neighboring Messina. Nerello Mascalese wines resemble Pinot Noirs but with greater acidity. Back in the Etna zone, the indigenous white variety called Carricante makes some of Italy's finest white wines, including Etna Bianco — of which Pietramarina, made by Benanti, is the stellar example.

  Sicily's long-established wineries, such as Duca di Salaparuta (also known as Corvo) and Regaleali, now have the company of exciting, new wineries, such as Planeta, COS, Morgante, Palari, and Benanti. Many of Sicily's best reds come from Sicily's superb variety, Nero d'Avola.

- ✔ **Campania:** The Avellino province, near Naples, produces some of the best wines in southern Italy. A full-bodied, tannic red, Taurasi — a DOCG wine from the Aglianico variety — is one of the great, long-lived red wines in Italy. Premium producers are Mastroberardino (look for his single-vineyard Taurasi, called Radici), Feudi di San Gregorio, and Terredora. The same producers also make two unique whites, Greco di Tufo and Fiano di Avellino. They're flavorful, viscous wines with great aging capacity that sell in the $16 to $24 range. Falanghina ($13 to $19) is another exciting white Campania wine.

- ✔ **Basilicata:** Mountainous, cool Basilicata is the home of southern Italy's greatest red variety, Aglianico, which produces Aglianico del Vulture. The wine is similar to Taurasi but not quite so intense and full-bodied. D'Angelo and Paternoster are leading producers.

- ✔ **Apulia:** Better known by its Italian name, Puglia, this generally hot region makes more wine than any other in Italy — mainly inexpensive, full-bodied red wines, such as Salice Salentino (from the native variety, Negroamaro) and Primitivo, a cousin of red Zinfandel. Leading producers include Cosimo Taurino, Leone de Castris, Agricole Vallone, and Antinori (whose Puglia estate and wines are named Tormaresca).

Snapshots from the Rest of Italy

Italy's wines are by no means confined to the regions we discuss individually in the earlier sections of this chapter. A quick tour of some of Italy's other regions proves the point. (For more complete info on the wines of these other regions, see *Italian Wine For Dummies*.) Refer to Figure 11-1 for the location of each of the following regions:

- **Lombardy:** Italy's most populated region, with its chic fashion capital, Milan, huge Lombardy (known as *Lombardia* in Italian) is the source of a vast array of wines. In the northern part of this northerly region, near the Swiss border, the Valtellina wine district produces four relatively light-bodied red wines from the Nebbiolo grape: Sassella, Inferno, Grumello, and Valgella. Most of these wines are moderately priced ($18 to $30) and, unlike Barolo, can be enjoyed young. Lombardy is also the home of Italy's best sparkling wine district, Franciacorta.

- **Emilia-Romagna:** This region in central-western Italy is the home of Lambrusco, one of Italy's most successful wines on export markets. Lambrusco also comes as a delicious, dry wine, which complements the rich Bolognese *salumi* (dried meats). Bologna and Parma, two gastronomic meccas, are in this region.

- **Liguria:** This narrow region south of Piedmont, along the Italian Riviera, is also the home of Cinque Terre, one of Italy's most picturesque areas. The region's two fine white wines, Vermentino and Pigato, are ideal with Liguria's pasta with pesto, its signature dish.

- **Marches (or Marche):** Verdicchio is a dry, inexpensive white wine that's widely available and seems to improve in quality with every vintage. Try the Verdicchio from Villa Bucci, Fazi-Battaglia, Colonnara, Garofoli, Sartorelli, Tavignano, Bonci, or Umani Ronchi, great values at $10 to $18. Marche's best red wine, Rosso Cònero, made mainly from Sangiovese, is one of Italy's fine red wine buys at $15 to $21.

- **Umbria:** Home to the towns of Perugia and Assisi, Umbria makes some good reds and whites. Orvieto, a white, is widely available for $10 to $11 from Tuscan producers, such as Antinori and Ruffino. Two interesting red wines are Torgiano, a Chianti-like blend (try Lungarotti's Rubesco Riserva DOCG), and Sagrantino di Montefalco DOCG, a medium-bodied, characterful wine made from the local Sagrantino grape.

- **Latium (or Lazio):** This region around Rome makes the ubiquitous, inexpensive Frascati, a light, fairly neutral wine from the Trebbiano grape; Fontana Candida is a popular brand.

- **Abruzzo:** Montepulciano d'Abruzzo, an inexpensive, easy-drinking, low tannin, low-acid red wine, comes from here; it's a terrific everyday red, especially from a quality producer such as Masciarelli. Abruzzo is also home to two other fine producers, Cataldi Madonna and the late, great Edoardo Valentini, whose sought-after Trebbiano d'Abruzzo is perhaps the world's greatest white wine from the otherwise ordinary Trebbiano grape; the Valentini family also makes a fantastic rosé, Cerasuolo, from the Montepulciano d'Abruzzo variety.

- **Sardinia:** This large Mediterranean island off the eastern coast of Italy makes delicate white wines and characterful reds from native grape varieties and from international varieties, such as Cabernet Sauvignon. Sella & Mosca, Argiolas, and Santadi are three leading producers. Two of the more popular Sardinian wines are the white Vermentino and the red Cannonau (a local version of Grenache), both of which sell in the $11 to $16 range.

Chapter 12

Spain, Germany, and Elsewhere in Europe

. . . .

In This Chapter

▶ Spain on the rise

▶ Great finds from Portugal

▶ Germany's unique ways

▶ Austria's exciting dry whites and unique reds

▶ The Greek renaissance

. . . .

*I*n the past, no one ever used the phrase *European wine* when talking generally about the wines of France, Italy, Spain, Portugal, and Germany. The wines had nothing in common. But today, two factors have changed the way we look at the wines of these countries. First, the wines of the European Union member countries now share a common legislative umbrella, within the European Union. Second, non-European wines — from California, Australia, Chile, and Argentina — have inundated the U.S. market, popularizing a nomenclature (varietal names, such as Chardonnay) and flavors (fruity, fruitier, fruitiest) foreign to the European, or "Old World," model.

When we compare Europe's wines to non-European, or "New World," wines (see Part IV), we notice that the diverse wines of Europe have many things in common after all. Most European wines are usually named for their place of production rather than their grape (see Chapter 4); European winemaking is tethered to tradition and regulations; the wines, for the most part, have local flavor instead of conforming to an international concept of how wine should taste (although, sadly, we're seeing an emerging "internationalization" of wine styles); and these wines are relatively low in fruitiness. European wines tend to embody the traditions of the people who make them and the flavors of the place where their vines grow — unlike New World wines, which tend to embody grape variety and a general fruitiness of flavor.

Despite these similarities among European wines, the countries of Europe each make distinctly different wines. The importance of France and Italy has earned each of these countries a whole chapter (see Chapters 10 and 11, respectively). Here, we concentrate on the next five most important wine-producing countries: Spain, Portugal, Germany, Austria, and Greece.

Intriguing Wines from Old Spain

Spain is a hot, dry, mountainous country with more vineyard land than any other nation on earth. It ranks third in the world in wine production, after France and Italy.

Spanish wine has awakened from a long period of dormancy and under-achievement. Spain is now one of the wine world's most vibrant arenas. For decades, only Spain's most famous red wine region, Rioja (ree-*oh*-ha), and the classic fortified wine region, Sherry, had any international presence for fine wines. (For more on Sherry, see Chapter 16.) Now, many other wine regions in Spain are making seriously good wines. Besides Rioja, the following regions, which we explore in the next sections, are an important part of the wine quality picture in Spain today, and their wines are generally available (see Figure 12-1):

- **Ribera del Duero** (ree-*bear*-ah dell *dwair*-oh), now famous for its high quality red wines, has helped to ignite world interest in Spanish wines.

- **Priorato** (pree-oh-*rah*-to), mountainous and inaccessible, and one of the world's "hot" new regions for red wine, is north of the city of Tarragona, in northeast Spain.

- **Penedés** (pen-eh-*dais*) is a large producer of both red and white wines and famous for its sparkling wines (known as *Cava;* see Chapter 15).

- The **Rías Baixas** (*ree*-ahse *byche*-ahse) region of Galicia (gah-*leeth*-ee-ah) is gaining acclaim for its exciting white wine, Albariño.

- **Navarra** (nah-*var*-rah), an area long known for its dry rosé wines, is an increasingly strong red wine region.

- **Bierzo** (bee-*ur*-zoh), in northwestern Spain, boasts an exciting native grape called Mencia that makes vibrant red wines.

- **Toro** is quickly emerging as one of Spain's best red wine regions.

- **Rueda** (roo-*ae*-dah) is known for well-made, inexpensive white wines.

Figure 12-1:
The wine
regions of
Spain.

Illustration by Lisa S. Reed

Spain's wine laws provide for a multilevel Protected Designation of Origin (PDO) category — or, as they call it in Spain, the *Denominación de Origen Protegida (DOP)* category:

- ✔ The fundamental level is *Denominación de Origen (DO);* 67 wine regions hold this status.

- ✔ A higher classification, *Denominación de Origen Calificada (DOCa),* "Qualified Designation of Origin," has existed since 1991; so far, Rioja and Priorato are the only two regions that have been awarded the DOCa.

- ✔ *Vino de Calidad con Indicación Geográfica,* or "Quality Wine with a Geographic Indication," applies to six wine areas, and ranks lower than DO in status.

- ✔ The *Vino de Pago* designation refers to individual wine estates *(pago)* that have earned special status apart from whichever DO zone the estate is located within. Thirteen wine estates are in this category, including the very fine Dominio de Valdepusa estate.

Other Spanish wines with geographic indications fall into the Protected Geographic Indication (PGI) category, or *Indicación Geográfica Protegida (IGP)* in Spain — or, in the traditional parlance, *Vino de la Tierra.* See Chapter 4 for more about appellation systems.

Spain's classic wines start with Rioja

Rioja, in north-central Spain (see Figure 12-1), has historically been the country's major red wine region (even if today Ribera del Duero and Priorato are catching up — fast!). Red wines dominate in La Rioja. About 80 percent of its wines are red, 10 percent *rosado* (rosé), and 10 percent white.

The principal grape in Rioja is Tempranillo (tem-prah-*nee*-yoh), Spain's greatest red variety. But regulations permit another three varieties for reds — Garnacha (known elsewhere as Grenache), Graciano (known elsewhere as Carignan), and Mazuelo — and red Rioja wine is typically a blend of three or more varieties. Some producers also use Cabernet Sauvignon in their red Rioja. The Marqués de Riscal is one of the few wineries legally allowed to use Cabernet Sauvignon in its Rioja blend, because this variety had been growing on its property before regulations for Rioja existed.

The Rioja region has three districts: the cooler, Atlantic-influenced Rioja Alavesa and Rioja Alta areas and the warmer Rioja Baja zone. Most of the best Riojas are made from grapes in the two cooler districts, but some Riojas are blended from grapes of all three districts.

Traditional production for red Rioja wine involved many years of aging in small barrels of American oak before release, which created pale, gentle wines that lacked fruitiness. The trend has been to replace some of the oak aging with bottle aging, resulting in wines that taste much fresher. Another trend, among more progressive winemakers, is to use barrels made of French oak along with barrels of American oak — which has traditionally given Rioja its characteristic vanilla aroma. (See Chapter 5 for a discussion of oak barrels.)

Regardless of style, red Rioja wines have several faces, according to how long they age before being released from the winery.

- Some wines receive no oak aging at all and are released young; the name for these fresh, youthful wines is *joven,* which means "young." (Sometimes producers use the term *sin crianza,* "without aging.") About 90 percent of all *rosado* and white wines are *joven.*

- Some wines age in oak and in bottle for two years at the winery and are labeled *crianza;* these wines are still fresh and fruity in style.

- Other wines age for three years and carry the designation *reserva.*

- The finest wines age for five years or longer, earning the status of *gran reserva.*

These terms appear on the labels — if not on the front label, then on a rear label, which is the seal of authenticity for Rioja wines.

Prices start at $10 to $12 for the youngest Riojas, including *rosados* and whites, $13 to $15 for *crianza* reds, and go to $60 and up for some *gran reservas*. The best recent vintages for Rioja are 2009, 2008, 2005, 2004, 2001, 1995, and 1994. Both 2004 and 2001 are exceptional Rioja vintages and are ready to drink.

The following Rioja producers are particularly consistent in quality for their red wines:

- CVNE (Compañía Vinícola del Norte de España), commonly referred to as CUNE (*coo*-nay)
- Bodegas Muga
- R. Lopez de Heredia
- La Rioja Alta
- Marqués de Murrieta Ygay
- Marqués de Riscal
- Roda

Most white Riojas these days are fresh, clean, fairly neutral wines, but Marqués de Murrieta and R. Lopez de Heredia still make a traditional white Rioja, golden-colored and oak-aged, from a blend of local white grape varieties, predominantly Viura. We find both of these traditional whites fascinating: flavorful, voluptuous, with attractive traces of oxidation, and capable of aging. They're not everybody's cup of tea, true, but the wines sure have character! They have so much presence that they can accompany foods normally associated with red wine, as well as traditional Spanish food, such as paella or seafood. The Murrieta white sells for about $23. The Lopez de Heredia whites, which are aged for ten years or more before being released, sell for about $27 for the Viña Tondonia Crianza, $40 for the recently released Viña Tondonia 1996 Blanco Reserva, and more than $100 for the Viña Tondonia Blanco Gran Reservas. Lopez de Heredia also produces a less expensive white, Viña Gravonia; the current Viña Gravonia Reserva sells for about $25.

Ribera del Duero's serious red wines

Ribera del Duero, two hours north of Madrid by auto, is one of Spain's most dynamic wine regions. Perhaps nowhere else in the world does the Tempranillo grape variety (called Tinto Fino here) reach such heights, making wines with body, deep color, and finesse. For many years, one producer, the legendary Vega Sicilia, dominated the Ribera del Duero area. In fact, Spain's single most famous great wine is Vega Sicilia's Unico

(Tempranillo, with 20 percent Cabernet Sauvignon) — an intense, concentrated, tannic red wine with enormous longevity; it ages for ten years in casks and then sometimes ages further in the bottle before it's released. Unico is available mainly in top Spanish restaurants. The 2000 Unico, the last vintage generally available in U.S. retail stores, sells in the $350 to $400 price range — per bottle, that is. Even Unico's younger, less intense, and more available sibling, the Vega Sicilia Tinto Valbuena, retails in the $150 to $200 range.

But the days when Vega Sicilia was the only renowned red wine in Ribera del Duero are long gone. Alejandro Fernández's Pesquera, entirely Tempranillo, has earned high praise over the past 20 years. Pesquera is a big, rich, oaky, tannic wine with intense fruit character that ages amazingly well. The reserva sells for about $42 to $50 while the younger Pesquera Crianza is $27. The reserva of Fernández's other winery in the area, Condado de Haza, sells in the $34 to $49 range — depending on the vintage. Three other fine producers of Ribera del Duero are Bodegas Mauro, Viña Pedrosa, and Bodegas Téofilo Reyes, who all make red wines that rival Pesquera.

Priorato: Emerging from the past

Back in the 12th century, monks founded a monastery (or "priory") in the harsh, inaccessible Sierra de Montsant Mountains, about 100 miles southwest of Barcelona in the Catalonia region, and planted vines on the steep hillsides. As time passed, the monastery closed. The vineyards became abandoned because life was simply too difficult in this area. In time, the area became known as Priorat, or Priorato.

Cut to the 20th century — in fact about 30 short years ago. Enterprising winemakers, among them Alvaro Palacios, rediscovered the area and decided that conditions were ideal for making powerful red wines, especially from old vines planted by locals early in the 20th century.

All of a sudden, previously unheard of Priorato became the Spanish wine region in the spotlight. Yet Priorato hasn't become a tourist destination, because it's so difficult to reach. The region's volcanic soil, composed mainly of slate and schist, is so infertile that not much other than grapes can grow there. The climate is harshly continental: very hot, dry summers and very cold winters. The steep slopes are terraced, and many vineyards, therefore, can be worked only by hand. And grape yields are very low.

Amazingly rich, powerful red wines — made primarily from Garnacha and Carignan, two of Spain's native varieties — have emerged from this harsh landscape. Many are as rugged as the land, with high tannin and alcohol; some wines are so high in alcohol that they have an almost Port-like sweetness. Because winemaking in Priorato isn't cost-effective, to say the least, and the quantities of each wine are so small, the wines are necessarily quite expensive (prices begin at about $40). Clos Erasmus, arguably the finest Priorato, retails in the $175 to $185 range.

Priorato reds to look for include Clos Mogador, Clos Erasmus, Alvaro Palacios, Clos Martinet, Morlanda, Mas d'En Gil, and Pasanau. For us, Pasanau Priorato is a particularly good value.

Other Spanish regions to know

The action in Spanish wines — especially when value is your concern — definitely doesn't end with Rioja, Ribera del Duero, and Priorato. Here, we discuss a few more noteworthy Spanish wine regions.

Penedés

The Penedés wine region is in Catalonia, southwest of Barcelona (refer to Figure 12-1). It is the home of most Spanish sparkling wines, known as *Cava*, which we discuss in Chapter 15.

Any discussion of Penedés's still wines must begin with Torres, one of the world's great family-owned wineries. Around 1970, Miguel Torres pioneered the making of wines in Spain from French varieties, such as Cabernet Sauvignon and Chardonnay, along with local grapes, such as Tempranillo and Garnacha.

All the Torres wines are clean, well made, reasonably priced, and widely available. They start around $9 or $10 for the red called Sangre de Toro (Garnacha-Carignan), $11 for Coronas (Tempranillo–Cabernet Sauvignon) and $10 for the white Viña Sol. The top-of-the-line Mas La Plana Black Label, a powerful yet elegant Cabernet Sauvignon, costs about $60.

Freixenet, the leading Cava producer, is now also in the still wine business. Its wines include the inexpensive René Barbier brand of varietal wines and a fascinating $20 wine from Segura Viudas (a Cava brand owned by Freixenet). Creu de Lavit, as it's called, is a subtle but complex white that's 100 percent Xarel-lo (pronounced sha-*rel*-lo), a native grape used mainly for Cava production.

Rías Baixas: The white wine from Galicia

Galicia, in northwest Spain next to the Atlantic Ocean and Portugal, was not a province known for its wine. But from a small area called Rías Baixas (*ree*-ahse *byche*-ahse), tucked away in the southern part of Galicia (refer to Figure 12-1), an exciting, new white wine has emerged — Albariño, made from the Albariño grape variety. Rías Baixas is, in fact, one of the world's hottest white wine regions. We use *hot* to mean "in demand," and not to describe the climate, because Rías Baixas is cool and damp a good part of the year, and verdant year-round.

This region now boasts nearly 200 wineries, compared to only 60 just 15 years ago. Modern winemaking, the cool climate, and low-yielding vines have combined to make Albariño wines a huge success, especially in the United

States, its leading market. We love this lively, (mainly) unoaked white, with its vivid, floral aromas and flavors reminiscent of apricots, white peaches, pears, and green apples. It's a perfect match with seafood and fish. The Albariño grape — known as Alvarinho in northern Portugal (south of Rías Baixas) — makes wines that are fairly high in acidity, which makes them fine *apéritif* wines.

Albariños to look for include Bodega Morgadío, Pazos de Lusco, Fillaboa, Pazo de Señorans, Pazo San Mauro, Pazo de Barrantes, Condes de Albarei, Terras Gauda, Valminor, and Vionta; all are in the $14 to $24 range.

Navarra

Once upon a time, the word *Navarra* conjured up images of inexpensive, easy-drinking dry rosé wines (or, to the more adventurous, memories of running the bulls in Pamplona, Navarra's capital city). Today, Navarra, just northeast of Rioja, is known for its red wines, which are similar to but somewhat less expensive than the more famous wines of Rioja.

Many Navarra reds rely on Tempranillo, along with Garnacha, but you can also find Cabernet Sauvignon, Merlot, and various blends of all four varieties in the innovative Navarra region. Look for the wines of the following three Navarra producers: Bodegas Julian Chivite (*hoo*-lee-ahn cha-*vee*-tay), Bodegas Guelbenzu (gwel-ben-*zoo*), and Bodegas Magana. Prices start in the $9 to $12 range for all three wines.

Bierzo

This small region is in northwest Spain, east of Rías Baixas, and we mention it more because we're so fond of its wines than for the quantity of wine it produces, which is fairly small. Bierzo is a mountainous region with steep vineyard slopes, growing the red Mencia grape. The wines are what we would call "spicy reds," with lively acidity and aromas and flavors of red fruits.

El Toro

The Toro region in northwest Spain, northwest of Ribera del Duero, made wines in the Middle Ages that were quite famous in Spain. But it's a hot, arid area with poor soil, so winemaking was practically abandoned there for centuries. In Spain's current wine boom, Toro has been rediscovered. Winemakers have determined that the climate and soil are actually ideal for making powerful, tannic red wines — mainly from the Tempranillo variety (called Tinto del Toro here) — which rival the wines of Toro's neighbors in Ribera del Duero. Toro wines to buy include those of Bodegas Fariña, Vega Sauco, Estancia Piedra, Bodegas y Viñas Dos Victorias, Gil Luna, and Dehesa La Granja (owned by Pesquera's Alejandro Fernandez).

Decoding Spanish wine labels

You may see some of the following terms on a Spanish wine label; here's what they mean:

✔ **Blanco:** White.

✔ **Bodega:** Winery.

✔ **Cosecha (coh-*say*-cha) or Vendimia (ven-*dee*-me-yah):** The vintage year.

✔ **Crianza (cree-*ahn*-zah):** For red wines, this means that the wine has aged for two years with at least six months in oak; for white and rosé wines, *crianza* means that the wines aged for a year with at least six months in oak. (Some regions have stricter standards.)

✔ **Gran reserva:** Wines produced only in exceptional vintages; red wines must age at least five years, including a minimum of two years in oak; white *gran reservas* must age at least four years before release, including six months in oak.

✔ **Reserva:** Wines produced in the better vintages; red *reservas* must age a minimum of three years, including one year in oak; white *reservas* must age for two years, including six months in oak.

✔ **Tinto (*teen*-toe):** Red.

The Verdejo from Rueda

The Rueda region, west of Ribera del Duero, produces one of Spain's best white wines from the Verdejo grape. The wine is clean and fresh, has good fruit character, and sells for an affordable $9 to $11. The Rioja producer Marqués de Riscal makes one of the leading and most available examples.

Other emerging Spanish regions

Spanish wines are in demand more than ever in international markets because they're such great values — often selling for $10 to $15. Look for wines from the regions of Jumilla, Valdepeñas, Alicante, Valencia, and La Mancha — all offering excellent, good-value wines. Although Jumilla does make many low-priced wines, a few of its finest wines sell for up to $50.

Portugal: More Than Just Port

Portugal is justifiably famous for its great dessert wine, Port (which we discuss in Chapter 16). But gradually, wine lovers have been discovering the other dimensions of Portuguese wine — the country's dry wines, especially its reds. Most of these wines come from native Portuguese grape varieties, of which the country has hundreds. We do expect Portugal's well-priced wines to play a larger role in world wine markets in the 21st century — especially if Portugal itself does more to promote them. Find out more about Portuguese wines in the following sections.

The E.U.'s highest, Protected Designation of Origin (PDO) level of protected-origin wines is called *Denominação de Origem Protegida* in Portuguese, or *Denominação de Origen* (DOC), the traditional term. At the E.U.'s Protected Geographic Indication (PGI) level, where wine producers have more flexibility in their grape varieties and winemaking techniques, Portugal has the category of *Indicação Geográfica (IG), also called Vinho Regional (VR)*.

Portugal's "green" white

On hot summer evenings, the most appropriate wine can be a bottle of bracing, slightly effervescent, white Vinho Verde (*veen*-yo *vaird*). The high acidity of Vinho Verde refreshes your mouth and particularly complements grilled fish or seafood.

The Minho region, Vinho Verde's home, is in the northwest corner of Portugal, directly south of the Rías Baixas wine region of Spain that we talk about earlier in this chapter. (The region is particularly verdant because of the rain from the Atlantic Ocean — one theory behind the wine's name.)

Two styles of white Vinho Verde exist on the market:

- ✔ One style is that of the most commonly found brands (Quinta Da Aveleda and Casal Garcia); these sell for $6 to $9 and are medium-dry wines of average quality that are best served cold.

- ✔ The more expensive Vinho Verdes ($15 to $20) are varietal wines made from either the Alvarinho grape (Rías Baixas's Albariño), or the Loureiro or Trajadura grapes. They're more complex, dryer, and more concentrated than basic Vinho Verde, and are Portugal's best whites. Unfortunately, these finer wines are more difficult to find than the inexpensive ones; look for them in better wine shops or in Portuguese neighborhoods — or check out the importer Broadbent Selections (`www.broadbent.com`), who specializes in Portuguese wines.

At one time, the majority of wines from Vinho Verde were red. Now, due to the success of white Vinho Verde wines, only one-third is currently red. However, these red Vinho Verde wines are *highly* acidic; you definitely need to acquire a taste for them. (We haven't acquired it yet!)

Noteworthy Portuguese red wines

The Douro in northern Portugal is the region for sweet Port wine, but it also makes very good dry reds. The Port house of Ramos Pinto (now owned by Roederer Champagne) makes inexpensive, top-quality, dry red Douro wines that are fairly easy to find. Ramos Pinto Duas Quintas ($12 to $14) has ripe, plummy flavors and a velvety texture; it's surprisingly rich but supple, and it's a great value.

The Douro region boasts other terrific dry red wines, most of them fairly new and based on grapes traditionally used for Port. Brands to look for include Quinta do Vallado, Quinta do Vale D. Maria, Quinta do Crasto, Quinta de la Rosa, Quinta do Vale Meão (over $50), Quinta de Roriz, and Chryseia.

Here are some other good red Portuguese wines to try:

- ✔ **Quinta do Carmo:** This huge, beautiful estate, which dates back to the 17th century, is in the dynamic Alentejo region in southern Portugal. Its red *reserva,* a rich, full-bodied wine, sells in the $25 to $30 range. Quinta do Carmo also produces a white wine and a less expensive red named Don Martinho.

- ✔ **Quinta de Pancas:** One of the few Cabernet Sauvignons in Portugal, Quinta de Pancas comes from the Alenquer region, north of Lisbon; it sells for $12 to $14.

- ✔ **Quinta da Bacalhôa:** An estate-bottled Cabernet Sauvignon–Merlot from the esteemed Portuguese winemaker Joào Pires in Azeitao (south of Lisbon), Bacalhôa has the elegance of a Bordeaux; it sells for $25 to $30.

- ✔ **Joao Portugal Ramos:** A tireless winemaker who consults for various wineries and also owns three properties, Ramos has a golden touch and yet maintains typicity in his wines. Some wines sell under his own name; others include Marquês de Borba and Vila Santa, both in Alentejo.

Arguably the best dry red wine in Portugal, Barca Velha, comes from the Douro region. Made by the Ferreira Port house, Barca Velha is a full-bodied, intense, concentrated wine that needs years to age — Portugal's version of Vega Sicilia's Unico. Like Unico, not much is made, and it's produced only in the best vintages. The last vintage of Barca Velha available is the 2000, and it retails at about the same price as Unico — around $350.

Recognizing Portuguese wine terms

The following terms may appear on Portuguese wine labels:

- ✔ **Colheita (col-*yay*-tah):** Vintage year

- ✔ **Garrafeira (gar-ah-*fay*-ah):** A *reserva* that has aged at least two years in a cask and one in a bottle if it's red; six months in a cask, six months in a bottle if it's white

- ✔ **Quinta (*keen*-ta):** Estate or vineyard

- ✔ **Reserva:** A wine of superior quality from one vintage

- ✔ **Tinto (*teen*-toe):** Red

Germany: Europe's Individualist

German wines march to the beat of a different drummer. They traditionally have come in mainly one color: white. They're fruity in style, low in alcohol, rarely oaked, and many of them are off-dry or sweet. Their labels carry grape names, which is an anomaly in Europe.

Germany is the northernmost major wine-producing country in Europe — which means that its climate is cool. Except in warmer pockets of Germany, red grapes don't ripen adequately — at least they didn't before the current global warming trend began, around 1997. The climate is also erratic from year to year, meaning that vintages do matter for fine German wines. Many of Germany's finest vineyards are situated along rivers such as the Rhine and the Mosel, and on steep, sunny slopes, to temper the extremes of the weather and help the grapes ripen. Find out more about German wines in the following sections.

Riesling and its cohorts

In Germany's cool climate, the noble Riesling (*reese*-ling) grape finds true happiness. Riesling represents 22 percent of Germany's vineyard plantings, the largest of any variety.

A less distinguished German variety is Müller-Thurgau (pronounced *mool-lair-toor*-gow), a man-made crossing between the Riesling and Madeleine Royale grapes. It used to be the country's largest-growing variety (and is still second in plantings at 13 percent) but is losing ground because it's becoming less popular. Its wines are softer than Riesling's and less flavorful, with little potential for greatness.

After Riesling and Müller-Thurgau, the most-planted grape in Germany now, believe it or not, is Pinot Noir (called Spätburgunder). When we wrote the first edition of *Wine For Dummies* back in 1995, Pinot Noir was an afterthought in Germany — accounting for 2 to 3 percent of the country's plantings. Pinot Noir now represents 11.5 percent of Germany's grapevines. After Pinot Noir, another red variety, the native Dornfelder, is fourth in plantings with 8 percent.

Of the next five most-planted varieties, four are white; in order of production, the grapes are Silvaner, Ruländer (Pinot Gris), Blauer Portugieser (a red variety, probably of Austrian origin), Weissburgunder (Pinot Blanc), and Kerner.

The modern trends in Germany, wine-wise, are clear:

  ✔ Rieslings still rule, but a majority of them are now dry.

  ✔ Müller-Thurgau, once very popular, is falling out of style.

  ✔ Red wine, especially Pinot Noir, has become much more popular, accounting for 37 percent of all German wines.

Germans continue to consume huge quantities of beer, but they also drink a good deal of wine — both white and red. Until recently, most of its red wines were imported from neighboring countries, primarily Italy and France. Now Germany can look to its own vineyards to supply at least some of its red wine needs — with a big thanks to Mother Nature for providing the recent wave of warmer weather. Baden and the Pfalz, Germany's two warmest wine regions, are leading the way in red wine production. (We talk about Germany's wine regions in more detail later in this chapter.)

Today, 44 percent of Baden's wines are red — primarily Pinot Noir. While tasting in Germany, we were astounded by the quality of Baden's Pinot Noirs, certainly a far cry from the very light, thin German Pinot Noir wines of the past. One Baden producer, Weingut Bernhard Huber, is making Pinot Noirs that compare favorably to France's Côte de Beaune Burgundies, and at a lower price. Huber's Pinot Noirs start at $30.

The huge winemaking region Pfalz is making both fine Rieslings and red wines. Some of Germany's best dry Rieslings come from the cooler, northern part. But almost 40 percent of the Pfalz's wines are now red, and they come from the warmer southern part. Dornfelder, a dark-colored, fruity, tannic, quite full-bodied wine, is the largest-planted red variety in the Pfalz, followed by Pinot Noir. Other red wines you can find from the Pfalz include Blauer Portugieser, Trollinger (Italy's Schiava), and Lemberger (also known as Blaufränkisch).

Germany's wine laws

Like most European wines, German wines are, in fact, named after the places they come from — in the best wines, usually a combination of a village name and a vineyard name, such as Piesporter (town) Goldtröpfchen (vineyard).

Unlike most European wines, however, the grape name is also usually part of the wine name (as in Piesporter Goldtröpfchen *Riesling*). And the finest German wines have yet another element in their name — a *Prädikat* (pray-di-cat), which is an indication of the ripeness of the grapes at harvest (as in Piesporter Goldtröpfchen Riesling *Spätlese*). Wines with a Prädikat hold the highest rank in the German wine system.

Germany's system of assigning the highest rank to the ripest grapes is completely different from the concept behind most other European systems, which is to bestow the highest status on the best vineyards or districts. Germany's system underscores the country's traditional grape-growing priority: Ripeness — never guaranteed in a cool and variable climate — is the highest goal.

German wine law divides wines with a Prädikat into six levels, from the least ripe to the ripest (that is, from the lowest to the highest):

- ✔ Kabinett (*kab*-ee-net)
- ✔ Spätlese (*shpate*-lay-seh)
- ✔ Auslese (*ouse*-lay-seh)
- ✔ Beerenauslese (*beer*-en-*ouse*-lay-seh), abbreviated as *BA*
- ✔ Eiswein (*ice*-vine)
- ✔ Trockenbeerenauslese (*troh*-ken-*beer*-en-*ouse*-lay-seh), abbreviated as *TBA*

At the three highest Prädikat levels, the amount of sugar in the grapes is so high that the wines are inevitably sweet. Many people, therefore, mistakenly believe that the Prädikat level of a German wine is an indication of the wine's sweetness. In fact, the Prädikat is an indication of the amount of sugar in the *grapes at harvest,* not the amount of sugar in the wine. At lower Prädikat levels, the sugar in the grapes can ferment fully, to dryness, and for those wines, there's no direct correlation between Prädikat level and sweetness of the wine.

Wines whose (grape) ripeness earns them a Prädikat are categorized as *Prädikatswein,* translated as "wines with special attributes" (their ripeness). They are Protected Designation of Origin (PDO) wines in the eyes of the European Union (see Chapter 4 for more about this and other designations, including the phrases in German). When the ripeness of the grapes in a particular vineyard isn't sufficient to earn the wine Prädikat status, the wine can still qualify as a PDO (protected place-name) wine in Germany's second tier, called *Qualitätswein,* translated as "quality wine"; each label carries the name of one of Germany's 13 wine regions in addition to the word *Qualitätswein* and usually the name of a grape variety. (See the later section "Germany's wine regions" for the names of the main regions.)

A small amount of Germany's wine production falls into the looser Protected Geographic Indication (PGI) category. These are called *Landwein* in Germany, and carry a geographic indication that's broader than a region name.

German wine styles

Although the common perception of German wines has been that they're sweet, and although a movement toward dry wines is sweeping over Germany, the truth is that many German wines have always tasted dry, or fairly dry. In fact, you can find German wines at just about any sweetness or dryness level you like. The following sections cover German wine styles in more detail.

Gentle, half-dry, and dry wines

Most inexpensive German wines, such as Liebfraumilch, are light-bodied, fruity wines with pleasant sweetness — wines that are easy to enjoy without food. The German term for this style of wine is *lieblich,* which translates as "gentle" — a poetic but apt descriptor. The very driest German wines are called *trocken* (dry). Wines that are sweeter than trocken but dryer than lieblich are called *halbtrocken* (half-dry). The words *trocken* and *halbtrocken* sometimes appear on the label, but not always.

You can make a good stab at determining how sweet a German wine is by reading the alcohol level on the label. If the alcohol is low — about 9 percent, or less — the wine probably contains grape sugar that didn't ferment into alcohol and is, therefore, sweet. Higher alcohol levels suggest that the grapes fermented completely, to dryness.

Although we generally prefer dry white wines, we find that a bit of sweetness in German wines can be appealing — and, in fact, can improve the quality of the wine. That's because sweetness undercuts the wines' natural high acidity and gives the wines better balance. In practice, most off-dry German wines don't really taste as sweet as they are, thanks to their acidity.

One way that German winemakers keep some sweetness in their wines is called the *süssreserve* (sweet reserve) method. In this method, a winemaker holds back as much as 25 percent of his grape juice and doesn't allow it to ferment. He then ferments the rest of his juice fully, until it's dry wine. Later, he blends the unfermented grape juice into his dry wine. The grape juice (the süssreserve) contributes a natural, juicy sweetness to the wine. Alternatively, some winemakers ferment all their Riesling juice and then block the fermentation of the juice before all the sugar has converted to alcohol.

What's noble about rot?

Wine connoisseurs all over the world recognize Germany's sweet, dessert-style wines as among the greatest wines on the face of the earth. Most of these legendary wines owe their sweetness to an ugly but magical fungus known as *botrytis cinerea* (pronounced bo-*try*-tis sin-eh-*ray*-ah), commonly called *noble rot.*

Noble rot infects ripe grapes in late autumn if a certain combination of humidity and sun is present. This fungus dehydrates the berries and concentrates their sugar and their flavors. The wine from these infected berries is sweet, amazingly rich, and complex beyond description. It can also be expensive: $100 or more per bottle.

Wines at the BA and TBA Prädikat levels are usually made entirely from grapes infected with noble rot (called *botrytised* grapes) and are generally richly textured and sweet. *Auslese*-level wines often come from some partially botrytised grapes, and when they do, they are likely to be sweet, although never to the extent of a BA or TBA.

Another way that nature can contribute exotic sweetness to German wines is by freezing the grapes on the vine in early winter. When the frozen grapes are harvested and pressed, most of the water in the berries separates out as ice. The sweet, concentrated juice that's left to ferment makes a luscious sweet Prädikat-level wine called *Eiswein* (literally, ice wine). Eisweins differ from BAs and TBAs because they lack a certain flavor that derives from botrytis, sometimes described as a honeyed character.

Both botrytised wines and Eisweins are referred to as *late-harvest wines*, not only in Germany but all over the world, because the special character of these wines comes from conditions that normally occur only when the grapes are left on the vine beyond the usual point of harvest.

Germany's wine regions

Germany has 13 wine regions — 11 in the west and 2 in the eastern part of the country (see Figure 12-2).

The most famous of these 13 are the Mosel region, named for the Mosel River, along which the region's vineyards lie, and the Rheingau region, along the Rhine River. The Rhine River lends its name to three other German wine regions, Rheinhessen, the Pfalz (formerly called the Rheinpfalz), and the tiny Mittelrhein region. The Nahe and Baden are two other renowned regions.

Mosel

The Mosel, formerly known as Mosel-Saar-Ruwer (*moh*-zel-zar-*roo*-ver) to include the names of the two tributaries, is a dramatically beautiful region. Its vineyards rising steeply on the slopes of the twisting and turning Mosel River. The wines of the region are among the lightest in Germany (usually containing less than 10 percent alcohol); they're generally delicate, fresh, and charming. Riesling dominates the Mosel with 57 percent of the plantings. Wines from this region are instantly recognizable because they come in green bottles rather than the brown bottles that other German regions use. The Mosel is Germany's fourth-largest wine-producing region.

Figure 12-2:
The wine regions of Germany.

Illustration by Lisa S. Reed

The Mosel boasts dozens of excellent winemakers who produce really exciting Riesling wines. Some of our favorites include, in alphabetical order:

Egon Müller
Dr. Fischer
Friedrich Wilhelm Gymnasium
Karlsmühle
Dr. Loosen
Maximin Grünhauser
Merkelbach

Meulenhof
J.J. Prüm
Reichsgraf Von Kesselstatt
Willi Schaefer
Selbach-Oster
Zilliken

Rheingau

The Rheingau (*ryne*-gow) is among Germany's smaller wine regions. It, too, has some dramatically steep vineyards bordering a river, but here the river is Germany's greatest wine river, the Rhine. The Riesling grape occupies more than 80 percent of the Rheingau's vineyards, many of which are south-facing slopes that give the Riesling grapes an extra edge of ripeness. Rheingau wine styles tend toward two extremes: trocken wines on the one hand and sweet late-harvest wines on the other. Recommended Rheingau producers include Georg Breuer, Knyphausen, Franz Küntsler, Schloss Schönborn, Leitz, and Robert Weil.

Rheinhessen

Rheinhessen (*ryne*-hess-ehn) is Germany's largest wine region, producing huge quantities of simple wines for everyday enjoyment. Liebfraumilch originated here, and it's still one of the most important wines of the region, commercially speaking. The Rheinhessen's highest-quality wines come from the Rheinterrasse, a vineyard area along the river. The Rheinhessen's image today has greatly improved, because it now produces many exciting, dry Rieslings. Producers from that area who are particularly good include Gunderloch, Heyl Zu Herrnsheim, and Strub.

Pfalz

Almost as big as the Rheinhessen, the Pfalz *(fallz)*, Germany's second-largest wine producer, has earned a great deal more respect from wine lovers for its dry, full-bodied white wines and its very good reds — all of which owe their style to the region's relatively warm climate. The Pfalz has more Riesling planted than any other wine region in the world! Other major grape varieties of the Pfalz include Silvaner, Kerner, and Müller-Thurgau, but qualitatively, Spätburgunder (Pinot Noir) and the white Scheurebe are important. To experience the best of the Pfalz, look for wines from Dr. Bürklin-Wolf, Rainer Lingenfelder, Müller-Catoir, and Basserman-Jordan.

A secret code of German place-names

If you're like most of us and don't speak German or know German geography intimately, deciphering German wine names can be tricky, to say the least. But here's a bit of information that can help. In the German language, the possessive is formed by adding the suffix *-er* to a noun. When you see names like Zeller or Hochheimer — names that end in *-er* — on a wine label, the next word is usually a vineyard area that "belongs" to the commune or district with the *-er* on its name (Zell's Swartze Katz, Hochheim's Kirchenstück). The name of the region itself always appears on labels of Qualitätswein and Prädikatswein wines.

Nahe

Another German region of importance for the quality of its wines, especially Riesling, is Nahe (*nah*-heh), named for the Nahe River and situated west of Rheinhessen. The Riesling wines here are relatively full and intense. Favorite producers include Diel, Kruger-Rumpf, Prinz zu Salm-Dahlberg, and Dönnhoff.

Baden

Now Germany's most important region for Pinot Noir, Baden (*bah*-den), Germany's third-largest wine producer, is celebrating the recent warm climate that undoubtedly has played a large role in its greatly improved red wines. The somewhat cooler, northern part of Baden produces some fine Weissburgunders (Pinot Blancs) and Rülanders (Pinot Gris) as well as dry Rieslings. Although co-ops make 80 percent of Baden's wines, independent producers to look for in Baden include Bernhard Huber (for Pinot Noirs), Weingut Heitlinger (for Riesling), and Weingut Dr. Heger (for Weissburgunder and Riesling).

Austria's Exciting Whites (And Reds)

Austria is one of the wine countries that most excites us. Apart from the gorgeous vineyard regions, the warmth of the people, and the classic beauty of Vienna, we love many of the wines. What makes Austrian wines all the more interesting is how they are evolving, as winemakers gradually discover how to best express their land and their grapes through wine.

Austria makes less than 1 percent of all the wine in the world — about 27 million cases a year. All of it comes from the eastern part of the country, where the Alps recede into hills, and most of it comes from small wineries. Although some inexpensive Austrian wines do make their way to export markets, the Austrians have embraced a high-quality image; therefore, many of their wines command premium prices.

Although the excellence of Austria's sweet whites has long been recognized, her dry whites and reds have gained recognition only in the past three decades.

✔ Reds are still in the minority, claiming about 30 percent of the country's production, because many of Austria's wine regions are too cool for growing red grapes. Red wines hail mainly from the area of Burgenland, bordering Hungary, one of the warmest parts of the country. They're medium- to full-bodied, often engagingly spicy, with vivid fruity flavor — and often the international touch of oaky character. Many of them are based on unusual, native grape varieties such as the spicy Blaufrankish (Lemberger), the gentler St. Laurent, or Blauer Zweigelt (a crossing of the other two).

> ✔ Austria's white wines — apart from the luscious, late-harvest dessert wines made from either botrytised, extremely ripe, or dried grapes — are dry wines ranging from light- to full-bodied, and are generally unoaked.

Find out more about the world of Austrian wine in the following sections.

Grüner Veltliner and company

The country's single most important grape variety is the native white Grüner Veltliner. Its wines are full-bodied yet crisp with rich texture and herbal or sometimes spicy-vegetal flavors (especially green pepper). They're extremely food-friendly and usually high quality. Some people in the wine trade have nicknamed Grüner Veltliner "GruVe"; we agree with that characterization!

Riesling, grown mainly in the region of Lower Austria, in the northeast, is another key grape for quality whites. In fact, some experts believe that Austria's finest wines are its Rieslings (while others prefer Grüner Veltliner).

Other grape names that you may see on bottles of Austrian wine include Müller-Thurgau, which makes characterful dry whites; Welschriesling, a grape popular in Eastern Europe for inexpensive wines that achieves high quality only in Austria; Pinot Blanc, which can excel here; and Muscat. Sauvignon Blanc is a specialty of the region of Styria, in the south, bordering Slovenia; among all the Sauvignon Blanc wines in the world, these are among the finest.

Austrian wine names and label terms

In some parts of Austria, for example in the Wachau district, along the Danube River, wines are named in the German system — a town name ending in *-er* followed by a vineyard name and a grape variety. In other parts of Austria, the wine names are generally a grape name (or, increasingly, a proprietary name) followed by the name of the region.

Austria's wine classification laws draw from the German model that we describe earlier in this chapter, with PDO wine divided into *Qualitätswein* and *Prädikatswein* categories, and Protected Geographic Indication (PGI) wine classified as *Landwein*. (One difference is that *Kabinett* falls into the *Qualitätswein* category.) But a new system, based on *terroir* rather than ripeness levels and thus more similar to regulations in the rest of Europe, coexists with the German-type classification. Authorities introduced the *Districtus Austria Controllatus (DAC)* system in early 2003, and it now falls under the E.U.'s PDO category. The following seven DAC zones now exist (their permitted grape varieties are noted in parentheses):

- ✔ Weinvertel (Grüner Veltliner)

- ✔ Traisental (Grüner Veltliner or Riesling)

- ✔ Kremstal (Grüner Veltliner or Riesling)

- ✔ Kamptal (Grüner Veltliner or Riesling)

- ✔ Mittelburgenland (Blaufrankish)

- ✔ Eisenberg (Blaufrankish)

- ✔ Leithaberg (for white wines, Pinot Blanc, Chardonnay, Neuburger, Grüner Veltliner, or a blend of these varieties; and for reds, Blaufränkisch)

The Glory That Is Greece

We find it hard to comprehend that a country that practically invented wine, way back in the 7th century BC, could be an emerging wine region today. But that's the way it is. Greece never stopped making wine for all those centuries, but her wine industry took the slow track, inhibited by Turkish rule, political turmoil, and other real-life issues. The modern era of Greek winemaking began only in the 1960s, and it has made particularly strong strides in the past decade. Today, Greek wines are worth knowing; we introduce you to them and all their glory in the following sections.

Greek grapes

Although Greece is a southern country and famous for its sunshine, its grape-growing climate is actually quite varied, because many vineyards are situated at high altitudes where the weather is cooler. (Most of Greece is mountainous, in fact.) Its wines are mainly (60 percent) white; some of those whites are sweet dessert wines, but most are dry.

One of Greece's greatest wine assets — and handicaps, at the same time — is its abundance of native grape varieties, more than 300 of them. Only Italy has more indigenous grape varieties. These native grapes make Greek wines particularly exciting for curious wine lovers to explore, but their unfamiliar names make the wines difficult to sell. Fortunately for the marketers, Greece also produces wines from internationally famous grape varieties, such as Chardonnay, Merlot, Syrah, and Cabernet Sauvignon, and those wines can be very good. These days, however, producers seem more committed than ever to their native varieties rather than to international grapes.

Of Greece's many indigenous grape varieties, four in particular stand out as the most important — two white and two red varieties:

- **Assyrtiko (ah-*seer*-tee-koe):** A white variety that makes delicate, bone-dry, crisp, very long-lived wines with citrusy and minerally aromas and flavors. Although Assyrtiko grows in various parts of Greece, the best Assyrtiko wines come from the volcanic island of Santorini. Any wine called Santorini is made from at least 90 percent Assyrtiko. Two outstanding Santorini producers are Domaine Sigalas and Gaia (*yea*-ah).

- **Moschofilero (mos-cho-*feel*-eh-roe):** A very aromatic, pink-skinned variety that makes both dry white and pale-colored dry rosé wines grows mainly around Mantinia, in the central, mountainous Peloponnese region. If a wine is named Mantinia, it must be at least 85 percent Moschofilero. Wines made from Moschofilero have high acidity and are fairly low in alcohol, with aromas and flavors of apricots and/or peaches. Because they're so easy to drink, Moschofilero wines are a great introduction to Greek wines.

- **Agiorghitiko** (eye-your-*yee*-tee-koe): The name of this grape translates in English to "St. George," and a few winemakers call it that on the labels of wines destined for English-speaking countries. Greece's most planted and probably most important native red variety, it grows throughout the mainland. Its home turf, where it really excels, is in the Nemea district of the Peloponnese region; any wine with the place-name Nemea is entirely from Agiorghitiko. Wines from this variety are medium to deep in color, have complex aromas and flavors of plums and/or black currants, and often have a resemblance to Cabernet Franc or spicy Merlot wines. Agiorghitiko also blends well with other indigenous or international varieties.

- **Xinomavro (ksee-*no*-mav-roe):** The most important red variety in the Macedonia region of northern Greece. Xinomavro produces highly tannic wines with considerable acidity that have been compared to Nebbiolo wines of Piedmont, Italy. Wines made from Xinomavro have complex, spicy aromas, often suggesting dried tomatoes, olives, and/or berries. Xinomavro wines are dark in color but lighten with age and have great longevity. Their home base is the Naoussa district of Macedonia; any wine named Naoussa is entirely from Xinomavro.

Other important white indigenous varieties in Greece include Roditis (actually a pink-skinned grape), which makes Patras white; and Savatiano, the most widely planted white grape. Retsina, a traditional Greek wine made by adding pine resin to fermenting grape juice (resulting in a flavor not unlike some oaky Chardonnays), is made mainly from Savatiano. Mavrodaphne is an indigenous Greek red variety that's becoming increasingly important, both for dry and sweet red wines.

Wine regions, producers, and label lingo in Greece

Some of the wine regions of Greece whose names you're likely to see on wine labels include

- **Macedonia:** The northernmost part of Greece, with mountainous terrain and cool climates. Naoussa wine (from the Xinomavro grape) comes from here.

- **The Peloponnese:** A large, mainly mountainous, peninsula in south-western Greece with varied climate and soil. Noteworthy wines include the soft, red Nemea; the dry whites Patras and Mantinia; and the sweet wines Mavrodaphne de Patras (red) and Muscat de Patras (white).

- **Crete:** The largest Greek island, which makes both white and red wines, many of which are varietally named along with the place-name of Crete.

- **Other Greek islands:** Besides Crete, the four most important islands that make wine are Santorini, Rhodes, Samos, and Cephalonia.

Many Greek wines today are top quality, especially the wines of small, independent wineries. The following are some of our favorite Greek wine producers (listed alphabetically within regions):

- From Macedonia: Alpha Estate, Domaine Gerovassilou, Kir Yianni Estate, and Tsantali-Mount Athos Vineyards

- From the Peloponnese: Antonopoulos Vineyards, Gaia Estate (pronounced *yea*-ah, has wineries also in Santorini), Katogi & Strofilia (with operations also in Macedonia), Mercouri Estate, Papantonis Winery, Domaine Skouras, Domaine Spiropoulos, and Domaine Tselepos

- From the islands: Boutari Estates (six estates throughout Greece, including Crete and Santorini), Gentilini (in Cephalonia), and Domaine Sigalas (Santorini)

Greece's appellation system for wine, which had involved separate tiers for dry wines and sweet wines, has been simplified by the country's complete adaptation of the new E.U. system. Thirty-three wine zones fall into the PDO category, and most will carry the phrase *Protected Designation of Origin* in English. PGI wines mainly carry the phrase *Protected Geographic Indication* in English.

Other terms that have formal definitions under Greek wine regulations include *reserve* (PDO wines with a minimum one or two years aging, for whites and reds respectively), *grande reserve* (two years of aging for whites and four years for reds), and *cava* (non-PDO wines with one year of aging for whites and three years for reds). All these terms require that a specified portion of the wines' aging take place in barrel.

Part IV

Discovering the "New World" of Wine

"I'm trying to remember the type of California white wine I like, but my mind keeps drawing a blanc."

In this part . . .

Like Columbus in 1492, we set sail for the land of opportunity, where winemakers grow whichever grapes they like and make fresh, modern, flavorful wines that electrify wine drinkers.

This part contains only two chapters, but the countries covered in them are big players in the wine marketplace — the United States, Australia, New Zealand, Chile, Argentina, and South Africa, for example. We guide you to the most exciting wines and explain what makes them special.

Chapter 13

The Southern Hemisphere Arises

*W*hat do the wines of North and South America, South Africa, Australia, and New Zealand have in common? For one thing, none of them are produced in Europe. In fact, you could say that they are the wines of "Not Europe."

The name most often used in wine circles for Not Europe is the *New World.* Undoubtedly, this phrase, with its ring of colonialism, was coined by a European. Europe, home of all the classic wine regions of the world, producer of more than 60 percent of the world's wine, is the Old World. Everything else is nouveau riche.

When we first heard the expression *New World* applied to wines, we thought it was absurd. How can you lump together wine regions as remote as California's Napa Valley, the Finger Lakes of New York, Australia's Coonawarra, and Chile's Maipo Valley? But then we started thinking about it. In Europe, they've been making wines for so long that grape-growing and winemaking practices have become codified into detailed regulations. Which hillsides to plant, which grapes should grow where, how dry or sweet a particular wine should be — these decisions were all made long ago, by the grandparents and great-great-grandparents of today's winemakers. But in Not Europe, the grape-growing and winemaking game is wide open; every winery owner gets to decide for himself where to grow his grapes, what variety to plant, and what style of wine to make. The wines of the New World do have that freedom in common.

The more we thought about it, the more similarities we found among New World wine regions as they compared to Europe. We concluded that the New World is a winemaking entity whose spirit, legislative reality, and winemaking style are unique from those of the Old World — as generalizations go.

We could easily fill 400 pages on the wines of the United States, Chile, Argentina, Australia, New Zealand, and South Africa alone, if only we had the space. Fortunately, New World wines are easy for you to explore without a detailed road map: In the New World, there's little encoded tradition to decipher and relatively little historical backdrop against which the wines need to be appreciated.

In this chapter, we explore the wines of Australia, New Zealand, Chile, Argentina, and South Africa. We devote Chapter 14 to the wines of the United States.

Australian Wine Power

Australia is one of the world powers of wine. The wine industry of Australia is one of the most technologically advanced, forward thinking on earth, and the wines of Australia have experienced runaway success all over the world.

Australia has no native vines. Vinifera grapevines first came to the country in 1788, from South Africa. Historically, most Australian wines were rich and sweet, many of them fortified with alcohol. But today, Australia is famous for its fresh, fruity, flavorful red and white table wines. Australia now ranks seventh in the world in wine production — making slightly more than half as much wine as the United States — and fourth in exports.

Approximately the same size as the continental United States, Australia has about 2,000 wineries. Many of these wineries are small, family-owned companies, but four mega-companies — together with one family-owned winery, Casella Wines (producer of the popular brand called [yellow tail]), are responsible for about two-thirds of Australia's wine production.

The dramatic sales growth of inexpensive wine brands from these large Australian producers drove the worldwide popularity of Aussie wine for close to two decades. But that success has backfired, resulting in overproduction and low profitability. Australia's wine industry is now refocusing and is shifting attention to the country's smaller-production wines as well as to its many unique wine regions. This is an exciting time for wine drinkers to explore the depth of what Australia has to offer. You can start investigating Australian wines with the help of the following sections.

The old and the new

In wine terms, the New World is not just geography but also an attitude toward wine. Some winemakers in Europe approach wine the liberated New World way, and some winemakers in California are dedicated Old World traditionalists. Keep that in mind as you look over the following comparison between the Old World and the New World. And remember, we're talking generalizations here — and generalizations are never *always* true.

New World	**Old World**
Innovation	Tradition
Wines named after grape varieties	Wines named after region of production
Expression of the fruit is the primary winemaking goal	Expression of *terroir* (the particular place where the grapes grow, with its unique growing conditions) is the winemaking goal
Technology is respected highly	Traditional methods are favored
Wines are flavorful and fruity	Wines have subtle, less fruity flavors
Grape-growing regions are broad and flexible	Grape-growing regions are relatively small and fixed
Winemaking resembles science	Winemaking resembles art
Winemaking processes are controlled	Intervention in winemaking is avoided as much as possible
The winemaker gets credit for the wine	The vineyard gets credit for the wine

Winemaking, grapes, and terroir

Australia's wine regions are mainly in the southern, cooler part of the country, with many of them clustered in the state of Victoria, the southern part of South Australia, the southern part of Western Australia, the cooler parts of New South Wales, and Tasmania.

The success of Australia's wines stems from a generally warm, dry climate, which provides winemakers with excellent raw material for their work — although drought has seriously challenged winemakers in recent years. The country's renowned research programs in grape growing and winemaking also contribute greatly by enabling winemakers to stay on the cutting edge of their craft.

Australia's number-one grape for fine wine is Syrah, locally called *Shiraz,* followed by Cabernet Sauvignon, Chardonnay, Merlot, Semillon (pronounced *sem*-eh-lon in Australia, as opposed to the French seh-mee-yohn elsewhere in the world), Pinot Noir, Riesling, and Sauvignon Blanc. The wines are generally labeled with the name of their grape variety, which must constitute at least 85 percent of the wine.

Shiraz wines are particularly interesting because they come in different styles, from inexpensive, juicy wines brimming with ripe plum and blackberry fruit to serious wines that express specific regional characteristics, such as spice and pepper from cool-climate areas (such as Yarra Valley and the Adelaide Hills) or sweet-fruit ripeness from warmer areas (such as McLaren Vale, Barossa Valley, and Clare Valley).

The wines of Australia have two distinct faces:

✔ Most Australian wines in export markets are inexpensive varietal wines that sell for $10 a bottle or less. These wines are generally labeled simply as coming from *South Eastern Australia,* meaning that the grapes could have come from any of three states, a huge territory. Often sporting whimsical labels, they are user-friendly wines that preserve the intense flavors of their grapes and are soft and pleasant to drink young.

✔ Higher-priced wines carry more focused regional designations, such as single states (South Australia or Victoria, for example) or even tighter region-specific designations (such as Barossa Valley, Coonawarra, or Yarra Valley). Although these wines are also enjoyable when released, many of them are more serious wines that can also age.

Australia now has more than 60 wine regions and more than 100 Geographic Indications (GIs) whose names are becoming more visible on wine labels abroad. We mention some of the more famous regions of Australia, state by state, in the following section. If you're interested in finding out about these regions — and the many others that we don't mention — in more detail, consult James Halliday's *The Australian Wine Encyclopedia* (Hardie Grant Books) and his *Wine Atlas of Australia* (University of California Press).

Odd couples

Although winemakers all over the world make blended wines — wines from more than one grape variety — generally the grape combinations follow the classic French models: Cabernet Sauvignon with Merlot and Cabernet Franc, for example, or Sémillon with Sauvignon Blanc. Australia has invented two completely original formulas:

✔ Shiraz with Cabernet Sauvignon

✔ Semillon with Chardonnay

The grape in the majority is listed first on the wine label for wines sold in the United States, and the percentages of each grape are indicated.

Australia's wine regions

Australia has five major wine regions. In order of importance, they consist of South Australia, Victoria, New South Wales, Western Australia, and Tasmania. We explore these regions in the following sections.

South Australia

Australia's most important state for wine production is South Australia, whose capital is Adelaide (see Figure 13-1). South Australia makes about 51 percent of Australia's wine. While many vineyards in South Australia produce inexpensive wines for the thirsty home market, vineyards closer to Adelaide make wines that are considered among Australia's finest. Its main fine wine subregions include the following:

- **Barossa Valley:** north of Adelaide, this is one of Australia's oldest areas for fine wine; it's a relatively warm area famous especially for its robust Shiraz, Cabernet Sauvignon, and Grenache, as well as rich Semillon and Riesling (grown in the cooler hills). Most of Australia's largest wineries, including Penfolds, are based here.

- **Clare Valley:** North of the Barossa Valley, this climatically diverse area makes the country's best Rieslings in a dry, weighty yet crisp style, as well as fine Shiraz and Cabernet Sauvignon.

- **McLaren Vale:** south of Adelaide, with a mild climate influenced by the sea, this region is particularly admired for its Shiraz, Cabernet, Sauvignon Blanc, and Chardonnay.

- **Adelaide Hills:** Situated partially within the Adelaide city limits, this fairly cool region sits between the Barossa Valley and McLaren Vale areas and is the home to some very good Sauvignon Blanc, Chardonnay, Pinot Noir, and Shiraz.

- **Limestone Coast:** This unique zone along the southern coast of South Australia is an important area for fine wine, both red and white, thanks to the prevalence of limestone in the soil. Two of the six subregions within the Limestone Coast zone are famous in their own right — the warm **Coonawarra** area for some of Australia's best Cabernet Sauvignon wines, and **Padthaway** for its popular Chardonnay, as well as Shiraz and Cabernet Sauvignon.

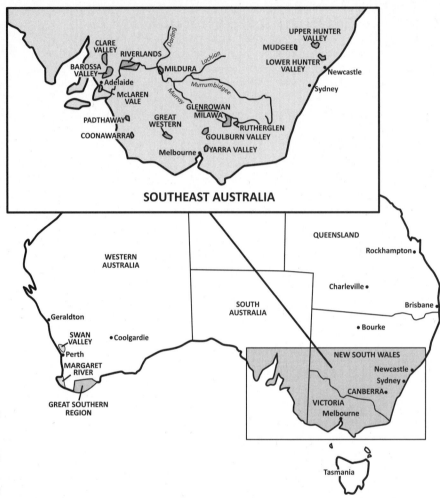

Figure 13-1:
The wine regions of Australia.

Victoria

Bordering South Australia to the east is Victoria, a smaller state that makes 15 percent of Australia's wines. Although South Australia is home to most of Australia's largest wineries, Victoria has more wineries (more than 600) than any other Aussie region, most of them small. Victoria's fine wine production ranges from rich, fortified dessert wines to delicate Pinot Noirs. Principal subregions include the following, from north to south (refer to Figure 13-1):

 ✔ **Murray River:** This area stretching into New South Wales includes the Mildura region, where Lindemans, one of Australia's largest wineries, is situated. This region is particularly important for growing grapes for Australia's good-value wines.

- **Rutherglen:** In the northeast, this long-established, warm climate zone is an outpost of traditional winemaking and home of an exotic Australian specialty, fortified dessert Muscats and Tokays (now renamed as Topaque) that are world renowned.

- **Goulburn Valley:** In the center of the state, Goulburn Valley is known especially for its full-bodied reds, especially Shiraz.

- **Heathcote**: East of Goulburn and due north of Melbourne (the capital of Victoria), this area boasts unusual soils that make distinctive, rich yet elegant Shirazes and also Cabernet.

- **Yarra Valley:** In southern Victoria, and close to Melbourne, Yarra Valley boasts a wide diversity of climates due to altitude differences of its vineyards. The Yarra is noted for its Cabernet, Pinot Noir, Shiraz, Chardonnay, and Sauvignon Blanc, as well as its sparkling wines.

- **Mornington Peninsula and Geelong**: South of Melbourne and separated from each other by Port Phillip Bay, these two cool, maritime regions specialize in fine Pinot Noir and Chardonnay.

New South Wales

New South Wales, with its capital, Sydney, is Australia's most populous state, and the first to grow vines; today it makes about 30 percent of Australia's wine. High-volume production of everyday wines comes from an interior area called the Riverina. (We get a kick trying to pronounce its alternate name, Murrumbidgee.) Fine wine, for now, comes from three other areas (refer to Figure 13-1):

- **Hunter Valley:** A historic grape-growing area that begins 80 miles north of Sydney. The Lower Hunter, with a warm, damp climate and heavy soils, produces long-lived Semillon as its best wine. The Upper Hunter is a drier area farther from the coast.

- **Mudgee:** An interior area near the mountains. Mudgee specializes in reds such as Merlot and Cabernet Sauvignon but also makes Chardonnay.

- **Orange:** A cool, high-altitude area making distinctive white wines and also very good reds.

Western Australia

Western Australia, the largest state, has the country's most isolated wine area, in its southwest corner. It makes little wine compared to the preceding three states, but quality is very high. The warm, dry Swan Valley is the state's historic center of wine production, but two cooler climate regions have become more important (refer to Figure 13-1):

- ✔ **Margaret River:** This is a fairly temperate region near the Indian Ocean. Among the wines that various wineries here excel in are Sauvignon Blanc–Semillon blends (especially Cape Mentelle), Chardonnay (especially Leeuwin Estate), and Cabernet Sauvignon (from Mosswood, Voyager, Cape Mentelle, and Howard Park).

- ✔ **Great Southern:** Cooler than Margaret River, Great Southern's specialty is crisp, age-worthy Riesling — a favorite of ours. This huge, diverse region also produces intense, aromatic Cabernet Sauvignon as well as fine Shiraz and Chardonnay; on the southern coast, Pinot Noir is successful.

Tasmania

Tasmania, an island south of Victoria (refer to Figure 13-1), has some cool microclimates in both its northern and southern sections. Producers are increasingly proving what potential exists for delicate Pinot Noirs, Chardonnays, and sparkling wines. Two of the better-known producers are Pipers Brook and Pirie.

The Rise of New Zealand

The history of fine winemaking in New Zealand is relatively short, having been hampered by conservative attitudes towards alcohol. In the 1980s, New Zealand finally began capitalizing on its maritime climate, ideal for producing high-quality wines, and started planting grapes in earnest. Today, it makes about one-sixth of the wine of its nearest neighbor, Australia, but its production is increasing every year. And, unlike Australia, New Zealand has managed to maintain an elite image for its wines, as opposed to a good-value-for-everyday image, which enables New Zealand wine producers to obtain sustainable prices for their wines.

Four large producers dominate New Zealand's wine production: Montana (sold in the United States under the Brancott label, to avoid confusion with the state of Montana), Corbans, Villa Maria, and Nobilo. But in the past 25 years, numerous small, boutique wineries have sprung up, especially on the South Island.

In the following sections, find out more about the world of wine in New Zealand.

Kiwi geography

New Zealanders are nicknamed "Kiwis," because for a long time this country led the world in kiwi production (Italy is now the largest producer, followed by New Zealand). Situated farther south than Australia, New Zealand is, in general, cooler. Of New Zealand's two large islands, the North Island is the warmer. Red grapes grow around the capital city, Auckland, in the north and around Hawke's Bay (especially known for its Cabernet Sauvignon, grown on gravelly soil farther south on the North Island); Müller-Thurgau, Chardonnay, and Sauvignon Blanc are the North Island's main white varieties. Martinborough, a cooler district at the southern end of North Island, makes excellent Pinot Noir.

On the South Island, Marlborough — the country's largest and commercially most important wine region — is New Zealand's largest production zone for Chardonnay and, especially, Sauvignon Blanc. The interior, hilly Central Otago zone is famous for its Chardonnay and Pinot Noir.

Sauvignon Blanc, Pinot Noir lead the way

The first New Zealand Sauvignon Blancs to be exported were generally unoaked wines with pronounced flavor, rich texture, and high acidity. They were so distinctive — pungent, herbaceous, with intense flavors suggestive of asparagus, lime, or cut grass — that New Zealand became recognized almost overnight in the late 1980s for a new prototype of Sauvignon Blanc. This style of New Zealand Sauvignon Blanc is still very popular worldwide. These are the least expensive Kiwi Sauvignon Blancs, retailing for $12 to $20, with many priced around $15 to $16.

Another style of New Zealand Sauvignon Blanc involves the use of oak barrels and/or blending with Semillon. Riper, less assertive, and softer in texture, these wines have fruitier flavors, usually passion fruit or ripe grapefruit. New Zealand wine producers correctly foresaw that wine drinkers may need an alternative to the herbaceous style. The riper, fruitier, less herbaceous New Zealand Sauvignon Blancs are frequently labeled as *Reserve* wines or as single-vineyard wines. They generally retail for $20 to $30.

Pinot Noir is increasingly significant in New Zealand — and New Zealand is increasingly significant in the world of Pinot Noir. In fact, this grape has now surpassed Cabernet Sauvignon as New Zealand's most planted red variety. In addition to its stronghold in Martinborough, on the North Island, Pinot Noir is now being made throughout the South Island. Many wine producers in Marlborough make Pinot Noir in addition to Sauvignon Blanc. And the small, inland Central Otago wine zone, farther south on the South Island, has emerged as a key site for Pinot Noir.

Central Otago is home of the world's most southerly grapevines. Vines are planted on hillsides for more sunshine and less frost risk. The low-yielding vines here produce highly concentrated Pinot Noir wines. Mt. Difficulty and Felton Road, both from Central Otago, are currently two of New Zealand's best Pinot Noir producers.

Current trends in Kiwi Land

New Zealand Sauvignon Blancs are still hot and Pinot Noir seems to be the next "big thing." But New Zealand is more than just a two-grape country. In the white wine category, we're impressed with the improved Chardonnays, Rieslings, and Pinot Gris wines. The biggest surprise could be New Zealand's really fine Cabernet Sauvignons, Merlots, and Bordeaux-blends, not only from established warmer-climate North Island regions such as Hawke's Bay and its Gimblett Road zone, but also from Waiheke Island, a few miles east of the city of Auckland, where the climate is mild enough to grow Cabernet Franc and Petit Verdot.

New Zealand's final surprise is that it's making excellent sparkling wines by using the classic method (see Chapter 15 for an explanation of this winemaking system). Most of the better New Zealand sparkling wines use the two main grape varieties of Champagne, Pinot Noir, and Chardonnay. Highfield Estate is one of New Zealand's many fine sparkling wine producers.

New Zealand Pinot Noirs vary in taste from region to region; the wines of Martinborough, for example, are a bit more savory and minerally than those of Marlborough, which tend to be soft and fruity, while the wines of Central Otago tend to have more weight and concentrated fruit character. In time, as the producers of each region refine their styles, the regional differences should become more evident.

Chile's Rapid Wine Development

Chile's wine industry wears the mantle *New World* somewhat uncomfortably. The Spanish first established vineyards in Chile in the mid-16th century, and the country has maintained a thriving wine industry for its home market for several centuries. Nothing new about that. What *is* new about Chile, however, is the growth of her wine industry since the mid-1980s, her rapid development of a strong export market, and her embrace of French grape varieties such as Cabernet Sauvignon, Merlot, and Chardonnay — with an almost-forgotten red Bordeaux variety called Carménère definitely in the running, on the outside post position.

Yet another, even newer, aspect of Chilean wine is the expansion of the country's wine regions into outlying areas where growing conditions enable the production of styles of wine — fresher, crisper whites and more powerful reds — that are new to the national repertoire.

With the Pacific Ocean to its west and the Andes Mountains to the east, Chile is an isolated country. This isolation has its advantages in terms of grape growing: The Phylloxera louse hasn't yet taken hold in Chile — as it's done in just about every other winemaking country — and vinifera vines can, therefore, grow on their own roots. (For an explanation of phylloxera, see Chapter 3.) Chile's other viticultural blessings include the ocean's general tempering influence on a relatively hot climate and a range of mountains along the coast, which blocks the ocean dampness from most vineyards.

Red grape varieties represent 70 percent of Chile's production, with Cabernet Sauvignon accounting for 47 percent of those red grapes, followed by Merlot at 12 percent and Carménère, Chile's signature red, at 10 percent. Among white varieties, Chardonnay and Sauvignon Blanc are almost equally significant, representing 37 and 34 percent of white grape plantings respectively.

The following sections describe Chile's wine regions and specific wines in more detail.

Chile's wine regions

As in every other country, grape growers and wine producers in Chile originally planted vineyards in the most obvious locations, where vines would grow prolifically. Experience has gradually enabled them to discover the less obvious locations — many of them cooler, or hillier and thus less accessible — that offer the opportunity to make truly distinctive wines.

Initially considered the ideal place to plant grapes, and still the source of excellent wines, Maipo Valley surrounds Santiago, which is Chile's capital and its largest and only important city. (Convenience undoubtedly played a large role in the early development of this region.) Maipo Valley marks the northern part of Chile's vast Central Valley, which lies between the coastal range and the Andes. Even today, most of Chile's vineyards are in the Central Valley, but now vineyards also exist in regions that no one had heard of just ten years ago.

From north to south, here's a summary of Chile's wine regions today, both old and new:

- ✔ **Elqui Valley:** Close to the Atacama Desert, which covers much of northern Chile, this valley runs east to west. The climate of this tiny, fairly undeveloped region is cool and damp near the ocean and much warmer inland, where cloudless skies enable astronomical research. For the past decade, the pioneering Falernia winery has been making impressive Syrah wines from this area.

- ✔ **Limarí Valley:** A small, semiarid region about 250 miles northwest of Santiago, near the Pacific Ocean. Proximity to the Pacific brings cool morning fog and ocean breezes that blow through the Valley during the day. Chile's three largest wineries, Concha y Toro, San Pedro, and Santa Rita, all have bought land in Limarí. Promising wines so far are Sauvignon Blanc, Chardonnay, and Syrah. This is one of the country's "hot" emerging regions.

✔ **Aconcagua Valley:** North of Santiago, the dramatic Aconcagua Valley is named for the continent's highest mountain, Mount Aconcagua, and is one of the warmest areas for fine grapes. But Aconcagua also includes many cooler high-altitude sections. Cabernet Sauvignon grows especially well here, and more recently, Syrah. A new development is white wine from vineyards planted near the coast. Viña Errázuriz is Aconcagua Valley's most important winery.

✔ **Casablanca Valley:** This region was the first of Chile's newer coastal wine regions to be developed. Some of Chile's finest Chardonnays and Sauvignon Blancs grow in one part of Casablanca, while good Merlots and Pinot Noirs come from a higher-altitude part. Veramonte is Casablanca's best-known winery; Casas del Bosque and Loma Larga are two other noteworthy wineries. Many wineries elsewhere in Chile own vineyards in this region or buy grapes from here, and they turn to this area particularly for Chardonnay.

✔ **San Antonio Valley and Leyda Valley:** These two coastal areas (technically Leyda is part of San Antonio, but you can find it mentioned in its own right on wine labels) are south of Casablanca Valley and are perhaps Chile's most exciting new wine zones. The maritime influence produces impressive Sauvignon Blancs and Chardonnays in Leyda, while Pinot Noir and Syrah are growing especially well on the cool, steep slopes. Now making one of the world's better Pinot Noirs outside of Burgundy and perhaps even a better Syrah, Viña Matetic is a winery to watch in San Antonio Valley. Viña Leyda and Garces Silva are standouts in Leyda.

✔ **Maipo Valley:** Chile's most established wine region, almost surrounding Santiago, Maipo Valley is home to most of the country's famous wineries. Concha y Toro, Santa Rita, Carmen, Almaviva, and Viñedos Chadwick are a few of Maipo's premium producers. Cabernet Sauvignon is king in this region, and Merlot also does very well.

✔ **Cachapoal Valley:** The large Rapel Valley, south of Maipo Valley, has two main wine regions, Cachapoal Valley and Colchagua Valley. Cachapoal Valley, nearer the Andes, is a red wine region whose soil and climate vary according to proximity to the mountains. Cabernet Sauvignon is particularly significant here, followed by Merlot and Carménère. Morandé and Altair are two rising star wineries here.

✔ **Colchagua Valley:** This is a very diverse region because it features vineyards on the slopes of the Andes and all the way westward toward the sea. Cabernet Sauvignon, Merlot, Carménère, and Syrah grow especially well here, and the region abounds with well-known wineries. Colchagua's leading wineries include Casa Lapostolle, Montes, MontGras, Casa Silva, and Emiliana.

- **Curicó Valley:** One of Chile's oldest and largest wine regions, the Curicó Valley is directly south of Rapel Valley. Because of its diverse microclimates, both red and white varieties grow well here. The huge San Pedro Winery and Viña Miguel Torres are located in Curicó.

- **Maule:** Maule Valley is Chile's largest wine region in area, and also the southernmost of its important wine regions. Because it's so huge, it has many diverse microclimates, and both red and white varieties grow well, especially Sauvignon Blanc, Cabernet Sauvignon, and Merlot. Two wineries making very good wine here are O. Fournier and J. Bouchon.

Technically, under Chile's appellation system, most of the country's wine regions are grouped under fewer than a handful of DOs *(Denominación de Origen),* or official regions, and the remaining areas are subregions.

- The DO of **Coquimbo** encompasses the northern regions of Elqui, Limarí, and the tiny region of Choapa.

- The **Aconcagua** DO includes the western areas, namely the Aconcagua subregion, as well as Casablanca and San Antonio.

- The **Central Valley** DO covers Maipo, Rapel, Cachapoal, Colchagua, Curicó, and Maule.

- One additional DO is the **Southern Regions**, which encompasses Itata, Bío Bío, and Malleco; we don't address these southern regions because their wines are scarce abroad.

The face and taste of Chilean wines

Before Chilean wineries began making wines from grapes grown in the country's cooler regions, the style of Chilean wines was a bit easier to generalize: The wines could be described as generally lacking the exuberant fruitiness of Californian and Australian wines, while being not quite so subtle and understated as European wines. That generalization is still applicable to many of Chile's red wines, especially from the Central Valley areas, but you can now find many an exuberantly fruity Sauvignon Blanc or Pinot Noir from cooler regions.

Chile's Sauvignon Blanc wines are generally unoaked, while most of the Chardonnays are oaked. Red wines vary from simple everyday styles to elite, age-worthy wines.

Like most New World wines, Chile's wines are usually named for their grape varieties. The reasonable prices of the basic wines — mainly from $9 to $14 in the United States — make these wines excellent values. The wineries whose wines are easiest to find in export markets include, in alphabetical order, Calina, Caliterra, Carmen, Casa Lapostolle, Concha y Toro, Cousiño Macul, Errázuriz, Los Vascos, Mont Gras, Montes, Santa Carolina, Santa Rita, and Undurraga.

Surprising Syrah from Chile

In a recent visit to Chile, we saw clear signs of a rising star, Syrah wines from Chile's cooler regions. The Errázuriz winery in Aconcagua and the Montes winery in Colchagua Valley were pioneers in growing Syrah, but now the grape has caught on with winemakers in coastal areas such as San Antonio, Leyda Valley, Casablanca, and Limarí and in the northern region of Elqui. Syrah wines from these cool areas tend to be lean and firm in structure with vibrant flavors of black fruit, minerals, and spice. At Chile's annual Wines of Chile Awards in 2012, three cool-climate Syrah wines took prominent trophies, including the Best of Show wine, 2010 Viña Tamaya Winemaker's Selection Syrah from Límari. Maybe someone should warn Carménère?

Many wineries produce multiple tiers of wine that rise in price (and ideally, in quality) from a basic line to a higher-level line and ultimately what the wineries call their *icon wine,* a super-premium wine, usually a red. Ironically, many of the basic-level reds are labeled as *Reserve* wines (a regulated term but with a rather broad application).

The super-premium reds tend to be in the $45 to $90 price range. These elite Chilean wines are often blends rather than varietal wines, and many are styled along international lines — made from very ripe grapes that give rich, fruity flavors and high (14 percent or higher) alcohol levels and aged in small French oak barrels. What many (but not all) of them have lacked is a sense of place: They don't taste particularly Chilean. But as the wineries push the envelope of growing regions into the hilly foothills of the mountains and increasingly focus on soil types, Chile is beginning to produce fine wines that merit their high prices.

Keep an eye out for some of Chile's top super-premium red wines:

- Concha y Toro's Don Melchor Cabernet Sauvignon (about $65)
- Errázuriz's Don Maximiano Founder's Reserve (mainly Cabernet Sauvignon, about $80 to $85)
- Haras de Pirque Albis, a wine from a joint venture between the Chilean Haras de Pirque winery and the Italian Antinori company (Cabernet Sauvignon and Carménère, about $60)
- Montes Alpha M (a "Bordeaux blend," $75 to $90)
- Almaviva (a sleek and subtle red, mainly Cabernet Sauvignon with Carménère and Cabernet Franc, $90 to $100)
- Santa Rita's Casa Real Cabernet Sauvignon, one of Chile's pioneering elite wines (about $65)
- Casa Lapostolle's Clos Apalta (a blend of Carménère, Merlot, and Cabernet Sauvignon, about $60)

> ✔ Seña, from an estate in Aconcagua that was originally a partnership between the Robert Mondavi and Eduardo Chadwick (of Viña Errázuriz) families and is now owned by the Chadwicks (Cabernet Sauvignon, Merlot, and Carménère, $85 to $95)

For us, a particularly good value among Chile's super-premium wines is Casa Lapostolle's Clos Apalta.

Argentina, a Major League Player

Argentina boasts the largest wine production in South America and the sixth-highest wine production in the world. Although Argentina has long been a major wine-producing country in terms of its volume of production, its wines have become successful outside of Argentina only in this century. And they have become so successful and so popular that we would have to describe Argentina's ascendancy as meteoric. Not only is Argentina now a major player in the world wine market, but it's also one of the world's most exciting countries for wine production.

Wine grapes have grown in Argentina since the mid-16th century, as they have in Chile (we talk about Chile earlier in this chapter). Argentina's source of vines was more diverse, however; for example, many vines came to Argentina with the vast numbers of Italian and Basque immigrants. As a result, Argentina boasts grape varieties, such as Bonarda and Malbec, that are insignificant in Chile.

The following sections describe Argentina's wine regions, grapes, and wines in more detail.

Regions and grapes

Argentina's wine regions are situated mainly in the western part of the country, where the Andes Mountains divide Argentina from Chile. High altitude tempers the climate, but the vineyards are still very warm by day, as well as cool by night, and desert dry. Rivers flow through the area from the Andes and provide water for irrigation.

The vast majority of Argentina's vineyards are in the province of Mendoza, Argentina's largest wine region, which lies at roughly the same latitude as Santiago, Chile. Within the Mendoza region are various wine districts (the names of which sometimes appear on wine labels) such as Maipú, San Martín, Tupungato, and Luján de Cuyo. (Although winemakers are playing up district-based distinctions in their wines, we find that, for the most part, the wines express little differentiation.) Most of Argentina's oldest wineries and their vineyards are clustered close to Mendoza city, but the Uco Valley, south of the city, has attracted many newcomers who are building impressive wineries.

The province of San Juan, just north of Mendoza and considerably hotter, is Argentina's second-largest wine region. La Rioja province, Argentina's oldest wine-producing region, is east of San Juan, while the Salta province and wine region sits at the extreme northwest of the country.

San Juan is particularly famous for Torrontés, a white variety that's probably indigenous to Galicia, Spain. It produces an inexpensive ($9 to $14), light-bodied, high-acid, aromatic white wine that is fast becoming Argentina's signature white. It's especially fine with appetizers, seafood, and fish.

The mountainous Salta region has also emerged as a top area for Torrontés. Salta's subregion, Cafayate, has many vineyards growing at altitudes over 5,000 feet. The Torrontés wines made from the grapes of these vineyards have bracing acidity and are gaining a reputation as Argentina's best Torrontés. We think that Torrontés will be the new "hot" white wine coming from South America.

Argentina's newest wine area is in the southerly Patagonia region, including the provinces of Rio Negro and, farther south, Neuquén. This remote part of the country is slowly emerging as a favorable area for Pinot Noir, Chardonnay, and sparkling wines — all of which do best when their grapes grow in cool climates. So far, Patagonia's sparkling wines are doing particularly well and are arguably the best bubblies in all of South America.

Argentina's red wines are generally more interesting than its whites and far more numerous. Apart from Torrontés, most of the white wines are Chardonnay and Sauvignon Blanc. Red wines include Malbec, Cabernet Sauvignon, Bonarda (which actually exceeds Cabernet in plantings but is less evident among exports), and several Italian varieties, such as Barbera, Dolcetto, and Sangiovese, which also are uncommon in exported wines.

For red wines, the once little-known Malbec grape variety — now seldom used in Bordeaux, where it originated — has emerged as Argentina's flagship variety. Malbec has adapted extremely well to the Mendoza region, and winemakers are learning how it varies in the region's subzones. Debates continue as to whether Malbec or Cabernet Sauvignon makes Argentina's greatest red wines, but the fact remains that Malbec is Argentina's signature wine, while good Cabernet wines come from almost every wine-producing country.

Names to know

Thanks in part to its high altitudes and sunny days, Argentina's natural resources for grape growing are among the strongest in the world. Foreign investment continues to bring the capital and the winemaking know-how to make the most of these natural resources.

Malbec: From France to Argentina

At one point in the 19th century, the Malbec grape variety was a major player in France's Bordeaux region. But natural disasters have all but wiped out Malbec in Bordeaux. The first of these was the phylloxera affliction in the late 19th century, which practically destroyed all the vines. (See Chapter 3 for an explanation of phylloxera.) When the vineyards were replanted, many producers planted less Malbec because that grape needs lots of sun and warmth to fully ripen — conditions that Bordeaux, near the Atlantic Ocean, didn't always get. In addition, Malbec is prone to vine diseases and is vulnerable to frost. In fact, the second natural disaster, the 1956 frost in Bordeaux, wiped out 75 percent of the Malbec crop. Very few Bordeaux producers bothered to replant Malbec after that. (Ironically, a similar fate happened to Bordeaux's Carménère variety, which ripens too late for Bordeaux's climate;

Carménère found a new home in Argentina's next-door neighbor, Chile). In France, Malbec is still the important grape variety in the Cahors region in southwestern France, where it makes dark-colored, tannic wines.

Meanwhile, Malbec has been flourishing in Argentina's Mendoza region — where a French agronomist introduced it in the mid-19th century. Today, more Malbec grows in Mendoza than any other wine region in the world, and this grape is now Argentina's most important variety. Mendoza's warm, dry climate is perfect for Malbec, and the grape does particularly well in districts, such as Lujan de Cuyo and the Uco Valley, and in the foothills of the Andes, where some vineyards are up to 5,000 feet in altitude. Malbec makes dark, fruity wines in Argentina that are less tannic than the Malbec wines in Cahors, France, and more immediately drinkable.

- ✔ Bodega Norton, a winery that was purchased by Austrian crystal producer Swarovski in 1989, now makes some of the country's best wines.

- ✔ Moët & Chandon, another immigrant, is already Argentina's largest sparkling wine producer and it makes the Terrazas varietal table wines.

- ✔ A Dutchman owns the state-of-the-art Bodegas Salentein winery and its sister winery, Finca El Portillo.

- ✔ Bordeaux's Lurton family owns Bodega J. & F. Lurton.

- ✔ Bordeaux enologist Michel Rolland has created Clos de los Siete, an enclave of wineries in the Uco Valley, most of which are owned by Bordeaux families, including one property owned by Rolland himself. (He also makes a collective red wine from the group of wineries called Clos de Los Siete, a very refined wine, for about $16.)

On the homegrown front, Catena Zapata has emerged as one of Argentina's top wine producers. At $9 to $12 a bottle, its Alamos Malbec is one of the greatest wine values around. Catena Cabernet Sauvignon or Malbec (both $15 to $18), and the super-premium Malbec Alta or Cabernet Sauvignon Alta, both about $50, are higher-end wines, among the finest being made in South America today.

Trapiche is Argentina's leading export brand, and its wines offer very good quality with amazing value at the lower price points. Trapiche's Oak Cask Cabernet Sauvignon and Oak Cask Malbec, for example, are each about $10.

Argentine producers we recommend include, in alphabetical order, Achaval Ferrer, Alamos, Bodega J. & F. Lurton, Bodega Norton, Bodega Weinert, Bodegas Salentein, Catena, Cheval des Andes, Clos de LosSiete, DiamAndes, Dona Paula, El Portillo, Etchart, Finca Sophenia, Las Terrazas, Mendel, Michel Torino, Navarro Correas, Santa Julia, Trapiche, and Valentín Bianchi.

Some of Argentina's basic wines are priced the same as Chile's, in the $8 to $12 range, but a few wineries make pricier wines over $20. Cheval des Andes, a joint venture between Bordeaux's super wine, Château Cheval Blanc, and Argentina's Terrazas de los Andes, is a magnificent red Bordeaux-type blend (Malbec, Cabernet Franc, and Petit Verdot) that might be Argentina's best wine. It retails in the $65 to $75 range.

The South African Wine Safari

Vines came to South Africa in the 1650s with the Dutch, the first European settlers; in the same period, French Huguenots (Protestants) escaping religious persecution brought winemaking expertise. At the end of the 18th century, South Africa was producing a luscious fortified wine called Constantia, which became sought after in European royal courts. The country began focusing seriously on table wine production only in the 1980s, however. Today, South Africa ranks eighth in the world in wine production.

Most of South Africa's table wines come from an area known as the Coastal Region, around the Cape of Good Hope. Traditionally, large firms dominated South Africa's wine industry, and they continue to do so. KWV, formerly a wine growers' cooperative, is one of the country's largest wineries. South Africa's largest winery, the gigantic Distell firm, owns two groups of wineries that had been among the country's largest wine companies — Stellenbosch Farmers' Winery Group and the Bergkelder Group.

You can find out more about South Africa's regions and wines in the following sections.

South Africa's principal wine regions

South Africa has some vineyard areas with cool microclimates, especially around the southern coast, near the Cape of Good Hope (most of its vineyards are within 32 miles of the ocean) and in higher altitudes, but the climate in its wine regions is generally warm and dry.

South African style

Although we technically place South Africa in the New World, we must admit that its wines are rather reminiscent of European wines. The taste of a South African Cabernet Sauvignon, for example, may remind you of a French wine — but not quite. On the other hand, it doesn't really resemble a New World red from California or Australia, either. South African wines manage to combine the subtlety and finesse of French wines along with a touch of the voluptuous ripeness of California wines. In short, they are somewhat between both worlds.

South Africa's Wine of Origin legislation in 1973 created various wine regions, districts, and wards. Almost all the country's vineyards are near its southwestern coast, in Cape Province, within 90 miles of Cape Town, the country's most fascinating and picturesque city.

Following are the five major districts — mainly in the Coastal Region area:

- **Constantia:** The oldest wine-producing area (also known as *ward*) in the country, located south of Cape Town

- **Stellenbosch:** East of Cape Town; the most important wine district in quantity and quality

- **Paarl:** North of Stellenbosch; home of the KWV and the famous, beautiful Nederburg Estate; the second-most important wine district

- **Franschhoek Valley:** Used to be a ward of Paarl but is now a recognized district in its own right; many innovative winemakers here

- **Robertson:** East of Franschhoek, the only major district not in the Coastal Region; a hot, dry area, known mainly for its Chardonnays

The small, cool Hermanus/Walker Bay area, bordering the Indian Ocean, is also showing promise with Pinot Noir and Chardonnay, led by the innovative Hamilton Russell Winery. A relatively new wine district, Elgin, is on the coast between Stellenbosch and Walker Bay; a cool plateau area, Elgin shows promise for its intensely flavored Sauvignon Blancs and for Pinot Noirs. The latest area to show promise is Darling Hills, north of Cape Town, led by an up-and-coming winery, Groote Post. Two other emerging districts, dominated mainly by cooperatives, are Swartland, north of Capetown, and Worcester, inland from Capetown.

Varietal wines in South Africa must contain at least 75 percent of the named grape variety; exported wines (complying with the stricter European Union regulations) must contain 85 percent of the named variety. About 35 percent of South Africa's wines qualify as Wine of Origin (WO). WO wines must be made 100 percent from grapes of the designated area on the label. Wine of Origin regulations are based on the French *Appellation Contrôlée* laws (see

Chapter 10), and they strictly designate vineyards, allowable grape varieties, vintage-dating, and so on.

Steen, Pinotage, and company

The most-planted grape variety in South Africa is Chenin Blanc, often locally called *Steen*. This versatile grape primarily makes medium-dry to semisweet wines but also dry wines, sparkling wines, and late-harvest botrytis wines.

Cabernet Sauvignon, Merlot, Shiraz, and Pinot Noir have become increasingly important red varieties, while Sauvignon Blanc and Chardonnay are popular white varieties. Cabernet Sauvignon and Sauvignon Blanc do particularly well in South Africa's climate. (Producers here make a very assertive version of Sauvignon Blanc.)

And then you have Pinotage. Uniquely South African, Pinotage is a grape born as a crossing between Pinot Noir and Cinsaut (the same as Cinsault, the Rhône variety) back in 1925. However, Pinotage didn't appear as a wine until 1959. Pinotage wine combines the cherry fruit of Pinot Noir with the earthiness of a Rhône wine. It can be a truly delicious, light- to medium-bodied red wine that makes for easy drinking, or it can be a more powerful red. Although many good Pinotage wines sell for $15 to $20, the best Pinotages cost more. Kanonkop Estate, a specialist in this variety, makes classic Pinotages in the $30 to $35 range. Simonsig Estate makes a fine Pinotage for $16 to $18.

While Pinotage is a pleasant wine, certainly worth trying, we believe South Africa's future is with Cabernet Sauvignon, Merlot, and Shiraz (and blends of these grapes) for its red wines and Sauvignon Blanc and Chardonnay for its whites.

South Africa: The future

Chenin Blanc and Pinotage represent South Africa's recent past — although both are undergoing a revival today. Cabernet Sauvignon, Merlot, and Chardonnay are its present and are definitely making fine wines now. But Sauvignon Blanc and Shiraz seem to hold the most promise for the future.

✔ Sauvignon Blanc is a no-brainer; some of the world's best Sauvignon Blanc varietal wines are already being made here. The flavorful character of Sauvignon Blanc asserts itself in South Africa, especially in Constantia and in a new cool-climate ward, Elim, in Cape Agulhas. Although South African Sauvignon Blancs resemble those from New Zealand, they are easier to drink and not quite as assertive.

✔ Shiraz has become the hot, new variety of the Southern Hemisphere and indeed throughout the world. What South African winemakers love about Shiraz is its versatility: It can grow well in cool and in warm climates. Right now, Shiraz is the fastest-growing variety being planted in South Africa. In ten years or less, it may be the country's biggest-selling varietal wine.

Chapter 14

America, America

• •

In This Chapter

▶ The U.S.A.'s most famous wine address: Napa Valley

▶ The Golden Gate to Sonoma and beyond

▶ Oregon's Pinots

▶ Mister Red comes to Washington

▶ Islands, rivers, and lakes of New York wine

• •

*W*hen the *conquistadors* came to the New World of America in search of gold, Spanish missionaries accompanied them and planted the first wine grapevines in what is now Southern California. These "Mission" grapes, as they were called, still exist, but the noble grape varieties — Cabernet Sauvignon, Chardonnay, and the rest of the gang — have supplanted them to produce today's fine wines. One thing that hasn't changed is that California is still the focus of the American wine scene, although most of the wine business has moved to the northern part of the state; Southern California is now mainly filled with cars and people!

In this chapter, we cover American wines, paying particular attention to California's special wine regions, Napa Valley and Sonoma, but also discussing California's other wine regions, along with Oregon, Washington, and New York.

The New World of American Wine

Even though the United States produced wine commercially in the 19th century, the U.S. wine industry really only made it big beginning in the 1970s. Prohibition from 1919 to 1933, the Great Depression, and World War II were serious blows to the wine business — and recovery was slow.

Before 1970, only a few dozen operating wineries existed in California. By 2010, the state had 3,364 bonded wineries (about a dozen or so "giants," but mainly small, family-owned operations) — about four times as many wineries as existed just 14 years before, in 1996!

The growth of California's wine business has stimulated interest in wine all across the country. Today, wineries exist in all the 50 United States. But wine production is an important industry in only four states: California (the largest wine producing state, by far), Washington, Oregon, and New York. The United States currently is fourth in world wine production — although well behind the two leaders, Italy and France. (Spain is a distant third.) The following sections cover two interesting aspects of the world of American wine: the emphasis on a wine's grape variety and an appellation system that's different from the European model.

Homegrown ways

The wines of the United States — especially California — are the essence of New World wine-think. Winemakers operate freely, planting whatever grape variety they want, wherever they want to plant it. They blend wines from different regions together as they want. (Blending among states is trickier, because of federal rules.)

U.S. wines have elevated grape varieties to star status. Until California began naming wines after grapes, Chardonnay, Merlot, Pinot Noir, and Cabernet Sauvignon were just behind-the-scenes ingredients of wine — but now they *are* the wine. Lest anyone think that all wines from a particular grape are the same, however, winemakers have emerged as celebrities who put their personal spin on the best wines. In the California scenario especially, the land — the *terroir* — can often be secondary. With time, California wineries have bought into the European idea that *terroir* — the vineyard itself — is an essential part of a wine's character, but mainly for their finer wines.

American winemakers have embraced technology in their efforts to create wines that taste like fruit. California's two important universities for wine-making — California State University at Fresno and, especially, the University of California at Davis — have become world leaders in the scientific study of wine. Even European winemakers make pilgrimages to California to study at UC Davis.

Playing by their own rules

An appellation system for wines does exist in the United States, and like the classic French model (see Chapter 10), it identifies various vineyard regions. But the U.S. system of American Viticultural Areas (AVAs) establishes only the geographical boundaries of wine zones; it doesn't stipulate which grape varieties can be planted, the maximum yield of grapes per acre (see Chapter 5), or anything else that would link the geography to a particular style of wine. Therefore, AVA names, the names of the regions of production, logically have secondary importance on wine labels after the name of the grape.

A smorgasbord of AVAs

In naming their wines, winemakers often choose to use a broader AVA designation rather than a smaller, more specific one, in order to widen their options in buying grapes and wine. A winery in Alexander Valley, within Sonoma County, for example, may use the broader *Sonoma County* AVA rather than *Alexander Valley* if it buys grapes from (or owns vineyards in) other areas of the county and wants to use those grapes in its wine. It can use the larger *North Coast* AVA if it blends in grapes or wine from neighboring counties, like Napa. And if low price is a goal, the winery will use the even broader *California* AVA in order to buy less expensive grapes from the industrially farmed vineyards of the Central Valley (the San Joaquin Valley) or other parts of the state where grapes and wine are less expensive than in Sonoma County.

Sometimes, wineries use the *California* appellation even for their better wines, to give themselves complete freedom in sourcing their grapes. (This practice doesn't occur in smaller viticultural areas, such as southern Pennsylvania, where there are few alternative sources of grapes.) While specificity of place is admired, on the one hand, making a good wine at a good price through geographical blending is also admired. The relative merits depend on who's doing the admiring.

Traditional or not, America's way of making and naming wine sits just right with its local wine drinkers: American wines now account for about 70 percent of all wine sales in the United States, and of that 70 percent, 61 percent are California wines.

Wines labeled with the name of a grape variety in the United States must contain at least 75 percent of that grape variety, according to federal law. Wines with an AVA indication must be made from at least 85 percent of grapes from that viticultural area. Wines with vintage years must derive at least 85 percent from the named vintage.

California, U.S.A.

When most wine drinkers think about American wine, they think of California. That's not surprising — the wines of California make up about 90 percent of U.S. wine production.

California's Gallo Winery is the largest winery in the state — in fact, until recently, it was the largest wine company in the world — producing one out of every four bottles of wine sold in the United States. (Within the last decade, a large New York–based corporation, Constellation Brands, became the world's largest wine company through a series of acquisitions.)

It was another California company, the Robert Mondavi Winery, however, that stimulated fine wine production in the United States. In 1966, Robert Mondavi left his family's winery (Charles Krug Winery) to start his own operation, a winery dedicated to making premium wines. These finer wines — his own, and those of the many producers who would follow in his steps — would be varietally named Cabernet Sauvignon, Chardonnay, and so on. Identifying the wines by their grape varieties was a reaction against the low-priced jug wines that were then popular, wines labeled with names borrowed from Europe's wine regions, such as Burgundy and Chablis. Today, even Gallo is very much in the varietal wine business. And Robert Mondavi Winery is now part of the huge Constellation Brands corporation.

In the following sections, we name the state's most important wine regions and note the effects of weather on the variation of its wines.

Where California wines grow

In sunny California, there's no lack of warm climate for growing grapes. For fine wine production, the challenge is to find areas cool enough, with poor enough soil, so that grapes don't ripen too quickly, without full flavor development (see Chapter 5). Nearness to the Pacific Coast and relatively high altitudes are more important determinants of cooler climates than latitude is. Fine wines, therefore, come from vineyards up and down almost the whole length of the state.

The most important fine wine areas and districts include the following (see Figure 14-1):

- **North Coast:** Napa Valley, Sonoma County, Mendocino County, and Lake County
- **North-Central Coast:** Livermore and Santa Clara Valleys (San Francisco Bay area), Santa Cruz Mountains, Monterey County
- **Sierra Foothills**
- **South-Central Coast:** San Luis Obispo County, Santa Barbara County

We discuss all these regions in this chapter, but we cover them in even more detail in our book *California Wine For Dummies* (Wiley).

Signifying nothing

The words *reserve, special selection, private reserve, barrel select, vintners reserve, classic,* and so on have no legal definition in the United States. Although many premium wineries use these terms to indicate their special or better wines, most of the larger wineries use the same terms on their inexpensive bottlings as marketing tools (see Chapter 4).

Illustration by Lisa S. Reed

Figure 14-1:
The wine
regions of
California.

When the wines are good

Weather variations from year to year are far less dramatic in California
than they are in most European wine regions. One major reason is that rain
doesn't fall during the growing season in much of California. (Rain at the
wrong time is the usual cause of Europe's poorer vintages.) Using irrigation,
winemakers in effect control the water to their vines. Ironically, one factor
that can cause vintage variation in California is lack of water for irrigation
due to drought.

That said, the effects of global climate change have certainly impacted
California in recent years, and the future could see more vintage variation
than the past has.

Red wines finally catching up with Chardonnay

Chardonnay has been the perennial sales leader among domestic varietal wines in the United States for the past 20 years or so. But Americans are drinking more red wine these days, and red wine sales are finally catching up. In addition to Cabernet Sauvignon (still the leading red domestic varietal wine in sales) and Merlot, other red wines are gaining in popularity. These include Pinot Noir, red Zinfandel, and various other red wines.

Napa Valley: As Tiny as It Is Famous

Napa Valley is about a 90-minute drive northeast of the beautiful bay city of San Francisco. Many of California's most prestigious wineries — and certainly its most expensive vineyard land — are in the small Napa Valley, where about 400 wineries have managed to find space. (In 1960, Napa Valley had only 25 wineries.) The region's wine production is actually much tinier than its reputation: Napa Valley produces 4 percent of California's wine.

The southern part of the valley, especially the Carneros district, is the coolest area, thanks to ocean breezes and mists from the San Pablo Bay. Carneros — which extends westward into Sonoma County — has become the vineyard area of choice for grape varieties that enjoy the cool climate: Chardonnay, Pinot Noir, Merlot, and grapes for sparkling wines. North towards Calistoga — away from the bay influence — the climate can get quite hot (but always with cool nights).

Wineries and vineyards occupy almost every agricultural part of Napa Valley. Many vineyards are on the valley floor, some are in the hills and mountains to the west (the Mayacamas Mountains), and some are in the Vaca Mountains to the east (especially Howell Mountain). Napa winemakers and grape growers have established 16 AVAs besides the broad Napa Valley AVA itself (which always appears on the label beside the other AVAs) and the even broader, six-county North Coast AVA:

- Spring Mountain, Diamond Mountain, and Mt. Veeder (all in the Mayacamas Mountains)

- Howell Mountain, Stags Leap District, and Atlas Peak (all hilly or mountainous areas in eastern Napa Valley)

- Chiles Valley (in the easternmost part of Napa County)

- Oak Knoll District, Yountville, Oakville, Rutherford, St. Helena, and Calistoga (from south to north along the valley floor)

- Wild Horse Valley (in southeastern Napa Valley)

- Coombsville (east of the city of Napa)

- Los Carneros (part in Napa Valley, part in Sonoma)

The following sections discuss the wines, grapes, and important producers found in Napa.

The grapes of Napa

Almost everyone in Napa who makes table wine makes a Cabernet Sauvignon and a Chardonnay, and many Napa producers also make Merlot.

The six most important wines in Napa are the two whites, Chardonnay and Sauvignon Blanc (often labeled Fumé Blanc), and the four red wines, Cabernet Sauvignon, Merlot, Pinot Noir (mainly from cool Carneros), and Zinfandel. Cabernet Sauvignon is Napa Valley's most important wine in terms of production, followed by Chardonnay, Merlot, Sauvignon Blanc, Pinot Noir, and Zinfandel. Most critics regard Cabernet Sauvignon as Napa Valley's finest varietal wine.

But blended wines, which do not carry the name of a single grape variety, are also important. If red, these blends are usually made from red Bordeaux varieties (Cabernet Sauvignon, Cabernet Franc, Merlot, and sometimes even Malbec and Petit Verdot). If white, they're usually made from the white Bordeaux grapes (Sauvignon Blanc and Sémillon). Some of these blends are referred to as Meritage wines — not just in Napa but across the United States — although few carry the word *Meritage* on their labels. (The term *Meritage* can be used only for red or white wines that utilize grape varieties traditional for making red or white Bordeaux wine; see Chapter 10 for info on Bordeaux.)

From less than $10 to more than $200

You can find a few Chardonnays, Cabernets, Pinot Noirs, and Merlots from California at prices less than $10 a bottle. Better wines can be quite expensive, however. Most mid-range varietal wines are in the $25 to $60 range. Reserves, single-vineyard wines, and special selection wines generally can cost $60 to $200 and up.

Sauvignon Blancs — somewhat less in demand than Chardonnay, Cabernet, Pinot Noir, and Merlot — are the best values among California's premium wines. You can find some Sauvignon Blancs for less than $16, with many good ones from $18 to $20, although a few are priced as high as $30. Red Zinfandels are also still a bargain, but their prices are climbing as they become more popular. You can still buy many red Zins from $15 to $20, although a few premium Zinfandels are well over $20. If you like White Zinfandels, which are distinctly sweeter than the reds, you can save yourself a bundle; they're in the $7 to $10 range.

Who's who in Napa (and for what)

If just about every winery in Napa makes a Chardonnay and a Cabernet Sauvignon, how can you distinguish the wineries from one another? Good question — with no easy answer. The following alphabetical list indicates some of the better wine producers in Napa Valley, as well as their best wines, and can help steer you in the right direction. We know the list looks overwhelming, but . . . that's Napa!

Our list includes Napa classics as well as some personal favorites. We cover sparkling wine producers in Chapter 15.

Although all the wineries in the following list are situated in Napa Valley, their wines are not necessarily always made with Napa-grown grapes; the geographic name on the label tells you where the grapes came from.

- **Anderson's Conn Valley:** Cabernet Sauvignon, Chardonnay

- **Araujo Estate:** Cabernet Sauvignon (Eisele Vineyard), Syrah

- **Beaulieu Vineyard:** Cabernet Sauvignon Private Reserve (Georges de Latour), Cabernet Sauvignon (Rutherford)

- **Beringer Vineyards:** Cabernet Sauvignon (single-vineyard wines), Chardonnay Private Reserve, Merlot (Bancroft Ranch)

- **Cain Cellars:** Cain Five (five Bordeaux varieties), Cain Cuvée

- **Cakebread Cellars:** Cabernet Sauvignon, Sauvignon Blanc, Chardonnay

- **Caymus Vineyard:** Cabernet Sauvignon (especially *Special Selection*)

- **Chappellet:** Chenin Blanc, Cabernet Sauvignon

- **Charles Krug:** Cabernet Sauvignon, Chardonnay (Family Reserves)

- **Chateau Montelena:** Cabernet Sauvignon, Calistoga Cuvée Red, Chardonnay

- **Clos du Val:** Cabernet Sauvignon, Sémillon, Chardonnay

- **Corison:** Cabernet Sauvignon

- **Dominus Estate:** Dominus (mainly Cabernet Sauvignon), Napanook

- **Duckhorn:** Merlot, Cabernet Sauvignon, Sauvignon Blanc

- **Dunn Vineyards:** Cabernet Sauvignon (especially Howell Mountain)

- **Far Niente:** Cabernet Sauvignon, Chardonnay

- **Flora Springs:** Trilogy (blend of Cabernet Sauvignon, Merlot, Cabernet Franc), Cabernet Sauvignon Reserve, Soliloquy (Sauvignon Blanc)

- **Forman Vineyard:** Chardonnay, Cabernet Sauvignon

- **Franciscan Estate:** Chardonnay, Magnificat Red, Cabernet Sauvignon

- ✔ **Freemark Abbey:** Cabernet Sauvignon (Bosché and Sycamore)
- ✔ **Frog's Leap Winery:** Cabernet Sauvignon, Zinfandel, Sauvignon Blanc
- ✔ **Grgich Hills Cellar:** Chardonnay, Cabernet Sauvignon, Fumé Blanc
- ✔ **Harlan Estate:** Cabernet Sauvignon (small winery; very scarce)
- ✔ **Heitz Wine Cellars:** Cabernet Sauvignon (Martha's Vineyard)
- ✔ **Hess Collection Winery:** Cabernet Sauvignon, Chardonnay
- ✔ **Inglenook (formerly Rubicon; Niebaum-Coppola):** Rubicon (mainly Cabernet Sauvignon), Edizone Pennino Zinfandel
- ✔ **Joseph Phelps Vineyards:** Insignia (Cabernet blend)
- ✔ **Long Vineyards:** Chardonnay, Riesling, Pinot Grigio
- ✔ **Markham Vineyards:** Chardonnay, Merlot, Cabernet Sauvignon
- ✔ **Mayacamas Vineyards:** Cabernet Sauvignon, Sauvignon Blanc
- ✔ **Mount Veeder Winery:** Cabernet Sauvignon, Reserve Red
- ✔ **Newton Vineyard:** Chardonnay, Merlot, Cabernet Sauvignon
- ✔ **Nickel & Nickel:** Cabernet Sauvignon (all single-vineyard wines)
- ✔ **Opus One:** Opus One (mainly Cabernet Sauvignon)
- ✔ **Pahlmeyer Winery:** Red (Cabernet blend), Merlot, Chardonnay
- ✔ **Quintessa Estate:** Quintessa (Bordeaux blend)
- ✔ **Robert Mondavi Winery:** Cabernet Sauvignon Reserve, Pinot Noir Reserve
- ✔ **Saintsbury:** Pinot Noir (all), Chardonnay
- ✔ **Shafer Vineyards:** Cabernet Sauvignon, Merlot
- ✔ **Silver Oak Cellars:** Cabernet Sauvignon
- ✔ **Silverado Vineyards:** Cabernet Sauvignon, Chardonnay (Carneros)
- ✔ **Smith-Madrone:** Riesling, Chardonnay, Cabernet Sauvignon
- ✔ **Spottswoode Winery:** Cabernet Sauvignon, Sauvignon Blanc
- ✔ **Staglin Family Vineyard:** Cabernet Sauvignon
- ✔ **Stag's Leap Wine Cellars:** Cask 23 (Cabernet blend), Cabernet Sauvignon (Fay Vineyard and SLV), Chardonnay
- ✔ **Stony Hill Vineyard:** Chardonnay, Riesling
- ✔ **Swanson Vineyards:** Cabernet Sauvignon, Merlot, Syrah
- ✔ **Trefethen Vineyards:** Cabernet Sauvignon, Chardonnay, Riesling (dry)
- ✔ **Turley Wine Cellars:** Zinfandel (all single-vineyard Zinfandels)
- ✔ **Turnbull Cellars:** Cabernet Sauvignon, Turnbull Red "Black Label"

Down-to-Earth in Sonoma

If you leave San Francisco over the beautiful Golden Gate Bridge, you'll be in Sonoma in an hour. The differences between Napa and Sonoma are remarkable. Many of Napa's wineries are showy (even downright luxurious), but most of Sonoma's are rustic, country-like, and laid back. The millionaires bought into Napa; Sonoma is just folks (with some exceptions, of course).

On the other hand, the famously successful Gallo is also in Sonoma, and so are Sebastiani, Glen Ellen, Korbel, Kendall-Jackson, Simi, Francis Ford Coppola, and Jordan wineries — not exactly small-time operations! We have the sneaking suspicion that at some point in the future, Sonoma will bear a striking resemblance to Napa. We hope not; we like it just the way it is.

Find out more about Sonoma's viticultural areas, grapes, and important producers in the following sections.

Sonoma's AVAs

Sonoma is more than twice as large as Napa, it's more spread out, and it has almost as many wineries — more than 300. Its climate is similar to Napa's, except that some areas near the coast are definitely cooler. Although there's plenty of Chardonnay, Cabernet Sauvignon, and Merlot in Sonoma, the region's varied microclimates and terrain have allowed three other varieties — Pinot Noir, Zinfandel, and Sauvignon Blanc — to excel.

The following are the viticultural areas (AVAs) of Sonoma County listed roughly from south to north with their principal grape varieties and wines:

- **Los Carneros** (part in Napa Valley): Pinot Noir, Chardonnay, sparkling wine, and Merlot
- **Sonoma Valley:** Chardonnay (and to a lesser extent, Pinot Noir, Cabernet Sauvignon, Zinfandel)
- **Sonoma Mountain:** Cabernet Sauvignon
- **Bennett Valley:** Chardonnay, Sauvignon Blanc, Merlot
- **Fort Ross-Seaview** (new AVA, on the Extreme Sonoma Coast): Pinot Noir, Chardonnay
- **Russian River Valley:** Pinot Noir, Chardonnay, sparkling wine, Zinfandel
- **Sonoma-Green Valley** (within Russian River Valley): Sparkling wine, Chardonnay, Pinot Noir
- **Chalk Hill** (within Russian River Valley): Chardonnay, Sauvignon Blanc
- **Dry Creek Valley:** Zinfandel, Cabernet Sauvignon, Sauvignon Blanc

- **Alexander Valley:** Cabernet Sauvignon, Chardonnay, Sauvignon Blanc
- **Pine Mountain-Cloverdale Peak** (new, mountainous AVA, including some of Alexander Valley AVA, and extending north into Mendocino County): Cabernet Sauvignon, Merlot, Cabernet Franc
- **Knight's Valley:** Cabernet Sauvignon, Sauvignon Blanc
- **Rockpile** (in the northwestern part of the county): Zinfandel, Cabernet Sauvignon, Syrah, Petite Sirah

Sonoma County has two more AVAs: Northern Sonoma, a patchwork area encompassing Russian River Valley, Alexander Valley, Dry Creek Valley, and Knight's Valley; and Sonoma Coast, a hodgepodge of land in western Sonoma, along the coast. Also, the North Coast AVA takes in Sonoma County.

The True Coast

Called by its fans simply as "The True," the *True Sonoma Coast*, also known as the *Extreme Sonoma Coast*, refers to a section of the huge Sonoma Coast AVA along the Pacific Ocean, from the town of Fort Ross north to Annapolis. It includes the towns of Occidental and Freestone and the Sebastopol hills. Wine producers and growers with wineries and/or vineyards on the Extreme Sonoma Coast felt the need to distinguish their area from the rest of the Sonoma Coast AVA because their wines are unique, reflecting the *terroir* of the coastal area. Hence, the name True Coast evolved. The first step toward redefining the huge, nonspecific Sonoma Coast AVA just took place in January 2012, when the Fort Ross-Seaview AVA was created, covering an important vineyard area on the Extreme Sonoma Coast, close to the Pacific Ocean.

One of the main climactic influences in the True Coast area is the Petaluma Gap effect, a 15-mile virtual wind tunnel of ocean breezes that sweep through an opening in the mountain ranges at Bodega Bay (a village hugging the Pacific Ocean). This cool, windy effect, along with plenty of sun, makes an ideal growing climate for Pinot Noir and Chardonnay. Because of the cool climate, Pinot Noir grapes ripen later on the True Coast, and the wines are typically lower in alcohol than Pinot Noirs from other parts of Sonoma. True Coast Pinot Noirs tend to be lighter in color and in weight than most other California Pinot Noirs. But they possess elegance and balance, plus a delicacy and finesse not usually found in U.S. Pinots.

Quite a few top wineries specializing in Pinot Noir — such as Williams Selyem, Littorai, Hartford Coast, Failla, DuNah Vineyard, and Willowbrook — purchase grapes from True Coast growers and make their own single-vineyard Sonoma Coast Pinot Noirs. Because most of the wineries actually in the True Coast area are so miniscule, producing only a few thousand cases of wine annually (mainly Pinot Noir), we don't list their names in the section "Sonoma producers and wines." Flowers Vineyard & Winery is the largest producer on the Extreme Sonoma Coast, and its wines are thus easier to find than those of the smaller wineries. Other wineries whose wines we urge Pinot Noir lovers to seek out include Hirsch Vineyards, Cobb Winery (including Coastland Vineyard), Peay Vineyards, Wild Hog Vineyard, Freestone, Fort Ross Vineyard, Lioco, Drew Family Estate, B. Kosuge, Evening Land, and Red Car. Wines from this special area are difficult to find in retail shops; your best bet is to look for them online or contact the wineries directly.

Pinot Noir lovers should look for wines from Russian River Valley producers, such as Williams & Selyem, Rochioli, and Dehlinger. Another new, "hot" area for Pinot Noir — an area called the *Extreme Sonoma Coast* or *True Coast* — is ideal for growing Pinot Noir. See the nearby sidebar "The True Coast" for details.

Sonoma producers and wines

The following list of recommended producers includes some of Sonoma's better wineries, listed alphabetically, along with their best wines.

Although these wineries are all in Sonoma County, some wines are made from grapes grown elsewhere. Cline Cellars, for example, uses grapes from Contra Costa County, east of San Francisco. Check the labels to find out.

- ✔ **Arrowood Vineyards:** Chardonnay, Cabernet Sauvignon, Syrah
- ✔ **Benziger Family Winery:** Cabernet Sauvignon, Sauvignon Blanc
- ✔ **Chalk Hill Estate:** Sauvignon Blanc, Chardonnay, Cabernet Sauvignon
- ✔ **Chateau St. Jean:** Chardonnay (Robert Young, Belle Terre Vineyards), Cabernet Sauvignon (Cinq Cépages)
- ✔ **Cline Cellars:** Mourvèdre, Zinfandel
- ✔ **Clos du Bois:** Marlstone (Cabernet blend), Chardonnay
- ✔ **Dehlinger Winery:** Pinot Noir, Chardonnay, Syrah
- ✔ **Dry Creek Vineyard**, Fumé Blanc, Chenin Blanc, Zinfandel
- ✔ **Ferrari-Carano:** Chardonnay, Fumé Blanc, Cabernet Sauvignon
- ✔ **Fisher Vineyards:** Chardonnay, Cabernet Sauvignon
- ✔ **Flowers Vineyard & Winery:** Pinot Noir, Chardonnay
- ✔ **Foppiano Vineyards:** Petite Sirah, Cabernet Sauvignon, Merlot
- ✔ **Freestone Vineyards:** Pinot Noir, Chardonnay
- ✔ **Gallo Family Vineyards:** Chardonnay (Laguna Ranch), Zinfandel
- ✔ **Hanzell Vineyards:** Chardonnay
- ✔ **Hartford Court (also known as Hartford Family Winery):** Pinot Noir (all), Zinfandel
- ✔ **Jordan Vineyard:** Cabernet Sauvignon, Chardonnay
- ✔ **Kendall-Jackson:** Cabernet Sauvignon, Chardonnay, Zinfandel
- ✔ **Kenwood Vineyards:** Cabernet Sauvignon (Artist Series), Zinfandel
- ✔ **Kistler Vineyards:** Chardonnay, Pinot Noir

- **Joseph Swan Vineyards:** Pinot Noir, Zinfandel
- **La Crema Winery:** Chardonnay, Pinot Noir
- **La Follette Wines:** Pinot Noir, Chardonnay
- **Laurel Glen Vineyard:** Cabernet Sauvignon
- **Littorai Wines:** Pinot Noir, Chardonnay
- **Marcassin:** Chardonnay (all vineyards; very scarce, by mailing list)
- **Marimar Torres Estate:** Chardonnay, Pinot Noir
- **Martinelli Vineyard:** Zinfandel, Chardonnay (Russian River Valley)
- **Matanzas Creek Winery:** Chardonnay, Sauvignon Blanc, Merlot
- **Merry Edwards Winery:** Pinot Noir, Sauvignon Blanc
- **Paul Hobbs:** Cabernet Sauvignon, Chardonnay, Pinot Noir
- **Peter Michael Winery:** Chardonnay, Les Pavots (Cabernet blend)
- **Preston of Dry Creek:** Zinfandel, Syrah, Barbera
- **Quivira Vineyards:** Zinfandel, Syrah, Petite Sirah
- **A. Rafanelli Winery:** Zinfandel, Cabernet Sauvignon (mailing list)
- **Ramey Wine Cellars:** Cabernet Sauvignon, Chardonnay, Syrah
- **Ravenswood:** Zinfandel (single vineyards), Merlot (Sangiacomo Vineyard), Pickberry (Cabernet Sauvignon–Merlot blend)
- **J. Rochioli Vineyard:** Pinot Noir (all), Sauvignon Blanc, Zinfandel
- **Saint Francis Winery:** Zinfandel, Merlot, Cabernet Sauvignon
- **Sebastiani Vineyards:** Cabernet Sauvignon, Merlot, Chardonnay
- **Seghesio Family Estates:** Zinfandel (all), Sangiovese, Barbera
- **Sonoma-Cutrer Vineyards:** Chardonnay (all selections)
- **Stonestreet:** Cabernet Sauvignon (all), Chardonnay, Sauvignon Blanc
- **Williams Selyem Winery:** Pinot Noir (all), Zinfandel, Chardonnay

Mendocino and Lake Counties

Lake County, dominated by Clear Lake, is Napa's neighbor to the north, and Mendocino County is directly north of Sonoma.

If you have the chance, it's worth your while to drive up the beautiful California coastline from San Francisco on Route 1 to the quaint, old town of Mendocino — perhaps with a side trip to view the magnificent, giant redwoods of the Pacific Coast. Tourists are scarcer up here than in Napa or

Sonoma, and that makes it all the nicer: You'll be genuinely welcomed at the wineries.

The cool Anderson Valley in Mendocino County is ideal for growing Chardonnay, Pinot Noir, Gewürztraminer, and Riesling, and for the production of sparkling wine. The wily Louis Roederer Champagne house bypassed Napa and Sonoma to start its sparkling wine operation here and has done extremely well in a short time — as have Scharffenberger and Handley, two other successful sparkling wine producers in Anderson Valley (see Chapter 15 for more sparkling wine producers).

The following list includes recommended producers and their best wines. We list the producers alphabetically in each county.

- ✔ **Mendocino County:**
  - **Brutocao Cellars:** Zinfandel, Barbera, Dolcetto
  - **Edmeades:** Zinfandel (especially single vineyards)
  - **Elke Vineyards:** Pinot Noir
  - **Fetzer Vineyards:** Pinot Noir Reserve, Cabernet Sauvignon Reserve
  - **Frey Vineyards:** Petite Sirah, Zinfandel
  - **Goldeneye Winery (Duckhorn):** Pinot Noir
  - **Greenwood Ridge Vineyards:** Riesling, Pinot Noir, Zinfandel
  - **Handley Cellars:** Chardonnay, Gewürztraminer, Sauvignon Blanc
  - **Husch:** Pinot Noir, Sauvignon Blanc, Gewürztraminer, Chenin Blanc
  - **Lazy Creek Vineyards:** Gewürztraminer, Riesling
  - **Lolonis Winery:** Cabernet Sauvignon (all), Zinfandel
  - **McDowell Valley Vineyards:** Syrah, Viognier
  - **Navarro Vineyards:** Gewürztraminer, Chardonnay (Reserve)
- ✔ **Lake County:**
  - **Guenoc Winery:** Cabernet Sauvignon, Chardonnay, Langtry Meritage Red (Cabernet blend), Petite Sirah Reserve
  - **Langtry Estate & Vineyards:** Petite Sirah, Sauvignon Blanc
  - **Shannon Ridge Vineyards:** Sauvignon Blanc, Zinfandel
  - **Steele Wines:** Chardonnay, Zinfandel, Pinot Noir, Pinot Blanc
  - **Wildhurst Vineyards:** Cabernet Sauvignon, Chardonnay, Merlot

The San Francisco Bay Area

The San Francisco Bay area includes wine regions north, east, and south of the city: Marin County to the north; Alameda County and Livermore Valley to the east; and San Mateo County to the south.

The urban spread east and south of San Francisco, from the cities of Palo Alto to San Jose (Silicon Valley) and eastward, has taken its toll on vineyards in the Livermore and Santa Clara Valleys (all just about gone from Santa Clara Valley). Livermore Valley, cooled by breezes from the San Francisco Bay, is now relatively small. In Livermore, directly east of San Francisco, Sauvignon Blanc and Sémillon have always done well.

We list our recommended wineries alphabetically, by locality.

✔ **Marin County:**

- **Kalin Cellars:** Sauvignon Blanc, Sémillon, Chardonnay, Pinot Noir; grapes from diverse areas, including Livermore Valley

- **Sean H. Thackrey:** Orion Old Vines Red (Syrah blend), Sirius (Petite Sirah); grapes come from several different areas, including Napa

✔ **Alameda County/Livermore Valley:**

- **A Donkey and Goat Winery:** Grenache Rosé, Chardonnay, Mourvèdre

- **Concannon Vineyard:** Chardonnay, Petite Sirah

- **Dashe Cellars:** Zinfandel, Grenache, dry Riesling

- **Edmunds St. John:** Syrah, Rocks and Gravel (Rhône blend); grapes are sourced from throughout the state

- **Murrieta's Well:** Zinfandel, Red Meritage (Cabernet blend)

- **Wente Family Estates:** Chardonnay, Sauvignon Blanc

✔ **San Mateo County:**

- **Cronin Vineyards:** Chardonnay, Cabernet Sauvignon

- **Thomas Fogarty Winery:** Gewürztraminer, Chardonnay, Pinot Noir

The Santa Cruz Mountains

Standing atop one of the isolated Santa Cruz Mountains, you can quickly forget that you're only an hour's drive south of San Francisco. The rugged, wild beauty of this area has attracted quite a few winemakers, including some of the best in the state. (Paul Draper of Ridge Vineyards and Randall Grahm of Bonny Doon are but two.) The climate is cool on the ocean side, where Pinot Noir thrives. On the San Francisco Bay side, Cabernet Sauvignon is the important red variety. Chardonnay is a leading variety on both sides.

We list our recommended Santa Cruz Mountains wine producers alphabetically, along with their best wines:

- **Bargetto:** Chardonnay, Pinot Noir, Cabernet Sauvignon, Merlot (Bargetto is also in Monterey County; see the next section)
- **Bonny Doon Vineyard:** Le Cigare Volant Red (Rhône blend)
- **David Bruce Winery:** Pinot Noir
- **Cinnabar Vineyards:** Chardonnay, Cabernet Sauvignon
- **Kathryn Kennedy Winery:** Cabernet Sauvignon, Syrah
- **Mount Eden Vineyards:** Chardonnay Estate, Pinot Noir Estate, Cabernet Sauvignon Estate
- **Ridge Vineyards:** Cabernet Sauvignon Monte Bello, Geyserville (Zin blend), Zinfandel (all)
- **Santa Cruz Mountain Vineyard:** Pinot Noir, Cabernet Sauvignon

What's New in Old Monterey

Monterey County has a little bit of everything — a beautiful coastline, the chic town of Carmel, some very cool (as in temperature, not chicness) vineyard districts, and some very warm areas, mountain wineries and Salinas Valley wineries, a few gigantic wine firms, and lots of small ones. Like most California wine regions, Monterey has been changing rapidly during the past two decades, and now nine official viticultural areas (AVAs) exist here, covering about 85 wineries:

- Arroyo Seco
- Carmel Valley
- Chalone
- Hames Valley

✔ Monterey

✔ San Antonio Valley

✔ San Bernabe

✔ San Lucas

✔ Santa Lucia Highlands

Santa Lucia Highlands, in particular, is now one of the prime new Pinot Noir regions in California.

Chardonnay is the leading varietal wine in Monterey County — as it is in most of the state. But the cooler parts of Monterey are also principal sources of Riesling and Gewürztraminer. Cabernet Sauvignon and Pinot Noir are the leading red varieties in the mountain areas.

The following are our recommended producers in Monterey County, listed alphabetically, along with one producer from neighboring San Benito County:

✔ **Bernardus Winery:** Chardonnay, Sauvignon Blanc, Marinus (mainly Cabernet Sauvignon), Pinot Noir

✔ **Calera (San Benito County):** Pinot Noir (especially single-vineyard selections), Viognier, Chardonnay, Aligoté

✔ **Chalone Vineyard:** Chardonnay, Pinot Blanc, Pinot Noir

✔ **Chateau Julien:** Chardonnay, Merlot, Cabernet Sauvignon

✔ **Estancia Estates:** Chardonnay, Cabernet Sauvignon, Merlot, Pinot Noir

✔ **Hahn Estates/Smith & Hook Winery:** Chardonnay, Pinot Noir: Smith & Hook Cabernet Sauvignon

✔ **Jekel Vineyards:** Riesling, Chardonnay, Pinot Noir

✔ **Morgan Winery:** Chardonnay, Pinot Noir, Syrah

✔ **Paraiso Vineyards:** Pinot Noir, Chardonnay, Riesling, Syrah

✔ **Robert Talbott Vineyards:** Chardonnay

Gold Country: The Sierra Foothills

No wine region in America has a more romantic past than the Sierra Foothills. The Gold Rush of 1849 carved a place in history for the foothills of the Sierra Nevada Mountains. It also brought vineyards to the area to provide wine for the thirsty miners. One of the vines planted at that time was certainly Zinfandel — still the region's most famous wine. Many of the oldest grapevines in the United States, some more than 100 years old — mainly Zinfandel — are here in the Sierra Foothills.

In fact, very little has changed in the Sierra Foothills over the years. This is clearly the most rustic wine region on the West Coast — and perhaps in the country. Therein lies its charm. A visit to the Sierra Foothills is like a trip into the past, when life was simple.

The Sierra Foothills is a sprawling wine region east of Sacramento, centered in Amador and El Dorado Counties, but spreading north and south of both. Two of its best-known viticultural areas are Shenandoah Valley and Fiddletown. Summers can be hot, but many vineyards are situated as high as 1,500 feet — such as around Placerville in El Dorado — and evenings are very cool. Soil throughout the region is mainly volcanic in origin.

The following are our recommended producers in the Sierra Foothills (listed alphabetically), along with their best wines:

- **Amador Foothill Winery:** Zinfandel
- **Boeger Winery:** Zinfandel, Barbera, Sauvignon Blanc
- **Karly Winery:** Zinfandel, Sauvignon Blanc
- **Lava Cap Winery:** Barbera, Cabernet Sauvignon, Petite Sirah
- **Montevina Winery:** Zinfandel, Barbera, Syrah
- **Renaissance Vineyard:** Cabernet Sauvignon, Riesling (Late Harvest)
- **Shenandoah Vineyards:** Zinfandel, Sauvignon Blanc
- **Sierra Vista Winery:** Zinfandel, Syrah
- **Sobon Estate:** Zinfandel, Viognier
- **Stevenot Winery:** Syrah, Zinfandel

San Luis Obispo — from Warm to Cool

San Luis Obispo County is an area of vastly diverse viticultural areas. These include, for example, the warm, hilly Paso Robles region (north of the town of San Luis Obispo) where Zinfandel, Cabernet Sauvignon, and Syrah reign, and the cool, coastal Edna Valley and Arroyo Grande (south of the town), home of some very good Pinot Noirs and Chardonnays.

Paso Robles is one of California's fastest-growing wine regions, with more than 180 wineries — twice as many as it had just five years ago. It is in the heart of California's Central Coast, about equidistant from San Francisco and Los Angeles. Its wines are so different from those of the two coastal areas that we name the producers separately. We recommend the following producers in San Luis Obispo (listed alphabetically, along with their best wines):

- ✔ **Paso Robles:**

  - **Adelaida Cellars:** Pinot Noir, Zinfandel, Cabernet Sauvignon
  - **Caparone Winery:** Sangiovese, Aglianico, Nebbiolo
  - **Clayhouse Wines:** Petite Sirah, Syrah, Malbec
  - **Eberle Winery:** Zinfandel, Cabernet Sauvignon, Syrah, Viognier
  - **Justin Vineyards:** Isosceles (Cabernet blend), Cabernet Sauvignon, Syrah, Chardonnay
  - **J. Lohr Winery:** Chardonnay, Cabernet Sauvignon, Syrah
  - **Meridian Vineyards** (also has vineyards in Edna Valley and Santa Barbara): Chardonnay (especially Reserve), Syrah
  - **Peachy Canyon Winery:** Zinfandel
  - **Robert Hall Winery:** Rhône blends, Viognier, Sauvignon Blanc
  - **Tablas Creek Vineyard:** Mourvèdre, Grenache, Syrah, Roussanne
  - **Hope Family Wines/Treana:** Red (mainly Cabernet Sauvignon, Merlot, Syrah), White (mainly Marsanne and Viognier)

- ✔ **Edna Valley and Arroyo Grande:**

  - **Alban Vineyards:** Viognier (Estate), Roussanne, Syrah, Grenache
  - **Claiborne & Churchill:** Riesling, Pinot Gris, Pinot Noir
  - **Edna Valley Vineyard:** Chardonnay, Pinot Noir, Cabernet Sauvignon
  - **Laetitia Vineyard:** Chardonnay, Pinot Noir
  - **Saucelito Canyon Vineyard:** Zinfandel
  - **Talley Vineyards:** Chardonnay, Pinot Noir

Do you like Italian red wines but haven't had much luck finding good "Cal-Ital" wines in California? We have the winery for you! In their small winery outside of Paso Robles, Dave Caparone and his son Marc are making the most authentic California wines from Italian varieties that we have tasted. Caparone's Sangiovese and Aglianico are possibly the best examples of these challenging Italian varietal wines in the United States, in our opinion. Caparone's Nebbiolo is very good, although not quite up to the other two wines yet, but it's getting better all the time.

Location! Location!

Adelaida Cellars is blessed with one of the more remarkable settings in California for its winery and vineyards. It is situated almost 2,000 feet high on one of the hillsides of the Santa Lucia Mountains, 16 miles west of the town of Paso Robles, and 16 miles east of the Pacific Ocean. Its altitude enables Adelaida and its nearby vineyards to catch the cool afternoon breezes from the Pacific, creating a perfect environment for growing grapes. With plenty of sunshine during the day and a nighttime drop in temperature that can be as much as 50 degrees Fahrenheit, climate conditions are unique for making both an outstanding Pinot Noir from 48-year-old vines of the renowned HMR Estate Vineyard plus an equally outstanding Cabernet Sauvignon from its Viking Estate Vineyard. It is extremely rare throughout the world, let alone California, to find a winery that can make both a superior Pinot Noir and an excellent Cabernet Sauvignon in the same general area. Adelaida's Zinfandels are very fine as well. If you're in the area, Adelaida Cellars is a "must" visit.

Santa Barbara, Californian Paradise

The most exciting viticultural areas in California — if not in the entire country — are in Santa Barbara County. Even though Spanish missionaries planted vineyards there 200 years ago, it wasn't until 1975 that the first major winery (Firestone Vineyards) opened. In light of what we now know — that is, how well suited Santa Barbara County is to grape growing — 1975 was a late start.

The main growing areas of the county are the Santa Maria, Santa Ynez, and Los Alamos Valleys, which lie north of the city of Santa Barbara. These are cool valleys that — unusually in California — run east to west, opening toward the Pacific Ocean and channeling in the ocean air. The cool climate is ideal for Pinot Noir and Chardonnay. In the Santa Maria Valley, for example, one of the main sites of these varieties, the average temperature during the growing season is a mere 74 degrees Fahrenheit.

The southernmost of the three valleys, the Santa Ynez Valley, boasts a cool climate on its western end, while the eastern end of the valley is warm enough to grow red grapes, such as Grenache and Syrah. In the cool, western end is the Sta. Rita Hills AVA, an area that has been officially recognized fairly recently, although it encompasses some of the earliest vineyard plantings. It is particularly known for its Pinot Noir and Chardonnay.

Long before the film *Sideways* brought new attention and tourists to Santa Barbara wineries and restaurants, Pinot Noir had earned Santa Barbara much of its acclaim as a wine region. Santa Barbara is generally recognized as one of the six great American wine regions for this variety — the other five being Carneros, the Russian River Valley, the Sonoma Coast, Mendocino County's

Anderson Valley, and Oregon's Willamette Valley (which we discuss later in this chapter). In Santa Barbara, Pinot Noir wines seem to burst with luscious strawberry fruit, laced with herbal tones. These wines tend to be precocious; they're delicious in their first four or five years — not the "keepers" that the sturdier, wilder-tasting Russian River Pinot Noirs or the True Sonoma Coast seem to be. But why keep them when they taste so good?

The following are some recommended producers in Santa Barbara (listed alphabetically), and their best wines:

- **Alma Rosa:** Chardonnay, Pinot Gris, Pinot Noir

- **Au Bon Climat:** Pinot Noir, Chardonnay (especially single-vineyard bottlings of both), Pinot Gris/Pinot Blanc

- **Babcock Vineyards:** Sauvignon Blanc, Chardonnay, Pinot Noir

- **Beckmen Vineyards:** Syrah, Grenache

- **The Brander Vineyard:** Sauvignon Blanc

- **Byron Vineyard:** Chardonnay (especially Nielson Vineyard), Pinot Noir

- **Cambria Winery:** Chardonnay, Pinot Noir (Julia's Vineyard), Syrah

- **Clos Pepe Vineyards:** Pinot Noir, Chardonnay

- **Cottonwood Canyon:** Pinot Noir, Chardonnay

- **Daniel Gehrs:** Chenin Blanc, Dry Riesling, Gewürztraminer, Syrah

- **Fess Parker Winery:** Chardonnay, Syrah, Pinot Noir

- **Fiddlehead Cellars:** Pinot Noir, Sauvignon Blanc

- **Foley Estates:** Chardonnay, Pinot Noir

- **Foxen Vineyard:** Pinot Noir, Syrah, Chardonnay, Chenin Blanc

- **Gainey Vineyard:** Chardonnay, Pinot Noir, Sauvignon Blanc

- **Hitching Post:** Pinot Noir, Syrah

- **Lane Tanner Winery:** Pinot Noir

- **Longoria Wines:** Pinot Noir, Syrah

- **The Ojai Vineyard:** Pinot Noir, Syrah, Chardonnay

- **Qupé Cellars:** Syrah, Chardonnay, Roussanne, Marsanne, Viognier

- **Sanford Winery:** Pinot Noir (especially Sanford & Benedict Vineyard), Chardonnay

- **Santa Barbara Winery:** Pinot Noir, Chardonnay, Syrah, Sauvignon Blanc

- **Sea Smoke Cellars:** Pinot Noir

- **Sierra Madre Vineyard:** Chardonnay, Pinot Noir

- **Zaca Mesa Winery:** Syrah, Roussanne, Chardonnay, Viognier

Oregon: A Tale of Two Pinots

Because Oregon is north of California, most people assume that Oregon's wine regions are cool. And they're right. But the main reason for Oregon's cool climate is that no high mountains separate its vineyards from the Pacific Ocean. The ocean influence brings low temperatures and rain. Grape growing and winemaking are really completely different in Oregon and California.

Winemaking is a fairly new industry in Oregon, but it's growing rapidly. From five wineries in 1970, the state had 419 wineries in 2011 — almost four times as many as in 2000! Most of Oregon's wineries are small, family-owned operations. The exception in terms of size is King Estate, Oregon's largest winery, but even King Estate is relatively small compared to some of the wine behemoths of California.

Oregon first gained respect in wine circles for its Pinot Noir, a grape that needs cool climates to perform at its best (see Chapter 3). The Eyrie Vineyards released Oregon's first Pinot Noir in 1970, but national recognition for the state's Pinots came only after the excellent 1983 and 1985 vintages. Pinot Noir is still Oregon's flagship wine, and a vast majority of the state's wineries make this wine. Oregon's Pinot Noirs, with their characteristic black-fruit aromas and flavors, depth and complexity, have won accolades as some of the very best Pinots in the United States.

Red wine encompasses 60 percent of Oregon's wine production today; the 40 percent of production that is white wine features mainly Pinot Gris, Chardonnay, and Riesling. In recent years, Oregon's Chardonnays have surged in quality, thanks to the replanting of many vineyards with French clones of the Chardonnay grape, as opposed to the original plantings that were more suited to California's warmer climate.

In the following sections, we discuss Oregon's Pinot Gris, and we talk about the state's main wine regions: the Willamette Valley, the Umpqua Valley, and the Rogue River Valley.

Oregon's other Pinot

Because Chardonnay is the companion grape to Pinot Noir in France's Burgundy region (see Chapter 10), and because Chardonnay wine is hugely popular in America, it's an important variety in Oregon. However, a second white grape variety actually out produces Chardonnay in Oregon: Pinot Gris. A natural mutation of its ancestor, Pinot Noir, the Pinot Gris variety has grapes that are normally pale pink–yellowish in color when ripe. (Read about Pinot Gris in Chapter 3.)

David Lett, founder and winemaker of The Eyrie Vineyards and Oregon's Pinot Noir pioneer, is also the man who made Oregon's first Pinot Gris, around 1970, followed by Ponzi Vineyards and Adelsheim Vineyard. Today, almost every winery in the Willamette (wil-*lam*-et) Valley, Oregon's most important wine region, makes Pinot Gris, along with Pinot Noir.

Two styles of Oregon Pinot Gris exist:

- ✔ A lighter, fruity style (for which the grapes are picked early) — always made without oak; these wines can be consumed as soon as six to eight months after the autumn harvest.
- ✔ A medium-bodied, golden-colored wine from grapes left longer on the vine, which sometimes has a little oak aging; these wines can age for five or six years or longer.

In general, Oregon Pinot Gris is light- to medium-bodied, with aromas reminiscent of pears, apples, and sometimes of melon, and surprising depth for an inexpensive wine. It's an excellent food wine, even when it's slightly sweet; it works especially well with seafood and salmon — just the kind of food that it's paired with in Oregon. Most of Oregon's Pinot Gris wines are in the $10 to $19 range in retail stores.

Now, more and more California wineries are also making Pinot Gris. But in California, most wineries are producing a lighter wine in the style of Italian Pinot Grigio, and they usually call the wine by that Italian name — hoping, no doubt, to capitalize on the popularity of the Italian wine. Oregon's richest Pinot Gris wines resemble Alsace's flavorful Pinot Gris style.

Who's who in Willamette Valley

The main home of Pinot Noir and Pinot Gris in Oregon is the Willamette Valley, directly south of the city of Portland in northwestern Oregon. The Willamette Valley has established itself in the last 40 years as the most important wine region in Oregon; in fact, about two-thirds of the state's wineries are situated there.

Willamette Valley is a convenient wine destination to visit because the vibrant city of Portland, with all its fine restaurants, hotels, and shops, is 30 minutes north of this wine region.

Willamette Valley is huge and encompasses several counties. Yamhill County, directly southwest of Portland, has the greatest concentration of wineries, all of which produce Pinot Noir. But quite a few wineries are located in Washington County, west of Portland, and in Polk County, south of Yamhill. In addition to the general Willamette Valley AVA, six specific AVAs now exist in the Willamette Valley: Chehalem Mountains, Dundee Hills, Yamhill-Carlton District, Ribbon Ridge, McMinnville Foothills, and Eola-Amity Hills. The diverse soils of the Willamette Valley have inspired winemakers to differentiate the area and formalize these AVAs.

Here are some of the better producers in the Willamette Valley, primarily for Pinot Noir and Pinot Gris (but sometimes also Chardonnay or Riesling), listed alphabetically:

Adelsheim Vineyard	Hinman Vineyards/Silvan Ridge
Amity Vineyards	Ken Wright Cellars
Anne Amie	King Estate Winery
Archery Summit	Kramer Vineyards
Argyle Winery	Lange Estate Winery
Beaux Frères	Montinore Estate Vineyards
Benton Lane Winery	Oak Knoll Winery
Bethel Heights Vineyard	Panther Creek Cellars
Brick House Vineyards	Patricia Green Cellars
Broadley Vineyards	Penner-Ash Wine Cellar
Cameron Winery	Ponzi Vineyards
Chehalem Winery	Redhawk Vineyard
Cooper Mountain Vineyards	Rex Hill Vineyards
Cristom Vineyards	St. Innocent Winery
Domaine Drouhin Oregon	Shafer Vineyard Cellars
Domaine Serene	Sokol Blosser Winery
Duck Pond Cellars	Stangeland Vineyards
Edgefield Winery	Torii Mor Winery
Elk Cove Vineyards	Tualatin Vineyards
Eola Hills Wine Cellars	Van Duzer Wines
Erath Winery	WillaKenzie Estate
Evesham Wood Winery	Willamette Valley Vineyards
The Eyrie Vineyards	Witness Tree Vineyard
Firesteed Winery	Yamhill Valley Vineyards
Hamacher Wines	

Two other Oregon wine regions

Two other wine regions of note in Oregon are both in the southwest part of the state: the Umpqua Valley (around the town of Roseburg) and farther south, next to California's northern border, the Rogue River Valley.

Considerably warmer than Willamette, the Umpqua Valley is the site of Oregon's first winery, Hillcrest Vineyard, founded in 1962. The main grape varieties in Umpqua are Pinot Noir, Chardonnay, Riesling, and Cabernet

Sauvignon. Major wineries are Henry Estate and Girardet Wine Cellars, known for their Pinot Noir and Chardonnay.

The Rogue River Valley is warmer still; Cabernet Sauvignon and Merlot often perform better than Pinot Noir there. Chardonnay is the leading white wine, but Pinot Gris is becoming popular. Bridgeview Vineyards, the region's largest winery, is doing an admirable job with Pinot Gris as well as Pinot Noir. Four other vineyards to watch are Ashland Vineyards, Valley View Winery, Sarah Powell Wines, and Foris Vineyards — the latter a specialist in Merlot and Cabernet Sauvignon.

Wine on the Desert: Washington State

Although Washington and Oregon are neighboring states, their wine regions have vastly different climates due to the location of the vineyards relative to the Cascade Mountains, which cut through both states from north to south.

On Washington's western, or coastal, side, the climate is maritime — cool, plenty of rain, and a lot of vegetation. (In Oregon, almost all the vineyards are located on the coastal side.) East of the mountains, Washington's climate is continental, with hot, very dry summers and cold winters. Most of Washington's vineyards are situated in this area, in the vast, sprawling Columbia and Yakima Valleys. Because it's so far north, Washington also has the advantage of long hours of sunlight, averaging an unusually high 17.4 hours of sunshine during the growing season.

Washington's winemakers have found that with irrigation, many grapes can flourish in the Washington desert. The Bordeaux varieties — Merlot, Cabernet Sauvignon, Cabernet Franc, Sauvignon Blanc, and Sémillon — are the main players. Washington first became well known for the quality of its Merlots. (One winery, Columbia Crest, makes the largest-selling Merlot in the United States in the over-$8 price category.)

But Washington's Syrah wines are now gaining many of the accolades. In fact, Washington may be the single best region in the United States for this potentially exciting wine. Chenin Blanc and the ever-present Chardonnay also are doing well. Most recently, Riesling has taken off, and one winery, Chateau Ste. Michelle, makes the largest-selling Riesling wine in the United States.

Washington does have a few vineyards west of the Cascades, around Puget Sound, where Riesling and Gewürztraminer grow well. In fact, many of the larger wineries, such as Chateau Ste. Michelle and Columbia Winery, are located in the Puget Sound area, near the thriving city of Seattle (but they obtain almost all their grapes from the Columbia and Yakima Valleys). Running a business is a bit easier in Seattle than in the desert!

Chateau Ste. Michelle, along with the even larger Columbia Crest (both under the same corporate ownership), are the giants in the state; they account for more than 50 percent of all Washington's wines at present. Two other large Washington wineries are The Hogue Cellars and Washington Hills Cellars.

Like Oregon, Washington got off to a late start in the wine business. With the exception of Chateau Ste. Michelle and Columbia Winery, both founded in the 1960s, practically none of the current wineries existed before 1980. In 1981, Washington had 19 wineries; as of 2010, 638 wineries are in business, making Washington the second-largest wine producer of premium wines in the United States.

The types of wine produced in Washington have also dramatically changed during the past decade. In 1993, about two-thirds of Washington's wines were white, one-third red. Reflecting Americans' changing tastes in wine, Washington's wines are now about 60 percent red, 40 percent white.

Check out the following sections for more about Washington's wine regions, important producers, and wines.

Washington's wine regions

Washington has one gigantic AVA, Columbia Valley, which encompasses eight other AVAs within its macro-appellation (listed in order of their general importance):

- **Yakima Valley:** This region is the second largest in acreage, behind the huge Columbia Valley itself; more wineries are actually located here than in all the rest of Columbia Valley.

- **Walla Walla Valley:** Although only 5 percent of the state's _vinifera_ grapes grow here, this fast-growing region in the southeast corner of Washington, along the Oregon border, is home to some of the state's top wineries, such as Leonetti Cellar, Woodward Canyon, Waterbrook Winery, Canoe Ridge Vineyard, and L'Ecole No 41 — as well as some of the state's top red wines.

- **Red Mountain:** Red Mountain received its AVA in 2001. The tiny Red Mountain area is actually within the Yakima Valley AVA, but its red clay soil and high altitude earned it a separate appellation. About nine wineries, including Hedges and Kiona Vineyards, concentrate on red varieties: Cabernet Sauvignon, Merlot, Cabernet Franc, and Syrah. Some great vineyards are also located here.

- **Horse Heaven Hills:** Recognized as a separate AVA in 2005, this area in the southernmost part of the Columbia Valley, just north of the Columbia River, has long been known as an ideal location for Cabernet Sauvignon. Many of Washington's leading wineries, including Chateau Ste. Michelle, use grapes from vineyards here.

- **Wahluke Slope:** A fairly new AVA (2006), the Wahluke Slope is one of the state's warmer appellations, known for its Merlot and Cabernet Sauvignon, and home to Snoqualmie Vineyards.

- **Rattlesnake Hills:** A tiny appellation established in 2006, Rattlesnake Hills is actually a sub-appellation of Yakima Valley, with Yakima's highest elevation (more than 3,000 feet). The wineries number 17, all small. Temperatures are moderate in this beautiful region, thanks to the altitude.

- **Snipes Mountain:** Washington State's new AVA (2009), this is another sub-appellation of Yakima Valley. Snipes Mountain is the first region in the state of Washington to have grown wine grapes.

- **Lake Chelan:** Located in northern Columbia Valley, with 15 wineries, Lake Chelan became the state's tenth AVA in 2009. It boasts high elevation and temperate climate.

Columbia Gorge, a beautiful area in southwest Washington crossing into Oregon, is another Washington AVA; it actually has an equal number of Oregon and Washington wineries. The Greater Puget Sound/Seattle Area AVA encompasses the Puget Sound Islands and has more than 50 wineries; in this cool, moist climate, Pinot Gris and Pinot Noir are leading varieties, as well as Riesling and Gewürztraminer. Finally, 11 wineries, including Arbor Crest, are located in the Spokane area (currently waiting for its AVA) in eastern Washington.

A Washington oddity

When was the last time you had a Lemberger? No, we don't mean the cheese! Lemberger is a little-known grape variety from Germany that's also grown in Austria, where it's called Blaufränkisch. Don't feel bad if you haven't heard of it, because few people in the United States — outside of Washington — have tasted it. Lemberger is a hardy red variety that does well in the Yakima Valley; it makes a fruity but dry, medium-bodied inexpensive wine in the Beaujolais style. Hoodsport, Covey Run, Kiona Vineyards, and The Hogue Cellars are four good producers of Lemberger — the wine! The Hogue Cellars calls its version "Blue Franc."

Who's who in Washington

No, we're not talking about cabinet members and senators here! The following are our recommended wine producers in Washington, grouped alphabetically, along with some of their best wines:

- **Andrew Will Cellars:** Cabernet Sauvignon, Merlot
- **Arbor Crest Wine Cellars:** Sauvignon Blanc, Chardonnay, Riesling
- **Badger Mountain Winery:** Chardonnay, Cabernet Franc
- **Barnard Griffin Winery:** Sémillon, Chardonnay, Fumé Blanc, Merlot
- **Betz Family Winery:** Cabernet Sauvignon, Merlot blend, Syrah
- **Bookwalter Winery:** Cabernet Sauvignon, Merlot
- **Canoe Ridge Vineyard:** Merlot, Cabernet Sauvignon
- **Chateau Ste. Michelle:** Merlot, Cabernet Sauvignon, Chardonnay (especially Cold Creek Vineyard of all three), "Eroica" Riesling (with Dr. Loosen)
- **Chinook Winery:** Sauvignon Blanc, Sémillon, Chardonnay
- **Col Solare Winery:** Meritage (mainly Cabernet Sauvignon; a Chateau Ste. Michelle/Piero Antinori collaboration)
- **Columbia Crest Winery:** Reserve Red (Cabernet-Merlot blend), Sémillon, Syrah, Merlot, Cabernet Sauvignon, Sémillon-Chardonnay
- **Columbia Winery:** Cabernet Sauvignon, Cabernet Franc, Syrah, Merlot (especially Red Willow Vineyard of all four)
- **Covey Run Winery:** Chardonnay, Lemberger
- **DeLille Cellars:** Chaleur Estate (Bordeaux-style blend), Chaleur Estate Blanc (Sauvignon Blanc–Sémillon blend), D2 (second label of Chaleur Estate), Harrison Hill (Cabernet Sauvignon), Syrah
- **Gordon Brothers Cellars:** Chardonnay, Merlot, Cabernet Sauvignon
- **Gramercy Cellars:** Syrah, Cabernet Sauvignon
- **Hedges Cellars:** Red Mountain Reserve (Bordeaux-style blend), Cabernet/Merlot, Fumé/Chardonnay, Three Vineyard Red
- **The Hogue Cellars:** Merlot, Cabernet Sauvignon (Reserve), Blue Franc (Lemberger), Chenin Blanc, Sémillon-Chardonnay, Sémillon
- **Hoodsport Winery:** Lemberger, Sémillon
- **Hyatt Vineyards:** Merlot, Cabernet Sauvignon
- **Januik/Novelty Hill Winery:** Merlot, Cabernet Sauvignon

- **Kiona Vineyards:** Lemberger, Cabernet Sauvignon, Merlot
- **L'Ecole No 41:** Merlot (Seven Hills), Cabernet Sauvignon, Sémillon
- **Leonetti Cellar:** Cabernet Sauvignon (especially Seven Hills Vineyard), Merlot, Sangiovese
- **Long Shadows Winery:** Merlot, Syrah, Riesling
- **Matthews Cellars:** Merlot, Yakima Valley Red (Bordeaux-style blend)
- **McCrea Cellars:** Chardonnay, Syrah
- **Northstar Winery:** Merlot
- **O-S Winery (also known as Owen-Sullivan):** Syrah, Cabernet Franc, Merlot
- **Pacific Rim:** Riesling
- **Pepper Bridge Winery:** Cabernet Sauvignon, Merlot
- **Preston Wine Cellars:** Cabernet Sauvignon, Merlot (Reserves)
- **Quilceda Creek Vintners:** Cabernet Sauvignon, Merlot
- **Sagelands Vineyard:** Cabernet Sauvignon, Merlot
- **Seven Hills Winery:** Merlot, Cabernet Sauvignon
- **Snoqualmie Vineyards:** Cabernet Sauvignon, Merlot, Syrah
- **Tamarack Cellars:** Merlot, Cabernet Sauvignon, Firehouse Red
- **Tefft Cellars:** Sangiovese, Cabernet Sauvignon
- **Thurston Wolfe Winery:** Syrah
- **Washington Hills Cellars:** Cabernet Sauvignon, Merlot, Chardonnay, Sémillon, Cabernet Franc ("Apex" is this winery's premium label; it also uses the "W. B. Bridgman" label)
- **Waterbrook Winery:** Cabernet Sauvignon, Merlot, Chardonnay, Cabernet Franc, Sauvignon Blanc
- **Woodward Canyon Winery:** Chardonnay, Cabernet Sauvignon, Merlot

The Empire State

New York City may be the capital of the world in many ways, but its state's wines don't get the recognition they deserve, perhaps because of California's overwhelming presence in the U.S. market. New York ranks as the third-largest wine producing state in the United States, after California and Washington. Brotherhood, America's Oldest Winery, the oldest continuously operating winery in the United States, opened its doors in New York's Hudson Valley in 1839. And the largest wine company in the world, Constellation Brands, has its headquarters in the Finger Lakes region of western New York. Find out more about New York's world of wine in the following sections.

Upstate, downstate

New York's most important region is the Finger Lakes, where four large lakes temper the otherwise cool climate. This AVA produces nearly two-thirds of New York's wines and has well over 100 wineries. Riesling, the Finger Lakes Region's most renowned (and best) wine, is available under 200 wine brands, almost exclusively from small wineries.

The other two important regions are the Hudson Valley, along the Hudson River north of New York City, and Long Island, which has three AVAs: North Fork of Long Island (the most important); the Hamptons, on the island's South Fork; and Long Island itself, applicable to wines made with grapes from all over Long Island.

In the early days (prior to 1960), most of New York's wines were made from native American varieties, such as Concord, Catawba, Delaware, and Niagara, as well as French-American hybrid grapes, such as Seyval Blanc, Baco Noir, and Maréchal Foch.

Common wisdom held that the relatively cold New York winters could not support *Vitis vinifera* varieties. But a Russian immigrant, the late, great Dr. Konstantin Frank, proved all the naysayers wrong when he succeeded in growing Riesling (followed by many other vinifera varieties) in 1953 in Hammondsport, in the Finger Lakes region. (The first wines from vinifera grapes were made in 1961 at his winery, Dr. Frank's Vinifera Wine Cellars.) His son, Willy Frank, ran one of the most successful wineries in the state, with an entire line of fine vinifera wines and excellent sparkling wines; the winery carries on today under the leadership of Dr. Frank's grandson, Fred.

In 1973, Alec and Louisa Hargrave got the idea that Long Island's North Fork (about a two-hour drive east of New York City) had the ideal climate and soil for vinifera grapes. They founded Long Island's first winery, Hargrave Vineyards, which they sold in 1999. (The winery is now known as Castello di Borghese Vineyard.) Today, Long Island has 37 wineries and is still growing. Like Washington state, Long Island seems particularly suited to Merlot, but Chardonnay, Riesling, Cabernet Sauvignon, Cabernet Franc, and Sauvignon Blanc are also grown, plus some Gewürztraminer, Pinot Noir, and numerous other varieties.

Who's who in New York

The New York wine industry has grown from 19 wineries in 1976 to more than 200 today, most of them small, family-run operations. The following are lists of recommended producers in New York's three major wine regions, mentioned alphabetically.

The Finger Lakes Region

Anthony Road Wine Company

Atwater Estate Vineyards

Casa Larga Vineyards

Dr. Frank's Vinifera Wine Cellars (and its affiliate, Chateau Frank, for sparkling wines)

Fox Run Vineyards

Glenora Wine Cellars

Hazlitt 1852 Vineyards

Hermann J. Wiemer Vineyard

Heron Hill Vineyards

Hosmer Winery

Hunt Country Vineyards

Knapp Winery

Lakewood Vineyards

Lamoreaux Landing Wine Cellars

Lucas Vineyards

McGregor Vineyard

Prejean Winery

Sheldrake Point Winery

Standing Stone Vineyards

Swedish Hill Vineyard

Wagner Vineyards

Hudson River Valley Region

Adair Vineyards

Baldwin Vineyards

Benmarl Vineyards

Brotherhood Winery

Cascade Mountain Vineyards

Clinton Vineyards

Magnanini Winery

Millbrook Vineyards

Rivendell Winery

Long Island Region (North Fork, Unless Otherwise Noted)

Bedell Cellars

Castello di Borghese Vineyard

Channing Daughters (Hamptons)

Corey Creek Vineyards

Duck Walk Vineyards (Hamptons)

Jamesport Vineyards

Laurel Lake Vineyards

Lenz Winery

Lieb Family Cellars

Loughlin Vineyards

Macari Vineyards

Martha Clara Vineyards

Wolffer Estate (Hamptons)

Bouké Wines

Old Brookville-Banfi (Nassau County)

Osprey's Dominion

Palmer Vineyards

Paumanok Vineyards

Peconic Bay Vineyards

Pelligrini Vineyards

Pindar Vineyards

Pugliese Vineyards

Raphael

Shinn Estate Vineyards

Sparkling Pointe

Part V
Wine's Exotic Face

The 5th Wave   By Rich Tennant

"Ooh, see? Now this is a good Champagne. Check the bubbles."

In this part . . .

There's life beyond Pinot Grigio and Cabernet Sauvignon! In fact, there's a whole world of truly delicious wines to drink not so much at the table as at parties, on the patio before dinner, or by the fire after dinner. These wines include the most glamorous wine in the world — Champagne! — as well as bubbly wines from other regions, and the classic wines called Sherry and Port. (Nobody doesn't love Port.)

In the two chapters in this part, we tell you how these magical wines are made, which brands to look for, and when to drink the wines (including tips on how to use them in a meal — for an exotic touch).

Chapter 15

Champagne and Other Sparklers

. . . .

In This Chapter

▶ All champagne is not Champagne

▶ When *extra dry* means "not all that dry"

▶ The lowdown on the *Champagne method*

▶ Sparkling wines from $8 to $300-plus

▶ Marrying bubblies with food

. . . .

*I*n the universe of wine, sparkling wines are a solar system unto themselves. They're produced in just about every country that makes wine, and they come in a wide range of tastes, quality levels, and prices. Champagne, the sparkling wine from the Champagne region of France, is the brightest star in the sky, but by no means the only one.

Sparkling wines are distinguished (and distinguishable) from other wines by the presence of bubbles — *carbon dioxide* — in the wine. In the eyes of most governments, these bubbles must be a natural byproduct of fermentation in order for a wine to be officially considered a sparkling wine.

In many wine regions, sparkling wines are just a sideline to complement the region's table wine production, but in some places, sparkling wines are the main business. At the top of that list is France's Champagne region (where sparkling wine was — if not invented — made famous). Italy's Asti and Prosecco wine zones are other important regions as are France's Loire Valley, northeastern Spain, and parts of California.

All That Glitters Is Not Champagne

Champagne, the sparkling wine of Champagne, France, is the gold standard of sparkling wines for a number of reasons:

✔ Champagne is the most famous sparkling wine in the world; the name has immediate recognition with everyone, not just wine drinkers.

✔ A particular technique for making sparkling wine was perfected in the Champagne region.

✔ Champagne is not only the finest sparkling wine in the world but also among the finest wines in the world of any type.

Within the European Union, only the wines of the Champagne region in France can use the name *Champagne*. In some other places, because of Champagne's fame, the name *champagne* can appear on labels of all sorts of sparkling wines that don't come from the Champagne region and that don't taste like Champagne. Wineries call their bubbly wines *champagne* to make them more marketable. Despite tighter regulations regarding the use of the term, many wineries in the United States may still use *champagne* on their labels. Many wine drinkers also use the word *champagne* indiscriminately to refer to all wines that have bubbles.

Ironically, much of the sparkling wine sold in the United States that's called "champagne" is not even made with the same techniques as true Champagne. Most imitation champagnes are made by a process that takes only a few months from beginning to end (compared to a few years to make Champagne), is less costly, and works more effectively on an industrial scale.

Whenever we use the word *Champagne* (with a capital *C*), we are referring to true Champagne, from the region of the same name; we use the generic term *sparkling wine* to refer to bubbly wines collectively, and sparkling wines other than Champagne.

The cool rule

Many sparkling wine regions are very cool areas, where grapes generally don't ripen sufficiently for *still* (nonsparkling) wine production. Vinified normally, the wines of these regions would be extremely high in acid, disagreeably tart, and very thin; the reds would lack color. But the elaborate process of sparkling wine production (the *traditional method* of production as practiced in the Champagne region, described later in this chapter) turns the climate's deficits into virtues and transforms the ugly-duckling grapes into graceful swans.

Sparkling Wine Styles

All sparkling wines have bubbles, and nearly all of them are either white or pink (which is far less common than white). That's about as far as broad generalizations take us in describing sparkling wines.

Some sparkling wines are downright sweet, some are bone-dry, and many fall somewhere in the middle, from medium-dry to medium-sweet. Some have toasty, nutty flavors, and some are fruity; among those that are fruity, some are just nondescriptly grapey, while others have delicate nuances of lemons, apples, cherries, berries, peaches, or other fruits.

The sparkling wines of the world fall into two broad styles, according to how they're made, and how they taste as a result:

- ✔ Wines that express the character of their grapes; these wines tend to be fruity and straightforward, without significant layers of complexity.

- ✔ Wines that express complexity and flavors (yeasty, biscuity, caramel-like, honeyed) that derive from winemaking and aging instead of expressing overt fruitiness.

The sweetness factor

Nearly all sparkling wines are not (technically) completely dry, because they contain measurable but small amounts of sugar, usually as the result of sweetening added at the last stage of production. But all sparkling wines don't necessarily taste sweet. The perception of sweetness depends on two factors: the actual amount of sweetness in the wine (which varies according to the wine's style) and the wine's balance between acidity and sweetness.

Here's how the balance factor operates. Sparkling wines are usually very high in acidity, because the grapes, having grown in a cool climate, are not very ripe at harvest. The wine's carbon dioxide also accentuates the acidic impression in the mouth. But the wine's sweetness counterbalances its acidity and vice versa. Depending on the actual amount of sugar and the particular acid/sugar balance a sparkling wine strikes, the wine may taste dry, very slightly sweet, medium sweet, or quite sweet.

Champagne itself is made in a range of sweetness levels, the most common of which is a dry style called *brut* (see the section "Sweetness categories," later in this chapter). Sparkling wines made by the *traditional method* used in Champagne (see "How Sparkling Wine Happens," later in this chapter) are made in the same range of styles as Champagne.

Inexpensive sparkling wines tend to be medium-sweet in order to appeal to a mass market that enjoys sweetness. Wines labeled with the Italian word *spumante* tend to be overtly sweet. (See the section "Italian spumante: Sweet or dry," later in this chapter.)

The quality factor

When you taste a sparkling wine, the most important consideration is whether you like it — just as for a still wine. If you want to evaluate a sparkling wine the way professionals do, however, you have to apply a few criteria, such as the following, that don't apply to still wines (or are less critical in still wines than in sparkling wines):

- **The appearance of the bubbles:** In the best sparkling wines, the bubbles are tiny and float upward in a continuous stream from the bottom of your glass. If the bubbles are large and random, you have a clue that the wine is a lesser-quality sparkler. If you don't see many bubbles at all, you could have a bad bottle, a poor or smudged glass, or a wine that may be too old.

  Tiny variations in glassware can drastically affect the flow of bubbles. If the wine in your glass looks almost flat, but another glass of wine from the same bottle is lively with bubbles, blame the glass and not the wine. (In this case, you should be able to *taste* the bubbles, even if you can't *see* many of them.) See Chapter 8 for our recommendations about glasses for Champagne and other sparkling wines.

- **The feel of the bubbles in your mouth:** The finer the wine, the less aggressive the bubbles feel in your mouth. (If the bubbles remind you of a soft drink, we hope you didn't pay more than $5 for the wine.)

- **The balance between sweetness and acidity:** Even if a bubbly wine is too sweet or too dry for your taste, to evaluate its quality you should consider its sweetness/acid ratio and decide whether these two elements seem reasonably balanced.

- **The texture:** Traditional-method sparkling wines should be somewhat creamy in texture as a result of their extended lees aging. (See the next section for an explanation of *traditional method* and *lees*.)

- **The finish:** Any impression of bitterness on the finish of a sparkling wine is a sign of low quality.

How Sparkling Wine Happens

For all wines, when yeasts convert sugar into alcohol, carbon dioxide (CO_2) is a natural byproduct. If fermentation takes place in a closed container, the carbon dioxide cannot escape into the air. With nowhere else to go, the carbon dioxide becomes trapped in the wine in the form of bubbles.

Most sparkling wines actually go through *two* fermentations: one to turn the grape juice into still wine without bubbles (that's called a *base wine*) and a subsequent one (conveniently called the *second fermentation*) to turn the base wine into bubbly wine. The winemaker has to instigate the second fermentation by adding yeasts and sugar to the base wine. The added yeasts convert the added sugar into alcohol and CO_2 bubbles.

Beginning with the second fermentation, the longer and slower the winemaking process, the more complex and expensive the sparkling wine will be. Some sparkling wines are ten years in the making; others are produced in only a few months. The slow-route wines can cost more than $100 a bottle, while bubblies at the opposite end of the spectrum can sell for as little as $4.

Although many variations exist, most sparkling wines are produced in one of two ways: through *second fermentation in a tank* or through *second fermentation in a bottle*.

Tank fermentation: Economy of scale

The quickest, most efficient way of making a sparkling wine involves conducting the second fermentation in large, closed, pressurized tanks. This method is called the *bulk method, tank method, cuve close* (meaning "closed tank" in French), or *charmat method* (after a Frenchman named Eugene Charmat, who championed this process).

Sparkling wines made in the charmat (pronounced shar-mah) method are usually the least expensive. That's because they're usually made in large quantities and they're ready for sale soon after harvest. Also, the grapes used in making sparkling wine by the charmat method (Chenin Blanc, for example) are usually *far* less expensive than the Pinot Noir and Chardonnay typically

used in the *traditional* or *Champagne method* described in the next section.

The following occurs in the charmat method:

1. A base wine is seeded with sugar and yeast, and it ferments. The carbon dioxide created by the fermentation becomes trapped in the wine, thanks to the closed tank as well as pressure within the tank and cold temperature.

2. The wine — now a dry sparkling wine with higher alcohol than the base wine had — is filtered (under pressure) to remove the solid deposits (the *lees*) from the second fermentation.

3. Before bottling, some sweetness is added to adjust the wine's flavor, according to the desired style of the final wine.

The whole process can take just a few weeks. In some exceptional cases, it can be extended to a few months, allowing the wine to rest between the fermentation and the filtration.

Bottle fermentation: Small is beautiful

The charmat method that we describe in the preceding section is a fairly new way of producing sparkling wines, dating back about 100 years. The more traditional method is to conduct the second fermentation in the individual bottles in which the wine is later sold.

Champagne has been made in this way for more than 300 years and, according to French regulations, can be made in no other way. Many other French sparkling wines produced outside of the Champagne region use the same process and are allowed to use the term *Crémant* (a term used to refer to all French bubblies made outside of the Champagne region) in their names rather than *Champagne.* The best sparkling wines from Spain, California, and elsewhere also use Champagne's traditional method.

The technique of conducting the second fermentation in the bottle is called the *classic* or *traditional method* in Europe; in the United States, it's called the *Champagne method* or *méthode champenoise.*

Bottle fermentation (or, more correctly, second fermentation in the bottle) is an elaborate process in which every single bottle is an individual fermentation vessel, so to speak. Including the aging time at the winery before the wine is sold, this process requires a minimum of 15 months (in the case of Champagne) and usually takes 3 years or more. Invariably, bottle-fermented sparkling wines are more expensive than tank-fermented bubblies.

The elements of bottle fermentation are as follows:

1. Each bottle is filled with a mixture of base wine and a sugar-and-yeast solution, closed securely, and laid to rest in a cool, dark cellar.

2. The second fermentation slowly occurs inside each bottle, producing carbon dioxide and fermentation lees.

3. As the bottles lie in the cellar, the interaction of the lees and the wine gradually changes the wine's texture and flavor.

4. Eventually — 12 months to several years after the second fermentation — the bottles undergo a process of shaking and turning so that the lees fall to the neck of each upside-down bottle.

5. The lees are flash-frozen in the neck of each bottle and expelled from the bottle as a frozen plug, leaving clear sparkling wine behind.

6. A sweetening solution (called a *dosage,* pronounced doh-sahj) is added to each bottle to adjust the flavor of the wine, and the bottles are corked and eventually labeled for sale.

Actually, the classic method as practiced in Champagne involves several processes that occur way before the second fermentation. For example, the pressing to extract the juice from the grapes must be gentle and meticulous to prevent the grape skins' bitter flavors — and their color, in the case of black grapes — from passing into the juice. Another step crucially important to the quality of the sparkling wine is blending various wines after the first fermentation to create the best composite base wine for the second fermentation.

After the first fermentation, each Champagne *house* (as the producers are called) has hundreds of different still wines, because the winemaker keeps the wines of different grape varieties and different vineyards separate. To create his base wine, or *cuvée,* he blends these wines in varying proportions, often adding some *reserve wine* (older wine purposely held back from previous vintages). More than 100 different wines can go into a single base wine, each bringing its own special character to the blend. What's particularly tricky about blending the base wine — besides the sheer number of components in the blend — is that the winemaker has to see into the future and create a blend *not* for its flavor today but for how it will taste in several years, after it has been transformed into a sparkling wine. The men and women who blend sparkling wines are true artists of the wine world.

Taste: The proof of the pudding

Tank-fermented sparklers tend to be fruitier than traditional-method sparkling wines. This difference occurs because in tank fermentation, the route from grape to wine is shorter and more direct than in bottle fermentation. Some winemakers use the *charmat,* or tank, method precisely because their goal is a fresh and fruity sparkling wine. Asti and Prosecco, two of Italy's most famous sparkling wines, are perfect examples. You should drink charmat-method sparklers young, when their fruitiness is at its max.

Second fermentation in the bottle makes wines that tend to be less overtly fruity than charmat-method wines. Chemical changes that take place as the wine develops on its fermentation lees diminish the fruitiness of the wine and contribute aromas and flavors, such as toastiness, nuttiness, caramel, and yeastiness. The texture of the wine can also change, becoming smooth and creamy. The bubbles themselves tend to be tinier, and they feel less aggressive in your mouth than the bubbles of tank-fermented wines.

Champagne and Its Magic Wines

Champagne. Does any other word convey such a sense of celebration? Think of it: Whenever people, in any part of the world, want to celebrate, you can hear them say, "This calls for Champagne!" ("This calls for iced tea!" just isn't quite the same.)

Champagne, the real thing, comes only from the region of Champagne (sham-pahn-yah) in northeast France. Dom Pérignon, the famous monk who was cellar master at the Abbey of Hautvillers, didn't invent Champagne, but he did achieve several breakthroughs that are key to the production of Champagne as we now know it. He perfected the method of making white wine from black grapes, for example, and, most important, he mastered the art of blending wines from different grapes and different villages to achieve a complex base wine. (See the previous section to find out what base wine is.)

Champagne is the most northerly vineyard area in France. Many of the important Champagne houses are located in the cathedral city of Rheims (French spelling, *Reims*) — where 17-year-old Joan of Arc had Prince Charles crowned King of France in 1429 — and in the town of Epernay, south of Rheims. Around Rheims and Epernay are the main vineyard areas, where three permitted grape varieties for Champagne flourish. These areas, and the grapes they specialize in, are

- The Montagne de Reims (south of Rheims), where the best Pinot Noir grows

- The Côte des Blancs (south of Epernay), home of the best Chardonnay

- The Valleé de la Marne (west of Epernay), most favorable to Pinot Meunier (a black grape), although all three grape varieties grow there

Most Champagne is made from all three grape varieties — two black and one white. Pinot Noir contributes body, structure, and longevity to the blend; Pinot Meunier provides precociousness, floral aromas, and fruitiness; and Chardonnay offers delicacy, freshness, elegance, and aging potential.

In the following sections, we delve into the details of Champagne: what makes it special, different types and sweetness levels, and recommended producers (including growers).

What makes Champagne special

The cool climate in Champagne is marginal for grape growing, and the grapes struggle to ripen sufficiently in some years. Even in warmer years, the climate dictates that the grapes are high in acidity — a sorry state for table wine but perfect for sparkling wine. The cool climate and the region's chalky, limestone soil are the leading factors contributing to Champagne's excellence.

Three other elements help distinguish Champagne from all other sparkling wines:

- ✔ The number and diversity of vineyards (more than 300 *crus,* or individual vineyards), which provide a huge range of unique wines for blending
- ✔ The cold, deep, chalky cellars — many built during Roman times — in which Champagnes age for many years
- ✔ The 300 years of experience the *Champenois* (as the good citizens of Champagne are called) have in making sparkling wine

The result is an elegant sparkling wine with myriad tiny, gentle bubbles, complexity of flavors, and a lengthy finish. Voilá — Champagne!

Non-vintage Champagne

Non-vintage (NV) Champagne — any Champagne without a vintage year on the label — accounts for 85 percent of all Champagne. Its typical blend is two-thirds black grapes (Pinot Noir and Pinot Meunier) and one-third white (Chardonnay). Wine from three or more harvests usually goes into the blend. And, remember, the wines from 30 or 40 different villages (or more) from each year can also be part of the blend. The Champagne winemaker is by necessity a master blender.

Each Champagne house blends to suit its own house style for its non-vintage Champagne. (For example, one house may seek elegance and finesse in its wine, another may opt for fruitiness, and a third may value body, power, and longevity.) Maintaining a consistent house style is vital because wine drinkers get accustomed to their favorite Champagne's taste and expect to find it year after year.

Most major Champagne houses age their non-vintage Champagne for 2½ to 3 years before selling it, even though the legal minimum for non-vintage is just 15 months. The extra aging prolongs the marrying time for the blend and enhances the wine's flavor and complexity. If you have good storage conditions (see Chapter 17), aging your non-vintage Champagne for one to three years after you purchase it usually improves the flavor, in our opinion.

Most non-vintage Champagnes sell for $30 to $50 a bottle. Often, a large retailer buys huge quantities of a few major brands, obtaining a good discount that he passes on to his customers. Seeking out stores that do a large-volume business in Champagne is worth your while.

Vintage Champagne

Until the mid-1990s, only about five of every ten years in the Champagne region have had weather good enough to make a Vintage Champagne — that is, the grapes were ripe enough that some wine could be made entirely from the grapes of that year without being blended with reserve wines from previous years. Since 1995, the climate in Champagne (and throughout Europe) has been much warmer than normal, and Champagne producers have been able to make Vintage Champagne almost every year (2001 was an exception).

The early'90s were more typical; four years — 1991, 1992, 1993, and 1994 — were unremarkable, and few producers made vintage-dated Champagne. But even in the 1980s, the Champagne region had exceptionally good weather; many houses made Vintage Champagne every year from 1981 to 1990, with the exception of 1984 and 1987.

The Champagne region has had a string of really fine vintages since 1995, especially the 1996 vintage. The three years that followed — 1997, 1998, and 1999 — all have been good. Both 2000 and 2003 were no more than average (too hot, especially 2003), but 2002 and 2004 are fine vintages (with 2002 the best since 1996). Champagne lovers should seek out 1996 Vintage Champagnes; 1996 is exceptional, one of the best, long-lived vintages ever! And the 2002 vintage is close behind in quality.

Champagne houses decide for themselves each year whether to make a Vintage Champagne. Factors that might come into consideration — besides the quality of the vintage — include the need to save some wine instead to use as reserve wines for their future non-vintage Champagnes (85 percent of their business, after all), and/or whether a particular vintage's style suits the "house style." For example, although 1989 was a rather good vintage, a few houses decided that Champagnes made from this vintage would be too soft (low in acidity) for them and did not choose to make a Vintage Champagne in 1989. In the end, 1989 turned out to be better than expected.

The minimum aging requirement for Vintage Champagne is three years, but many houses age their Vintage Champagnes for four to six years in order to enhance the wines' flavor and complexity. Vintage Champagnes fall into two categories:

> ✔ Regular vintage, with a price range of $50 to $80 a bottle; these wines simply carry a vintage date in addition to the name of the house.
>
> ✔ Premium vintage (also known as a *prestige cuvée* or *tête de cuvée*), such as Moët & Chandon's Dom Pérignon, Roederer's Cristal, or Veuve Clicquot's La Grande Dame; the typical price for prestige cuvées ranges from $100 to $200, with a few even more expensive.

Vintage Champagne is almost always superior to non-vintage for the following reasons:

> ✔ The best grapes from the choicest vineyards are put into Vintage Champagne (this is *especially* so for prestige cuvées).
>
> ✔ Usually, only the two finest varieties (Pinot Noir and Chardonnay) are used in Vintage Champagne. Pinot Meunier is present mainly in non-vintage Champagne.
>
> ✔ Most Champagne houses age Vintage Champagnes at least two years more than their non-vintage wines. The extra aging assures more complexity.
>
> ✔ The grapes all come from a year that's above average, at least — or superb, at best.

Vintage Champagne is more intense in flavor than non-vintage Champagne. It is typically fuller-bodied and more complex, and its flavors last longer in your mouth. Being fuller and richer, these Champagnes are best with food. Non-vintage Champagnes — usually lighter, fresher, and less complicated — are suitable as apéritifs, and they are good values.

Blanc de blancs and blanc de noirs

A small number of Champagnes derive only from Chardonnay; that type of Champagne is called *blanc de blancs* — literally, "white (wine) from white (grapes)." A blanc de blancs can be a Vintage Champagne or a non-vintage. It usually costs a few dollars more than other Champagnes in its category. Because they are generally lighter and more delicate than other Champagnes, blanc de blancs make ideal apéritifs. Not every Champagne house makes a blanc de blancs. Four of the best — all Vintage Champagnes — are Taittinger Comte de Champagne, Billecart-Salmon Blanc de Blancs, Deutz Blanc de Blancs, and Pol Roger Blanc de Blancs.

Blanc de noirs Champagne (made entirely from black grapes, often just Pinot Noir) is rare but does exist. Bollinger's Blanc de Noirs *Vieilles Vignes Francaises* ("old vines") is absolutely the best, but it is very expensive (more than $500) and hard to find. The 1985 Bollinger Blanc de Noirs is one of the two best Champagnes we've ever had; the other is the 1928 Krug.

Refrigerator blues

Don't leave your Champagne — or any other good sparkling wine — in your refrigerator for more than a week! Its flavor will become flat from the excessively cold temperature. Also, long-term vibrations caused by the cycling on and off of the refrigerator motor are not good for any wine — especially sparkling wine. (See Chapter 17 for more on storing your wine properly.)

Rosé Champagne

Rosé Champagnes — pink Champagnes — can also be Vintage or non-vintage. Usually, Pinot Noir and Chardonnay are the only grapes used, in proportions that vary from one house to the next.

Winemakers create a rosé Champagne usually by including some red Pinot Noir wine in the blend for the base wine. A few actually vinify some of their red grapes into pink wines, the way that you would make a rosé still wine, and use that as the base wine. Colors vary quite a lot, from pale onionskin to salmon to rosy pink. (The lighter-colored ones are usually dryer.)

Rosés are fuller and rounder than other Champagnes and are best enjoyed with dinner. (Because they have become associated with romance, they're popular choices for wedding anniversaries and Valentine's Day.)

Like blanc de blancs Champagnes (see the previous section), rosés usually cost a few dollars more than regular Champagnes, and not every Champagne house makes one. Some of the best rosés are those of Roederer, Billecart-Salmon, Delamotte, Gosset, and Moët & Chandon (especially its Dom Pérignon Rosé).

For some people, rosé Champagne has a bad connotation because of the tons of sweet, insipid, cheap pink wines — sparkling and otherwise — on the market. But rosé Champagne is just as dry and has the same high quality as regular (white) Champagne.

Who's drinking Champagne?

Not surprisingly, France leads the world in Champagne consumption, drinking 59 percent of all the Champagne produced. The United Kingdom is the leading foreign market for Champagne. The United States is second, Germany is third, followed by Belgium, Japan, Italy, and Switzerland. But the United States buys the most prestige cuvée Champagne (especially Dom Pérignon), followed by Japan.

Sweetness categories

Champagnes always carry an indication of their sweetness on the label, but the words used to indicate sweetness are cryptic: Extra dry is not really dry, for example. In ascending order of sweetness, Champagnes are labeled

- **Extra brut, brut nature, or brut zero:** Totally dry
- **Brut:** Dry
- **Extra dry:** Medium dry
- **Sec:** Slightly sweet
- **Demi-sec:** Fairly sweet
- **Doux:** Sweet

The most popular style for Champagne and other serious bubblies is brut. Brut and, trailing well behind, extra dry are the two types of Champagne you find most nowadays. But recently, very dry Champagnes (extra brut, brut nature, or brut zero) have become popular among connoisseurs.

Recommended Champagne producers

The Champagne business — especially the export end of it — is dominated by about 25 or 30 large houses, most of whom purchase from independent growers the majority of grapes they need to make their Champagne. Of the major houses, only Roederer and Bollinger own a substantial portion of the vineyards from which they get their grapes — a definite economic and quality-control advantage for them.

Moët & Chandon is by far the largest Champagne house. In terms of worldwide sales, other large brands are Veuve Clicquot, Mumm, Nicolas Feuillate, Vranken, Laurent-Perrier, Pommery, Lanson, and Piper-Heidsieck. The following lists name some of our favorite producers, grouped according to the style of their Champagne: light-bodied, medium-bodied, or full-bodied. (For an understanding of the term *body* as it applies to wine, see Chapter 2.)

Light, elegant styles

Laurent-Perrier	G.H. Mumm
Ruinart	Perrier-Jouët
Jacquesson	J. Lassalle*
Ayala	Henriot
Pommery	Billecart-Salmon
Piper-Heidsieck	Bruno Paillard

Medium-bodied styles

Charles Heidsieck	Deutz
Pol Roger	Taittinger
Moët & Chandon	Philipponnat
Alfred Gratien	Lanson

Full-bodied styles

Krug	Veuve Clicquot
Louis Roederer	Delamotte
Bollinger	Salon*
Gosset	Paul Bara*

* Small producer; may be difficult to find.

The following list names, in rough order of preference, 28 Champagne houses whose vintage and prestige cuvées have been in top form lately. For more info on Champagne, see Ed McCarthy's *Champagne For Dummies* (Wiley).

- **Louis Roederer:** Cristal, Cristal Rosé
- **Krug:** Clos du Mesnil, Vintage, NV Rosé, Grande Cuvée
- **Bollinger:** Grande Année, Blanc de Noirs Vieilles Vignes
- **Philipponnat:** Clos des Goisses
- **Moët & Chandon:** Dom Pérignon
- **Salon:** Blanc de Blancs
- **Charles Heidsieck:** Blanc des Millenaires, Vintage
- **Henriot:** Cuveé des Enchanteleurs, Blanc de Blancs
- **Gosset:** Celebris, Celebris Rosé, NV Grande Réserve

- ✔ **Ayala:** La Perle d'Ayala Nature, Cuvée Rosé Nature
- ✔ **Bruno Paillard:** Blanc de Blancs Réserve Privée
- ✔ **Veuve Clicquot:** Vintage, La Grande Dame
- ✔ **Pol Roger:** Cuvée Sir Winston Churchill, Blanc de Blancs
- ✔ **Paul Bara:** Vintage, Comtesse Marie de France
- ✔ **Taittinger:** Comtes de Champagne, Comtes de Champagne Rosé
- ✔ **Billecart-Salmon:** Blanc de Blancs, Cuvée Elisabeth Salmon Rosé
- ✔ **Deutz:** Cuvée William Deutz, Cuvée William Deutz Rosé
- ✔ **Pommery:** Cuvée Louise, Cuvée Louise Rosé
- ✔ **Jacquesson:** All of its Champagnes
- ✔ **Laurent-Perrier:** Grand Siècle
- ✔ **Ruinart:** Dom Ruinart Blanc de Blancs
- ✔ **Perrier-Jouët:** Fleur de Champagne Blanc de Blancs, Fleur de Champagne, Fleur de Champagne Rosé
- ✔ **Lanson:** Noble Cuvée, Noble Cuvée Blanc de Blancs
- ✔ **Piper-Heidsieck:** Champagne Rare
- ✔ **Alfred Gratien:** Cuvée Paradis (NV)
- ✔ **G.H. Mumm:** Cuvée R. Lalou, Blanc de Blancs
- ✔ **Delamotte:** Vintage Blanc de Blancs, NV Rosé
- ✔ **Cattier:** Clos du Moulin (NV)

Madame Lily Bollinger's advice on drinking Champagne

When Jacques Bollinger died in 1941, his widow, Lily Bollinger, carried their famous Champagne house through the difficult years of the German occupation of France. She ran the company until her death in 1977. Bollinger prospered under her leadership, doubling in size. She was a beloved figure in Champagne, where she could be seen bicycling through the vineyards every day. In 1961, when a London reporter asked her when she drank Champagne, Madame Bollinger replied:

"I only drink Champagne when I'm happy, and when I'm sad. Sometimes I drink it when I'm alone. When I have company I consider it obligatory. I trifle with it if I am not hungry and drink it when I am. Otherwise I never touch it — unless I'm thirsty."

The redoubtable Madame Lily Bollinger died at the age of 78, apparently none the worse for all that Champagne.

Grower Champagnes

A phenomenon has occurred in the world of Champagne during the last two decades: the growth of so-called *grower Champagnes* in export markets. A *grower-producer* is someone who makes Champagne from the grapes that he has grown in his own vineyards — as opposed to a Champagne house, which purchases some of the grapes for its wines. (You can recognize a grower Champagne by the initials *RM* or *RC* in small print on the bottom of the label.)

A few growers in Champagne, such as Paul Bara, have actually been making and selling their own Champagne for many decades, but two-thirds of the region's 15,000 growers are content selling their grapes.

Around 5,000 growers now sell the Champagnes that they themselves have made, accounting for about 22 percent of all Champagne sales. Most of these sales take place in France; only a very small percentage of growers are large enough to export their Champagnes around the world. But the number is growing. When coauthor Ed wrote *Champagne For Dummies* in 1999, about 40 to 50 grower Champagnes were available in the United States. Today that number tops 200. But this category accounts for only 4 percent of U.S. Champagne sales (up from 2 percent 12 years ago) for two reasons: Their production is very small compared to that of the Champagne houses; and they sell in only a few markets in the United States — mainly in large cities. Another reason could be that only the more knowledgeable Champagne drinkers even know about these wines: Growers don't have the budget to do mass advertising.

Some of the better-known grower Champagnes in the United States include the following: Paul Bara, Henri Billiot, Guy Charlemagne, Gaston Chiquet, Diebolt-Vallois, Egly-Ouriet, René Geoffroy, Pierre Gimonnet, Guy Larmandier, Larmandier-Bernier, J. Lasalle, A. Margaine, Serge Mathieu, Pierre Peters, Alain Robert, Jacques Selosse, and Vilmart. Most of these producers make 7,000 or fewer cases per year, a pittance compared to the production of the Champagne houses. Pierre Gimonnet and Gaston Chiquet are the two largest in this group and are probably the most available.

Are all grower Champagnes inherently of better quality than other Champagnes? No, but they are consistently of high quality and have the distinctive taste of their own vineyard area. On the non-vintage level (by far the largest type of grower Champagne), prices are about the same as other Champagnes. But grower Champagnes generally are lower priced at the premium Champagne level compared to wines of the Champagne houses.

One word of warning about grower Champagnes: They are generally not aged as long at the winery as major brands, because growers don't have the storage facilities. When you buy these wines, they might taste a bit "green"; they are simply too young, and ideally you should hold on to them a while (we suggest about a year) before you open them.

Other Sparkling Wines

Wineries all over the world have emulated Champagne by adopting the techniques used in the Champagne region. Their wines differ from Champagne, however, because their grapes grow in *terroirs* different from that of the Champagne region and because, in some cases, their grapes are different varieties.

Other wineries in many parts of the world make their bubblies by using the tank fermentation rather than the bottle fermentation method specifically to attain a certain style or to reduce production costs. (We discuss these methods in the earlier section "How Sparkling Wine Happens.")

French sparkling wine

France makes many other sparkling wines besides Champagne, especially in the Loire Valley, around Saumur, and in the regions of Alsace and Burgundy. Sparkling wine made by the traditional method (second fermentation in the bottle) often carries the name *Crémant,* as in Crémant d'Alsace, Crémant de Loire, Crémant de Bourgogne, and so on. Grape varieties are those typical of each region (see Chapter 10).

Some of the leading brands of French sparkling wines are Langlois-Château, Gratien & Meyer, Bouvet Ladubay (all from the Loire Valley), Brut d'Argent, Kriter, and Saint Hilaire. These wines sell for $10 to $20 and are decent. (The last three brands are less expensive than the three from the Loire Valley.) They're perfect for parties and other large gatherings, when you may want to serve a French bubbly without paying a Champagne price. For more info on French sparkling wines, take a look at our book *French Wine For Dummies* (Wiley).

American sparkling wine

Almost as many states make sparkling wine as make still wine, but California and New York are the most famous for it. Chateau Frank, in the $20 to $25 retail range, is a fine producer of New York State sparkling wines made in the traditional method.

One sparkling wine, Gruet, deserves special mention because it hails, improbably, from New Mexico. Owned by France's little-known Champagne Gruet, the New Mexican winery makes three fine bubblies: a NV Brut and NV Blanc de Noirs, both $12 to $15, and a top Vintage Blanc de Blancs, $22 to $24. Another fine sparkling producer is Oregon's Argyle Winery. Its vintage bubblies start at $19.

California bubbly is definitely a different wine from Champagne and tastes fruitier even when made by a Champagne house, using the same methods and the same grape varieties as in Champagne. Good California sparkling wines, the ones made in the traditional Champagne method, cost as little as $14 on up to $40 and more.

Most of California's finest sparkling wines do not call themselves Champagne, but the less-expensive, best-selling ones do. In that second category, Korbel, less than $15, is the only brand that is actually fermented in the bottle.

We recommend the following California sparkling wine producers, listed in our rough order of preference within each category.

- ✔ **U.S.-owned producers:**

  - **Schramsberg Vineyards:** Now sourcing its grapes from the coolest areas in Napa and Sonoma, Schramsberg, with Hugh Davies at the helm, has emerged as one of the premium sparkling wine houses in the United States. From its Blanc de Blancs and Blanc de Noirs ($30 to $35) to its premium J. Schram Teté de Cuvée Brut ($90 to $110), its sparklers are superb.

  - **Iron Horse:** In Green Valley, the coolest part of Sonoma (temperature wise, that is), Iron Horse is clearly making some of California's finest sparkling wine. Look for its better cuvées, such as the Wedding Cuvée or Russian Cuvée, for about $30.

  - **J:** Not content with making some of America's most popular Cabernet Sauvignons and Chardonnays, the Jordan winery in Sonoma also makes one of the best sparkling wines in the country. Almost all its grapes come from the cool Russian River Valley. Quite fruity and fairly delicate, the wine comes in white or rosé and sells for about $35.

- ✔ **French- or Spanish-owned producers:**

  - **Roederer Estate:** Louis Roederer is such a fine Champagne house that we're not surprised at the smashing success that its Anderson Valley winery, near the town of Mendocino, has achieved. Some critics think it's California's best. Wines include a good-value brut ($24), a delicate rosé ($30) that's worth seeking out, and outstanding premium cuvées, L'Ermitage ($42) and L'Ermitage Rosé ($55).

  - **Mumm Napa:** Now owned by France's Pernod-Ricard, Mumm has established itself as one of California's best sparkling wine houses. Much of its production comes from the cool Carneros District; look especially for the Winery Lake Brut and the cherrylike Blanc de Noirs. The price range is $25 and up.

  - **Domaine Carneros:** Taittinger's California winery makes an elegant, high-quality brut and rosé ($25 to $30) in cool Carneros.

Its premium cuvée, Le Rêve, a $95 blanc de blancs, and Le Reve rosé ($110) are stunning but expensive. (Production is small; they sell out quickly.)

- **Domaine Chandon:** This Napa Valley winery is part of the Moët & Chandon empire. A must-stop for its restaurant alone, Chandon continues to make solid, consistent sparkling wines at reasonable prices ($17 to $20). Look especially for its premium Etoile (about $35), one of the most elegant sparkling wines in the United States, and the delicious Etoile Rosé ($38).

- **Gloria Ferrer:** Spain's Freixenet has built a beautiful winery in windswept Carneros. Most of its wines are priced right ($20 to $25), including its Royal Cuvée. Gloria Ferrer's premium sparkler, Carneros Cuvée ($30 to $35) is a great value. The winery is definitely worth a visit.

- **Scharffenberger:** From the cool Anderson Valley, Scharffenberger, now owned by Champagne Louis Roederer, makes a Chardonnay-based brut and a rosé brut ($15 to $20).

Italian spumante: Sweet or dry

Spumante is simply the Italian word for "sparkling." It often appears on bottles of American wines that are sweet, fruity spinoffs of Italy's classic Asti, once called Asti Spumante. Actually, Italy makes many fine, dry spumante wines and a popular, slightly sparkling wine called *Prosecco,* as well as sweet spumante. For more info on Italian sparkling wines, check out our book *Italian Wine For Dummies* (Wiley).

Asti and Moscato d'Asti

Asti is a delicious, fairly sweet, exuberantly fruity sparkling wine made in the Piedmont region from Moscato grapes, via the tank method. It's one bubbly that you can drink with dessert (fantastic with wedding cake!).

Because freshness is essential in Asti, buy a good brand that sells well. (Asti is not vintage-dated, so there's no other way to determine how old the wine is.) We recommend Martini & Rossi and Cinzano (about $10 to $13).

For Asti flavor with fewer bubbles, try Moscato d'Asti, a delicate and delicious medium-dry vintage-dated *frizzante* (slightly sparkling) wine that makes a refreshing apéritif. It's also good with dessert and is a great brunch wine. And it has just 5 to 7 percent alcohol! Vietti makes a good one, called Cascinetta, for about $12 to $13. Other good producers of Moscato d'Asti are Dante Rivetti, Paolo Sarocco, and Ceretto, whose wine is called Santo Stefano; all these sell for $14 to $16. Again, freshness is essential. With Moscato d'Asti, let the vintage date guide you; buy the youngest one you can find.

Dry spumante

Using the traditional method, Italy produces a good deal of dry sparkling wine in the Oltrepò-Pavese and Franciacorta wine zones of Lombardy and in the Trentino region. Italy's dry sparkling wines are very dry with little or no sweetening dosage. They come in all price ranges:

- A good mid-priced bubbly is Ferrari Brut (at $20 to $22).

- Two upscale (and very good) bruts, $35 to $40 and up, are Bellavista NV Franciacorta Brut and Cà del Bosco NV Franciacorta Brut. The premium sparklers of these two houses can be expensive. Vintage Giulio Ferrari, the superb top-of-the-line Ferrari spumante, likewise is in the $85 to $100 range. Bruno Giacosa, well known for his outstanding Barbarescos and Barolos, makes 100 percent Pinot Noir Brut (about $60) in his spare time, for kicks. Like everything else he produces, it's superb.

Prosecco

This quintessential Italian sparkling wine has become all the rage in parts of the United States, thanks to the fact that so many Italian restaurants serve it by the glass. Prosecco comes from grapes grown in the Veneto and Friuli regions; the grape variety used to be called Prosecco but is now known as Glera. Prosecco wine is a straightforward, pleasant apéritif, low in alcohol (about 11 to 12 percent), and it comes in dry, off-dry, and sweet styles. Prosecco is mainly a frizzante (slightly sparkling) wine, but it also comes as a spumante (fully sparkling), or even as a nonsparkling wine (which we don't recommend; it's better with bubbles). The best Prosecco bears the DOCG appellation of either Valdobbiadene or Conegliano (or, in some cases, both), which are two villages in the northern Veneto (see Chapter 11 for more about the DOCG appellation).

Prosecco is the perfect wine to have with Italian antipasto, such as pickled vegetables, calamari, anchovies, or spicy salami. Its fresh, fruity flavors cleanse your mouth and get your appetite going for dinner. And Prosecco is eminently affordable: It retails for $12 to $18 a bottle. Recommended producers (alphabetically) include Astoria, Bisson, Carpenè Malvolti, Mionetto, Nino Franco, Valdo, Zardetto, and Zonin.

Spanish sparkling wines (Cava)

What if you want to spend about $10 or less for a decent sparkling wine? The answer is Spain's sparkling wine, Cava, which sells mainly for $8 to $12 a bottle. Almost all of it comes from the Penedés region in Catalonia, near Barcelona.

Cava is a traditional method sparkling wine, fermented in the bottle. Most Cavas use local Spanish grapes, and, as a result, they taste distinctly different (a nicely earthy, mushroomy flavor) from California bubblies and from Champagne. Some of the more expensive wines do contain Chardonnay in their blend.

Baby Champagnes are "in"

Although Champagnes in small bottles — 375 ml half-bottles and 187 ml splits — normally don't stay as fresh as Champagne in larger bottles, size becomes less an issue when the bottles sell quickly. A few savvy Champagne houses have attractively packaged their Champagnes in small bottles and made them readily available in nightclubs and bars where young adults congregate. A decade ago, Pommery introduced its "POP," a bright blue split (187 ml) that comes with a straw so you can even drink it right out of the bottle. It's an extra-dry non-vintage Champagne, not quite as dry as a brut, which suits the casual occasions when this wine is drunk. Not to be outdone, Piper-Heidsieck followed with a bright red split of its non-vintage brut, which it calls "Baby Piper." Both Champagnes have been selling very well. Perrier-Jouët is now aggressively marketing its half-bottles and splits; ditto Lanson with its half-bottle.

Although Champagne is a serious wine, it obviously offers plenty of opportunity for fun!

Two gigantic wineries dominate Cava production — Freixenet (pronounced fresh-net) and Codorníu. Freixenet's frosted black Cordon Negro bottle has to be one of the most recognizable wine bottles in the world. Other Cava brands to look for are Mont Marçal, Paul Cheneau, Jaume Serra Cristalino, Marqués de Monistrol, and Segura Viudas. Juve y Camps, a vintage-dated, upscale Cava, is a worthwhile buy at $15 to $18.

Buying and Serving Bubbly

Sparkling wine is best cold, about 45 degrees Fahrenheit (7 to 8 degrees Celsius), although some people prefer it less cold (52 degrees Fahrenheit; 11 degrees Celisus). We like the colder temperature because it helps the wine hold its effervescence — and the wine warms up so quickly in the glass, anyway. Because older Champagnes and Vintage Champagnes are more complex, you should chill them less than young, non-vintage Champagne or sparkling wine.

Never leave an open bottle of sparkling wine on the table unless it's in an ice bucket (filled with half cold water, half ice) because it will warm up quickly. However, an exception to this rule is if you have a large group of drinkers (six or more), because they will finish the bottle in ten minutes or less. Use a sparkling wine stopper to keep leftover bubbly fresh for a couple of days — in the fridge, of course.

If you're entertaining, you should know that the ideal bottle size for Champagne is the _magnum,_ which is equivalent to two bottles. The larger bottle enables the wine to age more gently in the winery's cellar. Magnums (or sometimes double magnums) are usually the largest bottles in which Champagne is fermented; all really large bottles have had finished Champagne poured into them, and the wine is, therefore, not as fresh as it is in a magnum or a regular bottle.

Be wary of half-bottles (375 ml) and — chancier yet — splits (187 ml)! Champagne in these small bottles is often not fresh. If you're given a small bottle of Champagne or any sparkling wine as a wedding favor, for example, open it at the first excuse; do not keep it around for a year waiting for the right occasion!

Champagne and other good, dry sparkling wines are extremely versatile with food — and they are the essential wine for certain kinds of foods. For example, no wine goes better with egg dishes than Champagne. Indulge yourself next time you have brunch. And when you're having spicy Asian cuisine, try sparkling wine, particularly a fruity style. For us, no wine matches up better with spicy Chinese or Indian food!

Fish, seafood, pasta (but not with tomato sauce), risotto, and poultry are excellent with Champagne and sparkling wine. If you're having lamb (pink, not well done) or ham, pair rosé Champagne with it. With aged Champagne, chunks of aged Asiago, aged Gouda, or Parmesan cheese go extremely well.

Don't serve a dry brut (or extra dry) sparkling wine with dessert. These styles are just too dry. With fresh fruit and desserts that aren't very sweet, try a demi-sec Champagne. With sweeter desserts (or wedding cake!), we recommend Asti. (For more info on Champagne with food, see coauthor Ed's *Champagne For Dummies,* published by Wiley.)

Ten excuses to indulge

You don't really need an excuse to open a bottle of Champagne. Please don't save it for "a special occasion." Make your own occasion. Here are a few suggestions:

1. You have a bottle on hand.

2. Your demanding boss just left for vacation, or better yet, changed jobs.

3. The noisy neighbors next door finally moved out.

4. You finished your income taxes.

5. It's Saturday.

6. The kids left for summer camp (or college).

7. You just found $50 in your old coat pocket.

8. You didn't get a single telephone or e-mail solicitation all day.

9. The wire muzzle over the cork makes a great cat toy.

10. You have just finished revising a wine book!

Chapter 16

Wine Roads Less Traveled: Fortified and Dessert Wines

. . . .

In This Chapter

▶ Sherry: The world's most versatile wine

▶ Port: 80 grapes for one wine

▶ Madeira: A wine that lasts 200 years

▶ Sauternes: Liquid gold from rotted grapes

. . . .

*T*he wines we lump together as *fortified wines* and *dessert wines* aren't mainstream beverages that you want to drink every day. Some of them are much higher in alcohol than regular wines, and some of them are extremely sweet (and rare and expensive!). They're the wine equivalent of really good candy — delicious enough that you can get carried away if you let yourself indulge daily. So you treat them as treats: a glass before or after dinner, a bottle when company comes, a splurge to celebrate the start of your diet — tomorrow.

Pleasure aside, from a purely academic point of view, you owe it to yourself to try these wines. Seriously! Learning about wine is hard work, but it's also a lot of fun.

Timing Is Everything

Many wines enjoyed before dinner, as apéritif wines, or after dinner, as dessert wines, fall into the category of *fortified wines* (called *liqueur wines* by the European Union, or E.U.; see Chapter 1 for an explanation of E.U. terms). Fortified wines all have alcohol added to them at some point in their production, giving them an alcohol content that ranges from 16 to 24 percent.

The point at which alcohol is added determines whether the wines are naturally sweet or dry.

- ✔ When fortified with alcohol *during* fermentation, the wines are sweet, because the added alcohol stops fermentation, leaving natural, unfermented sugar in the wine. (See Chapter 1 for an explanation of fermentation.) Port is the classic example of this process.

- ✔ When fortified *after* fermentation (after all the grape sugar has been converted to alcohol), the wines are dry (unless they're subsequently sweetened). Sherry is the classic example of this process.

Some of the wines we call dessert wines don't have added alcohol. Their sweetness occurs because the grapes are at the right place at the right time — when noble rot strikes. (See the discussion of German wines in Chapter 12 for more about noble rot.) Other dessert wines are sweet because winemakers pick very ripe (but not rotten) grapes and dry them before fermentation to concentrate their juice, or they let the grapes freeze — just other ways of turning grape juice into the nectar of the gods.

Sherry: A Misunderstood Wine

The late comedian Rodney Dangerfield built a career around the line, "I get no respect!" His wine of choice should have been Sherry, because it shares the same plight. Sherry is a wine of true quality and diversity, but it remains undiscovered by most of the world. (In a way, we're not sorry, because the price of good Sherry is attractively low.)

The Jerez triangle

Sherry comes from the Andalucía region of sun-baked, southwestern Spain. The wine is named after Jerez (her-*eth*) de la Frontera, an old town of Moorish and Arab origin where many of the Sherry *bodegas* are located. (*Bodega* can refer to the actual building in which Sherry is matured or to the Sherry firm itself.)

Actually, the town of Jerez is just one corner of a triangle that makes up the Sherry region. Another corner is Puerto de Santa María, a beautiful, old coast town southwest of Jerez and home to a number of large bodegas. The third point of the triangle, Sanlúcar de Barrameda (also on the coast but northwest of Jerez), is so blessed with sea breezes that the lightest and driest of Sherries, *manzanilla* (mahn-zah-nee-yah), can legally be made only there. Aficionados of Sherry swear that they can detect the salty tang of the ocean in manzanilla.

Traveling from Sanlúcar to Jerez, you pass vineyards with dazzling white soil. This soil is *albariza,* the region's famous chalky earth, rich in limestone from fossilized shells. Summers are hot and dry, but balmy sea breezes temper the heat.

The Palomino grape — the main variety used in Sherry — thrives only here in the hot Sherry region on albariza soil. Palomino is a complete failure for table wines because it is so neutral in flavor and low in acid, but it's perfect for Sherry production. Two other grape varieties, Pedro Ximénez (*pay*-dro he-*main*-ehz) and Moscatel (Muscat), are used for dessert types of Sherry.

The phenomenon of flor

Sherry consists of two basic types: *fino* (light, very dry) and *oloroso* (rich and full, but also dry). Sweet Sherries are made by sweetening either type.

After fermentation, the winemaker decides which Sherries will become finos (*fee*-nos) or olorosos (oh-loh-*roh*-sohs) by judging the appearance, aroma, and flavor of the young, unfortified wines. If a wine is to be a fino, the winemaker fortifies it lightly (until its alcohol level reaches about 15.5 percent). He strengthens future olorosos to 18 percent alcohol.

At this point, when the wines are in casks, the special Sherry magic begins: A yeast called *flor* grows spontaneously on the surface of the wines destined to be finos. The flor eventually covers the whole surface, protecting the wine from oxidation. The flor feeds on oxygen in the air and on alcohol and glycerin in the wine. It changes the wine's character, contributing a distinct aroma and flavor and rendering the wine thinner and more delicate in texture.

Flor doesn't grow on olorosos-to-be, because their higher alcohol content prevents it. Without the protection of the flor (and because the casks are never filled to the brim), these wines are exposed to oxygen as they age. This deliberate oxidation protects olorosos against further oxidation — for example, after you open a bottle.

Communal aging

Both fino and oloroso Sherries age in a special way that's unique to Sherry making.

The young wine isn't left to age on its own (as most other wines would) but is added to casks of older wine that are already aging. To make room for the young wine, some of the older wine is emptied out of the casks and is added to casks of even older wine. To make room in those casks, some of the wine is transferred to casks of even older wine, and so on. At the end of this chain, four to nine generations away from the young wine, some of the finished Sherry is taken from the oldest casks and is bottled for sale.

This system of blending wines is called the *solera* system. It takes its name from the word *solera* (floor), the term also used to identify the casks of oldest wine.

As wines are blended — younger into older, into yet older, and eventually into oldest — no more than a third of the wine is emptied from any cask. In theory, then, each solera contains small (and ever-decreasing) amounts of very old wine. As each younger wine mingles with older wine, it takes on characteristics of the older wine; within a few months, the wine of each generation is indistinguishable from what it was before being refreshed with younger wine. Thus, the solera system maintains infinite consistency of quality and style in Sherry.

Because the casks of Sherry age in dry, airy bodegas above ground (rather than humid, underground cellars like most other wines), some of the wine's water evaporates, and the wine's alcoholic strength increases. Some olorosos aged for more than ten years can be as much as 24 percent alcohol, compared to their starting point of 18 percent.

Two makes 12

So far, so good: two types of Sherry — delicate fino aged under its protective flor and fuller oloroso aged oxidatively — and no vintages, because the young wines are blended with older wines. But now Sherry begins to get a bit confusing. Those two types are about to branch into at least 12. New styles occur when the natural course of aging changes the character of a Sherry so that its taste no longer conforms to one of the two categories. Deliberate sweetening of the wine also creates different styles.

Among dry Sherries, these are the main styles:

✔ **Fino:** Pale, straw-colored Sherry, light in body, dry, and delicate. Fino Sherries are always matured under flor, either in Jerez or Puerto de Santa María. They have 15 to 17 percent alcohol. After they lose their protective flor (by bottling), finos become very vulnerable to oxidation spoilage, and you must, therefore, store them in a cool place, drink them young, and refrigerate them after opening. They're best when chilled.

✔ **Manzanilla:** Pale, straw-colored, delicate, light, tangy, and very dry fino-style Sherry made only in Sanlúcar de Barrameda. (Although various styles of manzanilla are produced, *manzanilla fina,* the fino style, is by far the most common.) The temperate sea climate causes the flor to grow thicker in this town, and manzanilla is thus the driest and most pungent of all the Sherries. Handle it similarly to a fino Sherry.

- ✔ **Manzanilla pasada:** A manzanilla that has been aged in cask about seven years and has lost its flor. It's more amber in color than a manzanilla fina and fuller-bodied. It's close to a dry amontillado (see the next item) in style, but still crisp and pungent. Serve cool.

- ✔ **Amontillado:** An aged fino that has lost its flor in the process of cask aging. It's deeper amber in color and richer and nuttier than the previous styles. Amontillado (ah-moan-tee-*yah*-doh) is dry but retains some of the pungent tang from its lost flor. True amontillado is fairly rare; most of the best examples are in the $25 to $40 price range. Cheaper Sherries labeled *amontillado* are common, so be suspicious if it costs less than $15 a bottle. Serve amontillado slightly cool and, for best flavor, finish the bottle within a week.

- ✔ **Oloroso:** Dark gold to deep brown in color (depending on its age), full-bodied with rich, raisiny aroma and flavor, but dry. Olorosos lack the delicacy and pungency of fino (flor) Sherries. They're usually between 18 and 20 percent alcohol and can keep for a few weeks after you open the bottle because they have already been oxidized in their aging. Serve them at room temperature.

- ✔ **Palo cortado:** The rarest of all Sherries. In general, it starts out as a fino, with a flor, and develops as an amontillado, losing its flor. But then, for some unknown reason, it begins to resemble the richer, more fragrant oloroso style, all the while retaining the elegance of an amontillado. In color and alcohol content, palo cortado (*pah*-loe-cor-*tah*-doh) is similar to an oloroso, but its aroma is quite like an amontillado. Like amontillado Sherry, beware of cheap imitations. Serve at room temperature. It keeps as well as olorosos.

Sweet Sherry is dry Sherry that has been sweetened. The sweetening can come in many forms, such as the juice of Pedro Ximénez grapes that have been dried like raisins. All the following sweet styles of Sherry are best served at room temperature:

- ✔ **Medium Sherry:** Amontillados and light olorosos that have been slightly sweetened. They are light brown in color.

- ✔ **Pale Cream:** Made by blending fino and light amontillado Sherries and lightly sweetening the blend. They have a very pale gold color. Pale Cream is a fairly new style.

- ✔ **Cream Sherry:** Cream and the lighter "milk" Sherries are rich *amorosos* (the term for sweetened olorosos). They vary in quality, depending on the oloroso used, and can improve in the bottle with age. These Sherries are a popular style.

- ✔ **Brown Sherry:** Very dark, rich, sweet, dessert Sherry, usually containing a coarser style of oloroso.

- ✔ **East India Sherry:** A type of Brown Sherry that has been deeply sweetened and colored.

✔ **Pedro Ximénez and Moscatel:** Extremely sweet, dark brown, syrupy dessert Sherries. Often lower in alcohol, these Sherries are made from raisined grapes of these two varieties. As varietally labeled Sherries, they are quite rare today. Delicious over vanilla ice cream (really!).

Some wines from elsewhere in the world, especially the United States, also call themselves *Sherry*. Many of these are inexpensive wines in large bottles. Occasionally, you can find a decent one, but usually, they're sweet and not very good. Authentic Sherry is made only in the Jerez region of Spain and carries the official name, *Jerez-Xérès-Sherry* (the Spanish, French, and English names for the town) on the front or back label.

Serving and storing Sherry

The light, dry Sherries — fino and manzanilla — must be fresh. Buy them from stores with rapid turnover; a fino or manzanilla that has been languishing on the shelf for several months will not give you the authentic experience of these wines.

Although fino or manzanilla can be an excellent apéritif, be careful when ordering a glass in a restaurant or bar. Never accept a glass from an already-open bottle unless the bottle has been refrigerated. Even then, ask how long it has been open — more than two days is too much. After you open a bottle at home, refrigerate it and finish it within a couple of days.

Manzanilla and fino Sherry are ideal with almonds, olives, shrimp or prawns, all kinds of seafood, and those wonderful tapas in Spanish bars and restaurants. Amontillado Sherries can accompany tapas before dinner but are also fine at the table with light soups, cheese, ham, or salami (especially the Spanish type, *chorizo*). Dry olorosos and palo cortados are best with nuts, olives, and hard cheeses (such as the excellent Spanish sheep-milk cheese, Manchego). All the sweet Sherries can be served with desserts after dinner or enjoyed on their own.

We like to buy half-bottles of fino and manzanilla so that we don't have leftover wine that oxidizes. These, and all Sherries, can be stored upright. Try not to hold bottles of fino or manzanilla more than three months, however. The higher alcohol and the oxidative aging of other types of Sherry (amontillado, oloroso, palo cortado, all the sweet Sherries) permit you to hold them for several years.

Nut'n Sherry

The aroma of fino Sherry is often compared with almonds. Amontillados are said to smell like hazelnuts, and olorosos, like walnuts. And, by the way, the named nuts make ideal accompaniments to each particular Sherry.

Recommended Sherries

Sherries are among the great values in the wine world: You can buy decent, genuine Sherries for $8 to $10. But if you want to try the best wines, you may have to spend $15 or more. The following are some of our favorite Sherries, according to type.

- **Fino:** These fino Sherries are about $16 to $18:
    - González Byass's Tío Pepe (*tee*-oh *pay*-pay)
    - Pedro Domecq's La Ina (*een*-ah)
    - Emilio Lustau's Jarana (har-*ahn*-ah)
    - Valdespino's Inocente ($19 to $20 per half-bottle)
- **Manzanilla:**
    - Hidalgo's La Gitana (a great buy at $14 to $15 for 500-ml bottle); also, Hidalgo's Manzanilla Pasada, $25 to $28
- **Amontillado:** You find a great number of cheap imitations in this category. For a true amontillado, stick to one of the following brands:
    - González Byass's Del Duque (the real thing; half-bottle, $38 to $44)
    - Emilio Lustau (any of his amontillados labeled *Almacenista*, $35 to $40)
    - Hidalgo's Napoleon ($17 to $18 for a 500-ml bottle)
- **Oloroso:**
    - González Byass's Matusalem (half-bottle, $35 to $40)
    - Emilio Lustau (any of his olorosos labeled *Almacenista,* $35 to $40)
- **Palo cortado:** You find many imitations in this category, too. True palo cortados are quite rare.
    - González Byass's Apostoles (half-bottle, $38 to $40)
    - Emilio Lustau (any of his palo cortados labeled *Almacenista,* $35 to $40)
    - Hidalgo's Jerez Cortado (about $50)
- **Cream:**
    - Sandeman's Armada Cream (about $15 to $16)
    - Emilio Lustau's Rare Cream Solera Reserva ($27 to $28)
- **East India, Pedro Ximénez, Moscatel:**
    - Emilio Lustau (quality brand for all three Sherries; all $25 to $30)
    - González Byass's Pedro Ximénez "Noe" (half-bottle, $38 to $40)

Montilla: A Sherry look-alike

Northeast of the Sherry region is the Montilla-Moriles region (commonly referred to as Montilla, pronounced *moan-tee-yah*), where wines very similar to Sherry are made in fino, amontillado, and oloroso styles. The two big differences between Montilla and Sherry are

- ✔ Pedro Ximénez is the predominant grape variety in Montilla.
- ✔ Montillas usually reach their high alcohol levels naturally (without fortification).

Alvear is the leading brand of Montilla. Reasonably priced ($18 to $20 for a half-bottle), these wines are widely available as finos or amontillados.

Marsala, Vin Santo, and the Gang

Italy has a number of interesting dessert and fortified wines, of which Marsala (named after a town in western Sicily) is the most famous. Marsala is a fortified wine made from local grape varieties. It comes in numerous styles, all of which are fortified after fermentation, like Sherry, and aged in a form of the solera system (see the earlier section "Communal aging" for details). You can find dry, semi-dry, or sweet versions and amber, gold, or red versions, but the best Marsalas have the word *Superiore* or — even better — *Vergine* or *Vergine Soleras* on the label. Marsala Vergine is unsweetened and uncolored and is aged longer than other styles.

Marco De Bartoli is the most acclaimed producer of dry-style Marsala. His 20-year-old Vecchio Samperi (about $50 to $60 for a 500-ml bottle) is an excellent example of a dry, apéritif Marsala. Pellegrino, Rallo, and Florio are larger producers of note. (For more info on Marsala and all other Sicilian fortified or dessert wines, see our book *Italian Wine For Dummies,* published by Wiley.)

Two fascinating dessert wines are made on small islands near Sicily from dried grapes. One is Malvasia delle Lipari, from the estate of the late Carlo Hauner. This wine has a beautiful, orange-amber color and an incredible floral, apricot, and herb aroma ($25 to $27 for a half-bottle). The other is Moscato di Pantelleria, a very delicious sweet wine. De Bartoli is one of the best producers; look for his Bukkuram Passito Pantelleria (about $80 to $85 for a 500-ml bottle).

The region of Tuscany is rightfully proud of its Vin Santo (vin *sahn*-toh), a golden amber wine made from dried grapes, generally white Malvasia and Trebbiano, and barrel-aged for several years. Vin Santo can be dry, medium-dry, or sweet. We prefer the first two — the dry style as an apéritif and the medium-dry version as an accompaniment to the wonderful Italian almond cookies called *biscotti.*

Many Tuscan producers make a Vin Santo; four outstanding examples of Vin Santo (conveniently available in half-bottles as well as full bottles) are from Avignonesi (very expensive!), Badia a Coltibuono, Castello di Cacchiano, and San Giusto a Rentennano.

Greece's Santorini Island also makes a Vinsanto from Assyrtiko and Aidani grapes, which is similar to Italy's Vin Santo. Greek producers claim that this type of wine originated on Santorini, but Italians dispute this. The leading producers of Santorini Assyrtiko, such as Argyros and Sigalas, also produce Vinsanto.

Port: The Glory of Portugal

Port is the world's greatest fortified red wine. The British invented Port, thanks to one of their many wars with the French, when they were forced to buy Portuguese wine as an alternative to French wine. To ensure that the Portuguese wines were stable enough for shipment by sea, the British added a small amount of brandy to finished wine, and early Port was the result. The English established their first Port house, Warre, in the city of Oporto in 1670, and several others followed.

Ironically, the French, who drove the British to Portugal, today drink three times as much Port as the British! But, of course, the French have the highest per capita consumption of wine in the world.

Home, home on the Douro

Port takes its name from the city of Oporto, situated where the northerly Douro River empties into the Atlantic Ocean. But its vineyards are far away, in the hot, mountainous Douro Valley. (In 1756, this wine region became one of the first in the world to be officially recognized by its government.) Some of the most dramatically beautiful vineyards in the world are on the slopes of the upper Douro — still very much a rugged, unspoiled area.

Port wine is fermented and fortified in the Douro Valley, and then most of it travels downriver to the coast. The large shippers' wine is finished and matured in the Port lodges of Vila Nova de Gaia, a suburb of Oporto, while most small producers mature their wine in the Valley. From Oporto, the wine is shipped all over the world.

To stop your wine-nerd friends in their tracks, ask them to name the authorized grape varieties for Port. (More than 80 exist!) In truth, most wine lovers — even Port lovers — can't name more than one variety. These grapes are mostly local and unknown outside of Portugal. For the record, the five most important varieties are *Touriga Nacional, Tinta Roriz* (Tempranillo), *Tinta Barroca, Tinto Cão,* and *Touriga Franca.*

My full name is Porto

The term *Port* has been borrowed even more extensively around the world than *Sherry* has. Many countries outside the E.U. make sweet, red wine in the Port style and label it as Port. Some of it can be quite good, but it's never as fine as the genuine article that is made only in Portugal. The trick in identifying authentic Portuguese Port is to look for the word *Porto,* which always appears on the label.

Many Ports in a storm

Think Sherry is complicated? In some ways, Port is even trickier. Although all Port is sweet because it is fortified during fermentation, and most of it is red, a zillion styles exist. The styles vary according to the quality of the base wine (ranging from ordinary to exceptional), how long the wine is aged in wood before bottling (ranging from 2 to 40-plus years), and whether the wine is from a single year or blended from wines of several years.

Don't let all the complicated styles of Port deter you from picking up a bottle and trying it. If you've never had Port before, you're bound to love it — almost no matter which style you try. (Later, you can fine-tune your preference for one style or another.) Port is simply delicious!

The following sections feature brief descriptions of the main styles, from simplest to most complex.

White Port

This type of Port is an anomaly, because most Port wine is red. But white Port does exist. Made from white grapes, this gold-colored wine can be off-dry or sweet. We couldn't quite figure out why it existed — Sherries and Sercial Madeiras (discussed later in this chapter) are better as apéritifs and red Ports are far superior as sweet wines — until someone served us white Port with tonic and ice one day. Served this way, white Port can be a bracing warm-weather apéritif.

Non-vintage Ports

Most Port wine is not vintage-dated and is blended from wines of various years. The types of non-vintage Port that we describe in this list encompass the majority of Port wines that you can see in a wine shop:

✔ **Ruby Port:** This young, non-vintage style is aged in wood for about three years before release. Fruity, simple, and inexpensive ($12 to $15 for major brands), it's the best-selling type of Port. If labeled *Reserve* or *Special Reserve,* the wine has usually aged about six years and costs a few dollars more. Ruby Port is a good introduction to the Port world.

✔ **Vintage Character Port:** Despite its name, this wine is not single-vintage Port — it just tries to taste like one. Vintage Character Port is actually premium ruby blended from higher-quality wines of several vintages and matured in wood for about five years. Full-bodied, rich, and ready to drink when released, these wines are a good value at about $18 to $20. But the labels don't always say *Vintage Character;* instead, they often bear proprietary names, such as Founder's Reserve (from Sandeman), Bin 27 (Fonseca), Six Grapes (Graham), First Estate (Taylor Fladgate), Warrior (Warre), and Distinction (Croft). As if *Vintage Character* wouldn't have been confusing enough!

✔ **Tawny Port:** Tawny is the most versatile Port style. The best tawnies are good-quality wines that fade to a pale garnet or brownish red color during long wood aging. Their labels carry an indication of their average age (the average age of the wines from which they were blended) — 10, 20, 30, or over-40 years. Ten-year-old tawnies cost about $30 to $40; 20-year-olds sell for $50 to $55; 30-year-olds, $80 to $100; and over-40-year-old tawnies cost a lot more ($130 to $150). We consider 10- and 20-year-old tawnies the best buys; the older ones, for us, aren't always worth the extra bucks. Tawny Ports have more finesse than other styles and are appropriate both as apéritifs and after dinner. Inexpensive tawnies that sell for about the same price as ruby Port are usually weak in flavor and not worth buying.

A serious tawny Port can be enjoyed in warm weather (even with a few ice cubes!) when a Vintage Port would be too heavy and tannic.

Vintage-dated Ports

Although the Port wines described in the preceding section can be excellent, the Ports made from grapes grown in a single year are generally of a higher quality caliber and are more expensive. These vintage-dated Ports include the following styles (only one of which is actually called Vintage Port):

✔ **Colheita Port:** Often confused with Vintage Port itself because it is vintage-dated, colheita is actually a tawny Port from a single vintage. In other words, it has aged (and softened and tawnied) in wood for many years. Unlike an aged tawny, though, it's the wine of a single year. Niepoort is one of the few Port houses that specializes in colheita Port. It can be very good, but older vintages are quite expensive ($50 to more than $100, depending on the vintage). Smith Woodhouse and Delaforce offer some colheita Portos for $50 or less.

✔ **Late Bottled Vintage (LBV) Port:** This type is from a specific vintage, but usually not from a very top year. The wine ages four to six years in wood before bottling and is then ready to drink, unlike Vintage Port itself, which requires additional aging in bottle. Quite full-bodied, but not as hefty as Vintage Port, it sells for about $22 to $26.

✔ **Vintage Port:** The pinnacle of Port production, Vintage Port is the wine of a single year blended from several of a house's best vineyards. It's bottled at about two years of age, before the wine has much chance to shed its tough tannins. It requires, therefore, an enormous amount of bottle aging to achieve the development that didn't occur in wood. Vintage Port is usually not mature (ready to drink) until about 20 years after the vintage.

Because it's very rich and very tannic, this wine throws a heavy sediment and *must* be decanted, preferably several hours before drinking (it needs the aeration). Vintage Port can live 70 or more years in top vintages.

Most good Vintage Ports sell for $80 to $100-plus when they're first released (years away from drinkability). Mature Vintage Ports can cost well over $100. Producing a Vintage Port amounts to a *declaration of that vintage* (a term you hear in Port circles) on the part of an individual Port house.

✔ **Single Quinta Vintage Port:** These are Vintage Ports from a single estate (*quinta*) that is usually a producer's best property (such as Taylor's Vargellas and Graham's Malvedos). They're made in good years, but not in the best vintages, because then their grapes are needed for the Vintage Port blend. They have the advantage of being readier to drink than declared Vintage Ports — at less than half their price — and of usually being released when they're mature. You should decant and aerate them before serving, however. (Some Port houses, incidentally, are themselves single estates, such as Quinta do Noval, Quinta do Infantado, and Quinta do Vesuvio. When such a house makes a vintage-dated Port, it's a Vintage Port, as well as a single quinta Port. But that's splitting hairs.)

Storing and serving Port

Treat Vintage Ports like all other fine red wines: Store the bottles on their sides in a cool place. You can store other types of Ports either on their sides (if they have a cork rather than a plastic-topped cork stopper) or upright. All Ports, except white, ruby, and older Vintage Ports, keep well for a week or so after opening, with aged-stated tawny capable of keeping for a few weeks.

You can now find Vintage Ports and some Vintage Character Ports, such as Fonseca Bin 27, in half-bottles — a brilliant development for Port lovers. Enjoying a bottle after dinner is far easier to justify when it's just a half-bottle. The wine evolves slightly more quickly in half-bottles, and, considering the wine's longevity, that may even be a bonus!

Serve Port at cool room temperature, 64 degrees Fahrenheit (18 degrees Celsius), although tawny Port can be an invigorating pick-me-up when served chilled during warm weather. The classic complements to Port are walnuts and strong cheeses, such as Stilton, Gorgonzola, Roquefort, Cheddar, and aged Gouda.

Recommended Port producers

In terms of quality, with the exception of a few clunker producers, Port is one of the most consistent of all wines. We've organized our favorite Port producers into two categories — outstanding and very good — in rough order of preference. As you might expect, wines in the first group tend to be a bit more expensive. Taylor-Fladgate and Dow are two Port producers who make their ports in a drier style — compared to other Port producers. Our rating is based mainly on Vintage Port but can be generally applied to all the various Port styles of the house.

Outstanding

Taylor-Fladgate	Dow
Fonseca	Smith-Woodhouse
Graham	Cockburn (coh-burn)

Quinta do Noval "Nacional" (made from ungrafted vineyards; see Chapter 3)

Very Good

Ramos Pinto	Ferreira
Warre	Cálem
Quinta do Noval	Churchill
Niepoort	Delaforce
Croft	Gould Campbell
Sandeman	Martinez
Quinta do Infantado	Osborne
Quinta do Vesuvio	Offley
Rozes	

Recent good vintages of Vintage Porto to buy include 2009, 2007, 2000, 1994, 1992, and 1991. (For a complete list of Vintage Port vintages, see Appendix C.)

Another Portuguese classic

One of the great dessert wines made mainly from the white or pink Muscat grape is Setúbal (*shtoo*-bahl). Produced just south of Lisbon, Setúbal is made similarly to Port, with alcohol added to stop fermentation. Like Port, it's a rich, long-lasting wine. The most important producer is J. M. da Fonseca.

Long Live Madeira

The legendary wine called Madeira comes from the island of the same name, which sits in the Atlantic Ocean, nearer to Africa than Europe. Madeira is a subtropical island whose precarious hillside vineyards rise straight up from the ocean. The island is a province of Portugal, but the British have always run its wine trade. Historically, Madeira could even be considered something of an American wine, for this is the wine that American colonists drank.

Madeira can lay claim to being the world's longest-lived wine. A few years ago, we were fortunate enough to try a 1799 Vintage Madeira that was still perfectly fine. Only Hungary's Tokaji Azsu can rival Vintage Madeira in longevity, and that's true only of Tokaji Azsu's rarest examples, such as its Essencia.

Although Madeira's fortified wines were quite the rage 230 years ago, the island's vineyards were devastated at the end of the 19th century, first by mildew and then by the phylloxera louse. Most vineyards were replanted with lesser grapes. Madeira has spent a long time recovering from these setbacks. In the 19th century, more than 70 companies were shipping Madeira all over the world; now, only four companies of any size exist: Barbeito, H. M Borges, the Madeira Wine Company (the largest by far, a consolidation of four old companies — Blandy's, Cossart Gordon, Leacock's, and Miles — and only the Blandy family is still involved), and Pereira d'Oliveira.

The very best Madeira wines are still those from the old days, vintage-dated wines from 1920 back to 1795. Surprisingly, you can still find a few Madeiras from the 19th century. The prices aren't outrageous, either ($300 to $400 a bottle), considering what other wines that old, such as Bordeaux, cost. (Refer to Chapter 17 for sources of old Madeira.)

Timeless, indestructible, tasty, and baked

The best Madeira comes in four styles, two fairly dry and two sweet. The sweeter Madeiras generally have their fermentation halted somewhat early by the addition of alcohol. Drier Madeiras have alcohol added after fermentation.

A curiosity of Madeira production is a baking process called the *estufagem* (es-too-*fah*-jem), which follows fermentation. The fact that Madeira improves with heat was discovered back in the 17th century. When trading ships crossed the equator with casks of Madeira as ballast in their holds, the wine actually improved! Today's practice of baking the wine at home on the island is a bit more practical than sending it around the world in a slow boat.

In the estufagem process, Madeira spends a minimum of three months, often longer, in heated tanks, in *estufas* (heating rooms). Any sugars in the wine become caramelized, and the wine becomes thoroughly *maderized* (oxidized through heating) without developing any unpleasant aroma or taste.

A more laborious and considerably more expensive way of heating Madeira is the *canteiro* method, in which barrels are left in warm lofts or exposed to the sun (the weather stays warm year-round) for as long as three years. The same magical metamorphosis takes place in the wines. The *canteiro* method is best for Madeira because the wines retain their high acidity, color, and extract much better in the slow, natural three-year process; *the finer Madeiras use this method of aging*.

Endless finish

Technically, almost all the best Madeira starts as white wine, but the heating process and years of maturation give it an amber color. It has a tangy aroma and flavor that's unique and as long a finish on the palate as you'll find on the planet. When Madeira is made from any of the island's five noble grapes (listed in the next section), the grape name indicates the style. When Madeira doesn't carry a grape name — and most younger Madeiras don't — the words *dry, medium-dry, medium-sweet,* and *sweet* indicate the style.

Vintage Madeira must spend at least 20 years in a cask, but in the old days, the aging was even longer. Some of the most memorable wines we've ever tasted were old Madeiras, and so we're afraid we might get carried away a bit, beginning any time now. Their aroma alone is divine, and you continue tasting the wine long after you've swallowed it. (Spitting is out of the question.) Words truly are inadequate to describe this wine.

If you can afford to buy an old bottle of vintage-dated Madeira (the producer's name is relatively unimportant), you'll understand our enthusiasm. And maybe some day when Madeira production gets back on its feet, every wine lover will be able to experience Vintage Madeira. In the meantime, for a less expensive Madeira experience, look for wines labeled *15 years old, 10 years old,* or *5 years old.* Don't bother with any other type, because it will be unremarkable, and then we'll look crazy.

Madeira styles and grape varieties

You never have to worry about Madeira getting too old. It's indestructible. The enemies of wine — heat and oxygen — have already had their way with Madeira during the winemaking and maturing process. Nothing you do after it's opened can make it blink.

If a Madeira is dated with the word *Solera* — for example, *Solera 1890* — it is *not* a Vintage Madeira but a blend of many younger vintages whose original barrel, or solera, dates back to the date indicated. Solera-dated Madeiras can be very fine and are generally not as expensive — nor as great — as Vintage Madeiras. But Solera Madeiras are becoming obsolete today. In their place is a new style of Madeira, called *colheita* or Harvest. This style is modeled after *colheita* Porto (see the earlier section "Many Ports in a storm"), in that colheita Madeira is a single vintage-dated Madeira wine. Colheita Madeira doesn't have to spend a minimum of 20 years aging in cask, as does Vintage Madeira, but only five — or seven for the driest, Sercial. (For example, the 1994 colheita Madeira debuted in 2000 at only six years of age.) Colheita Madeira is much less expensive than Vintage Madeira. Most of the major Madeira shippers are now selling colheita; sales of vintage-dated Madeira have doubled since the introduction of this style.

Vintage, colheita, and solera-dated Madeiras are made from a single grape variety and are varietally labeled. The grapes include five noble white grape varieties and one less noble red variety. (Another noble red variety, Bastardo, is no longer used for commercial production.) Each variety corresponds to a specific style of wine; we list them here from driest style to sweetest:

- **Sercial:** The Sercial grape grows at the highest altitudes. Thus, the grapes are the least ripe and make the driest Madeira. The wine is high in acidity and very tangy. Sercial Madeira is an outstanding apéritif wine with almonds, olives, or light cheeses. Unfortunately, true Sercial is quite rare today.

- **Verdelho:** The Verdelho grape makes a medium-dry style, with nutty, peachy flavors and a tang of acidity. It's good as an apéritif or with consommé.

- ✔ **Bual (or Boal):** Darker amber in color, Bual is a rich, medium-sweet Madeira with spicy flavors of almonds and raisins and a long, tangy finish. Bual is best after dinner. Like Sercial, true Bual is rare today.

- ✔ **Malmsey:** Made from Malvasia grapes, Malmsey is dark amber, sweet, and intensely concentrated with a very long finish. Drink it after dinner.

Here are two rare varieties, whose names you may see on some very old bottles:

- ✔ **Terrantez:** Medium-sweet, between Verdelho and Bual in style, this is a powerful, fragrant Madeira with lots of acidity. For some Madeira lovers, Terrantez is the greatest variety of all. Unfortunately, very little Terrantez is available today. Drink it after dinner.

- ✔ **Bastardo:** This is the only red grape of the noble varieties. Old Bastardos from the last century are mahogany-colored and rich, but not so rich as the Terrantez.

The less-noble red Tinta Negra Mole variety is the dominant grape for today's Madeira production (used for more than 85 percent of Madeira wines), because it grows more prolifically than the five noble varieties (Sercial, Verdelho, Bual, Malmsey, and Terrantez) without the diseases to which they are prone. Also, it is less site-specific; it can grow anywhere on the island, unlike the noble varieties, which grow in vineyards close to the sea where the urban sprawl of Funchal, Madeira's capital city, impinges on them. Previously, the less-regarded Tinta Negra Mole wasn't identified as a variety on bottles of Madeira, but now, the huge Madeira Wine Company is beginning to varietally label Tinta Negra Mole Madeiras.

Sauternes and the Nobly Rotten Wines

Warm, misty autumns encourage the growth of a fungus called *botrytis cinerea* in vineyards. Nicknamed *noble rot,* botrytis concentrates the sugar and acid in the juice of the grapes, giving the winemaker amazingly rich juice to ferment. The best wines from botrytis-infected grapes are among the greatest dessert wines in the world, with intensely concentrated flavors and plenty of acidity to prevent the wine from tasting excessively sweet.

The greatest nobly rotten wines are made in the Sauternes district of Graves (Bordeaux) in France, in Germany (see Chapter 12), and in the Tokaji district in Hungary, but they are also produced in Austria and California, among other places.

Sauternes: Liquid gold

Sauternes is a very labor-intensive wine. Grapes must be picked by hand; workers pass through the vineyard several times — sometimes over a period of weeks — each time selecting only the botrytis-infected grapes. Yields are low. Harvests sometimes linger until November, but now and then, bad weather in October dashes all hopes of making botrytis-infected wine. Often, only two to four vintages per decade make decent Sauternes (but the 1980s decade was exceptional, and the 2000s decade was phenomenal; see the vintage chart in Appendix C).

Consequently, good Sauternes is expensive. Prices range from $45 to $50 a bottle up to $750 (depending on the vintage) for Château d'Yquem (d'ee-kem). The greatest Sauternes, Yquem has always been prized by collectors (see Chapter 17). It was the only Sauternes given the status of *First Great Growth* in the 1855 Bordeaux Classification (see Chapter 10).

Sauternes is widely available in half-bottles, reducing the cost somewhat. A 375-ml bottle is a perfect size for after dinner, and you can buy a decent half-bottle of Sauternes or Barsac, a dessert wine similar to Sauternes, like Château Doisy-Védrines (dwahs-ee-veh-dreen) or Château Doisy-Daëne (dwahs-ee-dah-en) for $25 to $30.

Mining the gold

The Sauternes wine district includes five communes in the southernmost part of Graves (one of them named Sauternes). One of the five, Barsac, is entitled to its own appellation; Barsac wines are slightly lighter and less sweet than Sauternes. The Garonne River and the Ciron, an important tributary, produce the mists that encourage *botrytis cinerea* to form on the grapes.

The three authorized grape varieties are Sémillon, Sauvignon Blanc, and Muscadelle — although the latter is used by only a few châteaux, and even then in small quantities. Sémillon is the king of Sauternes. Most producers use at least 80 percent of Sémillon in their blend.

Wine that is called *Sauterne* (no final *s*) is produced in California and other places. This semi-sweet, rather insipid wine is made from inexpensive grapes and usually sold in large bottles. It bears absolutely no resemblance to true, botrytis-infected Sauternes, from Sauternes, France. California does make late-harvest, botrytis-infected wines, mainly Rieslings, and while they are far better than California Sauterne (and even worth trying), they are very different wines from the botrytis wines of Sauternes or of Germany.

Recommended Sauternes

All the Sauternes in the following list range from outstanding to good. (Wines specifically from Barsac are labeled as such.) In Sauternes, vintages are just as important as in the rest of Bordeaux; check our vintage recommendations in Appendix C.

- ✔ **Outstanding:**
  - **Château d'Yquem:** Can last for 100 years or more
  - **Château de Fargues:** Owned by Yquem; almost as good as Yquem, at one-fifth the price ($150)
  - **Château Climens (Barsac):** At $125, a value; near Yquem's level
  - **Château Coutet (Barsac):** A great buy ($80)
- ✔ **Excellent:**
  - **Château Suduiraut:** On the brink of greatness ($85 to $90)
  - **Château Rieussec:** Rich, lush style ($90)
  - **Château Raymond-Lafon:** Located next to Yquem ($40 to $50)
- ✔ **Very Good:**
  - **Château Lafaurie-Peyraguey**
  - **Château Latour Blanche**
  - **Château Guiraud**
  - **Château Rabaud-Promis**
  - **Château Sigalas-Rabaud**
  - **Château Nairac (Barsac)**
  - **Château Doisy-Védrines (Barsac)**
  - **Château Doisy-Daëne (Barsac)**
  - **Château Clos Haut-Peyraguey**
- ✔ **Good:**
  - **Château Bastor-Lamontagne**
  - **Château Rayne Vigneau**
  - **Château d'Arche**
  - **Château de Malle**
  - **Château Lamothe-Guignard**

- Château Romieu-Lacoste (Barsac)
- Château Doisy-Dubroca (Barsac)
- Château Filhot

Letting baby grow

Sauternes has such balance of natural sweetness and acidity that it can age well (especially the better Sauternes mentioned here) for an extraordinarily long time. Unfortunately, because Sauternes is so delicious, people often drink it young, when it's very rich and sweet. But Sauternes is really at its best when it loses its baby fat and matures.

After about 10 to 15 years, Sauternes's color changes from light gold to an old gold-coin color, sometimes with orange or amber tones. The wine loses the perception of sweetness and develops flavors reminiscent of apricots, orange rind, honey, and toffee. This stage is the best time to drink Sauternes. The better the vintage, the longer Sauternes takes to reach this stage, but once there, it stays at this plateau for many years — sometimes decades — and very gradually turns dark amber or light brown in color. Even in these final stages, Sauternes retains some of its complex flavors.

In good vintages, Sauternes can age for 50 to 60 years or more. Château d'Yquem and Château Climens are particularly long-lived. (We recently had a half-bottle of 1893 Château d'Yquem that was glorious!)

Sauternes is best when served cold, but not ice cold, at about 52 to 53 degrees Fahrenheit (11 degrees Celsius). Mature Sauternes can be served a bit warmer. Because the wine is so rich, Sauternes is an ideal companion for *foie gras,* although, ordinarily, the wine is far more satisfying after dinner than as an apéritif. As for desserts, Sauternes is excellent with ripe fruits, lemon-flavored cakes, or pound cake.

Sauternes look-alikes

Many sweet, botrytis-infected wines similar to Sauternes exist; they sell for considerably less money than Sauternes or Barsacs. These wines are not as intense or as complex in flavor, but they are fine values at $20 to $30.

Directly north and adjacent to Barsac is the often overlooked Cérons wine region. You can probably convince many of your friends that a Cérons, served blind, is a Sauternes or Barsac. From the Entre-Deux-Mers district of Bordeaux, look for wines with the Cadillac, Loupiac, or Sainte-Croix-du-Mont appellations — all less expensive versions of Sauternes.

Part VI
When You've Caught the Bug

The 5th Wave   By Rich Tennant

SACRAMENTAL WINE TASTING

©RICHTENNANT

"It has a nice, divine quality without being overly liturgical."

In this part . . .

The gestation period of the wine bug is unpredictable. Some people no sooner express interest in wine than they become engrossed in the subject. Other people exhibit mild symptoms for many years before succumbing to the passion. (And believe it or not, a lot of people are immune.)

But as soon as you've been bitten by the wine bug, you know it. You find yourself subscribing to magazines that your friends never heard of, making new friends with whom you have little in common other than an interest in wine, boycotting restaurants with substandard wine lists, and planning vacations to wine regions!

However quickly you got to this stage, the three chapters in this part provide fuel for your fire. We discuss, in detail, buying and collecting wine, educating yourself further with wine courses and travel, and describing and rating wine.

Chapter 17

Buying and Collecting Wine

. . . .

In This Chapter

▶ Playing hardball with hard-to-get-wines

▶ Keeping your own little black book of wine retailers

▶ Shopping virtually

▶ Collecting wine

▶ Helping your wine stay healthy

. . . .

*Y*ou read about a wine that sounds terrific. Your curiosity is piqued; you want to try it. But your local wine shop doesn't have the wine. Neither does the best store in the next town. Or maybe you decide to balance your wine collection by buying some mature wines. But the few older wines you can find in wine shops aren't really what you want. What's a wine lover to do?

Fortunately, the world of serious wine buying now extends far beyond your local wine shop. Within the last decade, two factors have changed the way we and our friends buy fine wines, whether older vintages or current releases: the burgeoning opportunities on the Internet and the growth of wine auctions. We still rely on our local wine merchants to satisfy most of our everyday wine needs. But when we're looking for that hard-to-find bottle, we're on the Net, searching. And our geeky wine-collector friends haunt the wine auctions — both in person and on the Internet — looking for special older bottles. Getting what you want is mostly a question of knowing where to look.

In this chapter, we show you exactly where to find rare and collectible wines; in addition, we explain how to balance, organize, and store your collection.

Finding the Rare and Collectible Wines

There's a Catch-22 for wine lovers who have really caught the bug: The more desirable a wine is, the harder it is to get; and the harder a wine is to get, the more desirable it is.

This situation exists for several reasons. The main reason is that some of the best wines are made in ridiculously small quantities. We wouldn't say that quantity and quality are necessarily incompatible in winemaking, but at the very highest levels of quality, there usually isn't much quantity to go around.

Sometimes when we search for a fairly scarce wine (most recently it was a special Italian white), we discover that it's available in only one store on the other side of the country, and that store has only three bottles in stock!

Today, many small-production wines sell *on allocation,* which means that distributors restrict the quantity that any one store can purchase, sometimes limiting stores to as few as six bottles of a particular wine. Most stores, in turn, limit customers to just one or two bottles. Certain wines are allocated in such a way that they're available primarily at restaurants. It's often the wine producer's wish to sell his scarce wine mainly in restaurants, figuring that the wine will get more exposure that way.

The issue of allocations brings us to the second factor preventing equal opportunity in wine buying: Wine buying is a competitive sport. If you're there first, you get the wine, and the next guy doesn't. Buying highly rated wines is especially competitive. When a wine receives a very high score from critics, a feeding frenzy results among wine lovers, not leaving much for Johnnies-come-lately. (See Chapter 18 for information on wine critics and Chapters 19 and 21 for more on wine ratings.)

A final factor limiting availability of some wines is that wineries usually sell each wine just once, when the wine is young. In the case of many fine wines, such as top Bordeaux wines, the wine isn't at its best yet. But most wine merchants can't afford to store the wine for selling years later. This means that aged wines are invariably hard to get.

When the wine you want plays hard to get, you have to play hardball; you have to look beyond your normal sources of supply. Your allies in this game are the Internet, wine shops in other cities, wine auction houses, and, in the case of domestic wines, the wineries themselves.

Buying fine and collectible wines on the Internet

As we mention in Chapter 6, the Internet is now a standard venue for wine buying, along with your local wine specialty shops and supermarkets. For sourcing collectible wines, however, online channels are all the more important. Sometimes, the *only* way to buy certain wines is on the Internet, because sought-after wines made in small quantities aren't available in every city.

Some of the online resources for finding and purchasing hard-to-find wines are the websites of actual brick-and-mortar wine shops, and we list many of them in the next section. Other online resources include sites that direct you to merchants who stock a specific wine you're seeking; obviously these sites can save you lots of time and trouble in hunting down wines. A few other sites sell wine online only.

Here are a few Internet sites worth checking out as a first step when you want to purchase wine online. Besides its search capacity, each site also features information about wine, wine reviews, and so forth.

- ✔ **Wine-Searcher** (www.wine-searcher.com): This site is indispensible to us. It searches for wines that you name and it lists stores and prices for them. You can use it to compare prices and to find the most suitable store for purchasing the wine you want. Depending on the criteria you input, the search results can include merchants outside the United States as well as auction sites that list specific wines (see the later section "Buying wines at auctions"). The site is free, but purchasing the Pro Version ($39 per year) enables you to see results beyond those merchants who are sponsors of the site; we find it a good investment.

- ✔ **WineAccess** (www.wineaccess.com): This is a multipurpose site that sells some wines itself — a few at a time, rather similar to a flash sales site — and also directs you to retailers who sell specific wines. Search results deliver relatively few results, just a store or two, probably because the geographic range is limited by your zip code.

- ✔ **The WineWeb** (www.wineweb.com): This site encompasses what it calls "the largest directory of wineries from all over the world" and enables you to buy wine directly from those wineries or from participating retailers. Search results include only those wineries or merchants that can ship into your state.

- ✔ **Snooth** (www.snooth.com): This site is the home of a large community of wine lovers who recommend wines, chat, and engage, but it also provides search capabilities for specific wines and links you to stores or websites carrying those wines.

Another Internet site worth knowing is Vinfolio (www.vinfolio.com). This company bills itself as "the fine wine source" and specializes in fine and collectible wines, although its offerings include some less exalted wines as well. You can purchase wine from the site, either from its inventory or from its peer-to-peer marketplace, where individuals list wines that they want to sell, subject to inspection by the Vinfolio team. Thanks to this collector-sourced marketplace, you can actually find older vintages to buy. The site also offers wine cellar management services; we discuss that aspect of wine collecting in the section "Organization is peace of mind," later in this chapter.

Crossing state lines

Because wine contains alcohol, it doesn't move as freely through commercial channels as other products do. Each state must decide whether to permit wineries and stores outside its borders to ship wine to state residents and under which conditions. By requiring consumers to buy wine only from local, licensed retail stores or wineries, a state government can be sure it's getting all the tax revenue it's entitled to on every wine transaction in its jurisdiction.

Most wine shops and wineries are sympathetic to out-of-state customers, but out-of-state deliveries are risky for their businesses, depending on the regulations in their state and the destination state. The risk is all theirs, too;

the store or winery can lose its license, while all the buyer loses is any wine that's confiscated by the authorities.

If you want to buy wine from an out-of-state winery or merchant, discuss the issue with the people there. If shipping to you isn't legal, they can sometimes find a solution for you, such as holding the wine for you to pick up personally or shipping to a friend or relative in a legal state.

Buy all the wine you want when you visit a winery: Different rules apply, and wine drinkers may legally ship home wines that they purchase during visits to out-of-state wineries.

Some U.S. wine stores worth knowing

We can't possibly list *all* the leading wine stores that sell fine wine, but the following purveyors are some of the best. Most of them specialize in certain kinds of fine wine that can be difficult to obtain elsewhere. We name the stores' main wine specialties here:

- Acker Merrall & Condit, New York, NY; www.ackerwines.com — Burgundy, California Cabernets
- Astor Wines & Spirits, New York, NY; www.astorwines.com — French, Italian, Spanish
- Brookline Liquor Mart, Allston, MA; www.blmwine.com — Italian, Burgundy, Rhône
- Burgundy Wine Company, New York, NY; www.burgundywinecompany.com — Burgundy, Oregon Pinot Noir, Rhône
- Calvert Woodley Wine & Spirits, Washington, D.C.; www.calvertwoodley.com — California, Bordeaux, other French
- Chambers Street Wines, New York, NY; www.chambersstwines.com — French, Italian, biodynamic/organic wines
- Corti Brothers, Sacramento, CA; www.cortibros.biz — Italian, California, dessert wines
- Crush Wine & Spirits, New York, NY; www.crushwineco.com — French, German, Champagne

- Garnet Wines & Liquors, New York, NY; www.garnetwine.com — Bordeaux, Champagne

- Hart Davis Hart Wine Co., Chicago, IL; www.hdhwine.com — Bordeaux, Burgundy

- Kermit Lynch Wine Merchant, Berkeley, CA; www.kermitlynch.com — French country wines, Burgundy, Rhône

- K&L Wine Merchants, San Francisco, CA; www.klwines.com — French, California, Champagne

- MacArthur Beverages, Washington, D.C.; www.bassins.com — California, Burgundy, Bordeaux, Italian, Rhône, Alsace, Australian, German, Vintage Port

- McCarthy & Schiering Wine Merchants, Seattle, WA; www.mccarthy andschiering.com — Washington, Oregon

- Mills Fine Wine & Spirits, Annapolis, MD; www.millswine.com — Bordeaux, other French, Italian

- Moore Brothers Wine Company, New York, NY; www.moorebrothers. com — French, German, Champagne

- Morrell & Co., New York, NY; www.morrellwine.com — California, Italian, French

- North Berkeley Wine, Berkeley, CA; www.northberkeleyimports.com — French, Italian

- Pop's Wines & Spirits, Island Park, NY; www.popswine.com — California, Italian, Bordeaux, Long Island

- The Rare Wine Co., Sonoma, CA; www.rarewineco.com — Italian, French, Port, Madeira

- Rosenthal Wine Merchant, New York, NY; www.madrose.com — Burgundy, Rhône, Loire, Italian

- Royal Wine Merchants, New York, NY; www.royalwinemerchants.com — French (especially rare Bordeaux), Italian, Burgundy, hard-to-find wines

- Sherry-Lehmann Wine & Spirits, New York, NY; www.sherry-lehmann. com — Bordeaux, Burgundy, California

- Sotheby's Wine, New York, NY; www.sothebyswine.com — Bordeaux, Burgundy, Champagne

- Table & Vine, West Springfield, MA; www.tableandvine.com — French, California

- TwentyTwenty Wine Merchants, West Los Angeles, CA; www.2020 wines.com — Bordeaux (especially rare, old), California, rare wines

- Wally's, Los Angeles, CA; www.wallywine.com — Italian, California, French, Champagne

- ✔ The Wine Club, Santa Ana, CA; San Francisco, CA; `www.thewineclub.com` — Bordeaux, California

- ✔ The Wine Library, Springfield, NJ; `www.winelibrary.com` — Bordeaux, California, Champagne

- ✔ Wine Warehouse, Los Angeles, CA; `www.winewarehouse.com` — California, French, Italian

- ✔ Zachys Wine & Liquor, Scarsdale, NY; `www.zachys.com` — Bordeaux, Burgundy

Buying wines at auctions

The clear advantage of buying wine through auction houses is the availability of older and rarer wines. In fact, auction houses are the principal source of mature wines — their specialty. (In general, you can obtain younger wines at better prices elsewhere.) At auctions, you can buy wines that are practically impossible to obtain any other way. Many of these wines have been off the market for years — sometimes decades!

The main disadvantage of buying wine at auction is that you don't always know the storage history, or *provenance,* of the wine you're considering buying. The wine may have been stored in somebody's warm apartment for years. And if the wine does come from a reputable wine collector's temperature-controlled cellar, and thus has impeccable credentials, it will sell for a very high price.

Also, almost all auction houses charge you a buyer's premium, a tacked-on charge that's 10 or 15 percent of your bid. In general, prices of wine at auctions range from fair (you rarely ever find bargains) to exorbitant.

You can attend an auction personally or submit bids by phone or online. To plan your attack, you can obtain a catalog for the auction ahead of time, sometimes for a small fee. The catalog lists wines for sale by lots (usually groupings of 3, 6, or 12 bottles) with a suggested minimum bid per lot.

If you're personally present at an auction, be careful not to catch auction fever. The desire to win can motivate you to pay more for a wine than it's worth. Carefully thought-out, judicious bidding is in order.

New York is currently one of the hottest wine auction markets in the United States. (You can either sell or buy wines at auction.) Four retail stores lead the crusade: Morrell & Company (`www.auction.morrellwineauctions.net`), Zachys (`www.zachys.com/auctions`), Sotheby's Wine (`www.sothebyswine.com`), and Acker Merrall & Condit (`www.ackerwines.com`). Christie's Auction House, `www.christies.com` (along with Sotheby's, one of the grand auction houses based in the United Kingdom), is also a major player.

Buying time: Wine futures

Every so often, you may notice ads urging you to buy *futures* of certain wines (usually Bordeaux, but sometimes California wines). The ads suggest that, to ensure getting a particular wine at the lowest price, you should buy it now for future delivery. In other words, "Give us your money now; you'll get the wine in due course, probably sometime next year when the winery releases it."

Generally, we recommend that you *don't* buy futures. Often, the wine will be the same price, or only slightly higher, when it hits the market. To save little or nothing, you will have tied your money up for a year or more, while the store has made interest on it or spent it. You face the risk that the store could go bankrupt before delivering your wine. And during recessionary economies in the past, some people who bought wine futures actually paid more for their wine than they would have paid if they had waited for the wine to arrive before purchasing it.

Futures are useful in only two situations: For wines that are made in such small quantity that you're pretty sure the wine will sell out before it reaches the stores; and for a wine that receives an extraordinarily high rating in the wine press before its release, assuring that its price could double and even triple by the time the wine reaches the market.

Here's the bottom line: Buy futures only when you must have a particular wine and buying futures might be the only way you can get it. For most wines, though, keep your wallet in your pocket until the wine is actually available.

In Illinois, The Chicago Wine Company (www.tcwc.com) and Hart Davis Hart Wine Co. (www.hdhwine.com) are leading auction houses. In California, leaders include Bonhams & Butterfields Auction House (www.bonhams.com), The Rare Wine Co. (www.rarewineco.com), and Christie's Los Angeles (www.christies.com).

You can also bid for wine online. WineBid.com (www.winebid.com) conducts auctions at its website and is the most established such service. Other online wine auction houses include Cellar Bid (www.cellarbid.com), WineCommmune (www.winecommune.com), WineGavel (www.winegavel.com), and Spectrum Wine Auctions (www.spectrumwine.com). The online store Vinfolio (www.vinfolio.com) also sells some wines in an auction format.

Wine counterfeiting is becoming big business these days, but mainly for the world's very rarest, priciest, most elite wines. This trend underscores the need to work only with reputable auction houses.

Improving your odds of getting a *good,* old bottle

Acquiring and drinking old wines requires you to be a bit of a gambler. But you *can* reduce the odds against buying a bottle well past its peak by following a few easy tips:

- Buy from reputable wine merchants and auction houses. They often know the history of their older wines and most likely acquired the wines from sources that they trust.

- Trade bottles with only wine-savvy friends who know the storage history of their wines.

- Stick to well-known wines with a proven track record of longevity.

- Inspect the wine if you can. Look at the *ullage* (the airspace between the wine and the cork). Ullage of an inch or more can be a danger sign indicating that evaporation has occurred, either from excessive heat or lack of humidity — both of which can spoil the wine. (On a very old wine, say 35 or more years old, an inch of ullage is quite acceptable, though.) Another sign of poor storage is leakage or stickiness at the top of the bottle, suggesting that wine has seeped out through the cork.

- Inspect the wine's color, if the bottle color permits. A white wine that is excessively dark or dull or a red wine that has become quite brown can be oxidized and too old. (Shine a penlight flashlight through the bottle to check the color of red wines.) But some red wines and Sauternes can show quite a bit of brown and still be very much alive. If you're not sure about the color, get advice from someone who knows about older wines before plunking down your money.

- If you buy at auction by telephone or online, ask the seller to inspect the bottle and describe its fill level and color.

- Be wary if the price of the bottle seems too low. Often, what appears to be a bargain is a damaged or over-the-hill wine.

- Ask wine-knowledgeable friends or merchants about the particular wines you're considering buying. Frequently, someone will be familiar with them.

- Say a prayer, take out your corkscrew, and plunge in. Live dangerously!

The Urge to Own: Wine Collecting

Most people consume wines very quickly after buying them. If this is your custom, you have plenty of company. But many people who enjoy wine operate a bit differently. Oh, sure, they buy wine because they intend to drink it; they're just not exactly sure *when* they'll drink it. And until they do drink it, they get pleasure out of knowing that the bottles are waiting for them. If you count yourself in this second group, you're probably a wine collector at heart. The chase, to you, is every bit as thrilling as the consummation.

If you're a closet wine collector, developing a strategy of wine buying (with the help of this section) can prevent a haphazard collection of uninteresting or worthless bottles from happening to you. (Even if you never intend to have a wine collection, it's worthwhile to put at least a little thought into your wine purchases.)

The first step in formulating a wine-buying strategy is to consider the following:

- ✔ How much wine you drink
- ✔ How much wine you want to own (and can store properly)
- ✔ How much money you're prepared to spend on wine
- ✔ What types of wine you enjoy drinking

Unless you strike a balance on these issues, you can end up broke, bored, frustrated, or in the vinegar business!

Balancing your inventory

Unless your intention is to fill your cellar with wines that bring you the greatest return on investment when you later sell them — in other words, unless you aren't interested in actually drinking the wines you own — you should like a wine before buying it. (We're not talking about all those bottles you buy while you're playing the field and experimenting with new wines — just those that you're thinking of making a commitment to by buying in quantity.) Liking a wine before you buy it sounds like the plainest common sense, but you'd be surprised at how many people buy a wine merely because somebody gave it a high rating!

A well-planned wine inventory features a range of wines. It can be heavy in one or two types of wine that you particularly enjoy, but it has other types of wine, too. If you like California Cabernet Sauvignons, for example, you may decide to make them your specialty. But consider that you may grow weary of them if you have nothing else to drink night after night. Boring! One of the greatest mistakes a novice collector can make is to buy mainly one type of table wine.

Table wines, of course, are the bulk of most wine collections. But it's a good idea to have some apéritif wines, such as Champagne or dry Sherry, and dessert wines, such as Port or sweet white wines, so you're prepared when occasions arise. (If you're like us, you'll invent plenty of occasions to open a bottle of Champagne!)

Another hallmark of a balanced collection is a healthy selection of both inexpensive wines ($15 to $25 a bottle) that can be enjoyed on casual occasions and important wines that demand a special occasion. Purchasing only expensive wines is unrealistic.

You also want to purchase wines that are ready to drink and those that require additional aging. We give you some pointers about doing so in the next two sections.

Is the sky the limit?

Some wine collectors own more than 10,000 bottles! This might be called taking one's hobby to the extreme. We believe that a collection of 1,000 to 1,500 bottles is definitely sufficient to handle most people's needs nicely. Then again, 100 bottles isn't so bad, either!

Everyday wines

What you stock as everyday wines will depend on your personal taste. Our candidates for everyday white wines include the following:

- Simple white Burgundies, such as Mâcon-Villages or St.-Véran
- Sauvignon Blancs from France (Sancerre and Pouilly-Fumé), New Zealand, Friuli and Alto-Adige in Italy, and California
- Pinot Gris/Pinot Grigio from Oregon, Alsace, and Italy
- Italian Pinot Bianco
- Flavorful Italian whites, such as Vermentino, Verdicchio, or Falanghina
- Grüner Veltliner from Austria
- Riesling from Germany, Austria, Alsace, Western Australia, or the United States
- Moschofilero from Greece
- Albariños from Spain
- Chablis (AOC Village) and Muscadet from France

For everyday red wines, we especially like Italian reds, such as Barbera, Dolcetto, Montepulciano d'Abruzzo, Valpolicella, and simple (under $20) Chianti. These red wines are enjoyable young, versatile enough to go well with the simple, flavorful foods many people eat every day, and sturdy enough to age for a couple of years if you don't get around to them (that is, they won't deteriorate quickly).

Other everyday red wines we recommend include Beaujolais, Côtes du Rhône, and lighter-bodied (under $15) Bordeaux. Plus inexpensive (under $15) Portuguese reds.

Age-worthy wines

In planning your own wine collection, include some age-worthy wines that you buy in their youth when their prices are lowest. Many of the better red wines, such as Bordeaux, Barolo, and Hermitage, often aren't at their best for at least ten years after the vintage — and some of them are difficult to find when they're ready to drink. Aging is also the rule for some fine white Burgundies (such as Corton-Charlemagne), better white Bordeaux, Hermitage Blanc and Châteauneuf-du-Pape Blanc, Sauternes, German Rieslings and late-harvest wines, plus Vintage Port, which usually requires about 20 years of aging before it matures!

Age-worthy white wines we recommend include

- ✔ Above all, Grand Cru and Premier Cru white Burgundies — such as Corton-Charlemagne, Bâtard- and Chevalier-Montrachets, Meursault, and Chablis Grand Crus (the latter is the best value)
- ✔ Better (over $30) white Bordeaux
- ✔ Great German and Austrian Rieslings
- ✔ Alsace Rieslings and Gewurztraminers

See Chapters 10 and 12 for explanations of these wines.

Among the many long-lived red wines, some likely candidates for *cellaring* (the term for letting wines mature) are

- ✔ Fine Bordeaux
- ✔ Grand Cru and Premier Cru Burgundies
- ✔ From the Rhône: Hermitage, Côte-Rôtie, and Cornas
- ✔ Powerful Italian reds, such as Barolo, Barbaresco, Chianti Classico Riserva, Brunello di Montalcino, Taurasi, and Super-Tuscan blends
- ✔ From Spain: Rioja, Ribeira del Duero (especially Vega Sicilia Unico), and Priorato wines
- ✔ Portugal's Barca Velha and other good Douro table wines
- ✔ Australia's Grange (Penfolds), the Henschke Shiraz wines, such as Hill of Grace, and other super-premium Shirazes
- ✔ From California: Better Cabernet Sauvignons (and Cabernet blends)

Parts III and IV discuss these wines in more detail.

Other age-worthy wines include

- ✔ Finer Champagnes (usually Vintage Champagnes and prestige cuvées; see Chapter 15)
- ✔ The finest dessert wines, such as late-harvest German Rieslings (see Chapter 12), French Sauternes, sweet Vouvrays from the Loire Valley (see Chapter 10), Vintage Port, and Madeira. (See Chapter 16 for Sauternes, Port, and Madeira.)

The charm of an aged wine

Aged wines are a thing apart from young wines — considering that some wines don't really reach their full expression until they've aged. Try drinking a highly acclaimed young red Bordeaux, say a 2008 Château Lafite-Rothschild. You taste a mouthful of tannin, and although the wine has concentration, you probably wonder what all the fuss is about. Try it in 10 to 15 years; the assertive tannins have softened, a wonderful bouquet of cedar, tobacco, and black currants emerges from the glass, and a natural sweetness of flavor has developed.

As a fine wine matures in the bottle, a series of chemical and physical changes occur. These changes are poorly understood, but their effects are evident in the style of a mature red wine:

✔ The wine becomes paler in color.

✔ Its aroma evolves from the fruity aromas (and often oakiness) it had when young to a complex, leathery and earthy bouquet.

✔ Its tannic, harsh texture diminishes, and the wine becomes silky.

Mature wines seem to be easier to digest, and they go to your head less quickly. (Perhaps that's because we tend to drink them slowly, with reverence.) Besides visceral pleasure, they offer a special emotional satisfaction. Tasting an aged wine can be like traveling back in time, sharing a connection with people who have gone before in the great chain of humanity.

Organization is peace of mind

When you're not only a wine drinker but also a wine collector, you become aware that you need to keep track of all your wine so that

✔ You can find a bottle quickly when you're looking for it.

✔ You know what you own. (Many a bottle has gone over the hill because the owner forgot that he had it!)

✔ You can show off your wine collection to your friends (something like showing your baby's pictures).

You can keep track of your wine in many different ways. At the very least, your wine inventory on paper or on a computer document, database, or spreadsheet should include a list of the specific wines in your collection, the number of each, and their location.

Many years ago, when we decided to catalog our wine collection by computer, we created a FileMaker database into which we typed, for each wine we own, all the details that we imagined we'd ever want to search for or sort by. We set up a separate field for each vintage, producer name, wine name, appellation, region, country, type (red, white, rosé, sparkling, apéritif, or dessert), quantity owned, price paid, and bottle size.

Two summary fields provided the total number of bottles in our inventory at any moment (or the total of any segment of our inventory, such as our red Bordeaux) as well as the current value of our inventory based on purchase price.

The world of wine cellar management has changed dramatically since then. Now, you can upload your inventory to the Internet so you can view it from any computer or even from a smartphone or tablet. Two excellent websites enable you to see lists of what you own, track your consumption, get current valuations of your collection, share tasting notes in a wine-community setting, and read expert tasting notes from major critics.

✔ The original of these cellar-tracking sites is named (logically) CellarTracker! (www.cellartracker.com). Microsoft veteran and wine lover Eric LeVine developed the tracking software in 2003 to record and manage his own wine collection, and in 2004, he made the website live for all to use. Today, more than 200,000 wine lovers participate in the CellarTracker! community to keep records of their collections (collectively, more than 32 million bottles) and share tasting notes. The site is free, but by making a voluntary payment, you gain access to additional features of the site, including professional tasting notes from major critics whose newsletters you subscribe to. Your voluntary price depends on the number of bottles you own; if you have fewer than 500 bottles, it's $36 a year.

✔ Another way to manage your wine cellar online is to enter your inventory with VinCellar (www.vincellar.com), the cellar management application of Vinfolio, which we mention in the section "Buying fine and collectible wines on the Internet," earlier in this chapter. This site launched in its current form in 2010 and now has more than 100,000 participating wine lovers. One of the key features of this site is its connection with Vinfolio, which enables you to buy wines online and seamlessly add them to your inventory, store wines at Vinfolio's warehouse, and sell wines from your collection via Vinfolio's store or peer-to-peer marketplace. The site also provides consulting services to collectors. VinCellar is free.

A Healthy Environment for Your Wines

If you've decided to collect wine — or if you discover that a wine collection is happening to you — please take heed: Poorly stored wines make disappointment after disappointment inevitable.

If you plan to keep wines indefinitely, you really need a wine storage facility with controlled temperature and humidity (the following sections offer different options). This is especially important if you live where the temperature exceeds 70 degrees Fahrenheit (21 degrees Celsius) for any length of time. Without proper storage, you may be tempted to drink those fine wines long before they reach their best drinking period (known in wine circles as infanticide), or worse yet, the wines may die an untimely death in your closet, garage, or warm cellar.

If you plan to build a wine cellar or buy a wine cabinet, allow for expansion in your wine collection. Like most waistlines, wine cellars inevitably grow larger with the passing years.

The passive wine cellar

You may be fortunate enough to have conditions suitable for a passive wine cellar (if you've recently inherited a castle in Scotland, for example, or if you live in one of the New England states in the cool Northeastern United States, or in Canada).

If the place where you intend to store your wine is very cool (below 60 degrees Fahrenheit, 15.5 degrees Celsius) and very damp (75 percent humidity or higher) year-round, you can be the lucky owner of a *passive cellar.* (It's called passive because you don't have to do anything to it, such as cool it or humidify it.) Usually, only deep cellars completely below ground level with thick stones or comparable insulation can be completely passive in temperate climates. Passive cellars are certainly the ideal way to store wines. And you can save a lot of money on their upkeep to boot.

If you don't have a space that's already ideal for a passive wine cellar, you might decide that you can dig one. For instructions on building your own passive wine cellar, see Richard M. Gold's authoritative book, *How and Why to Build a Wine Cellar* (Wine Appreciation Guild).

The issue of humidity

Some wine collectors aren't particularly concerned about the humidity level of their cellars. They argue that high humidity causes mold and disfigures labels. But dry air can dry the cork and allow the airtight seal to deteriorate, enabling oxygen to get in or causing your wine to evaporate or leech out around the cork, resulting in excessive *ullage* (space between the wine and the cork). The greater the ullage, the greater the chance of your wine's becoming oxidized.

Because we recommend humidity between 70 and 95 percent, we believe that air conditioners, which dehumidify the air to about 50 percent, aren't suitable for wine storage areas.

If you can't be passive, be bullish

Most of us are neither lucky enough to have a passive wine cellar nor fortunate enough to be able to create one without extraordinary expense and trouble (bulldozers, wrecking crews, and so on). But second best — a mechanically cooled and/or humidified room — is far better than a laissez-faire approach.

The following are key features of a good wine storage area:

- The temperature stays cool — ideally, in the 53 to 59 degrees Fahrenheit range (12 to 16 degrees Celsius).

- The temperature is fairly constant; wide swings in temperature aren't good for the wine.

- The area is damp or humid, with a minimum of 70 percent humidity and a maximum of 95 percent (mold sets in above 95 percent).

- The area is free from vibrations, which can travel through the wine; heavy traffic and motors cycling on and off — such as in refrigerators or washers/dryers — are detrimental to your wine.

- The area is free from light, especially direct sunlight; the ultraviolet rays of the sun are especially harmful to wine.

- The storage area is free from chemical odors, such as paints, paint remover, and so on.

We built a room in our basement for wine storage and installed a refrigeration device. Whatever area you use, your wine will keep well provided that the space has a climate control unit and is properly insulated (see the following sections).

Buy a hygrometer (an instrument that measures humidity) for your wine storage area. Our hygrometer gives us both the percentage of humidity and a digital reading of the temperature — information so valuable that we check it almost daily.

Avoid refrigerators for wine storage. Don't leave good wine or Champagne in the refrigerator for more than a week; not only is the refrigerator motor harmful, but the excessively cold temperature (as low as 35 degrees Fahrenheit, 1.6 degrees Celsius) tends to numb and flatten the flavors of the wine.

Climate control

You can find professional cooling devices advertised in wine accessory catalogs and wine magazines. These climate-control units humidify and cool the air of a room. They come in various capacities to suit rooms of different dimensions. Many require professional installation; they cost from $600 to $3,000, depending on their capacity.

Depending on where you live, you may not need to run your cooling unit all year. When we lived in Long Island, New York, we kept our refrigeration unit running from about mid-May to October. The additional expense for electricity was well worth it when we considered the value of the wine we were protecting. During the winter months when the air got dry, we often ran a humidifier in our wine room.

Wine racks

Racking systems vary from elaborate redwood racks to simple metal or plastic types. The choice of material and configuration really hinges on how much you want to spend and your own personal taste.

Large, diamond-shaped wooden (or synthetic composition) racks are popular because they efficiently store eight or more bottles per section and make maximum use of space (see Figure 17-1). Such racks permit the easy removal of individual bottles.

A rack configuration that gives each wine its own cubbyhole is more expensive; if you're checking out such racks, consider whether any of your oversized bottles (such as bulbous sparkling wine bottles) may be too large to fit the cubbyholes. (And consider whether your half-bottles may be too small!)

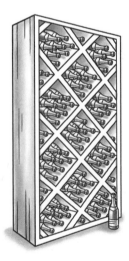

Figure 17-1:
Diamond-
shaped
wine rack.

Illustration by Lisa S. Reed

Some collectors prefer to store their wine in the wines' original wooden crates. (Many classic wines, such as Bordeaux and Vintage Port, come in these crates; you can also usually pick up empty wooden crates in wine stores.) The crates are beneficial for storing wine because the wine remains in a dark environment inside the case, and the temperature changes very slowly thanks to the mass of wine bottles packed together in the closed case. Retrieving a bottle from the bottom row of the case can really be inconvenient, though.

Cardboard boxes aren't suitable for wine storage. The chemicals used in the manufacture of the cardboard can eventually affect the wine. Also, the cardboard boxes become damaged, in time, from the moisture in the air, assuming that you're maintaining a proper humidity in your cellar.

Insulation

Far more important than your choice of racks is your choice of insulation.

We definitely don't recommend fiberglass insulation because it absorbs the moisture created by your cooling unit. We've heard of cases in which the weight of the moisture inside the insulation actually caused parts of ceilings to come tumbling down, creating quite a mess.

The ideal insulation is a 3-inch-thick, thermoplastic resin called polyurethane. It's odorless, doesn't absorb moisture, and makes a fine seal. Even when a cooling unit isn't running, temperatures will change extremely slowly in most wine rooms with this kind of insulation.

Wine caves for apartment dwellers

If you live in a house that has either a cellar or a separate area for your wine, consider yourself fortunate. What if you have no space — for example, what if you live in an apartment?

As an apartment dweller, you have three choices:

- Leave your wine in a friend's or relative's house (provided that he has adequate storage facilities — and that you trust him not to drink your wine!).
- Rent storage space in a refrigerated public warehouse.
- Buy a wine cave — also known as a wine cabinet — a self-contained, refrigerated unit that you plug into an electrical outlet.

We find the first two options barely acceptable because they don't give you immediate access to your wine. It's downright inconvenient to make a trip every time you want to get your hands on your own wine. And both of these options rob you of the pleasure of having your wines readily available in your home where you can look at them, fondle the bottles, or show them off to your friends.

We now live in an apartment, and we have a wine cave. Many wine caves resemble attractive pieces of furniture, either vertical or horizontal credenzas. Many have glass doors, and all of them can be locked.

Wine caves range in size and capacity from a tiny unit that holds only 24 bottles to really large units that hold up to 2,800 bottles, with many sizes in between. Prices range from $400 to about $10,000. You find wine caves advertised extensively in wine accessory catalogs and in the back pages of wine magazines. The two wine cave brands we recommend are Vinothèque (www.vinotheque.com) and Le Cache (www.lecachewinecabinets.com). You can buy less expensive brands, but they won't be of the same quality.

Chapter 18

Continuing Education
for Wine Lovers

- -

In This Chapter

▶ School was never such fun

▶ Phys Ed for your palate

▶ The magical places behind the labels

▶ Wine publications to keep you current

▶ Surfing the wine web

- -

*L*earning about wine is like space travel: Once you get going, there's no end in sight. Fortunately for those who choose to be educated wine drinkers, learning about wine is a fascinating experience, full of new flavors, new places, and new friends.

Although we teach others about wine, we are also avid students of wine. We can't imagine we'll ever reach the point where we say, "Now we know enough about wine; we can stop here." So off we go to another vineyard, to another wine tasting, or deep into the pages of another wine magazine or website. Every step brings not only more knowledge but also more appreciation of this amazing beverage. This chapter shows you how to educate yourself about wine with the help of classes, publications, and more.

Back to the Classroom

The best way to learn about wine and to improve your wine-tasting skills is to take a wine course. Wine classes provide the ideal combination of authoritative instruction and immediate, expert feedback on your tasting impressions. If you live in a medium-sized or large city, you're sure to find several wine courses offered by private wine schools, by universities as adult-education extension programs, or by local wine shops or restaurants. If you're out of reach of such courses, you can research wine online.

What do the initials MW mean?

You may have noticed that one of the coauthors of this book has *Master of Wine* (often shortened to MW) after her name. Wine professionals receive this title — which is the most respected wine credential in the world — by passing a grueling three-part exam. The Institute of Masters of Wine awards the credential; it offers preparatory programs and/or exams in Australia, the United States, the United Kingdom, and continental Europe. A high level of knowledge, at least five years of experience in the wine trade, and completion of any locally available wine courses (such as the WSET programs) are the normal prerequisites. As of this writing, there are 298 Masters of Wine in the world (30 in North America). For more information, visit the Institute online at www.masters-of-wine.org.

Most wine courses are *wine appreciation* courses — they don't teach you how to make wine, they don't usually provide you with professional credentials, and they're not accredited. The purpose of most wine courses is to provide both information about wine and practice in tasting wine. (For information on professional wine credentials, see the sidebar "What do the initials MW mean?")

Introductory classes generally deal with wine grape varieties and how to taste wine, while more advanced classes discuss in depth the various wine regions of the world or the wines of a particular region. Instructors are usually experienced professionals who work in the wine trade or who write about wine; in the best cases, they have also had some training in the principles of adult learning.

Brand promotion and education often enjoy too cozy a relationship in the wine field. Many wine instructors, such as distributor salespeople or winery reps, have a vested interest in the brands of wine that they offer as tasting samples in class. As long as the instructor has expertise beyond his or her own brands, you can certainly still benefit from the instruction. But you should request disclosure of any commercial affiliations at the first class. And when possible, consider taking classes from independent instructors instead.

One wine school in action

The following announcement is a shameless plug: We run a wine school in New York City called International Wine Center (www.internationalwinecenter.com). We offer the programs of the Wine & Spirit Education Trust (WSET), the world's leading wine education organization. The courses cover four levels of study (from beginner to very advanced) and range from 6 to 100-plus hours in duration; each course has a textbook or similar informational content, self-study aides, and an examination. Students who pass the exam corresponding to their level of study earn a certificate attesting to the knowledge they have gained. The same programs are available in other wine schools across the United States and in other countries.

Many other wine courses are less comprehensive or less formally structured — but most wine classes have a lot in common. A typical class usually lasts about two hours; students listen to a discussion of a particular topic and taste six to eight wines related to that topic. Maps of wine regions or slides reiterating key facts punctuate the discussion. The instructor encourages questions and guides students in tasting and understanding the wines that he presents.

At most wine classes, each student sits before a place setting of wine glasses — ideally one glass per wine to be tasted. Water and crackers are available to help students clear their palates between tastes of wine. Next to each student is a large plastic cup so that students can spit out the wines rather than swallow them and dump their leftover wine. (If the idea of spitting wine shocks you, read the section "To spit or not to spit?" later in this chapter.) Each student should receive a printed list of the wines being tasted as well as other material about the subject of that particular class session.

Wine tastings of all shapes and sizes

Wine tastings are events designed to give enthusiasts the opportunity to sample a range of wines. The events can be very much like classes (seated, seminar-like events), or they can be more like parties (tasters milling around informally). Compared to a wine class, the participants at a wine tasting are more likely to have mixed levels of knowledge. Tastings don't come in beginner, intermediate, and advanced levels — one size fits all.

Wine tastings are useful because they override the limitations of sampling wine alone, at home. How many wines can you taste on your own (unless you don't mind throwing away nine-tenths of every bottle)? How many wines are you willing to buy on your own? And how much can you learn, tasting wine in isolation — or with a friend whose expertise is no greater than yours?

At wine tastings, you can gain insight from your fellow tasters, as well as make new friends who share your interest in wine. Most important, you can taste wine in the company of some individuals who are more experienced than you, which is a real boon in training your palate.

We have led or attended literally thousands of wine tastings in our lives — so far. And it's fair to say that we've learned something about wine at almost all of them.

To attend a wine tasting in your area, contact your local wine merchant. Your local shop might sponsor wine-tasting events occasionally (apart from informal sampling opportunities in the store itself) and should also be aware of wine schools or other organizations that conduct wine tastings in your area.

Blind man's bluff

One of the favorite diversions of wine tasters is tasting wines blind. Before you conjure up thoughts of darkened rooms, blindfolded tasters, or other forms of hanky-panky, let us explain that the tasters aren't blind, the bottles are. Or anyway, the bottles have their faces covered.

In *blind tastings,* the tasters don't know the identities of the wines. The theory behind this exercise is that knowing the identities could prejudice the tasters to prefer (or dislike) a particular wine for its reputation rather than for "what's in the glass," as they say. Sometimes, extremely skilled tasters taste wines blind and try to identify them, in an effort to sharpen their tasting skills even further.

If you don't know enough about wine to be prejudiced by the labels, there's little point in tasting blind. Nevertheless, there's something about blind tasting that really helps you focus your concentration on what you're tasting — and that's always good practice.

Dinner with the winemaker

A popular type of wine event is the winemaker dinner, a multicourse dinner at which a winemaker or winery executive is the guest of honor. Wine drinkers pay a fixed price for the meal and taste various wines from the featured winery that are matched to each course.

As far as learning goes, winemaker dinners rank below seminar-style wine tastings but above many informal, reception-style tastings. These dinners offer the chance to taste wines under ideal circumstances — with food — but we find that most speakers disseminate very little information of any value and give you precious little opportunity to ask questions. In their potential for fun, however, winemaker dinners are right up there at the top of the list — even if you don't get to sit next to the winemaker.

Winery visits

One of the best — and most fun-filled — ways to find out about wine is to actually visit wineries and speak to the winemakers or other winery personnel about their wines. You get to immerse yourself in the region you visit — experiencing the climate firsthand, seeing the soil and the hills, touching the grapes, and so on. You can walk through the vineyards if you want, visit nearby towns or villages, eat the local food, and drink the wine of the region.

You discover that there's something special about the people who devote their lives to making wine. Maybe it's their creativity or their commitment to bringing pleasure to the world through their labor. Whatever the reason, they are exceptional people. We have found some of our dearest friends in wine regions throughout the world.

When you do plan to visit a winery, you usually need to call or write ahead for an appointment. The major exceptions are a few of the large wineries in California that offer scheduled tours or self-guided visits.

Many wineries in the United States do have tasting rooms that are open every day during the busy tourism months and on weekends during the winter, and you don't need an appointment for the tasting room. (But do check the hours in advance.) You can sample wines (often for a small fee), buy wine, and sometimes buy souvenirs, such as T-shirts imprinted with the logo of the winery, or wine paraphernalia.

If you visit wineries that are less geared toward tourism — which is the case in most of the rest of the wine world — you can simply sample the wines, talk to the winemaker or proprietor when he's available (you *have* made an appointment, right?), take an informal tour of the winery, and buy some wine if you want (an especially nice idea if the wine isn't available back home).

Don't let your limited (or nonexistent) ability to speak the local language prevent you from visiting wine regions. These days, English is the nearly universal language of the wine world. Even if the person you're visiting doesn't speak English, he invariably has someone available (his wife, his son, or his dog) who does. Besides, wine itself is a universal language. A smile and a handshake go a long way toward communicating!

When in Rome . . .

In case you've never been to a wine tasting or wine class, we should warn you that a few matters of etiquette apply at most tastings. Familiarizing yourself with the etiquette in the following sections will help you feel more comfortable. Otherwise, you're likely to be appalled by what you see or hear. Why are those people behaving like that?!

To spit or not to spit?

Professional wine tasters long ago discovered that if they swallow every wine they taste, they become far less thoughtful tasters by the time they reach the ninth or tenth wine. So spitting each wine after evaluating it became acceptable. In working wineries, professional tasters sometimes spit right onto the gravel floor or into the drains. In more elegant surroundings and in wine classes, tasters spit into a *spittoon,* usually a simple container like a large plastic cup (one per taster) or an ice bucket that two or three tasters share.

At first, some tasters are naturally loath to spit out wine. Not only have they been brought up to believe that spitting is uncouth, but they've also paid good money for the opportunity to taste the wines. Why waste them?

Well, you can drink all your wine at a wine tasting, if you want — and some people do. But we don't advise it, for the following reasons:

- Evaluating the later wines is difficult if you swallow the earlier ones. The alcohol you consume clouds your judgment.

- Swallowing is not really necessary in order to taste the wine fully. If you leave the wine in your mouth for eight to ten seconds (see Chapter 2), you are able to taste it thoroughly — while minimizing the effects of the alcohol.

- If you are driving to the tasting, you're taking a risk driving home afterward if you drink rather than spit. The stakes are high — your life and health, others' lives, and your driver's license. Why gamble?

The simple solution: Spit out the wine. Just about all experienced wine tasters do. Believe it or not, spitting will seem to be a very normal thing to do at wine tastings after a while. (And, in the meantime, it's one sure way to appear more experienced than you are!)

If you know that you can't bring yourself to spit, be sure to have something substantial to eat before going to a wine tasting. You absorb alcohol more slowly on a full stomach — and the simple crackers and bread at most wine tastings aren't sufficient to do the trick. And, of course, don't drive afterward.

What's with the sound effects?

Do you have to make that loud slurping or gurgling noise that you hear "serious" wine tasters make at tastings? Of course you don't. But drawing air into your mouth does enhance your ability to taste the wine (as explained in Chapter 2). With a little practice, you can gurgle without making loud, attention-getting noises.

More fine points of wine etiquette

Because smell is such an important aspect of wine tasting, courteous tasters try not to interfere with other tasters' ability to smell. This means

- Smoking (anything) is a complete no-no at any wine tasting.

- Using any scent (perfume, after-shave lotion, scented hair spray, and so on) is unacceptable. These foreign odors can really interfere with your fellow tasters' ability to detect the wine's aroma.

Courteous wine tasters also don't volunteer their opinions about a wine until other tasters have had a chance to taste the wine. Serious tasters like to form their opinions independently and are sure to throw dirty looks at anyone who interrupts their concentration.

Note: Most of these wine-tasting etiquette guidelines apply to wine classes as well — and are also relevant when you visit wineries around the world.

Horizontal or vertical?

Two of the goofiest expressions in the world of wine apply to wine tastings. Depending on the nature of the wines featured, wine-tasting events can be categorized as *vertical tastings* or as *horizontal tastings.* These categories have nothing to do with the position of the tasters themselves — they're usually seated, and they're never lying down (that went out of fashion after the Romans).

A vertical tasting is a wine tasting featuring several vintages of the same wine — Château Latour in various vintages from 1990 to 2005, for example. A horizontal tasting examines wines of a single vintage from several different wineries; usually the wines are of a similar type, such as 2007 Napa Valley Cabernet Sauvignons. There's no particular name for tastings with less disciplined themes, but we suggest *plaid.*

Armchair Travel

Traveling around the world takes time and money. Alternatively, you can travel through the wine world from the comfort of your living room or your home office, letting the written word carry you to faraway wine regions. Apart from bookstores themselves, many retail wine stores sell wine books, magazines, and newsletters. And with every passing month, the number of websites and smartphone or tablet apps about wine increases.

Recommended books

The following books are some of *the* established tomes; they take you into great depth on particular aspects of wine.

General knowledge

Hugh Johnson and Jancis Robinson, MW, *World Atlas of Wine,* 6th Edition, Mitchell Beazley, 2007. Johnson and Robinson, both English, are probably the world's most respected wine writers. Complete with detailed maps of all the world's wine regions, this book is essential for any serious wine lover's library. (*Hugh Johnson's Wine Companion* and *Hugh Johnson's Pocket Wine Book 2012,* both published by Mitchell Beazley, are two additional worthwhile books to check out.)

Oz Clarke, *Oz Clarke's New Encyclopedia of Wine,* 2nd Edition, Harcourt, 2003. Clarke is undoubtedly the wine world's most prolific writer — the Stephen King of winedom. This comprehensive encyclopedia is well organized and up-to-date. A great wine reference book. (*Oz Clarke's Grapes and Wines*, with coauthor Margaret Rand, published in 2010 in paperback by Sterling Epicure, is a recent book.)

Jancis Robinson, MW (editor), *The Oxford Companion to Wine,* 3rd Edition, Oxford University Press, 2006. This encyclopedic reference book sets the standard in the wine field. We would expect no less from Robinson, one of the truly brilliant wine writers. This book is a "must" for all serious students of wine!

Bordeaux

Robert M. Parker, Jr., *Bordeaux: A Consumer's Guide to the World's Finest Wines,* 4th Edition, Simon & Schuster, 2003. Robert Parker is certainly America's most famous wine critic. He earned his reputation for his knowledge of Bordeaux; he was also the first writer to use the 100-point wine rating system. This fourth edition covers all major Bordeaux wines from 1961 to 2001, with info on wines dating back to 1945. Although now dated, it's an essential book for any Bordeaux lover.

David Peppercorn, MW, *Wines of Bordeaux,* Revised Edition, Mitchell Beazley, 2006. England's David Peppercorn is rightfully regarded as one of the great Bordeaux experts. In this succinctly written wine guide, he offers his own ratings of Bordeaux wines, when to drink them, and which ones are particularly good values.

Benjamin Lewin, MW, *What Price Bordeaux?* Wine Appreciation Guild, 2009. Lewin explores developments in Bordeaux with scientific rigor and explains how Bordeaux wine has reached astronomical prices. A provocative book.

Burgundy

Anthony Hanson, MW, *Burgundy,* Mitchell Beazley, 2006. A succinct, excellent work on this very complicated wine region.

Clive Coates, MW, *The Wines of Burgundy,* Revised Edition, University of California Press, 2008. This is the updated version of Coates's *Côte d'Or: A Celebration of the Great Wines of Burgundy* about his favorite wine region. Coates, another in the fine corps of British wine writers, covers all the major districts of Burgundy, reviews the producers, and provides detailed information on vintages. A thorough reference book on Burgundy.

Champagne

Michael Edwards, *The Finest Wines of Champagne: A Guide to the Best Cuvées, Houses, and Growers,* University of California Press, 2009. A Champagne expert, Edwards explores 90 Champagne producers in depth. A Champagne lover's delight.

Ed McCarthy, *Champagne For Dummies,* Wiley, 1999. Your *Wine For Dummies* coauthor, a Champagne specialist, has written this comprehensive guide to the world of Champagne, including a section on touring Champagne and a directory of Champagne houses.

Tom Stevenson, *World Encyclopedia of Champagne & Sparkling Wine,* Revised Edition, Wine Appreciation Guild, 2003. England's Tom Stevenson knows more about Champagne than the Champenois themselves! A complete look at Champagne and all the major sparkling wines of the world.

Richard Juhlin, *4000 Champagnes,* Flammarion, 2005. Juhlin, an extremely knowledgeable Swedish lover of Champagne, gives his own personalized views of the Champagne houses. Thorough and comprehensive. (Also check out Richard Juhlin's *Champagne Guide,* Wine Appreciation Guild, 2008.)

Old and rare wines

Michael Broadbent, MW, *Michael Broadbent's Vintage Wine,* Harcourt, 2002. No one has tasted more great wines, especially old and rare ones, than England's Michael Broadbent. This guide to vintage wines, going back to the 19th century, concentrates on Bordeaux, Sauternes, and Burgundy. This book is for the advanced wine buff. Great stuff from one of the world's greatest French wine connoisseurs.

France

Ed McCarthy and Mary Ewing-Mulligan, MW, *French Wine For Dummies,* Wiley, 2001. Every French wine region is covered, with special emphasis on Bordeaux, Burgundy, and the Rhône Valley. Dare we say, "Eminently readable"?

James Turnbull, *Fine French Wines,* Flammarion, 2007. Turnbull selects and describes 220 of France's outstanding wines, covering just about every wine region. An excellent survey for the French wine connoisseur.

Andrew Jefford, *The New France: A Complete Guide to Contemporary French Wine,* Mitchell Beazley, 2007. A fresh look at the classic wine regions of France.

Italy

Mary Ewing-Mulligan, MW, and Ed McCarthy, *Italian Wine For Dummies,* Wiley, 2001. Every Italian wine region and every major Italian wine is covered, with special emphasis on Piedmont, Tuscany, northeastern Italy, and southern Italy.

Kerin O'Keefe, *Brunello di Montalcino: Understanding and Appreciating One of Italy's Greatest Wines,* University of California Press, 2012. *The* authoritative book on one of Italy's most important wines. O'Keefe does a thorough job that underscores her firsthand knowledge of the region.

Nicolas Belfrage, MW, *The Finest Wines of Tuscany and Central Italy: A Regional and Village Guide to the Best Wines and Their Producers,* University of California Press, 2009. Belfrage is one of the most knowledgeable writers on Italian wine today.

Spain

Jeremy Watson, *The New and Classical Wines of Spain*, Montagud Editores, 2002. Watson has performed a great service in providing the wine world with a comprehensive reference on one of the world's great wine countries.

Germany

Stuart Pigott, *The Wine Atlas of Germany: And Traveller's Guide to the Vineyards,* Mitchell Beazley, 1996. Although British, Pigott lives in Germany and is one of the leading experts on the intricacies of German wine. The series editor of this atlas is Hugh Johnson, another German wine lover and a man who knows something about putting together wine atlases. An excellent reference for German wines. Pigott's more current wine writing is in German.

California

Stephen Brook, *The Finest Wines of California: A Regional Guide to the Best Producers and Their Wines,* University of California Press, 2011. A respected British writer gives us a refreshing look at California's wines in this easy-to-read guide.

Charles E. Olken and Joseph Furstenthal, *The New Connoisseurs' Guide to California Wines,* University of California Press, 2010. An authoritative encyclopedia, atlas, and buying guide for California wines.

Ed McCarthy and Mary Ewing-Mulligan, MW, *California Wine For Dummies,* Wiley, 2009. Ed and Mary (yes, yours truly) take the varietal approach in this book, devoting a chapter to each of California's major varieties and recommending wines in various price categories.

Washington

Paul Gregutt, *Washington Wines and Wineries: The Essential Guide,* 2nd Edition, University of California Press, 2010. Washington State local Paul Gregutt writes the definitive guide for Washington's wines.

Argentina

Laura Catena, *Vino Argentino: An Insider's Guide to the Wines and Wine Country of Argentina,* Chronicle Books, 2010. The multitalented Laura Catena, director of Bodega Catena Zapata Winery, emergency room doctor, and author, writes an authentic guide to the wines of her native Argentina.

Australia and New Zealand

Oz Clarke, *Oz Clarke's Australian Wine Companion: An Essential Guide for All Lovers of Australian Wine,* Harcourt, 2004. The author's passion for Australian wines is enough to convert anyone. The book's authoritative information and clear maps are also top-notch.

James Halliday, *Australian Wine Companion,* 2012 Edition, Hardie Grant, 2011. This book is a compact but expert guide to the wine regions of Australia from the prolific James Halliday, wine writer, winemaker, and barrister.

Michael Cooper, *Wine Atlas of New Zealand,* 2nd Edition, Hatchette, 2010. Cooper is arguably the world's leading authority on New Zealand's wines. This comprehensive tome is required reading for all New Zealand wine lovers.

Winemaking and grape growing

Jamie Goode and Sam Harrop, MW, *Authentic Wine: Toward Natural and Sustainable Winemaking,* University of California Press, 2011. The authors question commercial, "industrial" wines and make the case for naturally made wine.

Alice Feiring, *Naked Wine: Letting Grapes Do What Comes Naturally,* Da Capo Press, 2011. Feiring attacks most New World wines as "made" and champions the cause of natural wines.

Katherine Cole, *Voodoo Vintners: Oregon's Astonishing Biodynamic Winegrowers,* Oregon State University Press, 2011. Cole explores biodynamic winemaking, using the vineyards of Oregon as an example.

Miscellaneous topics

Terry Theise, *Reading Between the Wines,* University of California Press, 2010. Wine importer and passionate wine expert, Theise writes a personal, opinionated tribute to wine, in all its glory.

Karen Page and Andrew Dornenburg, *Food Lovers Guide to Wine,* Hatchette, 2011. The authors, enthusiastic food lovers, explore the flavors of wine and their relationship to food.

Benjamin Lewin, MW, *Wine Myths and Reality,* Wine Appreciation Guild, 2010. Lewin goes behind the scenes in an authoritative account of how wine is really made. Compelling reading.

Randall Grahm, *Been Doon So Long: A Randall Grahm Vinthology,* University of California Press, 2012. Grahm, the humorous, irreverent owner of Bonny Doon Winery, pens a personal guide into his vision of the world of wine, in his own inimitable style.

Wine magazines and newsletters

Wine magazines and newsletters can provide more topical information about wine than books can. They keep you up-to-date on the current happenings in the wine world, give you timely tasting notes on newly released wines, profile the currently hot wines and winemakers, and so on. Also, the classified ads in the back of most wine magazines are a good way to hear about wine-related equipment for sale, wine tours, and other useful offers.

Magazines

Here, we name some wine magazines we recommend. Be sure to check out the websites of these magazines (some of them do require a subscription) for even more timely information.

- ✔ *Decanter* (`www.decanter.com`): One of the oldest and one of the best, this magazine covers the world but is especially strong on French and Italian wines. *Decanter* also frequently issues supplements on major wine regions as part of your subscription. It's published monthly in London.

- ✔ *Wine Spectator* (`www.winespectator.com`): Much of the current wine news is in the *Spectator,* but the magazine also includes rather extensive coverage of the world's major wine regions, with plenty of tasting notes. It's published twice monthly. Web access is $50 per year ($25 for print subscribers) and includes blogs and features not available in the print version.

- ✔ *Wine Enthusiast* (`www.winemag.com`): A colorful, newsy monthly that includes an extensive wine-buying guide.

- ✔ *Wine & Spirits* (`www.wineandspiritsmagazine.com`): This high-class magazine offers comprehensive, thoughtful coverage of wine and spirits. Extensive tasting notes are always included. It's published eight times a year.

- ✔ *World of Fine Wine* (`www.finewinemag.com`): The wine world's equivalent of a literary magazine, this truly fine quarterly published in the United Kingdom covers wine-related topics at the highest level of fine wine.

Newsletters

Wine newsletters usually express the personal opinion of authoritative critics. They contain mainly wine-tasting notes, whereas magazines contain feature-length articles along with tasting notes. Some newsletters accept no advertising and thus can maintain (in theory, at least) more impartiality than magazines. Most wine newsletters are intended for the intermediate to advanced wine buff. Also, you can check out the online versions of these newsletters. Here are the ones we recommend:

- ✔ *The Wine Advocate* (`www.eRobertParker.com`): Robert M. Parker, Jr., is an attorney-turned-wine critic who now has several other reviewers writing under his mantle. His approach to wine is methodical and thorough, complete with ratings of wine on a 100-point scale. Clear and easy to read with lots of charts and wine-buying tips, *The Wine Advocate* is published bimonthly and is for serious wine lovers (not for the complete beginner); it covers the world's major wine regions but is especially strong on French wines. The website includes blogs and lively discussion boards for an online subscription of $99 per year.

✔ *International Wine Cellar* (www.internationalwinecellar.com): Steve Tanzer combines thoughtful articles, interviews with major wine figures, and extensive tasting notes to make an intelligent guide for the advanced wine buff. Published bimonthly, online only.

✔ *Peter Liem's ChampagneGuide.net* (www.champagneguide.net): American journalist Peter Liem lives in the Champagne region. His authoritative comments on producers and Champagnes are incisive and clear, making him one of the best writers on Champagne today. The cost for this bimonthly newsletter subscription is $89 a year.

The blogosphere of wine

If you're thirsty for wine knowledge, you can spend hours and hours researching wine on Internet sites. Most wineries and wine importers have websites, as do the promotional boards of major wine-producing countries and wine regions, and those sites can be useful. But third-party websites and blogs provide more free-ranging information. Here are some of our favorite places to read about, or chat about, wine online. (Unless otherwise noted, the sites have free access.)

✔ **Wine Review Online** (www.winereviewonline.com): Robert Whitley, a San Diego–based wine writer and radio wine show host, is publisher of this weekly newsletter, edited by writer Michael Franz. Contributors include a very experienced group of wine writers from all over the United States, including both authors of this book. The site's articles are free, but access to the current and archived wine reviews requires a subscription of $59 per year or $39 for six months.

✔ **Jancis Robinson.com** (www.jancisrobinson.com): This site features articles and commentary from England's leading wine journalist and her contributing writers, as well as lively, active chat boards with international participation. Subscribers ($119 per year) gain access to the site's Purple Pages, where they can even search Robinson's authoritative *Oxford Wine Companion.*

✔ **Burghound.com** (www.burghound.com): Allen Meadows's comprehensive, quarterly review of red and white Burgundies has become *the* most respected newsletter on Burgundy, covering what is perhaps the most challenging wine of all to evaluate. Each issue averages 150 pages. A "must read" for Burgundy lovers. Subscription is $125 per year.

✔ **Wine Lovers' Page** (www.wineloverspage.com): One of the original wine websites, founded in 1994. It features online discussion groups, tasting notes, and feature articles.

✔ **Wine Anorak** (www.wineanorak.com): An online magazine from writer Jamie Goode with a distinctly British flavor. Strong in technical information about wine.

- ✔ **Vinography** (www.vinography.com): Alder Yarrow's wine blog was one of the first to gain fame, and understandably so, because it's one of the best-written and authoritative blogs we have come across.

- ✔ **Dr.Vino** (www.drvino.com): Tyler Coleman has established a reputation as the policeman of wine. He fearlessly goes after people in the wine business who make dubious claims. Not afraid to take on anybody, Coleman definitely has the pulse of the wine biz in his grasp.

- ✔ **1WineDude** (www.1winedude.com): Joe Roberts, wine dude, has a humorous, hip, and knowledgeable blog with lots of entertaining scoops about the wine business.

- ✔ **Wine Diarist** (www.winediarist.com): Mike Steinberger gained his reputation in wine journalism while writing for the online publication, *Slate,* for ten years and is one of the most respected wine writers in the business. The Wine Diarist is Steinberger's personal new wine site.

- ✔ **Do Bianchi** (www.dobianchi.com): Jeremy Parzen, PhD, is one of the most knowledgeable writers in the world on Italian wine. His incisive blog on Italian wine is not to be missed by Italian wine lovers or those who want to learn about Italian wine. (Two other blogs specializing in Italian wine are **Tom's Wine Line** at www.ubriaco.wordpress.com — which includes literary, thought-provoking articles from former English professor Tom Maresca — and **Charles Scicolone on Wine** at www.charlesscicolone.wordpress.com — where you can find casual but authoritative comments on Italian wines from another former teacher.)

- ✔ **The Feiring Line** (www.alicefeiring.com): Alice Feiring is another wine journalist who will take on anybody or any topic in wine in her blog — no matter how controversial — as she did when she wrote a recent book taking on Robert Parker. She's a particular advocate of natural wine.

- ✔ **Snooth** (www.snooth.com): Snooth claims to be the world's largest wine site; it's a lively site that features community reviews of wines, news feeds, discussion boards, wine recommendations, and more.

- ✔ **Palate Press** (www.palatepress.com): A fairly new, free site that features original articles and tasting notes from many writers and critics; active commentary from readers links you to dozens of individual wine blogs.

Chapter 19

Describing and Rating Wine

- -

In This Chapter

▶ Ways to be a more thoughtful taster

▶ Tips for writing tasting notes

▶ Numeric shorthand for wine quality

- -

*W*hen we first got excited about wine, we tried to share our enthusiasm with a friend who appeared to have some interest in the subject (well, he drank a glass now and then). Each time we served a wine, we'd talk about it in great detail. But he wasn't interested. "I don't want to talk about wine — I just want to drink it!" he proclaimed.

On some fundamental level where wine is just a generic beverage, it's certainly possible to drink wine without talking about it. But if you're the kind of person who likes to talk about food, or if you've been bitten by the wine bug, you know that it's difficult (if not impossible) to enjoy wine without talking about it at least a little. Wine is a social pleasure that's enhanced by sharing your opinions with others.

Ironically, the experience of a wine is highly personal. If you and three other people taste the same wine at the same time, each of you will have your own impression of that wine based on personal likes and dislikes, physiology, and experience. Maybe some day, if humans learn how to link their minds through Bluetooth, someone else will be able to experience your experience of a wine — but until then, your taste is singular. The only way you can share your impressions with others is through conversation; the guidelines in this chapter will help.

The Challenge of Putting Taste to Words

Language is our main vehicle for communicating our entire experience of life. Our vocabulary of taste is undeveloped, however. When we were young, we were taught a visual vocabulary: what green is, and what yellow, gold, and orange are — and for that matter, what pine green is, or jungle green, olive green, forest green, and sea green (thanks, Crayola!). No one ever taught us the precise difference in the words *bitter, astringent,* and *tart.* Yet to talk about wine taste, we use these words as if we all agree on what they mean. That's one reason wine descriptions can sound like mumbo jumbo.

Another reason wine descriptions are challenging is that a wine's taste is complicated. Wine is a complex beverage that gives us multiple taste sensations:

✔ Aromatic sensations (all those flavors we perceive by smelling them in our mouths — as we discuss in Chapter 2)

✔ Basic taste sensations (sweetness, sourness, and bitterness)

✔ Tactile sensations (the bite of astringency, for example, as well as the prickliness, roughness, smoothness, richness, or other textural impressions of a wine in our mouths)

✔ Sensations on the holistic level, a synthesis of all the wine's characteristics taken together

For example, say we just tasted an oaked Sauvignon Blanc from California. We may perceive the wine as intense in herbaceous and fruity, melon-like flavors (aromatic impressions), very slightly sweet, yet with firm acidity (basic taste impressions), smooth and rich (tactile impressions), a vibrant wine with personality to spare (holistic impression). That description might sound like some insufferable wine snob showing off, when it's actually just some poor wine lover trying his best to report the taste data the wine is sending him.

You've probably gotten many a laugh from wine descriptions you've read. At face value, they sound preposterous: *Unctuous, with butter and vanilla flavors that coat the sides of your mouth. Supple and smooth, showing some fatness in the mouth, and a long finish.* (Wait! They forgot to say wet and "liquidy.") Imperfect medium that language is, however, it's the only way we have of communicating the taste of wine.

Reading wine descriptions (or *tasting notes,* as they're often called) in wine newsletters or magazines can be as difficult as writing them. We must admit that our eyes often glaze over when we try to read tasting notes. And we're not alone. Frank Prial, former wine columnist of *The New York Times,* once wrote that ". . . a stranger's tasting notes, to me anyway, are about as meaningful as a Beijing bus schedule."

When It's Your Turn to Speak

Describing your experience or impression of a wine involves two steps: First, you have to form the impression; second, you have to communicate it.

What the words are worth

Once, we engaged in a humbling yet fascinating exercise. Several wine writers were given a wine to taste, along with eight published tasting notes from other writers, only one of which corresponded to that wine. We were asked to identify the corresponding tasting note, as well as the note that seemed the most off base. The description we all voted *least* appropriate for the wine turned out to be the description taken from the back label of the wine bottle! Not one of us had correctly matched the description's words to our taste experience. Again, with another wine, we each discovered that *our* taste and *their* words failed to correspond. Our only possible conclusions were either that we can't taste very well, that writers can't write very well (present company included), or that communicating taste is a hopeless exercise.

When you drink wine with friends purely for enjoyment and appreciation — over dinner, for example — simple impressions and silly comments are perfectly appropriate. If a wine strikes you as unusually full and voluptuous, why *not* say that it's like Kim Kardashian? If a wine seems tight and unyielding, go ahead and call it Ebenezer Scrooge. Everyone will know exactly what you mean.

In other circumstances, though, such as when you're attending a wine-tasting event, you probably want to form more considered impressions of each wine in order to participate in the discussion and gain the most from the event. To form a considered impression, you need to taste thoughtfully. The guidelines in the following sections will help.

Organizing your thoughts

The language you use to describe a wine starts with your own thoughts as you taste the wine. Thus, the process of tasting a wine and the process of describing it are intertwined.

Although wine tasting involves examining wine visually and smelling it as well as tasting it, those first two steps are a breeze compared to the third. When the wine is in your mouth, the multiple taste sensations — flavors, texture, body, sweetness or dryness, acidity, tannin, balance, length — occur practically all at once. In order to make sense of the information you receive from the wine, you have to impose some order on those impressions. (Turn to Chapter 2 for information on the steps involved in examining, smelling, and tasting wine.)

One way of organizing the impressions a wine sends you is to classify those impressions according to the nature of the "taste":

- The wine's *aromatics* (all the flavors you smell in your mouth)
- The wine's *structure* (its alcohol/sweetness/acid/tannin makeup and its basic tastes — the wine's bricks and mortar, so to speak)
- The wine's *texture* (the tactile data, how the wine feels in your mouth; texture is a function of the wine's structural components — a high acid, dry, low-alcohol white wine may feel thin or sharp, for example, whereas a high-alcohol red wine with low tannin may feel soft and silky)

Another way of organizing the impressions a wine sends you is by the sequence of your impressions, as we describe in Chapter 2. The words that tasters use to describe the sequence are

- **Attack:** The first impression of the wine, which may involve sweetness, dryness, richness or thinness of texture, or even fruitiness (although most of the wine's flavors register a few moments later).
- **Evolution:** The development of the wine in your mouth. You can think of this stage in two parts:
  - The *mid-palate impression,* a phase when you tend to notice the wine's acidity, perhaps get a first impression of its tannin (in red wines) and notice its flavors and their intensity
  - The *rear-palate impression,* which involves the degree of persistence that the wine's flavors have across the length of your mouth, the amount and nature of the wine's tannins, and any indication of a burning sensation from overly high alcohol
- **Finish or aftertaste:** Flavors or impressions that register after the wine has been spat or swallowed. Both the duration of the aftertaste and its nature are noteworthy. (A long finish is commendable, for example, and a bitter one is not.) A suggestion of concentrated fruit character on the finish often indicates that a wine is age-worthy.

Writing tasting notes

Some people have a special ability to remember tastes. But other people need to take notes in order to remember what wine they tasted, let alone what they thought of it. If you have the slightest difficulty remembering wine names, jot down the names of wines you try and like so you can enjoy them — or similar wines — again.

To taste, perchance to drink

In wine circles, tasting and drinking are two different activities. Tasting involves thoughtful evaluation of a wine's quality, flavors, texture, aging potential, and so on; if more than a couple of wines are being tasted comparatively, usually tasters spit the wine out (as we mention in Chapter 18) in order to keep their thinking clear. Drinking, on the other hand, involves consumption and sheer appreciation, without any particular analysis of the wine other than the judgment that you like it. (If you don't like it, you don't drink it.)

Unless you're a professional in the wine business, you don't ever have to taste a wine seriously; you can just drink it. However, many wine drinkers have discovered that wine tasting can be a fun way to discover more about wine.

It's a good idea to write comments about wines that you taste, too. Even if you're one of those lucky few who can remember everything you taste, we recommend that you write tasting notes now and then because the exercise of taking notes helps discipline your tasting methods.

When we take notes on wines, we automatically write the letters

- ✔ *C* (for color and appearance in general)
- ✔ *N* (for nose)
- ✔ *T* (for taste, or mouth impressions)

We put one below the other, under the name of each wine on our tasting sheet, leaving space to record our impressions.

When we taste, we take each wine as it comes: If a wine is very aromatic, we write lots of things next to *N,* but if the aroma is understated, we can just write *subtle* or even *not much.* When we taste the wine, we approach it sequentially, noting its attack and evolution, and we hold the wine long enough to note its balance and texture, too. Then (having spat), we often taste the wine again to determine what else it may be saying. Sometimes at that point, we arrive at a summary description of the wine, like *a huge wine packed with fruitiness that's ready to drink now,* or *a lean, austere wine that will taste better with food than alone.* Our tasting notes are a combination of fragmented observation — *high acid, very crisp* — and summary description.

At first, your own notes will be brief. Just a few words, like *soft, fruity* or *tannic, austere* are fine to remind you later what the wine was like. And as an evaluation of overall quality, there's absolutely nothing wrong with *yummy!*

Just keep in mind that the taste of a wine is more than a series of aromas and flavors. Instead of searching for ever more fruit or flower descriptors, move on to consider the dryness or sweetness, the body, or the texture, for example. As we mention in Chapter 9, these characteristics are at least as important in pairing wine with food as the wine's actual flavors are.

Describing wine: Purism versus poetry

Some people have the idea that there's a right way and a wrong way to describe wine. Many *enologists* (people who have earned a degree in the science of winemaking), for example, might favor a scientific approach to describing wine. This approach relies on descriptors that are objective, quantifiable, and reproducible — such as the level of acidity in a wine (which is measurable) or specific aroma and flavor descriptors (reproducible in laboratory tests). They dislike fanciful or unspecific terms, such as *rich, generous,* or *smooth.*

Other people who aren't scientists (ourselves included) believe that strictly scientific descriptions usually fail to communicate the spirit of a wine. We're all for noting the relative acidity, tannin, and alcohol levels of a wine, but we won't stop there; we like to describe the overall personality of a wine, even if we have to use language that's more personal than universal.

Sometimes, if a wine is really a great wine, tasters stumble into the most controversial realm of wine description: poetry. We never *try* to come up with picturesque metaphorical descriptions for wines, but sometimes a wine just puts the words in our mouths. One memorable wine in our early days of tasting was a 1970 Brunello di Montalcino that we described as a rainbow in the mouth, its flavors so perfectly blended that each one was barely perceptible individually. A friend of ours described a glass of great but too-young Vintage Port as "like rubbing a cat in the wrong direction."

If a wine inspires you to such fanciful description, by all means go with it. The experience of that wine will become memorable through the personal words you use to name it.

Beware of anyone who is moved to poetry over every wine, however. The vast majority of wines are prosaic, and their descriptions should be, too.

When you do lapse into metaphor over a wine, don't necessarily expect others to understand what you mean or even to approve. Literal types will be all over you, demanding to know what a rainbow tastes like and how a wine can possibly resemble a cat.

In the end, the experience of wine is so personal that the best any of us can do is to *try* to describe the experience to others. Your descriptions will be meaningful to people who share your approach and your language, especially if they're tasting the wine along with you. But someone else picking up your notes could find them incomprehensible. Likewise, you'll find some wine descriptions you read incomprehensible. Such is the nature of the exercise.

Rating Wine Quality

When a wine critic writes a tasting note, he usually accompanies it with a point score, a judgment of the wine's quality on a scale of 20 or 100. You see these numbers plastered all over the shelves in your wine shop, in wine advertisements, and in wine blogs.

Because words are such a difficult medium for describing wine, the popularity of number ratings is almost universal. Many wine lovers don't bother to read the descriptions in a critic's wine reviews — they just run out to buy the wines with the highest scores. (Hey, they're the best wines, right?) Wines that receive high scores from the best-known critics sell out almost overnight as the result of the demand generated by their scores.

Numbers do provide convenient shorthand for communicating a critic's opinion of a wine's quality. But number ratings are problematic, for a number of reasons:

- ✔ The sheer precision of a score suggests that the score is objective, when in fact it represents either the subjective opinion of an individual critic or the combined subjective opinions of a panel of critics.

- ✔ Different critics can apply the same scale differently. For example, some may assign 95 points only to wines that are truly great compared to all wines of all types, while others could assign the same score to a wine that's great in its own class.

- ✔ The score probably reflects an evaluation of a wine in different circumstances than those in which you'll taste it. Most critics rate wines by tasting them without food, for example, while most wine drinkers drink wine with food. Also, the wine glass the critic uses can be different from what you use, and even this detail can seriously affect the way the wine presents itself.

- ✔ Number scores tell you absolutely nothing about how the wine tastes.

This last point, for us, is the most important. You may hate a wine that's rated highly — and not only that, but you may end up feeling like a hopeless fool who can't recognize quality when it's staring him in the face. Save your money and your pride by deciding what kinds of wine you like and then trying to figure out from the words whether a particular wine is your style — *regardless of the number rating.* This advice is the principle behind our book *Wine Style:*

Using Your Senses to Explore and Enjoy Wine (Wiley); we urge you to read it so you can articulate what you like.

Despite the pitfalls of number ratings, you may be inclined to score wines yourself — and we encourage you to do that. Numbers can be meaningful to the person assigning them. Here are some basic steps to follow:

1. **To start, decide which scale you'll use.**

   We suggest a scale with 100 as the highest score, because it's more intuitive than a scale ending at 20, which many British writers use. (Most 100-point scales are actually only 50-point scales, with 50 points, not 0, representing the poorest conceivable quality.)

2. **After deciding your scale, create several groupings of points, and write down the quality level that each group represents.**

   It can be something like this:

   - 95–100: Absolutely outstanding; one of the finest wines ever

   - 90–94: Exceptional quality; excellent wine

   - 85–89: Very good quality

   - 80–84: Above-average quality; good

   - 75–79: Average commercial quality (a "C" student)

   - 70–74: Below average quality

   - Below 70: Poor quality

Until you get the hang of using this system, you may want to give each wine a range rather than a precise score, such as 80 to 84 (good) or 85 to 89 (very good). As you gain experience in tasting wine and rating wine quality, you become more opinionated and your scores will naturally become more precise.

Just remember that like every other critic, you have your own taste preferences that inevitably influence your scores, no matter how objective you try to be. Don't fall into the trap of thinking that all your wine friends should agree with you.

Part VII
The Part of Tens

The 5th Wave — By Rich Tennant

"We had an interesting wine last night that I can only describe as 'vacuum cleaner like.' It was big, came with a bag, and definitely sucked."

In this part . . .

This part is the place to turn for quick answers and easy solutions. The next time a friend tells you that expensive wines are always better, the next time you're wondering when to open that special bottle, the next time someone tells you that Champagnes don't age — check out the advice in this part.

Chapter 20

Answers to Ten Common Questions about Wine

. . . .

In This Chapter

▶ What to drink and when

▶ What the story is with *organic* wines and sulfites

▶ How to handle old wines

. . . .

*I*n our years of teaching about wine and helping customers in wine shops, we've noticed that the same questions about wine pop up again and again. In this chapter, we provide our answers to the ten most frequently asked questions about wine, from what's the best wine to when you should drink it.

What's the Best Wine?

This question is probably the one that customers ask most frequently in wine shops; they're asking, in other words, "Which wine should I buy?" The retailer usually responds with a barrage of questions, such as the following:

✔ "Do you prefer red wines or white wines?"

✔ "How much do you want to spend for a bottle?"

✔ "Are you planning to serve the wine with any particular dish?"

As all these questions suggest, the "best wine" depends on your taste and circumstances. No single wine can be the "best wine" for everyone.

These days, you can find hundreds of very good wines in most wine shops. A few decades ago, far fewer good wines existed — but winemaking and grape growing know-how has progressed dramatically, to the point that now you'll find few poor wines.

You won't necessarily like every one of those good wines, however. There's simply no getting around the fact that taste is personal. If you want to drink a good wine that's right for you, you have to decide what the characteristics of that wine could be and then get advice from a knowledgeable retailer. (Flip to Chapter 2 for more info on tasting wine.)

When Should I Drink This Wine?

Wine retailers frequently hear this question from customers, and the answer for most wines is, "Any time now."

The great majority of wines are ready to drink when you buy them. Only a small percentage of wines will actually improve with a year or two of age, but those wines won't improve enough for you to notice, unless you're a particularly thoughtful and experienced taster.

Some fine wines are an exception: They not only benefit from aging, but they also *need* to age in order to achieve their potential quality. For example, assuming that the wines are well stored (turn to Chapter 17 for specifics of wine storage):

- ✔ You can usually count on 20 to 30 years (or more) of life from top-quality red Bordeaux wines in good years such as 1986, 1989, 1990, 1996, 2000, 2005, 2009, and 2010 (2010 will be released in 2013).

- ✔ The best Barolos, Barbarescos, and Brunello di Montalcinos can age for 20 to 30 years in good vintages.

- ✔ The best white Burgundies and white Bordeaux improve with 10 to 15 years of aging or more, in good vintage years.

- ✔ Most of today's red Burgundies, with the *possible* exception of the 1999, 2005, and 2009 vintages, should be consumed within 10 to 15 years (the less expensive ones even earlier).

- ✔ Dessert wines, such as Vintage Port, Sauternes, Madeira, and Tokaji, will last for decades — and in the case of Vintage Madeira, centuries.

(For a listing of good vintage years and the approximate stage of readiness of the wines from those years, refer to Appendix C. For the names of some specific producers in each category whose wines we recommend, refer to Chapters 10, 11, 12, and 16.)

Unless the wine you own is one of the preceding types of wines, rest assured that you can drink it when you like, in the short term.

Is Wine Fattening?

A glass of dry wine contains 80 to 85 percent water, 12 to 14 percent ethyl alcohol, and small quantities of tartaric acid and various other components. Wine contains no fat.

A 4-ounce serving of dry white wine has about 104 calories, and 4 ounces of red wine has about 110 calories. Sweeter wines contain about 10 percent more calories depending on how sweet they are; fortified wines also contain additional calories because of their higher alcohol.

What Grape Variety Made This Wine?

Most New World wines (from the Americas, Australia, and other continents besides Europe) tell you what grape variety they're made from right on the front label — it's often the very name of the wine — or on the back label. Traditional European wines blended from several grape varieties usually don't give you that information because (a) the winemakers consider the name of the place more important than that of the grapes, anyway; and (b) often the grapes they use are local varieties whose names few people would recognize.

If you really want to know what grape varieties make a Soave, Valpolicella, Châteauneuf-du-Pape, Rioja, Côtes du Rhône, or other blended European wines, you'll generally have to look it up. (See our charts in Part III.) If you want to know more about that variety — and even those varieties that make varietal wines — turn to Chapter 3.

Which Vintage Should I Buy?

This question assumes that you have a choice among several vintages of the same wine. Most of the time, however, you don't. Nearly every wine is available in only one vintage, which is referred to as the *current* vintage.

For white wines, the current vintage represents grapes that were harvested as recently as nine months ago or as long as three years ago, depending on the type of wine; for red wines, the current vintage is a date one to four years ago. Sparkling wines often have no vintage date at all (they're blends of several vintages), but when they do, the date is generally three to eight years ago — or more, for the most elite Champagnes.

Classified-growth red Bordeaux wines (see Chapter 10) are a notable exception: Most wine shops feature several vintages of these wines. A few other fine wines — such as Burgundies, Barolos, or Rhône wines — may also be available in multiple vintages, but often they're not because the quantities produced are small and the wines sell out.

A red Rioja or a Chianti Classico might appear to be available in multiple vintages, but if you read the label carefully, you see that one vintage of the Rioja could be a *crianza* (aged two years before release), another may be a *reserva* (aged three years), and another may be a *gran reserva* (aged five years) — so they're actually different wines, not multiple vintages of the same wine. Likewise, a Chianti could be available in an aged *riserva* version as well as a non-*riserva* style.

Most of the time, for most wines, the vintage to buy is the vintage you *can* buy — the current vintage. For the exceptional cases, consult our vintage chart in Appendix C.

Are There Any Wines without Sulfites?

Sulfur dioxide exists naturally in wine as a result of fermentation. It also exists naturally in other fermented foods, such as bread, cookies, and beer. (Various sulfur derivatives are also used regularly as preservatives in packaged foods and dried fruits, such as apricots and figs.)

Winemakers use sulfur dioxide at various stages of the winemaking process because it stabilizes the wine (preventing it from turning to vinegar or deteriorating from oxygen exposure) and safeguards its flavor. Sulfur has been an important winemaking tool since Roman times.

Very few winemakers refrain from using sulfur dioxide, but some do. Your wine shop may carry a few wines whose sulfite content is so low that their labels don't have to carry the phrase *Contains Sulfites* (which the U.S. government requires on the label of any wine that contains more than 10 parts per million of sulfites). In some cases, these wines might be labeled as *organic wines* (in the United States, organic wines can't have added sulfur), which requires them to have also been made from grapes grown organically and certified as such. However, according to new E.U. regulations, organic wines can have added sulfur. Therefore, the lack of the *Contains Sulfites* phrase is your best assurance that the wine is extremely low in sulfites.

If you want to limit your consumption of sulfites, dry red wines should be your first choice, followed by dry white wines. Sweet wines contain the most sulfur dioxide. For more info, turn to Chapter 1.

What Are Organic Wines?

The standards of organic agriculture established by the U.S. Department of Agriculture in 2002 contain two categories for wine:

- ✔ **Wine made from organically grown grapes:** The grapes in these wines come from certified organic vineyards.
- ✔ **Organic wine:** These wines come from organically grown grapes and are also produced organically, that is, without the addition of chemical additives, such as sulfur dioxide, during winemaking.

Many more wines, by far, fall into the first category than the second, because most winemakers do use sulfur dioxide in making their wines. (See the preceding section for the reasons.)

But not all wines from organically grown grapes are labeled as such. Some winemakers whose vineyards are certified organic prefer to promote and sell their wines based on the wines' quality, not the incidental feature of their organic farming. For them, organic farming is a means to an end — better grapes, and therefore, better wine — rather than a marketing tool. Also, the fact that a national definition of *organic* didn't exist in the past disinclined some wineries from using that word.

Still other winemakers who are deeply committed to organic farming have chosen not to have their vineyards certified as organic. For some of them, the certification represents bureaucracy and extra paperwork. Therefore, their vineyards aren't organic, technically speaking, even if their farming practices are.

We have the impression that organic grape growing is more prevalent than ever, whether the *O* word appears on wine labels or not. But we expect the number of wines in the more rigid *organic wine* category to remain small, because of the sulfur dioxide restriction.

What Is a Wine Expert?

A wine expert is someone with a high level of knowledge about wine in general, including grape growing, winemaking, and the various wines of the world. A wine expert also has a high degree of skill in tasting wine.

Until fairly recently, most wine experts in the United States gained their expertise through informal study, work experience, or experience gained as *amateurs* (lovers) of wine. Although accredited wine courses did exist, they were university programs in *enology* (winemaking) and *viticulture* (grape growing) — valuable for people who plan to become winemakers or grape growers but scientific overkill for people whose goal is breadth of knowledge about wine.

Today, many people become wine experts through the programs of the Wine & Spirit Education Trust (or WSET; `www.wsetglobal.com`), or various professional sommelier organizations, which include examinations at the end of study. Some examinations entitle successful students to use letters after their names, such as CWE (Certified Wine Educator), MS (Master Sommelier), or MW (Master of Wine). MW is the oldest and most difficult credential for wine experts to earn.

Some people who write about wine or sell wine are truly experts in a particular aspect of wine, such as Spanish wines or Champagne, even if they hold no third-party credentials.

Today, when the digital channels for sharing information and experience about wine are so numerous, enthusiasm and passion often count for more than expertise does, which brings to mind a definition of *wine expert* that a friend of ours used to love: A wine expert is someone who knows more on the subject than you do!

How Do I Know When to Drink the Special Older Wines I've Been Keeping?

Unfortunately, no precise answer to this question exists because all wines age at a different pace. The aging curve of a wine is highly dependent on storage conditions. And even two bottles of the same wine that are stored under the same conditions can age differently.

When you have a specific wine in mind, you can get advice about its readiness to drink in several different ways:

- ✔ Consult the comments of critics, like Robert Parker, Michael Broadbent, or Steve Tanzer, who almost always list a suggested drinking period for wines they review in their newsletters and books (listed in Chapter 18); their educated guesses are usually quite reliable.

- ✔ Contact the winery; in the case of fine, older vintages, the winemaker and his staff are usually happy to give you their opinion on the best time to drink their wine — and they typically have more experience with the wine than anyone else.

- ✔ If you have several bottles of the same wine, try one from time to time to see how the wine is developing. Your own taste is really the best guide — you may enjoy the wine younger or older than the experts.

Do Old Wines Require Special Handling?

Like humans, wine can become somewhat fragile in its later years. For one thing, old wine doesn't like to travel. If you must move old wine, give it several days' rest before opening the bottle. (Red Burgundies and other Pinot Noirs are especially disturbed by journeys.)

Older wines, with their delicate bouquet and flavors, can easily be overwhelmed by strongly flavored foods. Simple cuts of meat or just hard cheeses and good, crusty bread are usually fine companions for mature wines.

If you're going to drink an older wine, don't over-chill it (whether it's white or red). Older wines show their best at moderate temperatures. Temperatures below 60 degrees Fahrenheit (15.5 degrees Celsius) inhibit development in the glass.

Decant red wines or Vintage Ports to separate the clear wine from any sediment that formed in the bottle. (For tips on decanting, see Chapter 8.) Stand the bottle up two or three days before you plan to open it so that the sediment can drift to the bottom. An important concern in decanting an old wine is giving the wine *too* much aeration: A wine in its last stages will deteriorate rapidly upon exposure to air, often within a half hour — sometimes in 10 or 15 minutes.

When you decant an old wine, taste it immediately and be prepared to drink it rapidly if it shows signs of fading.

Chapter 21

Ten Wine Myths Demystified

As you leaf through the pages of this chapter, you'll probably recognize several of the myths we mention. They all represent common thinking — and common misinformation — about wine. But don't worry: We set the record straight.

The Best Wines Are Varietal Wines

One advantage of *varietal wines* — wines named after a grape variety, such as Chardonnay or Merlot — is that you supposedly know what you're getting. (Actually, for most American wines, only 75 percent of the wine has to come from the named variety, and for most other wines, only 85 percent — so you don't know *exactly* what you're getting.) However, the presence of a grape variety name on the label, even a top-quality variety, such as Cabernet Sauvignon, tells you nothing about the quality of the wine.

Varietal wines range in quality from ordinary to excellent. Wines named in other ways (for their region of production or with a fantasy name) also range in quality from ordinary to excellent. Varietal wines in general are no better and no worse than other wines. (See Chapter 4 for more information about varietal wines.)

A More Expensive Wine Is a Wiser Choice

For wine, as for many other products, a high price often indicates high quality. Purchasing a high-priced wine shows others that you can afford "the very best" and that you have good taste. But for sheer pleasure, an expensive wine is rarely the best choice. For one thing, the highest quality isn't itself the best criterion for choosing a wine, for the following reasons:

- ✔ Your taste is personal, and you may not like a wine that critics consider very high in quality.
- ✔ Not all situations call for a very high-quality wine.

We certainly can enjoy a $10 to $12 wine in many circumstances. At large family gatherings, on picnics, at the beach, and so on, an expensive, top-quality wine can be out of place — too serious and important.

Likewise, the very finest wines are seldom the best choices in restaurants — considering typical restaurant prices. Instead, we look for the best value on the wine list (keeping in mind what we're eating), or we experiment with some moderately priced wine that we haven't tried before. (There will *always* be some wines you haven't tried.)

Quality isn't the only consideration in choosing a wine. Often, the best wine of all for your taste, or for a certain situation, will be inexpensive.

A Screw Cap Closure Indicates a Lower-Quality Wine

Not all that long ago, this statement was true, but that is no longer the case. Screw-off caps are still the closure on large "jug" bottles of those old-fashioned, really inexpensive domestic wines, but that type of wine is a dying breed. Meanwhile, sleek and modern screw-off caps have come on the scene as the closure of choice on many bottles of fine wine, especially white wines, from all over the world.

Winemakers know that using a metal cap to close their bottles can eliminate the risk of wine spoilage due to blighted corks, and thus solve a major quality-control issue for the wine industry. But many initially had concerns about how their wines would age with that type of closure. Research in New Zealand has now proven that wines can age and develop in bottles closed with screw caps, as wine does in cork-sealed bottles. Today's screw-cap closures are attractive, they're easy for wine drinkers to use, and they protect the wine from cork taint — all good reasons for winemakers to embrace them.

For now, you can find screw-cap closures on wines from New Zealand and Australia, on bottles of white wines (even high-quality whites) from many other countries, and on inexpensive and mid-priced bottles of red wines. You won't find screw caps on bottles of many red wines from classic European wine regions because, in some cases, the local regulations haven't caught up with scientific progress. And many of the world's most elite wine producers continue to favor the traditional closure — the cork.

When you encounter a wine with a screw-off cap, know that you have a wine from a conscientious producer who wants to protect his wine from off flavors that could derive from a cork.

Red Wines Are More Sophisticated than White Wines

We know: Something about red wine just says "serious." Maybe that's because many people enjoy white wines when they first start drinking wine, and then with experience, they progress to red wine. And good for them, if that's what they enjoy. But we can assure you from personal experience that, after years of drinking more red wine than white, many serious wine lovers rediscover the unique virtues of white wines, such as their compatibility with light meals and their easier drinkability. And some white wines can be serious indeed!

A corollary of this myth is, "The darker the red wine, the better." Many red wines today are extremely deep in color, almost to the point of being black rather than red. An opaque appearance in a red wine suggests that the wine's aromas and flavors are as concentrated as its color is, and for that reason, some people have begun to equate deep color with high quality.

Although it's true that some very great red wines have deep color, other great red wines don't. Wines made from lightly pigmented grape varieties, such as Pinot Noir, Nebbiolo, and Sangiovese, for example, will never be naturally opaque in color, yet they can certainly be great.

Winemakers today have ways of artificially deepening the color of red wines; therefore, even cheap, everyday wines can be deep in color if the winemaker wants to make them that way. Don't be fooled into thinking that dark equals high quality.

Whether you're deciding between red wine and white or judging the appearance of a particular red wine, dark color is no indication of quality and no measure of your good taste. Drink what you like.

White Wine Goes with Fish, Red Wine Goes with Meat

As guidelines go, this one isn't bad. But we said *guideline*, not rule. Anyone who slavishly adheres to this generalization deserves the boredom of eating and drinking exactly the same thing every day of his life!

Do you want a glass of white wine with your burger? Go ahead, order it. You're the one who's doing the eating and drinking, not your friend and not the server who's taking your order.

Even if you're a perfectionist who's always looking for the ideal food and wine combination, you'll find yourself wandering from this guideline. The best wine for a grilled salmon steak is probably red — like a Pinot Noir or a Bardolino — and not white at all. Veal and pork do equally well with red or white wines, depending on how the dish is prepared. And what can be better with hot dogs on the grill than a cold glass of rosé?

No one is going to arrest you if you have white wine with everything, or red wine with everything, or even Champagne with everything! No rules exist. (We offer a few additional suggestions for possible wine-food pairings in Chapter 9.)

Number Ratings Don't Lie

Turning to critics for advice is natural. We do it all the time — when we're deciding which movie to see, when we're choosing a new restaurant to try, or when we're wanting to find out what someone else thinks of a particular book.

In most cases, we weigh the critics' opinions against our own experience and tastes. Say a steakhouse just got three stars and a fabulous review from the dining critic. Do we rush to the telephone to make a reservation? Not if we don't like red meat! When the movie critics give two thumbs up, do we automatically assume that we'll like the movie — or do we listen to their commentary and decide whether the movie may be too violent, silly, or serious for us? You know the answer to that.

Yet when many wine drinkers hear that a wine just received a 90-plus points rating from a wine critic, they go out of their way to get that wine. The curiosity to try a wine that scores well is understandable. But the rigid belief that such a wine is (a) necessarily a great wine and (b) a wine you'll like is simply misguided.

The critics' scores are nothing more than the critics' professional opinion — and opinion, like taste, is *always* personal. (Chapter 19 tells you more about scoring wine.)

The Quality of a Wine Is Objectively Measurable

As wine critics, we constantly judge the quality of individual wines. Besides scribbling positive or negative comments about the wine's concentration or finesse or whatever, we quantify the quality by giving the wine a score. Usually, we're more or less in agreement with each other and our scores are fairly close, which reinforces the notion that we've properly pegged the quality of the wine. What we've actually pegged, however, is our individual and collective *impression* of the wine's quality.

If human beings were machines, maybe a person could taste a wine and, with repeated and reproducible accuracy, ascribe a quality ranking to that wine. As it is, however, the equipment we have to work with (our noses, mouths, and brains) is personal and varies in performance from one individual to the next. The experience of wine is always subjective, and the quality statement given to a wine is, therefore, always subjective.

Everything about the wine-tasting experience influences your subjective impression of a wine's taste. For example, the weather, your mood, and the ambiance of the situation all affect your reaction to a wine. Not only that: One bottle of a wine can be subtly different from another bottle of the same wine, and the same wine in a different glass can taste different. Not even the world's greatest experts can objectively measure the quality of a wine.

Wine Authorities Are Experts

Wine is an incredibly vast subject. It involves biochemistry, botany, geology, chemistry, climatology, history, culture, politics, laws, and business. How can anyone be an expert in all of that? To compound the problem, some people in authoritative positions within the wine field may have had little, if any, education, training, or background in wine before being thrust into situations, such as wine sales or critical commentary, that imply expertise.

Different aspects of wine appeal to different people. Depending on what they particularly like about wine, people tend to specialize in some of wine's disciplines at the expense of others. (Now you know why it takes two of us to write this book.)

Don't expect any one person to be able to answer all your questions about wine in the most accurate and up-to-date manner. Just like doctors and lawyers, wine professionals specialize. They have to.

Old Wines Are Good Wines

The idea of rare old bottles of wine being auctioned off for tens of thousands of dollars apiece, like fine art, is fascinating enough to capture anyone's imagination. But valuable old bottles of wine are even rarer than valuable old coins because, unlike coins, wine is perishable.

The huge majority of the world's wines don't have what it takes to age for decades. Most wines are meant to be enjoyed in the first one to five years of their lives. Even those wines that have the potential to develop slowly over many years will achieve their potential only if they're properly stored. (See Chapter 17 for information on storing wines.)

The purpose of wine is to be enjoyed — usually, sooner rather than later.

Champagnes Don't Age

We don't know who started this myth; to the contrary, Champagne *does* age well! Depending on the particular year, Vintage Champagne can age especially well. We've enjoyed two outstanding 1928 Vintage Champagnes, Krug and Moët & Chandon Dom Pérignon, neither of which showed any sign of decline. The oldest Champagne we've ever tasted, a 1900 Pol Roger, was also in fine shape.

But Champagne demands excellent storage. If kept in a cool, dark, humid place, many Champagnes can age for decades, especially in the great vintages. They lose some effervescence but take on a complexity of flavor somewhat similar to fine white Burgundy. Champagnes in magnum bottles (1.5 liters) generally age better than those in regular size (750 milliliters) bottles.

If you want to try some very fine, reliable, older bottles of Vintage Champagne, look for either Krug or Salon in the 1964, 1969, 1976, or 1979 vintage. If stored well, they'll be magnificent. Dom Pérignon is also reliable — the 1961 and 1969 are legendary.

The following houses produce Champagnes known to age well:

- ✔ **Krug:** All its Champagnes are remarkably long lived.
- ✔ **Pol Roger:** Especially Cuvée Sir Winston Churchill.
- ✔ **Moët & Chandon:** Cuvée Dom Pérignon, ageless when well stored.
- ✔ **Louis Roederer:** Cristal, Cristal Rosé, and Vintage Brut all age well.
- ✔ **Bollinger:** All its Champagnes, especially the Grande Année.
- ✔ **Gosset:** Grand Millésime and Celebris.
- ✔ **Salon:** Remarkable Blanc de Blancs; needs at least 15 years of aging.
- ✔ **Veuve Clicquot:** La Grande Dame and the Vintage Brut.
- ✔ **Taittinger:** Its Blanc de Blancs (Comtes de Champagne).
- ✔ **Billecart-Salmon:** The Vintage Blanc de Blancs.
- ✔ **Pommery:** Cuvée Louise.
- ✔ **Laurent-Perrier:** Cuvée Grand Siècle.
- ✔ **Philipponnat:** Clos des Goisses.

Recent great, age-worthy vintages for Champagne are 2002, 1996, 1988, 1985, 1982, and 1979. See Chapter 15 for more information on Champagne and other sparkling wines.

Part VIII
Appendixes

The 5th Wave   By Rich Tennant

"Wine reminds me of the opera. I enjoy it
even though I don't always understand
what's being said."

In this part . . .

We give you some useful tools of the trade in this part, like an extensive pronunciation guide to wine terms and names, a glossary of wine terms, and a vintage wine chart. (We were going to include a listing of every winery in the world that makes Chardonnay, but we ran out of space.)

Appendix A

Pronunciation Guide to Wine Terms

● ●

*N*othing will set a wine snob on your case more quickly than a mispronounced name of a famous wine or wine region. In order not to give snobs their smug satisfaction, we provide pronunciations of dozens of words here, for easy reference. This list is not exhaustive, however; the pronunciations of other, less common names and terms appear throughout this book. We place accented syllables, if any, in italics.

Name or term = Pronunciation
Agiorghitiko = eye-your-*yee*-tee-koe
Aglianico del Vulture = ah-lee-*ahn*-ee-coh del *vul*-toor-ay
Albariño = ahl-bah-*ree*-nyoh
Aligoté = ah-lee-go-tay
Aloxe-Corton = ah-luss-cor-tohn
Alsace = al-zass
(Alto)-Adige = *ah*-dee-jhae
amontillado = ah-moan-tee-*yah*-doh
Anjou = ahn-jhew
Arneis = ahr-*nase*
Assyrtiko = ah-*seer*-tee-koe
Au Bon Climat = oh bone klee-maht
Auslese = *ouse*-lay-seh
Auxerrois = aus-ser-whah
Auxey-Duresses = awk-see-duh-ress
Barbaresco = bar-bah-*res*-co

Name or term = Pronunciation
Barbera = bar-*bear*-ah
Barolo = bah-*ro*-lo
Batard-Montrachet = bah-tar-mon-rah-shay
Beaujolais = boh-jhoe-lay
Beaulieu (Vineyards) = bo-l'youh
Bianco di Custoza = bee-*ahn*-coh dee cus-*toez*-ah
Blanchot = blahn-shoh
botrytis = boh-*try*-tis
Bougros = boo-groh
Bourgogne = boor-guh-nyuh
Bourgueil = boor-guh'y
Brouilly = broo-yee
Brunello di Montalcino = brew-*nel*-lo dee mon-tahl-*chee*-no
brut = brute

(continued)

Name or term = Pronunciation
Cabernet Sauvignon = cab-er-nay saw-vee-nyon
Canaiolo = cahn-eye-*oh*-loh
Carmignano = car-mee-*nyah*-no
Chablis = shah-blee
Chardonnay = shar-dohn-nay
Chassagne-Montrachet = shah-sah-nyuh-mon-rah-shay
(Château de) Fieuzal = fee-oo-zahl
(Château) Grillet = gree-yay
(Château) Haut-Brion = oh-bree-ohn
(Château) Lafite-Rothschild = lah-feet-roth-sheeld
(Château) Margaux = mahr-go
(Château) Mouton-Rothschild = moo-tohn-roth-sheeld
(Château) Petrus = peh-troos
(Château) Trotanoy = trot-ahn-wah
Châteauneuf-du-Pape = shah-toe-nuf-doo-pahp
Chénas = shay-nahs
Chenin Blanc = shen-in blahnk
Chevalier-Montrachet = sheh-vah-lyay-mon-rah-shay
Chianti = key-*ahn*-tee
(Chianti) Rufina = *roo*-fee-nah
Chinon = she-nohn
Chiroubles = sheh-roob-leh
Clos du Val = clo dew val
Colheita = col-*yay*-tah
Condrieu = cohn-dree-uh
Corton-Charlemagne = cor-tawn-shahr-luh-mahn

Name or term = Pronunciation
Côte de Beaune = coat deh bone
Côte Chalonnaise = coat shal-oh-naze
Côte d'Or = coat dor
Côte de Nuits = coat deh nwee
Côte de Nuits-Villages = coat deh nwee-vee-lahj
Côte-Rôtie = coat-roe-tee
Côtes du Ventoux = coat due vahn-too
cuvée = coo-vay
Dolcetto = dohl-*chet*-oh
(Domaine) Leroy = lay-wah
Eisele Vineyard = *eye*-seh-lee
Entre-Deux-Mers = ahn-truh-duh-mair
Fleurie = flehr-ee
Fourchaume = for-chahm
Friulano = free-ou-*lah*-noh
Friuli-Venezia Giulia = free-*oo*-lee-veh-*netz*-ee-ah *joo*-lee-ah
Galicia = gah-*leeth*-ee-ah
Garrafeira = gar-ah-*fay*-ah
Gattinara = gah-tee-*nah*-rah
Gavi = *gah*-vee
Genevrières = jen-ev-ree-aire
Gewürztraminer = geh-*vairtz*-trah-mee-ner
Gigondas = jhee-gohn-dahs
Givry = gee-vree
Grands Crus Classés = grahn crew clas-say
Graves = grahv
Grenouilles = greh-n'wee
Grüner Veltliner = *grew*-ner *velt*-lee-ner
halbtrocken = *hahlb*-tro-ken
Haut-Médoc = oh-may-doc

Name or term = Pronunciation
Hermitage = er-mee-tahj
Juliénas = jhool-yay-nahs
Languedoc-Roussillon = lahn-gweh-doc-roo-see-yohn
Les Clos = lay cloh
Les Forêts = lay for-ay
Les Preuses = lay preuhz
Liebfraumilch = *leeb*-frow-milsh
Listrac = lee-strahk
Loire = l'wahr
Mâcon-Villages = mah-cawn-vee-lahj
Malvasia = mal-va-*see*-ah
Margaux = mahr-go
Médoc = meh-doc
Menetou-Salon = meh-neh-too-sah-lohn
Mercurey = mer-cure-ay
Merlot = mer-loh
Meursault = muhr-so
Moët = moh-ett
Mont de Milieu = mon deh meh-lyew
Montagny = mon-tah-nyee
Montepulciano d'Abruzzo = mon-tae-pul-chee-*ah*-noh dah-*brute*-zoh
Monthélie = mohn-teh-lee
Montlouis = mon-loo-wee
Montmains = mon-man
Montrachet = mon-rah-shay
Moschofilero = mos-cho-*feel*-eh-roe
Mosel = *moh*-zel
Moulin-à-Vent = moo-lahn-ah-vahn
Moulis = moo-lees
Müller-Thurgau = *mool*-lair-*toor*-gow
Muscadet = moos-cah-day

Name or term = Pronunciation
Muscat = moos-caht
Nahe = *nah*-heh
Nantais = nahn-tay
Nebbiolo = neb-bee-*oh*-lo
Niebaum-Coppola = *nee*-baum-*cope*-poh-lah
Niederosterreich = nee-der-*oz*-ter-ryke
Nuits-St.-Georges = nwee-san-johrj
Orvieto = or-vee-*ae*-toh
Pauillac = poy-yac
Pays d'Oc = pay-ee doc
Penedés = pen-eh-*dais*
Pernand-Vergelesses = per-nahn-ver-jeh-less
Perrier-Jouët = per-ree-yay-joo-ett
Pessac-Léognan = pay-sac-lay-oh-nyahn
Pfalz = fallz
Pinot Bianco = pee-noh bee-*ahn*-coh
Pinot Blanc = pee-noh blahnk
Pinot Grigio = pee-noh *gree*-joe
Pinot Gris = pee-noh gree
Pinot Noir = pee-noh nwahr
Pinotage = pee-noh *tahj*
Pouilly-Fuissé = pwee-fwee-say
Pouilly-Fumé = pwee-foo-may
Premier Cru = prem-yay crew
Priorato = pree-oh-*rah*-to
Puligny-Montrachet = poo-lee-nyee-mon-rah-shay
Qualitätswein = *kal*-ee-tates-vine
Quincy = can-see
Quinta = *keen*-ta
Regnie = ray-nyay

(continued)

Name or term = Pronunciation
Reuilly = reuh-yee
Rheingau = *ryne*-gow
Rheinhessen = *ryne*-hess-ehn
Rías Baixas = *ree*-ahse *byche*-ahse
Ribera del Duero = ree-*bear*-ah del *dwair*-oh
Ribolla Gialla = ree-*bohl*-lah *jahl*-lah
Riesling = *reese*-ling
Rioja = ree-*oh*-hah
Rueda = roo-*ae*-dah
Rully = rouh-yee
Saint-Amour = sant-ah-more
St.-Aubin = sant-oh-ban
St.-Nicolas-de-Bourgueil = san-nee-co-lah-deh-boor-guh'y
St.-Romain = san-roh-man
St.-Véran = san-veh-rahn
Sancerre = sahn-sair
Sangiovese = san-joe-*vae*-sae
Saumur = soh-muhr
Sauvignon Blanc = saw-vee-nyon blahnk
Savennieres = sah-ven-nyair
Savigny-lès-Beaune = sah-vee-nyee-lay-bone
Scheurebe = *shoy*-reb-beh
Semillon = *sem*-eh-lon (Australian)
Sémillon = seh-mee-yohn (French)
Sèvre-et-Maine = sev'r-et-mehn
Soave = so-*ah*-vay
Spanna = *spah*-nah
Spätlese = *shpate*-lay-seh
spumante = spoo-*mahn*-tay
St-Estèphe = sant-eh-steff

Name or term = Pronunciation
St.-Julien = san-jhoo-lee-ehn
St.-Emilion = sant-ay-meal-yon
Steiermark = *sty*-er-mark
Tempranillo = tem-prah-*nee*-yoh
Tinto = *teen*-toe
Tokaj-Hegyalja = toe-*kye*-heh-*jah*-yah
Torgiano = tor-gee-*ah*-no
Tre Venezie = trae veh-*netz*-ee-ae
Trebbiano = treb-bee-*ah*-noh
trocken = *troh*-ken
Vacqueyras = vah-keh-rahs
Vaillons = vye-yon
Valmur = vahl-moor
Valpolicella = val-po-lee-*chel*-lah
Vaudésir = voh-deh-zeer
Vendange Tardive = vahn-dahnj tahr-deev
Veneto = *ven*-eh-toh
Verdejo = ver-*day*-ho
Verdicchio = ver-*dee*-key-oh
Vernaccia di San Gimignano = ver-*nah*-cha dee san gee-mee-*nyah*-noh
Vinho = *veen*-yo
Vinho Verde = *veen*-yo *vaird*
(Vino) Nobile di Montepulciano = *no*-be-lay dee mon-tay-pul-chee-*ah*-no
Viognier = vee-oh-nyay
Vosne-Romanée = vone-roh-mah-nay
Vouvray = voo-vray
Wachau = va-*cow*
Weissburgunder = *vice*-boor-gun-der
Wien = vee-*en*
Willamette (Valley) = wil-*lam*-et
Xinomavro = ksee-*no*-mav-roe

Appendix B

Glossary of Wine Terms

. . . .

*H*ere, for handy reference, are definitions of dozens of the most common wine terms and wine-tasting terms.

acidity: A component of wine, generally consisting of tartaric acid (a natural acid in grapes) and comprising approximately 0.5 to 0.7 percent of the wine by volume.

aerate: To expose wine to air in preparation for drinking it, usually with the intention of allowing the most attractive aromas to reveal themselves in an older wine or softening the harshness of a younger wine.

alcohol level: The percentage of alcohol by volume that a wine has; most white wines have an alcohol level between 9 and 14 percent, and most red wines have an alcohol level between 12 and 15 percent.

American oak: Oak wood from a U.S. forest, of the species *quercus alba,* and the barrels made from such wood; some winemakers in certain wine regions (such as some in Spain and Australia) favor American oak for aging their wines.

ample: A descriptor for wines that give the impression of being full and expansive in your mouth.

AOC: Abbreviation for *Appellation d'Origine Contrôlée,* sometimes shortened to *Appellation Contrôlée* and abbreviated as AC; translates to "protected place-name"; France's original official category for its highest-ranking types of wine, whose name, origin, grape varieties, and other defining factors are regulated by law.

AOP: Abbreviation for *Appellation d'Origine Protégée*, the term that is equivalent to AOC in the European Union's new Designation of Origin system.

appellation: Name; often used to mean the official geographic origin of a wine, which is part of a wine's official name.

aroma: The smell of a wine. Some purists use the term *aroma* only for the straightforward, youthful smells of a wine, and use the term *bouquet* for the more complex smells of an aged wine. But we use *aroma* as a general term for all wine smells.

aromatic: A descriptor for a wine that has a pronounced smell, used particularly in reference to fruity and floral smells. Some white grape varieties are also dubbed *aromatic* because they are strong in aroma compounds.

aromatic compounds: Those substances in wine — derived from the grapes, from winemaking, or from aging — that are responsible for a wine's aromas and flavors.

astringent: A descriptor for the mouth-puckering, pore-tightening tactile character of some wines, caused by tannin, acid, or the combination of both. Generally not a positive trait.

attack: The first impression a wine gives you when you taste it. A wine's attack is related to sensations in the front of your mouth.

balance: The interrelationship of a wine's alcohol, residual sugar (if any), acid, and tannin; when no one component stands out obtrusively in your mouth, a wine is said to be well balanced; wines can also have balance between their aromas/flavors and their structure.

barrel: A relatively small wooden container for fermenting and/or aging wine, generally 60 gallons in size and generally made of oak.

barrel-aged: A term that applies to wines that are fermented in containers of inert material, such as stainless steel, and subsequently placed into wooden barrels for a period of maturation; the term also applies to the maturation period of wines that also fermented in the barrel.

barrel-fermented: A term that applies to white wines that are fermented in oak barrels; the oaky character of such wines is generally more subtle than that of wines that have been merely barrel-aged.

big: A general descriptor for wines that are either very full or very intense.

black fruits: A general term for wine aromas and flavors that suggest blackberries, blueberries, black cherries, black currants, or other black fruits.

black grapes: Wine grapes that have a reddish or blue pigmentation in their skins; used to make red wine.

blend: To mix together two or more individual lots of wine, usually wines from different grape varieties (but also applies to wines from different vineyards, different regions, or different vintages); a wine derived from the juice of different grape varieties is called a blend.

bodega: A winery in Spain; also the Spanish word for a building where wine is stored.

body: The impression of a wine's weight in your mouth. A wine's body is generally described as light, medium, or full.

bottle-age: Maturation of a wine after it has been bottled; most wines undergo a short period of bottle-age at the winery before release; fine wines can require additional bottle-age from the consumer.

bouquet: An evolved, complex, mature aroma.

bright: Indicates a wine whose characteristics are perceived as vivid by the senses. A wine can be visually bright, or it can have bright aromas and flavors; in both cases, the opposite is dull.

cask: A relatively large wooden container for making or storing wine.

castello: Italian for *castle;* refers to a wine estate.

cedary: Having aromas or flavors that resemble the smell of cedar wood.

character: An anthropomorphic descriptor for wines that give the impression of having substance and integrity.

charry: Having aromas or flavors that suggest burnt wood or charred wood.

château: A French name for a grand winery estate, commonly used in the Bordeaux region as well as other regions.

classico: An Italian term applicable to certain DOC/DOCG (or PDO) wines whose vineyards are situated in the original, classic part of the territory for that particular type of wine.

clone: A subvariety of a grape variety; a vine, or set of genetically identical vines, that exhibits characteristics specific to it as compared to other vines of the same variety.

colheita: Vintage, in Portuguese.

commune: A village, and its surrounding vineyard territory.

compact: A descriptor for wines that give the impression of being tight and concentrated, but not full.

complex: Having a multiplicity of aromas and flavors.

concentrated: A descriptor for wines with aromas and flavors that are dense rather than dilute.

concentration: A characteristic of wines whose flavors are tightly knit as opposed to being dilute or watery.

cosecha: Vintage, in Spanish.

crisp: A wine that feels clean and slightly brittle in your mouth; the opposite of *soft*. Crispness is usually the result of high acidity, and crisp wines, therefore, are usually relatively light in body and go well with food.

decant: To transfer wine from a bottle to another container, either for the purpose of aerating the wine or to separate a red wine from its sediment.

depth: A characteristic of fine wines that give the impression of having many layers of taste, rather than being flat and one-dimensional; a positive trait.

dilute: A descriptor for wines whose aromas and flavors are thin and watery, as opposed to concentrated; a negative characteristic.

district: A geographic entity more specific than a region and less specific than a commune.

DO: Abbreviation for *Denominación de Origen,* which translates to "place-name"; Spain's original, official category for wines whose name, origin, grape varieties, and other defining factors are regulated by law. Also an abbreviation for Portugal's highest official wine category, *Denominação de Origem,* translated similarly and having the same meaning.

DOC: Abbreviation for *Denominazione di Origine Controllata,* which translates to "controlled place-name"; Italy's original, official category for wines whose name, origin, grape varieties, and other defining factors are regulated by law. Also an abbreviation for *Denominacão de Origem Controlada,* Portugal's similar phrase.

DOCa: Abbreviation for *Denominación de Origen Calificada*, which is Spain's original category for wine regions of the highest status.

DOCG: Abbreviation for *Denominazione di Origine Controllata e Garantita,* which translates to "controlled and guaranteed place-name"; Italy's official category for its highest-ranking wines.

domaine: A French term for wine estate, commonly used in the Burgundy region.

DOP: Abbreviation for *Denominazione di Origine Protetta*, Italy's category in the new E.U. system of designating wine origin that encompasses DOC and DOCG wines; in Spanish, an abbreviation for *Denominación de Origen Protegida,* which is, in the new E.U. framework, Spain's category encompassing DO and DOCa wines; and in Portuguese, abbreviation for *Denominação de Origem Protegida*, Portugal's similar phrase.

dry: A wine that is not sweet. The word *dry* can also describe the texture of a wine that feels rough in your mouth, as in *dry texture* or *dry mouthfeel.* But when used alone, it refers specifically to lack of sweetness.

dull: A wine whose expression is muddled and unclear. This term can apply to a wine's appearance, to its aromas and flavors, or to its general style. It is a negative characteristic.

earthy: Having aromas and flavors that suggest earth, such as wet soil, dry earth, certain minerally aromas, and so forth. This term is sometimes used as a euphemism for wines that are rustic and lack refinement.

elegance: A somewhat overused descriptor for wines that express themselves in a fine or delicate manner as opposed to an intense or forceful way — considered a positive trait.

estate: A property that grows grapes and produces wines from its own vineyards; wines labeled *estate-bottled* are made from vineyards owned by (or in some cases, under the direct control of) the same entity that owns the winery and makes the wine; use of the term is regulated by law in most areas.

fermentation: The natural process by which the sugar in grape juice is transformed into alcohol (and the juice is, thus, transformed into wine) through the action of yeasts.

finish: The final impressions a wine gives in the rear of your mouth after you have swallowed it or spat it out; aftertaste.

firm: A descriptor for wines that are not soft but are not harsh and tough; generally relates to the tannic content of a red wine or the acidity of a white wine.

flabby: A pejorative term used to describe wines that taste too soft, generally due to a lack of acidity or tannin.

flavor intensity: The degree to which a wine's flavors are pronounced and easily perceived.

flavors: Aromatic constituents of a wine that are perceived in the mouth.

fleshy: A descriptor for a rich textural or tactile impression of some wines.

fortified wine: A wine that has had alcohol added to it.

French oak: Oak wood from the forests of France, of the species *quercus robur,* considered the finest type of oak for aging most white wines; the barrels made from such wood.

fruit character: Those characteristics of a wine that derive from the grapes, such as a wine's aromas and flavors.

fruity: Having aromas and flavors suggestive of fruit. This is a broad descriptor; in some cases, the fruity aroma or flavor of a wine can be described more precisely as suggestive of fresh fruit, dried fruit, or cooked fruit, or even more precisely as a specific fresh, dried, or cooked fruit, such as fresh apples, dried figs, or strawberry jam.

full: A descriptor for wines that give the impression of being large and weighty in your mouth. A wine's fullness can derive from high alcohol or from other aspects of the wine. A wine can be pleasantly full or too full, depending on one's taste preferences.

garrafeira: A Portuguese term for a reserva wine with specific aging requirements — for red wines, at least three years of aging in oak and bottle before release.

generous: A descriptor for wines whose characteristics are expressive and easy to perceive; usually describes fuller, rounder styles.

gran reserva: On Spanish red wines, a term indicating a wine that has aged at least five years before release, at least two of which were in oak.

grape tannin: Those tannins in a red wine that come from the grapes from which the wine was made, usually from the grapes' skins.

grape variety: A distinct type of grape within a species.

harmonious: A flattering descriptor for wines that are well balanced and also express themselves in a particularly graceful manner.

herbal: Having aromas and flavors that suggest herbs, such as fresh herbs, dried herbs, or specific herbs (rosemary, thyme, tarragon, and so forth).

IGP: Abbreviation for the French, Italian and Spanish phrases that mean "protected geographic indication," the E.U.'s secondary and looser category of place-name classification.

IGT: Abbreviation for the phrase that indicates Italy's original, lower tier of protected appellations for wine; translates as "typical geographic indication."

intense: Usually used in reference to a wine's aromas and flavors, to describe the volume of those aromas or flavors — how pronounced the smell of lemon is in the wine, for example, or how flavorful the wine is.

lees: Grape solids and dead yeast cells that precipitate to the bottom of a wine vessel after fermentation.

length: A characteristic of fine wines that give a sustained sensory impression across the length of the tongue.

maceration: The process of soaking the skins of red grapes in their grape juice to leach the skins' color, tannin, and other substances into the juice.

malolactic fermentation: A natural conversion of harsh malic acid into milder lactic acid, which weakens the total acidity of a wine; an optional process in white wine production.

maturation: The aging period at the winery during which a wine evolves to a state of readiness for bottling or for shipping; the process of development and evolution that fine wines undergo after they are bottled.

medium-dry: A term to indicate the perceived sweetness of wines that are very slightly sweet.

medium-sweet: A term to indicate the perceived sweetness level of wines that are sweeter than medium-dry, but not fully sweet.

minerally: Having aromas or flavors that suggest minerals (as opposed to organic substances, such as plants or animals). This is a broad descriptor; in some cases, the minerally aroma or flavor of a wine can be described more precisely as suggestive of chalk, iron, steel, and so forth.

new oak: Oak barrels that are used for the first time in making a particular wine; sometimes called *"first use"* oak.

New World: Collective term for those winemaking countries of the world that are situated outside of Europe.

nutty: Having aromas or flavors that suggest nuts. This is a broad descriptor; in some cases, the nutty aroma or flavor of a wine can be described more precisely as suggestive of roasted nuts, toasted nuts, nut butter, or cashews, almonds, hazelnuts, and so forth.

oaky: Having characteristics that derive from oak, such as toastiness, smokiness, a charry smell or flavor, vanilla aroma, or a higher tannin level than the wine might otherwise have. Usually, these oaky characteristics occur as the wine ages in oak barrels, but in very inexpensive wines, they may have been added as an actual flavoring.

off-dry: A generalized term for wines that are neither fully dry nor very sweet.

old oak: Oak barrels or casks that are old enough to have lost most of their oaky character, generally 3 years old and older.

old vines: An unregulated term for grape vines whose fruit quality presumably is quite good due to the fact the vines are old — generally 40 years old or older — and therefore produce a very small crop of concentrated grapes.

Old World: Collective term for the winemaking countries of Europe.

palate: A term used by wine tasters as a synonym for "mouth," or to refer to the characteristics of a wine that manifest in the taster's mouth.

PDO: Abbreviation for *Protected Denomination of Origin,* the E.U.'s higher category for wines with protected placenames.

petrol: Having aromas or flavors that suggest diesel fuel; can be a positive trait.

PGI: Abbreviation for *Protected Geographic Indication,* the E.U.'s lower category for wines from officially recognized regions.

phylloxera: A parasite louse that feeds on the roots of Vitis vinifera grape vines, resulting in the vines' premature death.

plummy: Having aromas or flavors that suggest ripe plums.

powerful: An anthropomorphic descriptor for wines that convey an impression of strength and intensity.

pretty: An anthropomorphic descriptor for wines that are attractive for their delicacy and finesse.

primary aromas: Fresh aromas in a wine that derive from the grapes used to make that wine.

region: A geographical entity less specific than a district but more specific than a country; for Italian wines, the term *region* applies to the political entity as well as to the wine zones within that area.

reserva: On a Spanish wine, a term indicating that the wine has aged longer at the winery (usually some specified combination of oak aging and bottle aging) than a non-reserva version of the same type of wine; red reserva wines must age at least three years (with a year in oak) before release. On a Portuguese wine, a wine of superior quality from a single vintage.

reserve: A designation for wines that are presumably finer than the non-reserve (normal) version of the same wine; use of the term is unregulated in the United States and in France.

residual sugar: Sugar remaining in the wine after fermentation.

rich: A descriptor of wines that offer an abundance of flavor, texture, or other sensory perceptions.

riserva: Italian word for *reserve,* indicating a wine that has aged longer before release from the winery than a non-reserve version of the same type of wine, and suggesting higher quality; whether a wine may use this term and the conditions of use are defined by individual DOC regulations.

round: A descriptor for wines that are perceived in the mouth to be neither flat nor angular. Roundness relates to the wine's structure — that is, its particular makeup of acid, tannin, sweetness, and alcohol, which dictates texture and mouthfeel.

second-label wine: A less-expensive, second wine (or a second brand of wine) made by a winery from grapes or wine not considered worthy of the winery's primary label.

sediment: The solid residue in a bottle of red wine that forms as the wine matures.

serious: A metaphorical descriptor for a wine that is of high quality, as opposed to a popularly styled, mass-market wine.

silky: Having a supple, smooth texture suggestive of silk.

single-vineyard wine: A wine that is made from the grapes of a single (presumably exceptionally good) plot of land and that usually carries the name of the vineyard on its label; the term is unregulated, in that *vineyard* is not defined as to size or ownership.

skin contact: The process during which the juice of grapes rests in contact with the grape skins; in red wine, the process by which the wines absorb color, tannin, and other substances; not normally used in white wine production, but occasionally used to enhance the aromatic character of the wine.

smoky: Having aromas or flavors that suggest smoke or smoked wood.

smooth: Descriptor for a wine whose texture is not rough or harsh.

soft: Textural descriptor for a wine whose alcohol and sugar (if any) dominate its acidity and tannin, resulting in a lack of hardness or roughness.

stemmy: Descriptor for red wines that give the impression of having dry, raspy, woody tannins, as if from the stems of grape bunches.

stems: The woody part of a grape bunch, which are high in tannin; usually the stems are removed and discarded prior to fermentation.

stony: Having minerally aromas or flavors that suggest stones. In some cases, the stony aroma or flavor of a wine can be described more precisely as suggestive of wet stones.

structural components: Principally, a wine's alcohol, acid, tannin, and sugar (if any).

structure: That part of a wine's taste that derives from perception of the wine's structural elements.

style: The set of characteristics through which a wine manifests itself.

supple: A descriptor for wines that seem fluid in texture in the mouth, without roughness or sharpness; a positive trait especially for red wines.

süssreserve: German for *sweet reserve;* unfermented grape juice that is added to a white wine to increase the wine's residual sugar and sweetness.

sweetness: The impression of sugary taste in a wine, which can be due to the presence of residual sugar or to other sweet-tasting substances in the wine, such as alcohol.

tannic: A word used to describe wines that seem to be high in tannin.

tannin: A substance in the skins, stems, and seeds of grapes; a principal component of red wines, which — unlike white wines — are made by using the grape skins. Tannin also is a component of oak barrels.

tarry: Having aromas or flavors that suggest fresh tar.

tart: A descriptor for aromas or flavors of under-ripe fruit. This term can also apply to a wine that is too high in acid.

taste: A general term for the totality of impressions a wine gives in the mouth; more specifically, the primary tastes found in wine: sweetness, sourness, and bitterness.

terroir: A French word that is the collective term for the growing conditions in a vineyard, such as climate, soil, drainage, slope, altitude, topography, and so on.

texture: A wine's consistency or feel in the mouth.

thin: A word used to describe wines that are lacking in substance or meager in texture.

tight: A descriptor for wines that seem to be inexpressive at the moment. This term can apply to a wine's aromas and flavors or to its structure.

underbrush: Aromas or flavors that suggest wet leaves, dampness, and slight decay; a welcome note in many older reds.

varietal: A wine named for the sole or the principal grape variety from which it was made.

varietal character: The characteristics of a wine that are attributable to the grape variety from which it was made.

vegetal: Having aromas or flavors that suggest vegetables, such as green peppers or asparagus; these can be pleasant or not, depending on the taster.

vin de pays: French phrase for *country wine;* in France's original regional classification system, a category that holds lower status than AOC wines.

vinification: The activity of making grape juice into wine.

vintage: The year in which a wine's grapes grew and were harvested; sometimes used as a synonym for the grape harvest.

viticulture: The activity of growing grapes.

Vitis vinifera: The species to which most of the world's wine grapes belong.

weight: The impression of a wine's volume in the mouth.

wood tannin: Those tannins in a wine that are attributable to the barrels in which the wine aged, as opposed to the grapes.

yeasts: One-cell microorganisms responsible for transforming grape juice into wine.

Appendix C

Vintage Wine Chart: 1991–2010

. . . .

*A*ny vintage wine chart must be regarded as a rough guide — a general, average rating of the vintage year in a particular wine region. Remember that many wines will always be exceptions to the vintage's rating. For example, some wine producers will manage to find a way to make a decent — even fine — wine in a so-called poor vintage.

Wine Region	1991	1992	1993	1994	1995	1996	1997	1998	1999	2000
Bordeaux										
Médoc, Graves	75c	75d	80c	85c	90b	90b	85c	85b	85b	90b
Pomerol, St.-Emil	60d	75d	85c	85b	90b	85b	85c	95b	85b	90b
Sauternes/Barsac	70c	65d	65d	70c	85b	85b	85c	85b	85a	85b
Burgundy										
Côte de Nuits	85c	70d	80d	75d	90c	90b	85c	80c	90b	85c
Côte de Beaune	70c	80c	75d	75d	85c	90c	85c	80c	90b	75c
Burgundy, White	70d	85c	70d	75d	90c	90c	85d	80c	85c	85c
Rhône Valley										
Northern Rhône	85c	75c	80c	60c	90b	85c	90c	90b	95b	85c
Southern Rhône	85c	75d	60d	80d	90c	80d	80d	95c	90c	90c
Other Wine Regions										
Alsace	75c	85c	85c	90c	85c	85c	85c	90c	85c	85c
Champagne	NV	NV	80c	NV	90b	100b	85c	85c	85c	80c
Germany	85c	80c	85c	90c	85c	90b	85c	90b	85c	70d
Rioja	75c	85c	85c	90c	90c	85c	85c	80d	85c	85c
Vintage Port	90b	95b	NV	90a	NV	NV	90a	95a	NV	95a
Italy										
Piedmont	75c	70d	80c	75d	85b	95a	85c	90b	90b	90c
Tuscany	75d	70d	80d	80d	85b	75c	90c	85c	85c	85c
California North Coast										
Cab. Sauvignon	95c	85c	85c	90c	85b	90b	90c	85c	85b	75c

Wine Region	2001	2002	2003	2004	2005	2006	2007	2008	2009	2010
Bordeaux										
Médoc, Graves	85b	85b	80b	85b	95b	85b	80c	85b	90a	95a
Pomerol, St.-Emil	85b	85b	80b	85b	95b	85b	85c	85b	90a	95a
Sauternes/Barsac	95a	90a	90a	80a	95a	85b	90b	90a	95a	?
Burgundy										
Côte de Nuits	80c	90b	85c	80c	95b	85b	85b	90a	95a	90a
Côte de Beaune	75c	90b	80c	75c	95b	80c	75c	90a	95a	90a
Burgundy, White	85c	90c	75d	85c	85c	85b	80c	90b	85b	90a

Wine Region	2001	2002	2003	2004	2005	2006	2007	2008	2009	2010
Rhône Valley										
Northern Rhône	90b	75c	95b	80c	85b	90b	85b	75b	95a	90a
Southern Rhône	95b	55d	90c	85c	95b	85b	95b	80b	90a	95a
Other Wine Regions										
Alsace	90c	85c	75c	90b	85c	75c	85c	90b	75c	?
Champagne	NV	95b	80c	90a	85b	?	?	?	?	?
Germany	95b	90b	85c	90b	90b	95a	85b	90b	95b	85a
Rioja	95b	70d	85c	90b	85b	80b	85b	90b	95a	?
Vintage Port	NV	NV	90a	90a	NV	NV	90a	90a	95a	?
Italy										
Piedmont	95a	75c	80b	90b	85b	90a	85b	90a	85a	?
Tuscany	95b	75d	80c	90b	85b	90a	85b	85b	85a	?
California North Coast										
Cab.Sauvignon	90b	85b	85b	85b	90b	85b	95b	90a	90a	?

Key:

100 = Outstanding	75 = Average	b = Can be consumed now, but will improve with time
95 = Excellent	70 = Below Average	
90 = Very Good	65 = Poor	c = Ready to drink
85 = Good	50–60 = Very Poor	d = May be too old
80 = Fairly Good	a = Too young to drink	NV = Non-vintage year
		? = Too soon; not rated yet

Wine Region	*Recent Past Great Vintages (prior to 1991)*
Bordeaux	
Médoc, Graves	1959, 1961, 1970, 1982, 1986, 1989
Pomerol, St.-Emilion	1961, 1964, 1970, 1975, 1982, 1989
Sauternes	1959, 1962, 1967, 1975, 1983,1986, 1988, 1990
Burgundy	
Côte de Nuits, Red	1959, 1964, 1969, 1978, 1990
Côte de Beaune, Red	1959, 1969, 1990
Burgundy, White	1962, 1966, 1969, 1973, 1978, 1989
Rhône Valley	
Northern Rhône	1959, 1961, 1966, 1969, 1970, 1972 (Hermitage), 1978, 1989, 1990
Southern Rhône	1961, 1967, 1978, 1988, 1990
Other Wine Regions	
Alsace	1959, 1961, 1967, 1983, 1989, 1990
Champagne	1961, 1964, 1969, 1971, 1975, 1979, 1982, 1985, 1988
Germany	1959, 1971, 1976, 1988, 1989, 1990
Rioja (Spain)	1964, 1970, 1981, 1982, 1989
Vintage Port	1963, 1966, 1970, 1977, 1983
Italy	
Piedmont	1958, 1964, 1971, 1978, 1982, 1989
Tuscany	1967, 1970 (Brunello di Montalcino), 1971, 1985, 1988
California North Coast	
Cabernet Sauvignon	1951, 1958, 1968, 1970, 1974, 1978

Index

• X •

• Y •

• Z •

Apple & Mac

iPad 2 For Dummies,
3rd Edition
978-1-118-17679-5

iPhone 4S For Dummies,
5th Edition
978-1-118-03671-6

iPod touch For Dummies,
3rd Edition
978-1-118-12960-9

Mac OS X Lion
For Dummies
978-1-118-02205-4

Blogging & Social Media

CityVille For Dummies
978-1-118-08337-6

Facebook For Dummies,
4th Edition
978-1-118-09562-1

Mom Blogging
For Dummies
978-1-118-03843-7

Twitter For Dummies,
2nd Edition
978-0-470-76879-2

WordPress For Dummies,
4th Edition
978-1-118-07342-1

Business

Cash Flow For Dummies
978-1-118-01850-7

Investing For Dummies,
6th Edition
978-0-470-90545-6

Job Searching with Social
Media For Dummies
978-0-470-93072-4

QuickBooks 2012
For Dummies
978-1-118-09120-3

Resumes For Dummies,
6th Edition
978-0-470-87361-8

Starting an Etsy Business
For Dummies
978-0-470-93067-0

Cooking & Entertaining

Cooking Basics
For Dummies, 4th Edition
978-0-470-91388-8

Wine For Dummies,
4th Edition
978-0-470-04579-4

Diet & Nutrition

Kettlebells For Dummies
978-0-470-59929-7

Nutrition For Dummies,
5th Edition
978-0-470-93231-5

Restaurant Calorie Counter
For Dummies,
2nd Edition
978-0-470-64405-8

Digital Photography

Digital SLR Cameras &
Photography For Dummies,
4th Edition
978-1-118-14489-3

Digital SLR Settings
& Shortcuts
For Dummies
978-0-470-91763-3

Photoshop Elements 10
For Dummies
978-1-118-10742-3

Gardening

Gardening Basics
For Dummies
978-0-470-03749-2

Vegetable Gardening
For Dummies,
2nd Edition
978-0-470-49870-5

Green/Sustainable

Raising Chickens
For Dummies
978-0-470-46544-8

Green Cleaning
For Dummies
978-0-470-39106-8

Health

Diabetes For Dummies,
3rd Edition
978-0-470-27086-8

Food Allergies
For Dummies
978-0-470-09584-3

Living Gluten-Free
For Dummies,
2nd Edition
978-0-470-58589-4

Hobbies

Beekeeping
For Dummies,
2nd Edition
978-0-470-43065-1

Chess For Dummies,
3rd Edition
978-1-118-01695-4

Drawing For Dummies,
2nd Edition
978-0-470-61842-4

eBay For Dummies,
7th Edition
978-1-118-09806-6

Knitting For Dummies,
2nd Edition
978-0-470-28747-7

Language &
Foreign Language

English Grammar
For Dummies,
2nd Edition
978-0-470-54664-2

French For Dummies,
2nd Edition
978-1-118-00464-7

German For Dummies,
2nd Edition
978-0-470-90101-4

Spanish Essentials
For Dummies
978-0-470-63751-7

Spanish For Dummies,
2nd Edition
978-0-470-87855-2

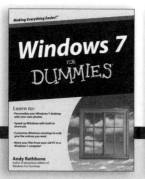

Available wherever books are sold. For more information or to order direct: U.S. customers visit www.dummies.com or call 1-877-762-2974.
U.K. customers visit www.wileyeurope.com or call (0) 1243 843291. Canadian customers visit www.wiley.ca or call 1-800-567-4797.

Connect with us online at www.facebook.com/fordummies or @fordummies

Math & Science

Algebra I For Dummies,
2nd Edition
978-0-470-55964-2

Biology For Dummies,
2nd Edition
978-0-470-59875-7

Chemistry For Dummies,
2nd Edition
978-1-1180-0730-3

Geometry For Dummies,
2nd Edition
978-0-470-08946-0

Pre-Algebra Essentials
For Dummies
978-0-470-61838-7

Microsoft Office

Excel 2010 For Dummies
978-0-470-48953-6

Office 2010 All-in-One
For Dummies
978-0-470-49748-7

Office 2011 for Mac
For Dummies
978-0-470-87869-9

Word 2010
For Dummies
978-0-470-48772-3

Music

Guitar For Dummies,
2nd Edition
978-0-7645-9904-0

Clarinet For Dummies
978-0-470-58477-4

iPod & iTunes
For Dummies,
9th Edition
978-1-118-13060-5

Pets

Cats For Dummies,
2nd Edition
978-0-7645-5275-5

Dogs All-in One
For Dummies
978-0470-52978-2

Saltwater Aquariums
For Dummies
978-0-470-06805-2

Religion & Inspiration

The Bible For Dummies
978-0-7645-5296-0

Catholicism For Dummies,
2nd Edition
978-1-118-07778-8

Spirituality For Dummies,
2nd Edition
978-0-470-19142-2

Self-Help & Relationships

Happiness For Dummies
978-0-470-28171-0

Overcoming Anxiety
For Dummies,
2nd Edition
978-0-470-57441-6

Seniors

Crosswords For Seniors
For Dummies
978-0-470-49157-7

iPad 2 For Seniors
For Dummies, 3rd Edition
978-1-118-17678-8

Laptops & Tablets
For Seniors For Dummies,
2nd Edition
978-1-118-09596-6

Smartphones & Tablets

BlackBerry For Dummies,
5th Edition
978-1-118-10035-6

Droid X2 For Dummies
978-1-118-14864-8

HTC ThunderBolt
For Dummies
978-1-118-07601-9

MOTOROLA XOOM
For Dummies
978-1-118-08835-7

Sports

Basketball For Dummies,
3rd Edition
978-1-118-07374-2

Football For Dummies,
2nd Edition
978-1-118-01261-1

Golf For Dummies,
4th Edition
978-0-470-88279-5

Test Prep

ACT For Dummies,
5th Edition
978-1-118-01259-8

ASVAB For Dummies,
3rd Edition
978-0-470-63760-9

The GRE Test For
Dummies, 7th Edition
978-0-470-00919-2

Police Officer Exam
For Dummies
978-0-470-88724-0

Series 7 Exam
For Dummies
978-0-470-09932-2

Web Development

HTML, CSS, & XHTML
For Dummies, 7th Edition
978-0-470-91659-9

Drupal For Dummies,
2nd Edition
978-1-118-08348-2

Windows 7

Windows 7
For Dummies
978-0-470-49743-2

Windows 7
For Dummies,
Book + DVD Bundle
978-0-470-52398-8

Windows 7 All-in-One
For Dummies
978-0-470-48763-1

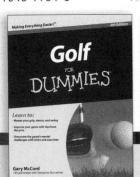

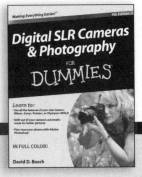

Wherever you are in life, Dummies makes it easier.

From fashion to Facebook ®, wine to Windows®, and everything in between, Dummies makes it easier.

Visit us at Dummies.com and connect with us online at www.facebook.com/fordummies or @fordummies